FOR ALL
WATERS

FOR ALL
WATERS

Finding Ourselves in
Early Modern Wetscapes

Lowell Duckert

UNIVERSITY OF MINNESOTA PRESS

MINNEAPOLIS • LONDON

An earlier version of chapter 1 was published as "Water Ralegh's Liquid Narrative: *The Discoverie of Guiana*," in *Literary and Visual Ralegh*, ed. Christopher M. Armitage (Manchester: Manchester University Press, 2013). An earlier version of chapter 2 was published as "Glacier," *postmedieval: A Journal of Medieval Cultural Studies* 4, no. 1 (2013). An earlier version of chapter 3 was published as "When It Rains," in *Material Ecocriticism*, ed. Serenella Iovino and Serpil Oppermann (Bloomington: Indiana University Press, 2014); copyright 2014 Indiana University Press. An earlier version of chapter 4 was published as "The Slough of Respond," *O-Zone: A Journal of Object-Oriented Studies* 1 (2014).

Published by the University of Minnesota Press
111 Third Avenue South, Suite 290
Minneapolis, MN 55401-2520
http://www.upress.umn.edu

ISBN 978-1-5179-0046-5 (hc)
ISBN 978-1-5179-0047-2 (pb)
A Cataloging-in-Publication record for this book is available from the Library of Congress.

Printed in the United States of America on acid-free paper

The University of Minnesota is an equal-opportunity educator and employer.

22 21 20 19 18 17   10 9 8 7 6 5 4 3 2 1

FOR MY FAMILY
turbulent and tranquil

How can we live without or against the four elements, without thinking like them, without turning toward them, through them, for them, with them?

—Michel Serres, *Biogea*

The world is turnin', I hope it don't turn away.

—Neil Young, "On the Beach"

Contents

Shivering, Wet

[Feste:] I am for all waters.

—William Shakespeare, *Twelfth Night* (1601)

Shiver is one installment in Colleen Ludwig's *Elemental Bodies* project. Made of thirty-five infrared sensors, seventy-one valves, and several frames of stretched fabric, this "cutaneous habitat" squirts short bursts of water down the wall nearest to any detected movement.[1] Despite the white room's one predictable feature, these water-walls retain their powers of surprise: whether one stands "out of" the cubicle's electronic reach or deliberately touches one of its three panels, jet streams are inevitably and accidentally triggered. *Shiver* is more event than exhibit, then; it invites participants to interact with water and break museums' mandatory distantiation. But while diverting, pooling, or impeding the waters' flows might serve as a facile metaphor for how human technology continues to disturb nonhuman waterways, the installation expresses a more complicated, because coimplicated, ensnarement of bodies and emotions. When Ludwig polled participants' experiences, many felt that they were "a part of it," that it uncannily "sort of knew about me"; they wondered if it "controls me" or if it were "alive"; some empathetically wanted "to please it." Over half felt improved and relaxed, although some found it "a bit unsettling." By its name, *Shiver* makes one think of the cold, of the automatic thermoregulatory attempt to generate heat, of catastrophic tales of wintering, but the assorted responses to feeling wet/ter also prove that touching water incurs delight and the curiosity of assemblage as well. A "shiver" houses both fears and desires in its shudders: the dizziness of disorientation, unsettling liberty, piloerection (goosebumps). As phenomenological architecture, *Shiver* shakes with water power; the first-century BCE classical architect Vitruvius, credited as the founder of Western architecture, knew this force well: "All things are composed of the power of water."[2] It is a feeling not just to be fought but embraced; the soft and hard aspects of water-space are to be explored rather than foreclosed.[3] Wetness is an architecture of feeling, the immanence of entrance, the effervescent ephemerality of bodies in touch.

"Skin flows like water," says the sensational philosopher of science Michel Serres, "a variable confluence of the qualities of the senses."[4] According to Ludwig, *Shiver* is meant to demonstrate the porosity of skin and the nonboundary between human and world, art and body, at the material level: its fabric was designed by looking at human skin under a microscope and watching subcutaneous flows of water. Mechanical and organic bodies of water converge here as "wetware" proudly displayed,[5] sponsoring questions not just of phenomenology but of ontology. To this point, Ludwig avoids the word "object" since it entails something for (human) use, preferring a subject–object "device" instead. Water *in* and *as* flesh: "this haptic feedback loop creates a sense of physical intimacy, within a space that functions as if it's a sentient organism." Skin acts as a mediator, a site of exchange in space, a "fluctuating borderland" in her

Colleen Ludwig, *Shiver*. Interactive sculptural installation, 10 x 14 x 14 feet, aluminum, polycarbonate, plumbing and filtration systems, solenoid valves, IR-bounce beam sensors, circuitry, wiring, fabric, and water. *SINEW*, dance collaboration with Lehrer Dance (Immanuel Naylor pictured). Burchfield Penney Art Center, Buffalo, New York, July 2014. Photograph by Colleen Ludwig.

words, "an atmosphere" without edges. The open-sided construction of the installation only helps to recognize water's constant presence: that "wall" of water vapor, also known as *air*, that takes up space (such as Buffalo's Burchfield Penney Art Museum, where I made first contact with Ludwig's in/organic machine). *Shiver* arrays the multisensory, affective space of human and nonhuman cutaneous commingling (indicated hereafter as "non/human") that wetness *is* by accentuating the shared skins of enfleshed things that flow, by examining their ever-expanding atmospheres that effect further envelopments of bodies. Entering Ludwig's showpiece is to discover that you have always been "inside" this watery atmosphere; it is to discard inside–outside boundaries altogether, replacing the "it" of objectivity with the "care" of curation for others (from the Latin *cura*): a water drop, partner, or stranger. Shivering wet, together, is not to dethrone the category of the human or, conversely, rearrange the prioritization of the classical senses (enthroning touch), but rather to disrupt these scales, to free up the actors involved to re/distribution and re/definition through cocorporeal expansion. All hierarchies, once wet, short circuit. *Shiver* shatters fantasies of human separability and extractability; in turn, this ontotechnological "sentience" of becoming wet presents a means of tactile symbiosis with an other instead of a (previously) human privilege to be given away. "Life," like touch, proves unlocatable and unknowable, only felt, fleetingly, across smooth spaces.

More than just working by "withdrawal," the ontographical "carpentry" of *Shiver* reveals our capacity to creatively converse with it:[6] that is, by touching water that touches back—as I did with my finger, writing droopy letters that dripped down the wall—we realize how non/human bodies of water are also bodies that write "onto-stories," or, to use a word that will reappear frequently throughout this project (and soon to be explained in better detail), compose "hydrographies."[7] The noun "shiver" is linked etymologically to the oldest form of writing, that of stone: it derives from Middle English "to split," and that from German *Schiefer* ("slate"). But water does not just respond dutifully to human activity, waiting, patiently, like a blank white wall (or slate) for a writer to project his or her emotions onto it. Nor is it confined to the aural dimension, as when the spigots announced each stream (and a gesture that provoked it) with a soft tapping sound. The verb "shiver" also comes from Middle English *chivere*, perhaps from dialectal *chavele* "to chatter," from Old English *ceafl* ("jaw"). Chattering is an instance in which a word expresses the physiological experience that bore it; "shivering" is therefore an embodied language, and not just confined to the ears or mouth—jaws open or clenched—but intrinsic to relationality itself: "noisy" chains of call and response, many movements, parasitic transmissions that travel along bodies and through hosts, wreaking their multisensorial affects.[8] *Shiver* chatters, and its vociferousness (which I heard, for I turned back to trace before exiting the museum) reconceives communication as a "chat" dissociated from (human) language and biased senses (sight, sound). Here is the very verb, the action, of the "verbal" that is not reliant upon words (the *verbum*) for meaning. Aurally, visually, and more (like temperature), *Shiver* says how water speaks. To enter, shivering, is to understand how all wet spaces are really compositional spaces—white, blank pages—that draw as much as are drawn upon, slates ready to be remade into cokinetic cocreations called art.

"Blank" spaces are never that, of course, just as geographically uncharted spaces are never "empty" and "white" is an innocuous, nonracialized descriptor. There are no "exits" in the open-ended atmosphere of collaboration that is *Shiver*—only entrances—and yet being cordoned off in a space of art (cultural capital) points up the violent "splits" that may be instantiated between things in a given watery space despite the fact that the non/human enmeshments it generates split this split. If "water is what we make of it"—Jamie Linton's answer to his own question in *What Is Water?*—we need to question what makes the "we."[9] *Shiver* is a hybrid art form that refutes the historical body-art "split" sociologist of science Bruno Latour claims is a condition of the "modern constitution," one that aims to divide humans from environments, nature from politics, and that repeatedly attempts (and fails) to occlude the reality that "ecology dissolves nature's contours."[10] Dissolution is both the greatest challenge and promise that water poses, an important reminder that all wet spaces are ethical sites of encounter, foregrounding, in Mick Smith's phrase, how "democracy is always already incomplete" and thus in need of representatives, advocates for "response(ability)" to others.[11] In short, *water might evenly flow but it does not flow evenly.* Flows are not materially obvious, their values universally established, their benefits equally enjoyed; certain flows (clean water) do not reach everyone (about one in six people currently), or harmful flows inundate certain groups (the poor). Water is rendered a resource, a commodity, vulnerable to "loss." It is warred over and upon.[12] Water bears the burden of human-created pollution (acidification via climate change), feels the "foreign burden" of neoliberalism as its cohabitants, predominantly from third-world countries of the Global South, suffer "slow violence."[13] Thus entering, and being entered by, water not only conveys "the role art can play in re-envisioning the world," Ludwig's hopeful *Shiver*, it also questions *which* bodies are more porous or "viscous" than others.[14] Yet just as importantly, a splitting feeling affords a chance to dream up future worlds, it enables bodies of water—and watery bodies politic—to enact social change by demanding restitution (recognition, at least) for the particularly unequal "ends" of environmental injustice they experience. Ludwig's wetspace showcases how ecology remains ever-susceptible to in- and exclusionary principles; it points up how humans are always "intermeshed with the more-than-human world," a mobile space Stacy Alaimo calls a "trans-corporeal landscape."[15] To make a wet entrance—shivering, wet—is to enter into non/human alliances of uncertain catastrophes and joys. To shiver is to gather in this way of experimental sensitization and sensation; splitting may magnify the moment at which collectives collect as well as disperse so that we may recognize that "we," the fragile we/t, are bodies of water capable of mobility and of assertive, vociferous protest.

Inventions

Wet happens, and while a drier book might end with that pronouncement, I intend to mystify this mundane fact by stressing the ontological, epistemological, and ethical complexity (matters of being, knowing, and doing) water retains;[16] my purpose throughout is to counteract water's denigrated definition through subtraction, negation, and binary systems— "When pure, it is transparent, colourless (except as seen in large quantity, when it has a blue tint), tasteless, and inodorous"[17]—by redefining wetness as a happening, one that propels the influential hydrosocial practices of the "everyday." *Shiver* introduces how water works within waterscapes and upon bodies—to repeat: through shaking (affect), splintering (dispersing as collecting), and chattering (conversing)—and thus it makes a fitting entrance for my study that takes acts of hydropoesis, inventive and invitational entrances, for its subject. If "meditation and water are wedded

for ever," as Herman Melville put it,[18] *Shiver* and the other watery media
herein are meditations on how water, far from being a passive and written-
upon medium (or oft-quoted adage for impermanence), actively *mediates*
in the production of corporeal and textual composition. Water is everywhere and all are drops to think: to meditate is to take the "hydrological
turn" that the editors of *Thinking with Water* advocate, writers who stress
the "co-constitution of water as a substance and water as poetics."[19] It is a
metathought about thinking, like *feeling* feeling, touching from the inside:
wet is weird. I have tried thus far to reacquaint us with what it feels like
to be and become wet; whether or not you have drowned this book (or
are about to) is not an issue, for the work is an instantiation already of
mediation by virtue of being my own meditation, my thoughts with (not
on) water and the possibilities available. The key is the *inter* ("between,
among"); to enter is to be, and to feel, caught in between transitional
states: right where I want us to be at this juncture, poised in and for positions in future.

　　Opacity is our ally in this process of thinking; it is a freeing up of
"analysis" (which comes from the Greek *analuein*, "unloose"). In getting
to know water since I began this project (from its dissertational source),
I have learned to un/know it, to see it as a continued discussion (which
is to "dissertate," actually). I have found that water is a good substance to
think-invent-create with because of its epistemological uncertainty and
endless interlocutions: the Hydra (Greek *hudros*, "water snake") of many
heads, of burgeoning, who is also Proteus (a minor sea god in Greek
mythology with the power of prophecy but who avoids answering questions by assuming different shapes). A liquid with unusually high heat
capacity, and that bizarrely expands as it freezes (at 39°F), whose hydrogen bonds expose only strangeness: while computers can generate models of how attractors between molecules grasp each other, the interaction
remains mysterious, random, and disorderly, turning water's cooperative
"'stickiness' . . . into a dynamic, ever-changing labyrinth."[20] These virtual
models of structure glimpse the virtuality, the generative surface effects,
of becoming-water. We actually know little about water, although we believe the opposite. Water secretes secrets in its amount: it covers approximately three-quarters of the earth, and is even on the sun; in its depths:
roughly 95 percent of the oceans are unmapped; in its immediacy: water's

movements and phase transitions are almost always apprehensible (clouds float above aridity below, ice floes harden upon seas' surface); in its necessity: the startling range of organisms that require water for survival; in its mutability: water holds endless variations of (Protean) forms, from the spell of the infinite snowflake to Heraclitus's famous adage that you cannot cross the same river twice; in its symbolic range: from purity to time; in its embodiment: the human body, born from amniotic fluid, may reach up to 75 percent water, and the human brain is approximately the same amount (right now your synapses are firing liquid sparks); and in language: it is only appropriate that some slippery thoughts come with water in mind, as many words in the English language do, their "liquid consonants" delivered by "stream of consciousness." Water is an ongoing relationship with a twist, multiple turns; the "labyrinth" never straightens or solves; some water is never water in sum.

We all know what happens when you try to catch water in your hands. If water follows any rules, it obeys the unruly "principles of the elements" by veering order out of order:[21] all of the classical elements do, according to Empedocles's (fifth-century BCE) arrangement of them un/tied through the forces of love-strife. Though no element ever acts alone, water (perhaps unlike the other elements) reveals this propensity in its exact atomic structure. It is possible to locate the ongoing onto-epistemological turns in which watery things relate in water's very materiality. Two atoms of hydrogen and one atom of oxygen are required to bond before water even happens. Water, we might say, is a bond that *bonds*, a relation that relates: it stresses the relationality necessary for existence, according to actor-network modes of inquiry, and those relations' inclination to congeal into other collectives. Water is, in action, "molecular" rather than "molar" despite its tidy symmetrical dyad (H_2O); messier, its bonding lines betray flows of accretion and secretion rather than segments of a fixed structure. Or, recalling the tubes and spheres of those atomic playsets (with which I modeled molecules), we should remember how bonds bend into others (at an angle of 104.5 degrees). Let the tubes, in length, become "lines of flight."[22] Uneasy assemblages are made easily, it seems, by a liquid that somehow glues, by a queer force that in- and declines away from the use value (and abuse value) humans attribute to it as the builder of civilizations.[23] Water's attractiveness to almost all living things puts it at the center of activity;

citizens are drawn around the well, enacting a true-blue Copernican counterrevolution. As a "quasi object . . . a tracker of the relations in the fluctuating collectivity around it,"[24] water runs between subject-object lines.
While water has always been associated with life in a symbolic sense, its
pulling and pulsing material forces lead us to ponder whether water possesses an in/organic life in its power of mediation and, in doing so, help
us challenge conceptions of life itself. Water activates thirsts—there is its
affluent "thing-power"[25]—and puts the "bio-" back in the "biography" of
water. In the hollow of the hand we wonder less at the magic of transcendent spirituality (an "anima" or carrier of life force), or the trickeries of
human craftiness (a promising "elixir"), but grasp living water with all its
vivacious inventions: the wizardry of energetic immanence.[26]

Ages

A preface is literally that which is "said before." This brief sketch of waters
that I have laid out, inaugurated by a *Shiver*, conveys my interests in water's
material agency rather than its categorical definitions; a bias for what water
enables, and becomes, than what it *is*. It is also intended to prepare us for
a turn into a specific history of inventiveness: liquid *early* modernity.[27]
By "history," I mean the "past" that has never really "passed"; just as conjoined environmental health and justice problematize the universal praise
of flows above, so it is with the untimely matter of time. "Time doesn't
flow; it percolates," says Serres, and "all of our difficulties with the theory
of history come from the fact that we think of time in this inadequate and
naive way."[28] The water tales told here are stowaways that cross vast passages of time; ever-adrift, they are fugitives on the fly who give us chase,
underwriting Manuel De Landa's point about effluxion: "reality is a single
matter-energy undergoing phase transitions of various kinds, with each
new layer of accumulated 'stuff' simply enriching the reservoir of nonlinear dynamics and nonlinear combinatorics available for the generation of
novel structures and processes."[29] This "stuff" bursts the timeline of conquest to which the moderns and their constitution would have us adhere:
water made predictable with Pierre Perrault's (ca. 1608–80) delineation of
the hydrological cycle in *On the Origin of Springs* (1674), problem solved;
water rendered inactive and inert by discovering it to be the scientific elements of H and O in Antoine Lavoisier's 1783 experiment, essence found;

its evaporation that announces the Anthropocene with James Watt's patented steam engine in 1784, matter coerced. Filtering water through the early modern is not to "recycle" one timeless substance and its unchanged linear laminae, but rather to think about repetition with a difference: what compositions have been formed, and what new configurations may come once we accept an invitation that early moderns took in wet page and stage. In order to intensify water's vibrancy today, to reincorporate steam as critique, I reenter the wet architecture of feeling known as the playhouse (a three-sided space in thrust form) and reexamine the wet spaces of encounter conveyed as travel literature (white pages). I argue that these art forms, these surfacings of invention, are shivering spaces that participate in, and exacerbate, the "*crisis of modern water*";[30] meaning, they do not stop at collapsing boundaries between human and nonhuman, past and present, but emphasize these categories' ontological inseparability and explore their alliances. And there is more: instead of upholding the modern, my analysis attempts to set the "modern" itself into crisis,[31] arguing that this age of influence, by flooding the "urgency of now," creates an eddy of encounter between times (past and present) as well as states, currently extending to us their unique powers of in/ter/vention.

Matter's performativity would make water suitable for the stage; indeed, water was an actor with agency, an adept "actant" in Latour's vocabulary, a collaborative force that enlists the human and brings forth wonders like a play.[32] Water's materiality refuses, as the recent "material turn" in ecocriticism demands, "to talk of matter in reductionist and essentialist terms."[33] When the clown Feste in William Shakespeare's (1564–1616) play *Twelfth Night* (1601) says, "I am for all waters" (4.2.56), he is figuratively claiming to be up for anything.[34] To take the preposition "for" seriously is not foolish, however; it signals a material interaction with water and not just an elemental metaphor about it. Early modern writers referenced Hippocratic humoralism—notably his fourth-century BCE treatise *Airs, Waters, Places*—that claimed human temperaments were composed of the four elements in various mixtures: too much exposure to water could produce a "phlegmatic" attitude, or it could lead to sickness, overflowing the body's "drier" components.[35] But water did much more than affect human mentality or health. Feste's stage, the Globe, was under construction along the Thames when it was nearly washed away during a rainstorm

in the spring of 1599: "The moneths of March, Aprill, and May cold and
dry, but on Whitsonday great haile and high waters, the like of long time
had not béene séene."[36] Water could enter human and nonhuman bodies
in violent ways, displace them, overflow them, outperform them. Feste
describes this fluctuating reality as he sings the play's epilogue, eternally
wandering: "For the rain it raineth every day" (5.1.379). The weather report from 1599 crucially continues: "the extreame violence of this Tempest
made London stréetes more fresh and faire then euer was séene before."[37]
Shakespeare's melancholic comedy suggests that early modern playgoers
knew the freshness and fairness of water's touch, the shiver of storms:
"And we'll strive to please you," Feste vows, "every day" (5.1.395). The
ecological circumstances surrounding the composition of *Twelfth Night*
demonstrate water's active role in the artistic process, that it could be called
upon as material of reciprocity, "cast" in both senses of the word. Shakespeare later requests soaked actors in two of his most oceanic plays: stage
directions for *Pericles* (1607–8) and *The Tempest* (1611) (the focus of the
introduction) summon characters who "Enter, wet." Littleworth in James
Shirley's (1596–1666) *The Lady of Pleasure* (1637) falls into the Thames,
unable to tell water from skin: "Pray doe not plucke off my skin, / It is
so wet, unless you have good eyes / You'le hardly know it from a shirt."[38]
Even domesticated and potable water could be put onstage, as the Wench
in Thomas Nabbes's (1605–41) *Totenham Court* (1633) "[p]owres the water
into the tub*" for the courtier, George.[39] The "Water Poet" John Taylor
(1578–1653) staged river pageants of sea battles, and Richard Brome (ca.
1590–1652), to "bring flouds of gaine to th' watermen," imagined a dramatic aquarium unreachable by the sedan-driving fad in 1632: "a new
Theatre or Playhouse / Upon the Thames on Barges or flat boats."[40] Early
modern writers knew what it meant to be a watery "I . . . for all waters"
palpably: to be real, roiled water-men and water-women in interchange
who ferried across those deepening ontological "middles" like London's
river. The Globe playhouse floats more than just figuratively; its scripts
are more than merely water-like. The riparian reaches under the Bankside's
banks, up- and degrades.

    It might seem counterintuitive, due to my amodern ambit, to think
about why water of the specific age of early modernity is good to think
with; in fact, its polychronic curves check the impulse merely to historicize

matter-movement, lend elemental "*re-story-ation*" to cultural-historical approaches of sedimentation.[41] As we will see, when Shakespeare imagined global travel for his romances, and when author-explorers entered similarly performative spaces (not just drama), they found water everywhere. Water found ways to endrench their compositional bodies and, later, their audiences. If we wrote a "liquid history" of this time, then, it would show the slickness with which early modern authors coinvented texts, tomes that incorporated—desirably or not—water's tumultuous vortices.[42] The early modern period is a useful and challenging ripple in time to study non/human composition, since the era makes significant splashes for reasons mainly to do with "trafficking": protoimperialistic and protocapitalistic exchanges that render humans and nonhumans as resources, objects, and commodities through violence and/of displacement. (1) The enlarging role of sea commerce and trade companies' competition sponsored increasing encounters with un/familiar places; as a result, the old maps were expanded as more water was met. But the charts were also redrawn to make room for new maps of relationships, those that detailed flowing explorations into actor-networks, burgeoning connections bordered by "fluctuating fluid."[43] (2) The rising role of colonization meant that these encounters were often fraught with violence (the rape of the wetland, the trafficking of human kidnapping) and protocapitalist exploitation ("blue" imperialism and its logic of extraction).[44] Voyages were primarily meant to gain imperial footholds for their respective nations and reap material profit, not to produce entertaining texts. These encounters, in turn, help us understand what is at stake when dividing not only early modern Englanders from indigenous others, for example, but separating non/human beings from their watery environments within which they are always enmeshed. (3) A period of unseasonably cold weather called the Little Ice Age (ca. 1300–1850) sponsored longer meditations on environmental catastrophe and their bodies that lingered in wetness.[45] For these admittedly broad historical reasons (and there are more),[46] the writers I include here negotiated any number of these influxes, and while their responses varied due to their initial agendas, they met splashes of water that swept their solid discourse off course and on into new routes. I aim to reopen the age of exploration—driven as it was by the lure of colonialism and commerce—as onto-epistemologically wide as possible,

underscoring the allure of water in their expanding maps that brimmed
with anticipation. I wish to dilute the powerful, but too-prevalent, scholarly interpretations of cartographic anxiety, while at the same time avoiding any nostalgia for a time before liquid became "liquid capital," a pitfall
of choosing between primordial substance and commodified asset. The
types of "trafficking" (of more than two hours of our global-local stage)
tracked here include commerce as a form of economic exchange and meteorological reports, but also, and more broadly, f/r/ictional sites of "rubbing
across" ("traffick" indebted to the Latin *transfricare*) and their generative
relationships that slip up and through time/s.

In its recurring and recrudescent creativity, early modern water proves
good to think with about the possibilities of collaboration: all wet texts
should, in fact, propel promiscuous partnerships rather than restrict their
access. To be clear: I am not interested in arguing why the early modern
period is *the* primary age of influence to study, or why it is the *most* liquid
historically.[47] There is no single age of influence. "[A]ll waters" are included.
In general, my readings are meant to be suggestive instead of definitive.
I hope they resonate with waterscapes different from faraway contact zones
mapped here, be it the Lea of Izaak Walton's (1593–1683) *The Compleat
Angler* (1653) or your own home. The *inter* of wetness works in the middle space of discipline, period, and genre; it even melts the university's
walls, seeing and seeking "action" broadly defined by actors and activists
alike. I wish this book to be a true place of confluence between specializa-
tions, departments, methodologies, and disciplines (such as ecocomposition). Proliferation is all: and yet I must admit, especially to the early
modern reader, that there are certain critical waters I am "for" more than
others. My overall goal is not just to combat landlocked criticism; there
I would only be pontificating the merits of watery studies over dry ones
rather than showing their prospective collaborations. My intervention is
designed to broaden early modern ecostudies' current horizons, excellent
studies that nonetheless risk congregating around specific sites.[48] I will use
(and laud) the critical shorelines from which others have launched before
me, yet my headings will be divergent: in blue cultural studies, beyond the
sea to freshwater, to solids (ice) and the gelatinous in-betweens (swamps);[49]
in ecotheory, beyond limit cases such as "deep ecology" to rhizome and
actor-network inquiries;[50] and, although he runs my introduction's ship,

beyond the authorship of Shakespeare.[51] And while postcolonial ecocrit-ics emphasize the need for "a broadly materialist understanding of the changing relationship between people, animals, and environment," early modern travel literature has been relatively unexplored ecocritically.[52] Thus this book is "for" many wet things: I trust it will add some flux to the ways in which scholars dam fields and periods (and more) into neat seg-ments; that it will stir up conversations between multiple fields just as it does between beings; that thinking with water recognizes the plurality that water *is*. Let us add to the critical reservoir of wet non/humanities, and may it overflow like the bodies who assemble there, a promulgation of erring, "like a drop of water / That . . . seeks another drop."[53]

A preface faces forward: my approach rephrases Patricia Yaeger's ques-tion, "How liquid are we?"[54] as both *were* and *will be*. To think about early modern liquid history is ultimately to think about liquid futures. Every-thing depends on the position, where we turn, including our willingness to participate with the non/human whom. Critiquing Walter Benjamin's Angel of History, Latour states that "fleeing from the past while continu-ing to look at it will not do."[55] Indeed, the past confronts us. Although feeling-thinking-shivering wet entails a process forward into the future, we process forward (movement) while going backward (direction) in time. In this sense, Robert N. Watson's early modern flight "back to nature" seems too unidirectional: backward. For him, early modern progress meant a "function of regress" that was perpetuated by fantasies of uncorrupted nature, unambiguous epistemology, and unmediation.[56] Mediation was an uncomfortable present for some early modern authors, certainly. Others, however, did not try to get back to the epistemological Garden of Eden whenever they could; in fact, some (like those here) welcomed a mediated environmental future. They took positions, delivered prospects—"look[s] forward"—that were prompted by water's touch. Published environmen-tal tracts on issues like deforestation prove that impending catastrophes did not always point to teleological endings (God).[57] Some took action; as rivers were lost (vaulted) and left to fester (cesspool), "conservation" began, a word sprung specifically from the Thames when late medieval statutes entrusted the mayor and aldermen of London with the estuary's "conservacie," a charge that "doth extend it selfe to the preservation of the streame, and the banks of the River; as also the Fish and Frie within the same."[58] In his conclusion to a "confessedly pastoral project," Todd A. Borlik remarkably puts early modernity's "nascent environmental ethic" in line with our own, and furthermore asks what happens when we consider "environment" as a "verb, a process."[59] But the radical intimacy I desire is too root-y a word (*radix*, Latin for "root") when circumscribed by green fields of study. If the pastoral mode's "'staying power,' its adaptability, is precisely what we need,"[60] wet art forms of intermixed genres give us a more tempestuous impulse to change, their flows supply our longed-for propulsion. The language of "backward" can serve to stigmatize timeless—because "uncorrupted" and hence uncivilized—places and peoples, be they the savages of America or hillbilly "trash." The Great Flood was not just biblical past to some; the rainy day after tomorrow was unsure, yet always poised on the brink of overflow (as it is today). If "time enmeshes, at an even greater level of intimacy . . . the confusion of humans and nonhumans," and this immersion "is not our past *but our future as well*," as Latour prognosticates,[61] I believe an enmeshment of times—early modern and our own, a "we" of plural time—can make us more intimate with non/human things as we enter uncertain futures with them, as our wet-world turns, and breaks, on the shores of multi-temporality. "The world is turnin'," but the ark of a literary archive, full of stories that survive, aids us in rewriting our covenants with wet, allows us to meditate upon living intracatastrophically (within them), and helps us become more *conversant* in addition to conservational, perhaps "turnin'" the world politically and poetically in the process.

In opening (not closing), and for the sake of shivering time, you may call my ecotheorizations "presentist."[62] It is fitting, then, to focus on a damply dramatic site: the Rose Theatre, built in 1587, that emerged from a boggy "grave" in 1989 only to be resubmerged soon after, thereby suffering the near-fate of its neighbor the Globe centuries before.[63] Red rope-lights running along the dank Bankside ground indicate where the stage once stood, the Rose's water paradoxically preserving the foundation of previous performance. This theatrical excavation illuminates our desire to enhance water's performativity that never left and, moreover, to re/en/act with it. Lethe has too long slaked our thirsts; the question becomes not how to restart water's playfulness but why we have forgotten, in Ivan Illich's words, "its seeming equivocation [to be] the quivering ambiguity of life"; why Mnemosyne, "a fluid memory," is intentionally replaced with "a fixed storehouse for past utterances," living water/s for "H_2O."[64] I deepen our thirsts for early modern waters in an effort to prove that we have never lost its feeling, only been numbed to its touch and assured of its disenchantment. To be sure, my project is not a plea for an impassioned rhetoric of "salvation" or a more commiserative yearning for lost water-worlds; doing so would only replicate the mistaken logic of relinquishment: to give up "mastery" (never held) in the former and technology (never automatous) in the latter. Nor is this is a call for a reinvigorated form of sustainability (such as recycling); like others who have argued for "postsustainability,"[65] I see sustainability as a fantasy, like the illusion of dryness, that presupposes a harmonious future tantalizingly out of reach. Plumbing the houses of drama and travel literature explores the problems and pleasures of becoming more-than-human; entering these shivering, wet spaces is to conduct amphibious archeology: of finding beginnings without ends and not *the* beginning ("archaeo-," from Greek *arkhē*) of the source, preferring geneses to Genesis—those inexplicable "waters" that precede God's creation in the second verse[66]—to sense how the artistic process with water works, how waters work upon us, and how they have always done so. We cannot think of time without thinking about water, or a time without water. "Hydrogen" means "water maker," and this is where I wish to start with you, with these waters that keep making: *fons sans*— instead of *et—origo*; "springs" that spring; currents that emphasize movement and mappability while digressing from questions of causation; molecules irreducible, antiessentialist, and infinite in variety that quest after the *more* of matter's addition and not its *lack*. If society is at "risk" it is also in re-creation.[67] The early modern ages of water are come, and their inventions not gone.

Meander

The word "meander"—a "winding course," later "a labyrinthine plan" and a verb denoting "to wander aimlessly with no or little purpose"— comes from the river of the same name (spelled Maeander and now Menderes) in Miletus, present-day southwestern Turkey and the home of the sixth-century BCE Greek philosopher Thales. As the first Western philosopher (according to Aristotle, who believed that Greek thought began with natural philosophy), Thales is widely known for proposing that the first cause of all things was water. His talents as a hydraulic engineer, his penchant for traveling the Nile, and his profitable marketing of olive oil are perhaps less known. One apocryphal story claims he diverted the Halys River in Anatolia so that Croesus's army could pass into Cappadocia. These proclivities cast Thales into dire straits of "domestication" that persist to this day, a sentence capped ultimately by the irony of his death: dehydration, nature's revenge. But each episode valuably illustrates how his metaphysics were conjoined with his physical encounters with wetness; as elemental philosopher David Macauley proposes, "as a result of his interactions with and investigations of this element, he may have been permitted and privileged to discover some of [water's] seemingly universal qualities, properties, and powers."[68] There is one more important story to tell: Thales, stargazing, once fell into a well. Imagining what shivers he met, and what thoughts transpired by being trapped by water for an indefinite time, retells the transportative thought process that *is* every meeting with water. Thales's spill is a model for the meanders that arise from meeting Meanders and the wanderings that lead to them: to run into chance encounters with water (a well) and then to reposition ourselves with new aims, aims that are still susceptible to veer and yet, in doing so, converge with another body of water. This book is my own story from the well; meandering is, and has always been, making hydrological turns upon turns in the labyrinth, and I hope that it influences. As its own wet space, a "wetware" of shivering architecture, this book is an entrance that invites the reader (you) to take the turn as well and thus be entered-entranced as I have been. So let us go down to these lines that seek to run. Here runs a story written in water; here run the stories that water writes. What f/ol/lows is a collaboration, a conversation with wet worlds and words together in flow, a discourse of and in cascade. We start with the Thames.

Enter, Wet

When you go into the river you discover a new entrance—and in yourself you uncover an exit, an unseen exit, your exit. (You brought it with you.)

—Roni Horn, *Another Water (The River Thames, for Example)*

[I]n the yeare 1574 on the fourth of September after a strong shower of rayne, a lad (of the age of 18 years) minding to haue leapt ouer the channell [at Downgate], was taken by the feete and borne downe with the violence of that narrow streame, and carried towarde the Thames with such a violent swiftnesse, as no man could rescue or stay him, till he came against a cart wheele that stood in the water gate, before which time he was drowned, and starke dead.

—John Stow, *The Survey of London* (1598)

Water wants a witness. Roni Horn's *Another Water (The River Thames, for Example)* is a set of approximately one hundred photographs of the river taken between January and May 1999, interspersed with actual police reports of suicide (one occurs roughly every week), and accompanied by reiterative footnotes that indirectly reference the water in the picture, oftentimes quoting song lyrics and cinematic dialogues surrounding the riverine. The reports, positioned opposite Horn's pictures with their infinite variegations and play, are clinically white; we witness drowned bodies through others' testimony such as the coroner or standers-by on bridges, piecing together lives that have been dismembered and dissolved-by-Thames. Liquefied, but not lost: these bodies are rewitnessed now—by Horn, by us—and their stories rereported through wet media, whether it be bureaucratic ink, an art print, a film. In "example," we witness the tragedy of water but also its allure: people taken and transformed by the oozy underbed, the black water signifying not the absence of activity but the enmeshment of commotion, questions sponsored by depths of full five fathoms or just a few inches. We are far from water's brighter qualities of reflection, for in this macabre maelstrom comes the clarity *of* opacity: the recognition that water is you and *another*, the othering of you, the self made self-aware of its solvency via its relation to something submerged. Witnessing the river, watching water, the mind meanders. Exit the solid "you" that was never really there: "If water is you, what are you? Or if water is you, who is water?"[1] Enter the dissoluble human self-in-motion in its stead—"(The Thames is you.)"[2]—a statement bounded and set free simultaneously, an insertion (like a stage direction) that points to grammatical and bodily in/completion: a true "parenthesis" (Greek *parentithenai*, "put in beside") that magnifies the interlude between entrance and exit waiting for you beside water, loves like suicide, the trauma and joys of un/coupling. The Thames is but one example; witnessing water counteracts its toted status as a space of mirrored reflection. Water is the reflection of diffraction, the body

Roni Horn, *Still Water (The River Thames, for Example)*, 1999 (detail). Lithograph on paper, 15 framed photographs and text, each 30.5 x 41.5 inches (77.47 x 105.41 cm); framed, each 33.07 x 44.09 x 1.97 inches (84 x 112 x 5 cm). Courtesy of the artist and Hauser & Wirth.

undergoing multiple acts of rippling into an other, goings out and in, always underway.

Thames

In a London theater in the early seventeenth century, water makes its way onto the stage. Enter, shipwrecked survivors from *Pericles* and *The Tempest*. The latter is William Shakespeare's wettest play. (The word "wet" appears four times, the most in all of his works.) It is easy to understand, then, why Steve Mentz opens his book of blue cultural studies, *At the Bottom of Shakespeare's Ocean*, with the oozy "sea-change" of this play obsessed with shipwrecks and storms, transformations and rebirth (1.2.404). For him, the "change" addresses "the physical and metaphorical qualities of the ocean . . . salt water's transformative impact on human flesh," and he rightly cautions that if we read this line purely as a demonstration of the dramatist's poetic prowess we lose the "real taste of ocean . . . a sharp tang of nonhuman immensity."[3] Mentz's work is a rich meditation on the powerful sea changes that the ocean performs in the early modern period. What is perhaps a little less noticeable than this critical "sea-change"— unless you happen to be the dramaturge—is a particular splash the ocean makes in the opening tempest: "*Enter Mariners, wet*" (1.1.45). The ocean's varying "impact on human flesh" that the play explores is performed, incredibly, right before our watery eyes. The stage direction attests to the ocean's transformative powers to "change" things, but in a slightly different register than in Ariel's song. The sailors do not merely act drenched; they are profoundly acted upon. Water performs, collaborates, and commingles with their "too too solid flesh" (*Hamlet*, 1600, 1.2.129). Enter, water. "*Enter Mariners, wet*." *Entertain*: a Latinate combination of the preposition *inter* ("between") and *tenēre* ("to hold"). They are, like the waterscape itself, held in between human and nonhuman. "*Enter Mariners, wet*" is both a stage direction and multiple directions bodies may take, bodies poised in potential: pitch, yaw, and roll.

In *Shakespeare's Ocean*, Dan Brayton fairly critiques the "terrestrial bias" of ecocriticism, early modern studies included.[4] Indeed, little attention has been paid to the materiality of water in a stage direction like "*Enter Mariners, wet*" apart from handbooks. *Pericles* and *The Tempest* are the only two Shakespearean plays in which specific stage directions call for the actors to not just act wet, but to literally enter wet (5.38; 1.1.45, 4.1.193, respectively). In these global plays where islands' locations and the Mediterranean's size are unresolved, wet runs of production draw attention to the turbulent relationships between oceans and humans, wet object and dry subject, and their supposed ontological divide in the early seventeenth century. Brayton's tale of "our aquatic ontogeny" reminds us that "we share a strange and ancient kinship with marine animals" since the sea is "the stuff of which we are made."[5] His book tests the waters of being; while sea creatures are "deeply part of human ontology," I think we can plunge deeper into (even below) the waters of ecological interconnectivity in order to ponder the difference between being "of the sea," being "compassed" by it, and being in a condition of "partial belonging."[6] Enter, wet actants: when watery bodies materialize on the early modern stage, they indicate embodiments that push our ontological categories into stranger waters, revealing the "human" to be always uncertain, yet constantly co-implicated with watery beings. It is a move not beyond water, but instead goes beyond the organic (piscatorial, mammalian, cetacean) kingdom of kinship: a "hypersea," we might say (*hyper-*, from Greek *huper* "over, beyond"), that encompasses "a very ancient and . . . strange fish" (*The Tempest*, 2.2.25–26) like Caliban, that always loops back from "dry" land to probiotic pools.[7] The stage favors these hydro/onto/genetic chains of becoming over the stiffer Great Chain of Being, choosing the metamorphosis of evolution over the echelons of prioritization.[8] Wet drama does not just rearrange the actors at play only to re-place them within impermeable hierarchies; wet discourse places heterogeneous beings along flat horizons of hydrological relations, at scales larger than molecules and smaller than oceans, reconceptualizing them in the process.

Shakespeare's stage, propped up as it was by the wet "stuff" of matter, absolutely roils in these plays. The difficulty is that we do not know exactly how the storms were portrayed and the actors were soaked. *The Tempest* had a wide theatrical range: it was performed at the court of James I, at Blackfriars, and at the Globe. Blackfriars afforded Shakespeare unique opportunities for special effects. Andrew Gurr believes the play was written specifically for the company's newly acquired indoor venue, listing the standard assortment of theatrics necessary to make a storm: thunder came from a "'roul'd bullet on a sheet of metal, or a 'tempestuous drum' . . .

lightning from squibs, and mists from smoke."[9] Certain senses take precedence in this explanation, however: storms are indicated by what they sound or look like. Yet stages *were* wet, whether in- or outdoors; out of the nearly fifteen stage directions (to the best of my knowledge) that call for water, most involve shipwreck.[10] What is singular about *The Tempest* is that it stages what the ocean feels like on the skin—its material touch upon the saturated bodies of the mariners—while *at* sea rather than after their wreck. The latter was a common enough convention that George Chapman (ca. 1559–1634), Ben Jonson (1572–1637), and John Marston (1576–1634) parodied it in *Eastward Ho!* (1605), a play that explicitly evokes the Thames and "a coil [it] keeps!" (4.1.14–15).[11] Staged shipwrecks typically operate according to the logic of before and after, cause and effect, positing a timeline from dry to wet (and, if lucky enough to survive, wet to dry). *The Tempest* interrupts this transition by suspending audiences in the middle, caught up in the moment of wetness's *doing*. Water is the main event here, and as such it reroutes predictable plot progressions in which an onstage storm produces an onshore arrival signaled by a stage direction or prompted by a playbook.

Shakespeare produced a tempest of unprecedented magnitude, certainly, and yet critics tend to diminish his achievement by evaluating it according to the more desiccated tenets of theatrical realism. A wet entrance is a "slight . . . devic[e]" that produces, says Gurr, "an emphatic though momentary illusion of reality" preceding Prospero's explanation to Miranda that "[t]here's no harm done" (1.2.15), and that all victims are, in fact, safe and dry.[12] Wetness, for him, is only a momentary lapse into reality: "The wetting of the mariners is a wonderfully literal-minded and yet strikingly minimal realization of the storm effects."[13] Gurr places water in a binary with reality on one side and representation on the other. Alan C. Dessen situates actors at the helm, choosing between "minimalist" (artistic) and "realist" (meteorological) productions.[14] Both offer viable, yet ultimately prescriptive choices, I think; when we read this way, we lose water's touch, understanding it solely as a backdrop for culture (art), waiting in the social constructivists' wings. If water cannot be severed from its social and cultural contexts because it shapes them, then arguing how society constructs water would suggest that culture is still separate from nature. Both present a prop for and of the "human." *The Tempest* meditates on the affective agency of water by calling for its material presence on stage. Our amazement definitely arises from expecting a shipwreck in the opening scene, only to be given, instead, dehydrated outcomes in act I, scene 2 and the act following—the sorcerer's explanatory "provision" (1.2.28) for his enemies' safety and Gonzalo's (sea) change of clothes, their "garments being, as they were, / drenched in the sea, hold notwithstanding their freshness and / glosses, being rather new-dyed than stained with salt water" (2.1.62–64)—but it just as importantly comes from realizing that actors playing wet characters *cannot* be believed to be dry, ever, even if "[t]ravellers ne'er did lie" (3.3.26). Gonzalo's gestic and deictic line ironically announces water's presence and not its absence, since, for one, their costumes might easily stay "stained" for the remainder of the performance. The dissolution of the "real," a disbelief in our ability to distinguish illusion (image, representation) from reality (matter, the prop): here audiences witness water's truly "special" effects.[15]

Admittedly, the mariners' entrance is an editorial dilemma. *The Tempest*'s manuscript was prepared by Ralph Crane and printed for the first time in the 1623 folio. Whether "*Enter Mariners, wet*" is an insertion of Crane's or Shakespeare's is impossible to determine. Trevor R. Griffiths's recent handbook to the play argues that the direction

> is more likely to describe either an author's thoughts on what he wanted to achieve or an audience's visual impression of the storm, rather than to act as an instruction to a stage manager, who is more likely to have needed to be reminded to have a bucket of water ready at an appropriate time and place than what the result of having the water available would be.[16]

But the "result[s]" are crucial: they move audiences away from a purely "visual impression" of oceans kept at a safe distance to a more embodied reaction to wetness, of bodies impressed (marked) by water. It allows us to think on how it was felt (phenomenologically), to what extent (in duration, in kind), and how it was interpreted once it entered the cultural imagination. The hue of blue is important, but so is the haptic and the aural; thus what *kinds* of water in the "bucket" were thrown on them and what aesthetic reactions resulted matter. Refreshing, from one of many "Conduits of fresh Water, serving the Citie" that John Stow surveys.[17]

Sickening, out of the thick Thames itself, its increasingly "noyant" nature desperately in need of reformation: "if any person after a great rain falleth, or at any other time sweepe any dung, ordure, rubbish, rushes, Seacole dust, or any other thing noyant, downe into the chanell of any street or lane, whereby the common course there is let . . . the same things noyant [are] driven downe into the said water of Thames."[18] Repulsive, skimmed off the River Fleet near Blackfriars, the Thames's treacly tributary and the source of Ben Jonson's odorous encomium in mock-epic form, "On the Famous Voyage" (1612–13):

> Ycleped Mud, which when their oars did once stir,
> Belched forth an air as hot as at the muster
> Of all your night-tubs, when the carts do cluster
> Who shall discharge first his merd-urinous load.[19]

Liquid (urine), solid (feces), and gas (air): a dip into the Fleet's ooze is to suffer a "shitten" change. Stagewater raises important awareness about *who* is wet: decisions onstage to drench characters of a lower class could support class divisions, even while there were bodily fluids being swapped through actors' clothes (like sweat) and between audience members (we can imagine the various discharges). Then there is the *where* and *when*: the venue can reinforce these wet-dry distinctions, especially when galleried gentry view a play on a rainy afternoon, looking across a muddy pit full of bottom-dwellers standing in their stew and soak. For these few reasons, the "result" of Griffiths's summation is less materiality and more art. Imagining this stage direction's startling and un/intended effects does all three things at once (and more): it cues the stagehand (a reminder), it gestures to the intended aesthetic effect (a storm), and it introduces an oceanic ecopoesis that breaks down, rather than widens, the separation between art and world while affording differences and examining their effects. In the language of what Nedra Reynolds calls "geographies of writing," the theater becomes an *inter* space of play, a "thirdspace" that exists somewhere between metaphor and materiality.[20] Swirling together "perceived, conceived, and lived space," it leaves binaries "floating in the middle."[21] Neither representation nor cultural construction, staged wetness is what Bruno Latour would call a "circulating reference," a "long chain of transformations" and "potentially endless sequence of mediators" that refuses to separate language and nature, world and word, into isolated domains.[22] Enter reality, wet. The cue is a handbook for dramaturges floating in, and writing as, whirling and widening middles. Wet matter infuses the dryness of metaphor to produce matter-phors: language that tells of non/humans in collaboration, garrulous alternatives to dead sea scrawls.

If, as Griffiths speculates, wet entrances could be achieved from "a judicious backstage application of water,"[23] watching water's performativity in Shakespeare's plays helps us disembark the ship of too-human authorial invention. From the opening scene, onstage water underscores *The Tempest's* theorization of humans becoming watery via their material entanglements. Drastic loss of control proves automatically damning; "*Enter Mariners, wet*" to utter one line in unison before they exit: "All lost! To prayers, to prayers! All lost!" (1.1.46). Water introduces confusion—Latin *confundere*, to "mingle together"—inviting attempts to quell its social destabilizations. There are many problems concerning chains of command on this boat; Antonio condemns the sailors for abandoning him, employing a gruesome image of pirates' rotting corpses, bodies that would have been noticeable on London's mud banks taking to/in the sea most earnestly by sloughing their skins: "We are merely cheated of our lives by drunkards. / This wide-chopped rascal—would thou mightst lie drowning / The washing of ten tides" (1.1.50–52). "He'll [the Boatswain] be hanged yet," promises Gonzalo, "Though every drop of water swear against it / And gape at wid'st to glut him" (1.1.52–54). In water's "swear[ing]" we hear a disruptive presence: the Boatswain understands their lack of authority amidst this swearing—"What cares these roarers / for the name of king?" (1.1.15–16)—and yet this conversation is coded as a competition versus voices, a jockeying for privileged positions of class, gender, human. Listening more carefully, it shows the little cares these upper-class Milanese and Neapolitans have for watery bodies: drops, "drunkards," and women, lunar beings "as leaky as an unstanched / wench" (1.1.43–44). It is misleading, however, to assume that these waters dethrone the "king" human, Alonso. If action is not about mastery, ecology is not about sovereignty: "You are a councillor," the Boatswain pleads hopelessly to Gonzalo, "if you can command these elements to silence and work / peace of the present, we will not hand a rope more" (1.1.18–20). The play is already questioning who speaks and how to *counsel* in its first sixty lines; the word, from the Latin *consilium*, is itself a confusion: a counselor (one who gives advice or council, from "consultation or advice") and a councillor (a member of a council, from "summon together"). Perhaps I am becoming Gonzalo myself—"winding the watch of my wit. . . . What impossible matter will I make easy next?" (2.1.12, 88)—but in this "councillor" is the portrait of parliaments at sea, of things speaking and thus taking their place/s, talking out of turn, adding to conversations and the body of stormy assembly that is act 1, scene 1.

"*A confused noise within*" (1.1.55). Wet entrances with others, sensations that may happen unannounced at any moment: "*within*" is within the tiring room and an ontological condition as well. The "Mariners [within]" respond: "We split, we split, we split!" (1.1.56). "*[W]ithin*" water announces a call-and-response dialogue, the sound of the self breaking apart, "split[ting]," and shivering within others: "What, must our mouths be cold?" (1.1.47). *No*: it is a call to abandon the anhydronous "we"— the human "we"—and we are almost there, reciting Antonio's line of last resort, "Let's all sink wi'th' King" (1.1.57). Let "wi'th" become "without": let us let sovereignty sink. Going "*within*" admits how swearing is a voice of water, how waters "gape" wide not just to swallow ("glut") but also to speak garrulously, and nears the truly noisy and nauseous meaning of conjuring, Latin *conjurare*, to "swear together." This clattering expands the critical attention given to music in the play, and draws closer to a parasitical noise of relationality, only to be usurped, unfortunately, in the very next scene by the water wizard Prospero, that great Tempestarian who uses his "staff"—or is it a dowsing rod?—to tease and tap the waters in the name of conjuration-domination. Narrated this way, water's (brief) realism is then handed over to the insubstantial realm of magic ("art") in this rhabdomancer who escapes dousing, believing his "magic cloak" of concealment to be waterproof. But if Prospero "[p]ut the wild waters in this roar" (1.2.2) he did it through hijacking: we know he did not put the "roar" in the "waters." The tempest cannot be silenced by his art; water takes the form of collaborative non/human playwriting, it is never Prospero's alone, and it is never still. "Lie there, my art" (1.2.25) is an empty command.

Prospero might try to cloak water's agency, but liquid remains in and at play on the island. It is not surprising that a story involving marooned Europeans in a semitropical locale proves to be a thirsty one: "water" is mentioned by name thirteen times. Drinking water is one of the first things given to Caliban, "When thou cam'st first, / Thou strok'st me and made much of me, wouldst give me / Water with berries in't" (1.2.335–37), a gesture that he then reciprocates ("I'll show thee the best springs; I'll pluck thee berries," 2.2.152), and it is Gonzalo's gift to Prospero and Miranda before they are sent adrift (1.2.161). But water is also used as a weapon to threaten others' bodies. (Prospero will offer only "[s]ea-water" to Ferdinand, 1.2.466.) Inside the play's vast reservoir of water references, potable water most frequently serves a social function, and nowhere is its dual entrancing of bodies and communities better displayed than as alcohol. Stefano comes ashore "upon a butt of sack which the sailors heaved o'erboard" and fashions a bottle of wood, "made of the bark of a tree with mine own hands" (2.2.113–15). His nausea—"My stomach is not constant" (2.2.6–7), filled with a cocktail of saltwater and Spanish wine—is just that, born from the sea. ("Nausea" comes from the Greek *nausia*, "ship," which is, in Stefano's case, a boat, or butt, of wine.) As a dropsy fool, he is overfull, flowing; his logorrhea a singing "to sea" (2.2.52) and another form of vomiting. Perhaps the sea adds a dash of its "roar" to his admixture, too, for "noise" comes from "nausea" as well. He enters, wet, only without a stage direction: and his wetness should remind us of another scene somewhere else in the Mediterranean, the shores of Laconia in Philip Sidney's (1554–86) *Arcadia* (1593), where a shipwreck survivor, Musidorus, arrives onshore holding a "square small coffer" and appearing to two shepherds as "a thing which floated."[24] Julian Yates reads this pastoral landing as an "event," observing how the sea refuses to separate man from "thing": "the world of tides proposes an alternative logic of existence, an alternative understanding of what it means to be 'human' . . . imagines a time solely of things endowed with movement through their parasitic relation to the elements."[25] But even shaken, he is never quite empty of seawater, and neither is Stefano after "*He dances . . . round*" (2.2.106). (Whereas Trinculo, also waterlogged, "can swim like a / duck," 2.2.120–21.) The anonymous play *Loves Changelinges Change* (1630) dramatizes the wet entrance Stefano might have had onstage; following Sidney's plot closely, stage directions in the first scene involve "Musidorus drawn in wet and half dead" and then Strephon and Claius "take him by the heels while water runs out of his mouth."[26] Are these coffers and butts, then, images of assemblage in re/birth or the "butt" of jokes, mere buffoonery? The question is, rather, how to fill the bottle of wood and the body anew, displayed in the ambiguous pronoun that fails to signify subject or object: "we'll fill *him* by and by again," says Stefano (2.2.168; emphasis added). The issue becomes how to get one's fill, by what means, and at what cost: "Tell not me. When the butt is out we will / drink water, not a drop before. Therefore bear up and board / 'em" (3.2.1–3). The language of entrance shifts: the "same black cloud" that follows Trinculo, that "cannot choose but fall by pailfuls" is a "foul bombard that would shed his liquor" (2.2.20–23). Wetting belies a military siege, whether it is the body bombarded (from celestial cannonade), boarded (by an invasive substance), or surrounded (fit into a drinking vessel known as a bombard, made resourceful). *All*: it is an event in which the body becomes bombard, where two vessels pull alongside ("near" or *para*), invent an in/organic engine of canals, sometimes queerly so: "I will pour some in thy other mouth [anus]" (2.2.89). The outcome is uncertain: a mutual slaking of thirsts, or a furthering of hostility over "the dregs of the storm" (2.2.38); to run and hide, or to open wide and receive "celestial liquor" (2.2.109). Never past, every body is in this tempest, *is* this tempest and *Tempest*, filtered, passed through.

It is hard to believe, after all of this, that the play wets not once but twice. The first instance is salty: the storm that stages the permeability of the human, its precariousness emphasized by the mariners' dripping prayers. The second is fresher, although still briny: Caliban, Stefano, and Trinculo also enter "*all wet*" (4.1.195) while they traipse "I'th'filthy-mantled pool beyond [Prospero's] cell" (4.1.182). Tactile water takes on qualities; it significantly stinks, "at which my / nose is in great indignation" (4.1.188–89), but immersion does not completely overwhelm. Even shallow waters hold open the imaginative possibilities of submersion: "There dancing up to th' chins . . . the foul lake / O'er-stunk their feet" (4.1.183–84). These three "smell all horse-piss," making reference perhaps to the horse-courser's wet entrance in Christopher Marlowe's (1564–93) *Doctor Faustus* (1592) and to Prospero's previous statement about "stale to catch these thieves"

(4.1.187), "stale" being both a decoy and urine (and quite possibly the smell of Thames water). There is a human-animal-elemental commingling happening here, and it turns tragic with the "infinite loss" (4.1.209), says Stefano, of their bottle in the pool. Trinculo, whose name obviously rhymes with "drink," replies, "That's more to me than my wetting" (4.1.210), meaning that the loss of drink matters more to him than falling in the pool, but also, and more tellingly, that "wetting" *incorporates* drinking. Stefano makes this connection clearer when he claims, "I will fetch off my bottle, / though I be o'er ears for my labour" (4.1.212–13): to drown in the filth is to drown in the drink. This scene is the bawdy reply to Ariel's "sea-change" song of metamorphosis (1.2.400–405); the actors' bodies, in fact, physically change on stage, bogging down even if drying and sobering up. Drink-ulo's body becomes a watery bottle of liquor, a movement accentuated by the actor's literal saturation. Interestingly, they cannot stop talking about drinking, orifices, and drowning: they approach the "mouth o'th' cell" (4.1.215), where Caliban will be their "foot-licker" (4.1.218), and they fill with "bloody thoughts" (4.1.219). They are getting wetter: Caliban calls for "[t]he dropsy [to] drown this fool [Trinculo]" (4.1.228), and Trinculo, for all his fluid identity, fittingly catches a disease in which the body retains water. And this is why the temptation, or tantalization, of changing *clothes* is so strong with them: as actors, they would want dry clothes, and we would expect them to, but the body stays wet even as it reaches for the "*glistening apparel*" Prospero hangs up (4.1.193). It is to the terrestrial "lime" tree they turn, yet the stage property quickly mutates into paste: "Monster, come," beckons Trinculo, "put some lime upon your fingers" (4.1.242), alluding to the sticky substance used to catch birds. Thus it might not be that this entrance "*all wet*" is simply a joke on the lower class in the play and in attendance, but proves the point that things are always stickier than they seem, for they, the actors "*all*," have been caught by water, no matter how high and dry above the pool or "beyond" the solid cell, how sumptuous the clothing, or how fervid their pleas to live a dry life or "die a dry death" like Gonzalo: "Now would I give a thousand furlongs of sea for an acre of barren ground" (1.1.58–60). Water is the solution that binds and dissolves, a glue that detaches schemas of wet and dry, the "strange" matter of skin—echoing the fairy's "rich and strange" (1.2.405)—of various and variable porosity in the pool of things.

At the same time that Shakespeare shows us the comical fantasy of human separation from these pooling and pullulating worlds, he also admits the real violence this fantasy permits: both the violence of water (1.1) along with the violence against it. Even more incredibly than the play's double dose of directed water, Prospero (the blue), the not-wet water wizard, believes himself to be a magically autonomous thing set apart. He wants his elixirs without the potion's solution, potency in dryness only ("elixir," the Greek *xērion*, a "powder for drying wounds"), an ability to speak spells with cracked lips: "Go charge my goblins that they grind their joints / With dry convulsions," he curses, wishing his enemies desiccated above water, higher than that which lives in the highest regions, the "cat o'mountain" (4.1.254–57). Despite the island's geographical mystery, it is a critical commonplace to view Caliban as a New World native. What is less noticed is Caliban's relation to a material patch of the island, the marsh:

> As wicked dew as e'er my mother brushed
> With raven's feather from unwholesome fen
> Drop on you both! A southwest blow on ye,
> And blister you all o'er! (1.2.324–27)[27]

Caliban's curse is from a "fen," producing swampy "dew" meant to infect his persecutor, Prospero, and it comes, notably, from the hot southern regions. While he is called "thou earth" (1.2.317)—and might even enter from below the stage because the text does not specify where his dwelling exactly is located—he is a wet/land "creature" like his liquid fellows, who "wear[s] a gaberdine" in act 2, scene 2, who learns how to drink and knows the feeling of rain.[28] Caliban is an example of swampy bodies forced onto dry land: "you sty me," he says to Prospero, "[i]n this hard rock" (1.2.345–46). But he also underscores Prospero's way of conflating toxic bodies with an alien swampscape. When Prospero calls him a "poisonous slave" (1.2.322), he could just as easily be talking to the water as well as those who dwell in it. By denigrating Caliban's body, Prospero voices early modern fears of fens and their standing water. Full of disease (dew), coded as foreign (southwest), and feminine (mother), swamps demanded territorialization (witnessed in chapter 4), a straightening-out into "segmentarity" and "strata."[29] All early modern waterscapes, actually, are susceptible "ecotones" in this way: transitional areas between two biological communities under pressure (from the Greek *tonos*, "tension"). Water might not always heal, either: those who believe to be separate from it, like usurpers anxious about losing their hard-earned dominion, "with bemocked-at stabs / Kill the still-closing waters" (3.3.63–64). Although Prospero lives in a dry cavernous "cell" (4.1.195), he and his company are there only infrequently; the failed assassination attempt only proves that the swampy things he abhors surround him. He believes himself to be beyond the swampscape, a sick place he ultimately abandons for "fair" Milan. Beyond but not *without*: "This thing of darkness I / Acknowledge mine" (5.1.279–80). If Caliban is a "thing of darkness" according to Prospero, so too, is the environment. In his material entanglements with one swamp "thing," Prospero must necessarily recognize his relationship with the other: both dark "thing[s]" are "mine." His puzzling phrase that "[e]very third thought shall be my grave" (5.1.314) begins to sound less like a relinquishment of authority and more like an acknowledgment of his material enmeshment with the ooze. If "we split" in the storm at the beginning of the play, Prospero will "drown [his] book" and "bury" his staff at its end (5.1.55–57). In other words, we sink, we sink, into more and more embeddedness. If Prospero ever leaves—it is unclear—it will be a moist farewell.

He cannot leave the marsh so fast: stuck at this sphagnous spot of not-yet-departure, a dream appears. It is worth revisiting Prospero's oft-quoted realization of ephemerality—"our little life / Is rounded with a sleep" (4.1.157–58)—for it betrays the tension of water's un/doing, an intimation of escape but also, even if briefly in the space of less than twenty lines, a conversion and embrace of dissolution. Prospero is surely "vex'd," as we have seen: caught between participating interdependently with a liquid isle and seeking dry cells at the cellular level. It is the same direction of a "*confused noise*" (4.1.140) that makes the actors of the agricultural masque "*heavily vanish*." While we might be tempted to hear this confusion as the noise of act 1, scene 1 and attribute it to "*within*" Prospero's mind only—a psychological tremor—it is a force that engages him climatically: "Your father's in some passion / That works him strongly" (4.1.143–44). His passion is more than just internal conditions; it is involved in an ecological interchange with a given environment, the confusion of commingling. Some matter "works" upon him, some "*noise*" that

I have been defining as wetness's powers of "*confus[ion]*." What is re-markable is that Prospero does not banish the thought; indeed, he follows it, and dreams up: "These our actors, As I foretold you, were all spirits, and / Are melted into air, into thin air" (4.1.148–50). While air (spirit) and the language of vanishing are definitely apparent here and through-out the rumination—"baseless fabric," "cloud-capped towers," "insubstan-tial pageant" (4.1.151, 152, 155)—I want to underscore the necessary wateriness of this scene illustrated in the word "melt." It takes an act of melting, even if they are spirits, to catalyze a metamorphosis into "thin air." Not just an amateur natural philosopher, Prospero repeats a widely held belief about transmutation: that as matter changed properties it changed elemental states in the process. (Hence he names "air" instead of steam, for instance, which is water.) If anything, then, he imagines a rudimen-tary hydrological cycle of melting and evaporation, centered on disso-lution: "the great globe itself, / Yea, all which it inherit, shall dissolve" (4.1.153–54). This circular image is a notable transformation, exchang-ing the circular form of perfection-harmony-sustainability for the circular motion of mind and matter ("stuff") that subsequently produces dreams: "We are such stuff / As dreams are made on, and our little life / Is rounded with a sleep" (4.1.156–58). Thus while other critics have interpreted Pros-pero's vision as an autobiographical farewell to the stage, a moment of metatheatrics, or self-referential dramaturgy disclosing how playwrights write, I believe that his dream is one that literally gives voice to how we make worlds with water, a powerful symbol of an open-ended cycle, the Globe and globe that is not the "O" of closure but the "O" of perme-ability and openness, the "O" of *oikos* and ecology. He had already med-itated on the reapers and sowers, the birth and death of romance (4.1.138). What is this "vision" if not a view of futurity, still part of environmental-ist rhetoric today, of what is given and left behind to future generations, "all which it inherit"? O, if only the verse would stay there; this would be a different departure, or even a willingness to stay. "Our [my] [his] revels are ended" too easily (4.1.148). He forecloses this possibility of dreaming futures: he will melt ("dissolve") the world, but in a deluge rather than a sensual act of house-building. The great melt will go on until it "[l]eave[s] not a rack behind" (4.1.156): a "rack" designating a "cloud" but also a "driving mist or fog." From this point on his thoughts "grave[ly]" thicken.

All we can say is what the startled onlookers do, "We wish you peace" (4.1.163). Or we can reply that nothing truly vanishes, retracing the mists of ontology, refusing to see racks as "baseless"—or worse—only a watery grave.

All of these scenes I have traversed deliquesce the insupportable idea of the human severed from its environment, and, in their moments of un/doing, offer ways of unthinking ecological sovereignty. To enter wet is to show the body being entered by water, directing our attention to the wetness of all things even if a stage direction is not given to or for them. These moments of entrance must be experienced collectively, and, in the case of the mariners, spoken as such. The question is to what ends: in the Epilogue, Prospero is never "free" (20), his final word, from his material bonds; his first line is more telling: "Be collected" (1.2.13). He redefines attachment to the elements, magically, as freedom: "Please *you*, draw near." "Then *to the* elements / Be free" (5.1.321–22, emphasis added). We are left with "bands" and "hands" at the end of the play, *yous*, symbols of cords and contracts that betoken better relationships with and toward oceanic matter rather than terms of enslavement (Epilogue 9, 10).[30] It is fitting that a play most known for its twice-mentioned "ooze" as a magical bed of transformation proves ontological purity impossible through mud and slimy wet/land, thereby dismantling codes of "fair" (Milan) and "filthy" (pool), along with our valuations and moral registers. The ooze is the material basis of de- and recomposition: from Old English *fÿlth*, "rotting matter." Intriguingly many of those in the audience (depending on venue) might have known this filth firsthand, in hand. Stow relates that on September 28, 1538, by order of Henry VIII's statute three years earlier, the "great shelves and other risings" made in the river Thames by "dung and other filth" were ordered to be cleansed by a unique method of recycling:

> that it shall be lawfull to every person or persons, to dig, carry away, and take away Sand, Gravell, or any Rubbish, Earth, or any thing lying or being in any Shelfe or Shelves within the said River of Thames, without let or interruption of any person or persons, and without anything paying for the same, and after that to sell the same away, or otherwise occupy or dispose the said Gravell, Sand, or other thing at their free liberty and pleasure.[31]

People flock "free[ly]" for free shit with which to re/build the social: literally themselves, for these "thing[s] lying or being," according to Stow's and his contemporaries' remonstrations about the river's health, included people's "Soylage, or filth." "Soylage" brown is people; in the slick "base" of river earth we witness the world in all its material ooze of engendering, not the "baseless fabric" of one magus's vision. Herein lies the original meaning of "pollute": not so much an invasion of previously uncontaminated essences but a commingling of substances and a trafficking across bodies, the Latin *pollut-* ("soiled, defiled") from the verb *polluere*, based on the root of *lutum* ("mud"). Ferried across "the said River," perhaps on the way to a play, they could think on aquatic ontogeny in the in/organic mud of the estuary, its primordial power of mediation and the vitality (life) it possessed, and they could build new structures in blue and brown, no less fragile, as their thoughts drifted away from impure and pure divisions toward unfathomable ontologies and what "rack[s]" are and will be left in time.

This sticky position was Prospero's, "defiled" Londoners', and finally our own. To unthink water as merely a grave—be it our first, second, or "third thought" (5.1.314)—is building "turf" with wetness: making worlds with water is also living, adrift, with it. Too often the way of longevity, of beating catastrophe, is to literally beat the waves.[32] Ferdinand's masochistic bodysurfing exemplifies this sort of conquest; Francisco tries to comfort Alonso by crediting his son's hypermasculinity:

> I saw him beat the surges under him
> And ride upon their backs. He trod the water,
> Whose enmity he flung aside, and breasted
> The surge, most swoll'n, that met him. (2.1.114–17)

And yet, we should remember that is Ariel who delivers Ferdinand safely from the tempest, not his breaststroke: "The King's son have I landed by himself" (1.2.222). The prince's arms are pent up "in [a] sad knot" when we actually see them (1.2.225), neither outstretched nor chopping water in defiant effort to stay alive. The ambiguity of endurance—how did he make it to shore, did he walk ("trod") on water, and at what "odd angle" of the island (1.2.224)—underscores what Mentz calls "swimmer poetics" occurring in shipwreck time: swimming as storytelling, without (and sometimes despite) a perceivable shoreline.[33] But we can see why Alonso, his father, would want to believe *this* tale: like Prospero's airy exhalation, of letting go, we just witnessed, it is difficult to dive deeper into immersion, to relinquish the "tread" of keeping water *beneath* the human and to embrace the "tread," so repetitive, of maintaining an upright position in deep water, without perceivable progress, dreading the chance of going nowhere, facing the fear of what you will find looking down: "Therefor my son I'th' ooze is bedded, and / I'll seek him deeper than e'er plummet sounded / And with him there lie mudded" (3.3.100–102). But you might also find a book, an eco-tome, a hydrography. It has been there all along. Before singing the song of sea change Ariel is dressed "*like a water-nymph*" (1.2.319), and upon hearing the sound waves, Ferdinand does not immediately think of water, although he hints at it: "Where should this music be? I'th' air [gas] or th' earth [solid]" (1.2.391); it is somewhere between, as he is, something *liquid*, water's voice: "This music crept by me upon the waters, / Allaying both their fury and my passion / With its sweet air" (1.2.395–97). Tales of drowning and tales with buoyancy, hope afloat: Iris, the rainbow, "wat'ry arch and messenger" (4.1.71), biblical and mythical transmitter, a covenant with water that could be, the noisy conversations with water that are, relations vanished but never disappeared.

"In this hope I live": "*Enter Pericles wet*" for a quick dip (6.48, 5.38). *Pericles* similarly theorizes what happens when human bodies enter and are entered by the sea. Within a "fish-story" like this one, enmeshment with the sea churns out non/human hybrids.[34] It is from the "finny subject of the sea" that the fishermen are able to tell their well-known moral about how fish are like men—the great ones swallow the smaller—and also how fish are men: the third fisherman "saw / the porpoise how he bounced and tumbled. . . . They say they're half fish, half flesh" (5.38, 5.63–64). It is from this oceanic mixture that Pericles enters. Tossed about on the waves, the hero eventually washes up on the shores of Pentapolis: "Wind, rain, and thunder, remember earthly man / Is but a substance that must yield to you" (5.42–43). A humbler statement than "Blow, winds, and crack your cheeks!" to be sure (*King Lear*, 1605, 3.2.1). But Pericles's wet entrance also calls the "substance" of the human into question: "What I have been, I have forgot to know, / But what I am, want teaches me to think on" (5.106–7). The stage direction is more than a Jacobean stage practice that signals to the audience that Pericles is shipwrecked. (Viola's entrance in act 1, scene 2 of *Twelfth Night*, for instance, is not "*wet*.") Stressing becomings over being, Pericles—soaked on shore and on stage—performs the contingent "am" that forever transforms. There is no perdurable substance known as identity, only a relationality tied to the ocean. More significantly, the play invites us to see this liquid nature of identity through the very substance that drenches the actor's body: "*Enter Pericles wet*." And exit Pericles, wet: in the end he asks to be

> put . . . to present pain,
> Lest this great sea of joys rushing upon me
> O'erbear the shores of my mortality
> And drown me with their sweetness! (21.178–81)

Pericles's body is still wet, still not quite dry from the shores of Pentapolis. More water, judiciously or not, is thrown on him. His oceanic body might risk personification here. Yet in a relatively obscure play full of "humming water" (11.62), transformative "ooze" (11.59), and a host of sea changes, the "humming water" is ultimately a non/human assemblage speaking to us: the wet body of the actor "humming" the lines onstage.

Shakespeare's dramatic dip-tych invites audiences to see the world as "trans-corporeal" waterscapes of watery bodies constantly on the move. Both plays materialize these bodies on the early modern stage because they engage the oceanic stage beyond them, mobile and material networks in which the English were (increasingly) participating. Andrew McRae argues that the literature of rivers helped situate "mobility within emergent models of nationhood."[35] Although enacted behind the seawalls of the "fluvial nation" known as England, the plays are dependent upon global travel and its waters that breached insular boundaries.[36] Even the sources closer to home sponsor the deterritorializing impulse of "eco-cosmopolitanism";[37] the Thames probably supplied the water for these stage directions, serving as but one facet (or faucet) of the "conduit community" Mark S. R. Jenner calls early modern London. The proof is in the pipes: civic engineering projects, including the ambitious New River aqueduct (completed 1613) were "social networks" in his estimation, "the first network technologies, binding thousands of households into a common system."[38] As a local river, the Thames is also tied to the global hydrosphere: a complex mixture of merchants' passages, explorers' discoveries, elemental atmospheres, and real-life wrecks. In their material interactions with wetness that *acts* as much as it is acted upon, the list of wet roles demonstrates how the human commingles with and is redefined by the ocean. It is no coincidence that these two plays—both fascinated with movement upon and within the sea—are the only two Shakespearean plays with inundated characters. With a splash of water, audiences could recognize the collapse of local, regional, and global distinctions; as places lapped in interplay, they could sense a push out to sea. Unanchored from place-specificity, they could reflect not only on the place of England in a world of increasing trade and travel, but also on the infinitely varying and variable nature of place itself. So could we: water's solvency continues to burst boundaries even as it supposedly subtends them. Our river-revels are not yet ended. Enter, braver new worlds.

As I have been suggesting, Shakespeare's geographical oceans had a role to play in the aquaria otherwise known as early modern theaters. The Globe in particular proves to be a moister "atmosphere" than ever before— from the Greek *atmos* ("vapor") and *sphaira* ("ball, globe")—a wetspace that significantly mist-ifies subject–object relations; within a single drop of water lies an art that disturbs ontology at the scale of globe and Globe— houses, both—offering constellations of disparate actants that swirl and dance, dis/aggregate and transform through contact. Here the opening drip of Peter Greenaway's luscious and liquefactive film *Prospero's Books* (1991) meets William Blake's "To see a World in a Grain of Sand" (ca. 1803), helping the latter regain its littoral nature so that it may extend its invitation to the waterscapes of the present. Any drop in our world offers a palmar "pluriverse" of activity where we may not just glimpse "a World" but imagine and bring about worlds-to-be.[39] *Pericles*, and by my extension, *The Tempest*, expands upon the "aquaman fantasy" Marina represents to Mentz: the hope that a "proto-ecological intermingling" will "demonstrate the power of coming to terms with the sea . . . [and] that living in an oceanic world may be possible."[40] The ocean may not be our home, he writes; it may be an "alien globe" instead: "The sea throws cold water on the happy dreams of environmentalism . . . destabilizes our fantasies

Hoh Rainforest, Olympic National Park, Washington. Receiving about 150 inches of rainfall a year on average, this is the wettest area in the continental United States. Photograph by author.

of sustainable growth and a harmonious relationship between human culture and the natural world." To study Shakespeare's oceans is to study
"limit cases."[41] Yet I believe this cold truth is the very reason why we need
to recompose our households (*oikos*) altogether. Shakespeare's wet entrances
speak of an ecotheoretical limit case: the limits of the human fantasy of
imperviousness. What is "alien" is precisely the idea of the human, the
subject, and the playwright alienated from the nonhuman, the object, and
the world. The human and the nonhuman are co-constitutive actors, never
discrete players oceans apart, and always on the verge of becoming. *Inter*
and *intra* ("within"), wet. Pericles's sea of both "pain" and "joys" proves
that Shakespeare thought in noneschatological, nonteleological waves
about the uncertainties of his time. And he helps us face those of our
own. Once we realize our always-already—and unpredictable—entanglement with water, the potential outcomes are bottomless. "*Enter Mariners, wet*" to tell us that all is not lost.

Potomac

In a theater outside Washington, D.C., in the spring of 2013, water fills
the bottom of the stage. Enter, slick spectators of *The Tempest*. The ninth
play in Synetic Theater's "Silent Shakespeare" series boasts a "stunning set
design complete with a water extravaganza"—*so wet*, in fact, that brave
patrons could save $15 for sitting in the "Splash Zone."[42] Or not so brave:
these front-row attendees are provided with ponchos to keep them dry
from the twenty-five hundred gallons of water on set, some assuredly from
the Potomac, including the four inches of water in which actors acro-
batically performed. By offering patrons the choice between wet and dry
seats—and anticipating their desires to be entered, wet—Synetic's eccen-
tric production reveals the stakes of this book to my own audience. To
enter, wet is to discard the poncho in order to feel s/plashes ranging "from
droplets to your daily recommended . . . intake" advertised at the online
box office, those water marks that go deeper than the human's protec-
tive skin, that touch our shared skins in onto-ecological flow. To enter,
wet is to hear the rebuttal to the theater series' "silent" moniker with every
drop that falls in the room, announcing and enunciating its capacity for
conversation. To enter, wet is to grasp the living water that cocreates "live"
theatre, to recognize the "vivaciousness" and "dripping . . . invention"

for which the company was praised. To enter, wet is to cohabit the sound/waves like those that gave Synetic its name, to ask what other synergetic relationships are possible with water, what waterworks will ensure our liquid journey of en/trances to be unfinished, forever, in the splash zones of the real.

Splash Zones

The ocean is not only Shakespeare's. Waters are wider: there are those who introduced their embodied narratives to Shakespeare-upon-Thames, who carried with them the living waters of influence. Enter, wet travel writing: in each of these episodes, water *influences* the compositional process (from the Latin *influere*, "to flow into"). Flowing into the writer's body, a drenched discourse is born: hydrographies, "water writings" that speak of beings coming into being, entrances like wet births. Theirs is a form of discourse propelled by water's physical courses. Indeed, "discourse" is runny writing (from the Latin *discursus*, "running to and fro"), and it is found in every waterscape; even swamps have their speed. In short, hydrographies narrate the interpenetrative flows of beings as they move through, and are moved by, others in their travels to and fro. They are compositions that collect. Put more imaginatively, they envision an environmental rhetoric, or rhea-toric, in full flood: a *syrrhèse* ("flow together") of conversations that engulfs genres as well.[43] Discussing the parallels between *The Tempest* and contemporary travel literature like William Strachey's (1572–1621) account of the *Sea Venture* wreck off the coast of Bermuda in 1609 (published by Samuel Purchas in 1625) is almost habitual; questioning how Strachey's embodied experiences with water may have influenced water's dramatic function is not. Thus I prefer to think more about *saturated* texts, the conditions for how they came into being, and the intimacies they created, rather than pinpoint sources or highlight generic differences. In order to take the "material turn" of ecocriticism, one must acknowledge that "matter [is] a text . . . a site of narrativity, a storied matter, a corporeal palimpsest in which stories are inscribed." Or, as these authors, Serenella Iovino and Serpil Oppermann, have most recently put it, "All matter . . . is a 'storied matter.'"[44] All authors included herein are hydrographers, cocorporeal composers, by this ecomaterial definition. Compositions commingle in ways more than one, affording a space between (*inter*) genres, just like the non/human mariners' bodies in onto-genetic intermingling; in sum, the historiographical reach of this project is limited in favor of an ongoing thought experiment that perceives wet matter as a text that bespeaks "worldly . . . emerge[nce] *together* as storied beings."[45] By sensing the real watermarks of immanence across differing degrees of ecomaterial encounter, the texts themselves draw us in, consti-tuting their own splash zones that do not simply narrate the experience of entering wet space, but affectively disseminate it. It is the ability to be a witness to an other and newer wor/l/ds. Travel narratives are the mun-dane ("of the world") partners to the dramatic "thirdspaces" of material narrativity. Through their greater nonhuman "articulation," they describe associations less familiar with subject-object distinctions and more loqua-cious with the liquid in/fusions of matter-meaning.[46]

"It's as if at some point you had to leave the solid land and go to sea."[47] Wet drama and travel literature both need water to roam, so it is not sur-prising that both swirl around the literary conventions of *romance* and the market culture of prose fiction surfacing at the time.[48] While criticism of texts that sail to the New World (my subjects in this book) have promi-nently noted the "interplay between . . . romance and colonial discourse," what is left unremarked is how travel-authors' material interactions with liquid imbued them, and eventually their dramatic counteracts, with ro/a/mantic movement.[49] Romance emphasizes travel as well as familial rela-tives, and by etymological association, *relations*: that which is "brought back" (from the Latin *referre*). These writers brought back the relations they created with the waterscape via the becoming-water processes they undertook. Bodies—and by now I mean those corporeal and textual assemblages known as hydrographies—return. So back to *Pericles*: though a late play only retroactively deemed a "romance," its protagonist under-goes a series of travails/travels upon the sea, yearns for the nearness and intimacy that being "related" entails, and eventually reunites with his rela-tives due to the same watery forces that caused their disintegration. Yet the "sea of joys" that "drown . . . with their sweetness" is a shared site of materiality as well as narrativity, a physical site as well as a metaphori-cal space in which early modern explorers converse with playwrights, where storied matter swells. These drowned books tell us that all is not yet written, not all is familiar. Refer to the stories that came before you, the palimpsest that you are, and create anew. Go roam, and may "[n]ew joy wait on you" (22.125). The true ro/a/mance of water illustrates, in Oppermann's oceanic phrase, "creative expressions contriving a creative ontology," and wet writing is where "we find [this] creative materiality encoded in a collective poetry of life."[50]

Any ode to emergence from immergence, however, must also think about those stories untold, or that are prevented from being told, or that disintegrate over time and by un/foreseen circumstances: splash zones are those "ecotones" abovementioned, tense material-discursive forms of *contact*, of "touching with."[51] Un/even flows of water are the nature of early modern discourse and not just ours, vortices that spiral up and down "as a duck for life that dives" (*Pericles*, 10.49). They, too, knew that water bodies might be synetic but are not always in sync. How bodies are inked, impressed, con- and inscribed—a trademark of postcolonial eco-criticism—takes a new trajectory here. We will witness the injustices of de-story-ation through watery imperial eyes—kidnappings, environmental degradation, attempted genocide—but we will see water worlds through the eyes of their human and nonhuman inhabitants who look back, and who, in doing so, demonstrate the deliberate efforts necessary to separate non/human becomings into structural, strictured hierarchies of human and nonhuman bondage: the deplorable steps required to render oneself "dry," or at least not as wet as one's inhospitable environment. Monique Allewaert places Ariel's ooze in the context of the American tropics, the song participating in "the origin of a minoritarian and anticolonial mode of personhood" within a plantation zone of disorganized and disorganiz-ing bodies, proving that "diversification and diversity became the origi-nary American story."[52] Imperial ideologies that exhibit an unwillingness to see shared materiality reflected by others write the world's inequalities and instabilities large. Another example is the un/containable vicissitudes of water itself. The Thames was such a site of vulnerable unpredictability: floods in 1626 and 1629, a "tempest of thunder and lightning" in 1626 that made a "strange spectacle" of a water tornado, a funnel that con-joined water and sky and verified vortical atmospheres as their reality.[53] Such events, then as now, can vivify water's ineluctable touch. But water always remains the third party in the struggle. Lethe (forgetfulness) can too easily and suddenly meet Styx (hatred) and Acheron (pain), turning the verses of textual composition into the *versus* of ontological antagonism. Enter, human versus water. Serres has ruminated over this struggle: "Turn the *against* into a *for*. . . . Turn the *against* into a *with*."[54] Look upon the eddy, he advises, a whirlpool whose circular flows run "again, back" (*ed-*) and counter to the main current. The turbulence inherent to the *inter* is likewise its greatest potential; it is the flux of the *flowing with*—the "con-fluence"—that carries things into newer positions; it is our own vorticose coexistence. Their weather-water reports are meditations upon living intra-catastrophically, of crafting resiliency with "all waters" in unpredictable times. But they also understood that there is a tide in the affairs of non/humans, and they sought desires despite the dangers of not knowing exactly what they were searching "for." So let us think back, again, on a different "spectacle" of the Thames and a tidal moment in time.

Another Thames

On February 4, 1641, a Friday afternoon about one o'clock and thus being "very fit to afford witnesse," "a wonderfull and vnusuall Accident . . . happened in the River of Thames," a double high tide: "There flow-ing two Tydes at London-Bridge, within the space of an houre and a halfe, the last comming with such violence and hideous noyse, that it not onely affrighted, but even astonished above 500. Water-men that stood beholding it, on both sides the Thames."[55] The anonymous author of the pamphlet quickly subsumes the strangeness under the more manageable rubric of theo-teleology, "True Newes from Heaven," a sign that people are to put away their uncivil disputes and pray "for the joyfull Union, and prosperous harmony between King and Parliament, wherein consisteth the onely happinesse of this Kingdome." The other astonishment the pam-phlet propounds is the water's stillness, caught between ebb and flow at high water, so that the ferrymen threw sticks, dishes, and buckets into it to no avail: "so that it seemed that the water was indeed asleep or dead, or had changed or borrowed the stability of the Earth." Transmutation, once more, to be feared. "[B]eing filled with amazement," but not water, a "new Tyde comes in, a new Tyde with a witness, you might easily take notice of him, so lowde he roared . . . that it was horror unto all that beheld it, and as it gave sufficient notice to the ear of its coming, so it left sufficient satisfaction to the eye." The rising tide that gave sufficient eyefuls of roaming and foaming demands the stemming of "Popish Idolatry" as well as water; as such, their hydropolitical nightmare plays into our climate change–fueled fears of high/er tides today: "Which latter Tyde rose six foote higher then the former Tyde had done," is similar to the modern-day dire prognostication of unstoppable rises in sea levels with disobedient authorities partly (or mainly) to blame. The oldest admit that they had not seen anything like it. The author unveils only one interpretation of apocalypse—Greek *apokaluptein*, "uncover, reveal"—reluctant to write any more. Cause and effect are delineated as assuredly as the water is placid, "seeming as plaine, quiet, even, and stable, as pavement, under the Arch." But it was not so rare: "this vnusuall, sudden, vnnaturall returne of the Tyde" had happened several times before. God re-creates the water, however, writes on the water, each time. The return of weird water can be read but one way—catastrophically—a dismal signification heaven-sent in a roaring rush, a world worse for the wetter, a reminder that water's un/predictability is (a) happening, again.

But the eye, seemingly full, alights on another water, another strange event "fit for witness" down by the river. Heaven's intentions and cause for political lamentation contrast with more material desires: "the Watermen not content with this evidence would needs make the vtmost of the tryall." Incredibly, they take the entrance into elemental borrowings and the chance for recreation; "they rowed under the very Arches, tooke up their Oares and slept there"; they move out of the linear to make an essay ("tryall") of encounter with the whirling rise-and-fall, their slumber harder to characterize as a symbol for political turgidity this time. Under the bridge's "Arches," between two architectural poles, they enter the middle space of dreams and being (imagination and materiality), resting in the meddling space of water's physical flows. We do not know what they dreamed in that hour and a half, but we can dream on that question and, in doing so, have our own: to peer into their "water mind-set" and imitate how they took on, as Gaston Bachelard writes in *Water and Dreams*, water as "complete poetic reality."[56] Their mental images materialized the oneiric, supplied another sketchbook open to scrutiny: "Elementary matter receives and preserves and exalts our dreams."[57] *Whose* dreams is what I wish to make more uncertain; who and what the receiver *is* and *can be* more extensive. What is communicated is the "hideous noyse" of nauseous

sea-speak we heard before, for it is also another waterman's dream, the
Boatswain's:

> We were dead of sleep,
> And—how we know not—all clapp'd under hatches;
> Where but even now with strange and several noises
> Of roaring, shrieking, howling, jingling chains,
> And more diversity of sounds, all horrible,
> We were awaked; straightaway, at liberty. (*The Tempest*, 5.1.233–38)

The Thames's anthropomorphized tide ("him") disturbs the *anthro*-
("human"). These watermen by vocation became vocalized water-men
(hyphenated since hybrid) because they saw unpredictability as an opportunity to explore; they talked in their sleep; they felt "at liberty"; they
willingly pushed out into the confusing within of embodiment.

The "Accident" is "fit" for underwriting my own "tryall"—this book—
for it witnesses water's strange happenings that have nothing to do with
destiny, a preordained "fall" or otherwise, only the aleatory; it attests to
water's live and luring ability to enter, mix, and imbue bodies, the senses,
and elements ("Earth" and all) to the point of satiation but never of satisfaction. On- and offshore witnesses' bodies are "filled" with "amazement"
as much as "horror"; the sight gives "satisfaction" to the eye, sound to the
ears, the body and the senses ferried to a point, then spilled out into the
images of language. As an instance of water's mutations that transmit and
transmute, the pamphleteer remains unidentified because whoever wrote
it cannot possibly be named: identity is distributed, becomes the watery
"I" anonymous that escapes the distinction between author and authored.
Drowned bodies are found at these junctions, too, it must be mentioned,
testimony to "violence": a "lad" killed by a "cart wheele," or, "like a creature
native and endued / Unto that element" (*Hamlet*, 4.7.150–51), Ophelia,
the bodies irretrievable. What we are witnessing here, ultimately, is a
performance of water that redefines "witnessing" as an active process: not
the passive reification of knowledge, but a welcome infusion in which the
mind ("wit") is shared, where epistemes flow and where stories are propelled in narrativity, in perpetuity, permeating "above 500" as well as those

few who ventured out into its precarious calm. They desired to sleep on the still waters that are never still, not "dead," turbulent even at rest. It is a dream of poetic *in*completion: it is ours.

"I am standing water" (*The Tempest*, 2.1.217). We might feel, like Sebastian, lazy between these tides. "[T]o ebb / Hereditary sloth instructs me" (2.1.218–19). To be "standing water" does not mean unwilling to act, necessarily; he is, rather, open to persuasion: "I'll teach you how to flow" (2.1.218), says Antonio. *So does water.* Coming one year before the closure of the theaters in 1642, the dream of the watermen is a watershed moment in London's history. But we might pause to consider water's own dreams for its future, however inconceivable it may seem, by thinking about how water of all stages changed minds ("wits"), wondering if the witnessing of waterlives led to more waterlives being shaped, and body-politic states, minds, and hearts to be altered. It was but twenty-five years before (1616, coincidentally, the year of Shakespeare's death) that city officials, those charged with enforcing the river's "conservacie," "tooke Barges at Belinsgate, and (within a few houres) arrived at Gravesend in Kent."[58] Did they speak of riparian justice on the river in this brief amount of time? (Stow is silent.) On what ecological futures did they dream? (We may.) Once they arrived, they held a session and were reminded of their duty "to reforme annoyances and offences . . . to inflict due punishment vpon the offenders."[59] The space is open to us; we have always been in this eddy of time/s, politics, and art. Instead of furthering policies of "standing water" in reserve, colluding with the political matter of water— in the polis of London and in the ecology of "another," for endless "example"—may convert mottos like "I am standing water" of neutrality into the standing of protest, the "stand" of "stead," of having a role in place and acting on another's behalf across multiple forms of ability. While the anonymous author hoped that his tract might "effect" political reunification and stanch the outbreak of civil war (1642–51), it is now, handed down to us, less an incitement to reunification than a recognition of non-bifurcation and a chance to dream (again) on the "stuff" we are made of and "on." Witnessing is awakening to this reality, working on a river-ie that arrives, sleeptalking, not knowing or caring whether we are awake or dreaming.

For All Waters

To quote Feste once more, "the whirligig," this whirlpool, "of time[s]" (5.1.364) is where I want you to be, dreaming, in the eddy known as everything. The wet stage is set. Enter *For All Waters*. My central argument runs like this: as early modern authors interact with the waterscape—rivers, glaciers, monsoons, and swamps—they compose fluid networks in which the human and nonhuman intermingle, creating bodily and textual assemblages of human and nonhuman things that dissolve notions of the human's autonomy and its singular narrativity. Wet authors navigated the disasters and desires that lurk in the onto-epistemological flux in which they found themselves, and in which we do now: rivers that will not stay their manufactured courses; icebergs that snap from the Ant/arctic poles; superstorms without a season; "viable" land slithering into swamps. Probing early modern waters helps us invent new directions to take within our current hydropolitical crises. Like those writers who took the chance and entered new wet-worlds, water offers us opportunities to conceive of newer ones. *For All Waters* does not merely imagine how to survive within a fluctuating world, but through its ontological humility describes a coimplication of water and human that has potential for more humane relations.[60] I advocate for a posthumanist ethics, one that enfolds both environmental justice and environmental health: water writes, and through that inscription we glimpse water's rights. By taking their soggy and storied matters to heart, we can learn much from early moderns' eco-ontological reveries. These dreams are truly delirious (Latin *delirare*: to "deviate," and, what is more, "from the furrow," the terrestrial). What is ultimately to discover, the waters told these authors, is that *you have never been dry*. *For All Waters* disputes fantasies of ecological solitude that would seek to maintain the opposite, or that attempt to sustain a political ecology that excludes beings like water, women, the poor. I wish to raise a particular point about troubling andro- and anthropocentricity at once, since water was (is) gendered in the process of domestication, and with damaging outcomes: after murdering Desdemona, for instance, Othello claims that "[s]he was false as water" in his defense (*Othello*, 1602–3, 5.2.143). But I am also aware of the fact that, while my ecotheorizations are informed by material feminist thought, my primary literature is written by men who often conflate the feminine with water.[61] Rather than see these areas as incommensurable, however, I wish to expose misogyny's harm, just as others have done in the period, thereby challenging patriarchy's persistence of influence.[62] This is the spirit of the volume: to consider ways in which the lives of both humans and waterscapes can be improved simultaneously through a direct engagement with the wetness that things are. It dreams how to be "for [the love of] all waters" by becoming them, by accepting water's invitation to enter wet and thus be entered. I would rather draw forth outpourings of newness; I would compose, with you, that impossible word "peace." It meanders like so; four curves will routinely be taken, my declarations distilled into drops (*stilla*) that move down (*de-*) these white walls.

> (*We express ourselves in ways that go with*
> *and against the flows of meaning.*)

Wet suits the early modern period well because of the ways they accented it: their measured lines of poetry and prose received "rhythm" from the water, a sixteenth-century word from the Greek *rhuthmos* ("to flow"). In general, waterscapes invoke the agency inherent in the very word "land-scape," a word that comes from the Old English *-sciepe*, *-scipe*, and *-scype* which means "to create, ordain, appoint."[63] "Land-scape" is land that has been created, though, syntactically, the land is also in a position to create. A "water-scape" does the same. Water synergizes wet words and things, spins its im/measurable rhythms in eddies undergoing speech acts. By narrating non/human experiences with water, hydrographies demonstrate the ways in which water works: rivers carry, ice slips, rain precipitates, and mud bogs. Jane Bennett defines vitality as "the capacity of things . . . not only to impede or block the will and designs of humans but also to act as quasi agents or forces with trajectories, propensities, or tendencies of their own."[64] Early modern authors expressed the vitality of water in the exact words they used to describe it. In doing so, they challenge us to re-think waterscapes (any -scape) in "vital materialist" ways and "articulate a vibrant materiality that runs alongside and inside humans."[65] As a dual vocality, language lets loose rather than circumscribes water's dynamism: "prospect," "glacier," "precipitation," and "swamp" carry in/organic vitality that we are just beginning to rediscover. In a word, their linguistic ecologies were "splashy." I use the word deliberately, for "splash" derives from "plash," first recorded in 1522 of unknown origin but probably born from imitation. In its onomatopoeic valences, "plash" precisely demonstrates the "word-making" power of water ("onomatopoeia" comes from Greek, "name-making"), how sounds beget sounds.[66] Thus my playfulness with w/etymologies actually harnesses the open-ended flows of language and the material slipperiness of the signifier-signified. These creations denote the inexpressive and unintelligible aspects that are translated into language—*splash!*—confirming that full fluency is beyond our reach, guaranteeing that the conversations continue. With a s/plash, early moderns could dwell on the unverifiable, singular origin of their reveries; more importantly, they could also bespeak their conversations with this elemental interlocutor by conveying them in print that spreads rather than encapsulates.

(We invent hydrographies that let slip the auto- of biography.)

Early modern hydrographies are really nonhuman-ifestos, compositions with the element that redefine the compositional act of writing as well as the composition of the "human." The -graphy of hydrography is not writing *about* water, thus rendering it an inert object separate from the human author, nor an illustrative drawing *of* it (such as a map), nor even writing *on* its physical surface, but a discourse that launches the *com-* of compose from the dry docks of logocentrism. Waterworks are where the terms "subjects" and "objects" themselves are transformed through the distributed agency of composition. I should say "de- and recomposed" rather, for as Latour lobbies in his "compositionist manifesto," connecting or reusing the allegedly bifurcated terms of nature and culture is misguided: "It is time to compose," he announces, "in all meanings of the word, including to compose with, that is to compromise, to care, to move slowly, with caution and precaution."[67] Composition therefore is a "slow process": it carefully traces how heterogeneous actants interact and construct, like "good" or "bad" composers; it notices how things fail, decompose, and recompose like compost; like compromise, it highlights how we move forward and also with (*com-*) things into new alliances. If compositionists agree that "we need to have a much more material, much more mundane, much more immanent, much more realistic, much more embodied definition of the material world if we wish to compose the common world," the water-writings here mark my attempt to reach a common *oikos*.[68] In their conspicuous imprints of mediation, early modern hydrographies avoid the tired argument that language is *either* human-made (thus anthropocentric) *or* a flawed method of communication (which instantiates subject-object distance and promotes nostalgia for a lost, unmediated correspondence between words and things). They resist strict metaphors or similes of fluidity—to be *like* water—and gather the ontological potential of being with it, "the ultimate medium for the conversations that continually create the world."[69]

Admittedly, the hydrography known as this book is indebted to, and yet differs from, two related fields of study. The first, cultural geography, is interested in the "complex interactions that take place between people and the spatial structures and concepts . . . that shape their understanding and practice of the world."[70] The early modern stage is no exception; Julie Sanders, for instance, has astutely demonstrated that Carolingian English playhouses were "networks" within "liquid landscapes": the drama of the 1620s and 1630s, she argues, is an "actor-agent" that challenges prior forms of spatial knowledge while offering up a more nuanced "sense of the literary and the material semiotics of space."[71] Attending to "the agency of the artistic form as much as its reflective or representational power" is slightly different from my task, however, which is to show (one layer deeper) how the flows of matter are responsible for the artistic work.[72] The -graphy is shared. Cultural geography risks privileging human culture in its unequal emphasis on human shapes and shaping. Reading the "theatrical potential of rivers" in the strange events noticed above, for example, Sanders hits on the "symbolic, political, cultural, and practical role that liquid landscapes played" as the "Thameside itself [was] a form of theatre" requiring "shared spectatorship," but relegates the potency of water to semiosis without alluding to the osmotic push behind this acculturation.[73] The "economical stage directions such as '*Enter X wet*'" remain just that: economical, and we have seen that the Thames could readily supply water that cost others (playgoers) and made money (assets).[74] The result, however, is one of ecological partition rather than connection, I think, imaginative projection rather than fleshy tangibility. The riverscape of London in these productions is a "richly suggested, yet never quite present, world just offstage in the commercial theatres."[75] It is not her intention to push further; still, the power of suggestion worries me in its proclivity to wedge divides between actor and the matter at hand.[76] Water is present in the wet-world on- and offstage, "quite literally everywhere"; dramatists like Shakespeare suggest that it cannot be other than irreducible through the directions they give for wet entrances. Sanders helps us think how much more uncontained these "uncontainable landscapes" are, how far "flow theory" can go once we realize wet matter flows' boundless theatrical-political potential.[77]

My work also dialogues with a second well-established field, "ecocomposition." In their conclusion to a definitive study, Sidney I. Dobrin and Christian R. Weisser move "toward ecocomposition," mentioning that "[it] must make uncomfortable natural discourse and see discourse and nature alike: neither 'Natural,' both constructed, and both reliant upon and affecting the other."[78] If ecocomposition is "all about" place and its relationship to writing, then this is what I wish to head *toward*.[79] But getting there proves perilous; I waver over accepting simple constructivist arguments. Preferring the social as a locus of culture, similar to cultural geography, risks, again, prioritizing culture. If nature is socially constructed according to these authors, we need to think about how the *social* itself is constructed as well, de- and recompose it. My watery ecocomposition that you are reading right now crucially varies from constructivism's methods in an additional way: while ecocomposition in rhetoric-composition disciplines maintains the inseparability of discourse and environment—and yet attempts to *produce* (keyword) texts that connect the two, oftentimes switching from environment-first to culture-first ontological explanations—the ecocompositionist drift I take here departs from dialectical waters since it recognizes the material agency of water as always present, ever-writing. The author flows with wet things and attains new material embodiments under the *influence* of composition. To its credit, this problem was endemic in the earliest stages of ecocomposition. I state my apprehensions not to belittle earlier work, but to note the field's expansive theoretical trajectories since its inception over a decade ago; to situate my research in this orbit so that ecocritical literary studies and ecocomposition studies may mutually reshape one another (so that the writing of theory influences the theory of writing); and to clarify my own point of view *toward* such horizons. Promisingly, in Dobrin's more recent edited collection, Laura Gries asks "*how* rhetoric matters," and by reviewing new materialist theorists (like those above), she outlines a "rhetorical actancy" of responsibility, asking us to see rhetoric *as* an assemblage in circulation: here is truly "the enduring *vitality* of discourse";[80] here are non/human "rhetorical bodies,"[81] hydrographies, themselves productions of nature-culture discourse that produce new "terministic sites" of composition theory,[82] fluid terminologies without terminations, an interminability that fundamentally increases the joys of composition.

(We thirst for ands that add.)

Entrances are also en-trances, and waterways are the love canals that emphasize these pleasures of encounter. "Never stop making love to Garonne," advises Serres.[83] But how does one make love to a river? Queerly.[84] Just as waterscapes do not presuppose distinctions between pure and impure (all pollution), their desires deviate from moral qualifications of purity that would problematically fashion the heteronormative body. Water ubiquitously brings out the affective motions of emotion. Similar to the false choice between human and nonhuman, I do not mean to posit a choice between the two poles of terror and titillation, pure and impure. I celebrate "ecosexuality" instead: "If queers don't have water they're not going to survive."[85] Simon C. Estok's "ecophobia," for example, has little to say about the possibilities for ecophilia, but choosing hydrophilia over "clorophilia," or even -philia over -phobia in general, is not the solution.[86] Watery discourse, now bedded with desire, shows us how we constantly run the middle course between love and strife. Conflux is, above all, this site of possibility. Thus early modern hydrographies privilege the open-ended company of confluence, noting the overflow of emotions that exceed any limits placed on them. The marketing strategy of *just add water* is actually a succinct principle by which to live; visiting the waterscape involves a metonymic relationship based on desire rather than lack, a desire to touch and be touched, to cohabit, what Gilles Deleuze and Félix Guattari call the "material process of connection."[87] Desire as movement, movement as desire. Within compositions, the waterscape moves and is moved in return; multipliable non/human bodies engage in rhizomatic processes of becoming; confluences go mobile. Across seemingly infinite locales—interminable rivers of Guiana, de/frosting archipelagos of the

Arctic, monsoonal cascades of India, and labyrinthine swamps of New England—waterways keep desiring-bodies going. "Becoming Wa/l/ter," "going glacial," "making (it) rain," and "mucking up" are dynamic processes that push desire-as-movement to the extreme. They propel, in a phrase, "water love."[88]

Desire has a wide affective range: drizzles differ from downpours. When Tim Ingold enjoins us to "sea" the landscape—to understand that even the most solid -scape is a fluid "weather-world"—he intimates a larger question I ask about how water *felt*.[89] I wonder how writers sensed and made sense of their water world. "Sea"-ing does not mean to privilege the visual. I carefully adhere to a form of ecophenomenology that marks "a return to the 'things' or 'matters' themselves, that is, the world as we experience it."[90] Sensing is not just a being-in; instead, being *with* enables the emergence of sense-experience. Likewise, writers do not merely write within a waterscape, they write with it and describe its various impressions. Their feelings expand the capabilities of sense (to hear ice, for instance) as well as scramble traditional ways of knowing and classifying the senses. To highlight how physical encounters with water dis/orient the senses, I prefer the faculty of touch throughout. Touch shores up the registers of intimacy, contact, and diffusion that wet entrances entail. Without an identifiable organ of origin—is it skin?—touch's indeterminacy is its greatest (and intensely pleasurable) advantage. Because of its protean nature, skin and its ever-deepening topographies of touch are paramount in Serres's book-length study on the senses. The medium is the mixture: "Everything meets in contingency, as if everything had a skin."[91] Sense is typified by variation, flow: wet, shivering skin. We always take in a myriad of other things when touching. The liquidity of skin and the plural/izing sense of touch provide us with a useful barometer for feeling wet. In vibrational vibrancy is "the murmur of the world."[92] Analyzing the sensible assemblages of non/human bodies as they commingle with the world, as I do here, is not a way of arresting water's affects; on the contrary, it is meant to enact proliferations, profusions of flowing feelings.

When early modern writers felt the material processes of connection with water and consequently composed their waterscapes of desire, like Prospero's passionate vexation, they negotiated an "ecology of the passions," contemporary beliefs involving "the relations of body to environment, of passions to their environmental surround," what Gail Kern Paster deems "an ongoing, continuous rectification of the body's appetites with the appetites of the natural world."[93] No mere pathetic fallacies on "sad," rainy days, human projections of subjective feeling turn into an exchange between psychology and the outside world: "This image of desire includes the human in its generous compass without making the human realm the origin of that desire or central to it."[94] Thus authors could illustrate their relationality with wetness in their exact emotions, "emotion . . . understood as a feature of the natural world, and is represented as fully shared between animate and inanimate objects within that world."[95] Joy, panic, the *confusion* of con-fusion (and all else) were all identifiable ways of "becoming the landscape" at the time;[96] for my purposes here, the "appetite" for the waterscape (or *thirst* for it) intensifies a desire both analogical and geographical, material and metaphorical, that once again disrupts inside and outside terms of human and nonhuman embodiment. It is a transcorporeal transfer that we are not supposed to witness but are beginning to see better, a perspicacity that early moderns knew well but were being told was outdated by the proponents of the New Science in the mid- to late seventeenth century. Mary Floyd-Wilson and Garrett A. Sullivan Jr. have insisted that even in their "mutual penetrability, the categories of 'body' and 'environment' prove remarkably resilient in maintaining their clarity of definition."[97] The ecological prospective I provide exposes these terms' already-shaky stature—I need only poke at a "resilient" structure that is not there—by underlining the ontological indistinguishability and murky definitions of "body" and "environment" to begin with. Antony, cloud-watching, reckons the loss of himself—now this, now that—as "indistinct / As water is in water" (*Antony and Cleopatra*, 1606, 4.15.10–11).[98] He voices a popular image at the time that visualized the world's rivers as human veins and vice versa, tapping into water's toted ability to mirror (since vain Narcissus) and serve as a place for self-reflection. William Caxton's (ca. 1422 – ca. 1491) *Mirrour of the World* (1481) accurately evidences the macro-, micro-, and hydrocosmic mix-up:

> Alle in lyke wyse as the blood of a man gooth and renneth by the vaynes of the body, and gooth out & yssueth in somme place, alle in lyke wyse renneth the water by the vaynes of therthe and sourdeth and spryngeth

out by the fontaynes and welles; fro whiche it gooth al aboute that, whan
one delueth in therthe depe in medowe or in montaygne or in valeye,
men fynde water salte or swete or of somme other maner.[99]

The surface of water need not simply reflect ("to bend back") or reproduce an original image, especially that of the human body or thought
process. It may inventively diffract ("break away"), breaking down ideas
of singularity and autonomy in stages instead of positing an ever-elusive
real.[100] (Antony's rippling identity seems to be something he enjoys.)
While the overlap between human and water veins works metaphorically
in the period, I will explore the assemblage that permits the resemblance
in the first place. Furthermore, as Floyd-Wilson has shown elsewhere,
clammy authors could draw upon pseudo-scientific traditions like "geohumoralism" to explain their emotions in environmental ways:[101] explain,
but not explain away, for in recounting their phlegmy feelings, their passions resurged, and their wet embraces led them to desire broader access
into the tumultuous space of emotions that being wet entails. We still
speak of arteries and vessels in the vein of networks; yet this physiological
non/human conjunction of bloodstreams supposedly collapsed once it was
demystified by mechanistic views of the universe. The blood-pumping
heart at the center of man, thanks to William Harvey's (1578–1657) theory of circulation (1628), sits at the center of the cosmos intact. I argue
that reinvigorating interest in these historic, though not outmoded, theories of water-bodies will strengthen our wet feelings of embodied and
emotive interrelations right now: for starters, to protest the break that has
been announced but never actually happened, yet still felt, dealt, and
suffered. If "I am a little world made cunningly / Of elements," as John
Donne put it, the making is through the immediacy of immanence, a
"we" of "unimaginable *causality*."[102]

   To pool my argument's rivulets from my fingertips so far: focusing
on wet embodiment shows how each author's body registers the agency
of "humming water" (vibrating materiality); produces a hydrography as
a result (composition); and now, how water "o'erwhelm[s] thy corpse"
(*Pericles*, 11.62) in ways that could both enhance their material imaginations as well as quicken their fears of the deep.[103] The melancholic message of "dark ecology" might be appropriate to this last point—Timothy

Morton's exhortation to mind the gap and "hang out in what feels like dualism"[104]—but *solastasia* wrought by environmental degradation, for example, need not invariably engender an unbearable feeling of loss. To be fair, its proponents do not always shy away from taking ethical stances: Morton's concept of the "strange stranger"—"realizing that we're always already responsible for the other"[105]—is a case in point. But this discussion means that I need to clarify my own motivation. Even Morton's radical "coexistentialism" (a lovely phrase) inspires an eerie feeling: "The ecological thought creeps over us to deliver a message of unbearable intimacy."[106] Intimacy brought by panic: and an "unbearable" kind at that. Though I think crises can help us become more attuned to things, I am curious about other kinds of relations that make intimacy a little more bearable, that make it, *yes*, desirable, even if we cannot fully understand water's intentions and even as we face uncertain futures. This leads us to the final curve: learning alternative ethical positions to take with the watery element in order find the reverence in the reverie. Morton claims, "everything is interconnected. And it sucks."[107] I rephrase: everything is interconnected. And it drips.

(We listen to waters that ask us how we will respond.)

At every moment, in unison, wet entrances constantly shout their clarion call: whither the *with*? While the human is caught up in water's energetic undertows at all times, "[t]h'unfriendly elements" (*Pericles*, 11.56) can be met in unfriendly ways by the corporeal body aquatic. Mutual entrancement is possible; yet all movements (or violations) might not be desirable. We must also "acknowledg[e] the often unpredictable and unwanted actions of human bodies, nonhuman creatures, ecological systems, chemical agents, and other actors," as Stacy Alaimo reminds us.[108] Reviewing water's role in environmental health does not presume an abled body; there is no clean bill of perfect health, just as there is no sustainable, balanced body. Admission of "violability" is an insight into the violence of interpenetration. But acceptance need not be the corollary; like satiated bodies that resist the fullness of fulfillment, our ethics are never finished as well. All entrances are "splash zones" of vortical flows that are the *precondition* for our radical coexistence, not a choice; we all act on wet stages of immanence, slippery planes of "smoothness" as well as "striation," our choice being whether or not to act any differently.[109] Water asks what positions we will take with the wet things that flow through us; it points out the increasing tugs between ecological war and peace that challenge non/humans alike. Since the prepositional *with* of writing is crucial to any compositionist effort, so it is essential to environmental ethics. Serres has noted that prepositions trace preestablished connections and also make additional routes; they beg directions to take: "Pre-positions—what better name for those relations that precede any position?"[110] I do not shy away from the harmful repercussions of human agency; I confront them, and I hold agents accountable for their actions, especially by placing texts in their historical contexts. Discourse is an unequal ability: early modern colonialist rhetoric, as we will see, can serve as origins for, and analogies to, present-day environmental movements. The efforts of environmental justice and health prove coterminous, I hope, because we find them conjoined in the fluid maps of non/human relationships the authors left behind, unfolded with all their potential: some are creased with commodification, of course, yet others unfurl uncharted positions, contouring their dreams of exalted, ecological futures. These material idealists tried to "*raise the status of the materiality of which we are composed,*" and so will I.[111]

Listen: we may grasp w/ethics that redefine rights and "personhood" altogether when we account for the fact that our voices are irrevocably tied to the beings that give us our noisy freedom. With early modern hydrographies in hand, I want to draft this water bill of rights. While I applaud legal efforts to protect drinking water and supplies—like the United Nations–sanctioned "human right to water and sanitation," and New Zealand's bestowal of "legal identity" upon the Whanganui River— these rights of water are often labeled as the human right *to* it.[112] I remain cautious, but hopeful, of the outcome:[113] rather than extending human rights to nonhumans, or bestowing human voice *onto* speechless things— to treat water as a human in both cases—we could do better by striking the discourse of silent running in total, by considering all things as speaking persons. Vociferous water means more-than-human-authored noise pollution. We must attend to how we have silenced nature, not how to hear it speak. The question of who is and who is not allowed to speak is also the question of who is and who is not excluded from a given ecology. Latour's imagined Parliament of Things grants both nonhumans and humans a say in global events. Julian Yates and Garrett Sullivan are optimistic:

> While policies might remain written or authored by human persons, there is every possibility that those persons will now, in truth, exist merely as factors or occasions by which the interests of the ozone layer, the coastline, sea lions, lichen, and so on, come to serve as co-authors in a collective writing of the world.[114]

As coauthors, early modern writers were remarkably attuned to the calls of living water, for better and for worse. If "a text truly speaks of the world," as Latour propounds, the question is "how [to] pack the world into words."[115] More than human amanuenses or translators of cacophony that nature "needs" in order to be represented, they articulated articulation, action at a distance, biosemiotic translations that describe the inseparability of meaning and matter, that burst the organic limits of *bios* and *techne*.[116] The touching vibrations of waterfalls, the hideous groans of living ice, the rattling booms of Bengali monsoons, the Puritans' silencing of swampspeak: all grapple with the essential question of what is heard, and what is done about it, when the wet-world speaks.

Respond: past violence should influence current policy, how we treat emplaced and displaced inhabitants, hear the desires they have and the stories they tell. By listening to those human and nonhuman voices, amplifying muted ones, and mourning for those that are lost, water's ways of writing propel a posthumanist ethics that attends to, and even redresses, the silenced creatures of the world. Émilie Hache and Latour have recently addressed how science delegates morality exclusively to the human dimension. Conducting "an experiment or exercise in sensitization and desensitization," they trace the ecological weight of matters of concern in the etymology of respond, *respondeo*: "I become *responsible* by *responding*, in word or deed, to the call of someone or something."[117] A response, then, is more than a mere speech act: it is a reply to "something," meaning that we must identify and heed the call. Here they bring us back to the feeling of my third curve: "sentient" and "sensitization" come from Latin *sentire* ("to feel"). Hache and Latour's significant contribution is that they attribute this calling capacity to the nonhuman, inorganic world: "One may become sensitive or increasingly insensitive to the call of certain beings, whether human or nonhuman: that is indeed an everyday experience."[118] The sound of silence is deafening to the ears of the trained respondents Hache and Latour would have us become. This final bend is thus the most future-oriented by virtue of being the most politically engaged: early modern hydrographies help us become more attuned, response-ible, and active activists by taking positions with and for water. Each of the ensuing chapters urges early modern ecostudies to compose in all senses of the word: positions (poses) that are creations (compositions) that anticipate peace (composure). Everything you have read thus far is my own meandering nonhuman-ifesto of water, an eco-ontological paean that I compose in ways that my premodern predecessors did before me: not to make clear the muddy waters of reality, but to delve deeper into their turbulent flows. *For All Waters* is a story of matter never solely my own, a conglomerate that conceives of ways in which humans and nonhumans may prosper together in the roiling entrances to come, my dream in drenched writing about the "pre-positions" we make and take with wet places.

Stories

My first chapter, "Becoming Wa/l/ter" explores Walter Ralegh's variegated relationships with the nonhuman world in the *Discoverie of Guiana* (1596) and, in doing so, identifies the key compositional themes for the rest of the book. For blue-blooded Ralegh, the Guianan waterscape is a capillary meshwork of non/human things, a place of unlimited horizons and sinuous pathways. Here are agential waters of attraction. Guiana's rivers and waterfalls permeate Ralegh and his narrative, and as he becomes Wa/l/ter by their courses, he displays how water connects diverse bodies, transforms them, and renders their relationships desirable. Living waters cocompose with him a seeping chart; left intentionally unfinished, it plots unstable connections upon a fluid map of relationships, spots the material and unforeseeable compositions that water designs. The *Discoverie* exemplifies the hydrographical process: how the subject writes about water and how water writes. But it also importantly details its dangers: Ralegh's Anglicized invasiveness pinpoints risky meetings between effusive selves and environmental ethics, in particular, the masculinity of ecological conquest (his incursion into Guiana's maidenhood) that curbs native bodies and their rushing desires. His undivided focus on influence's flows finally leads him, and us, to think on the wet stage of the scaffold as well as the life-blood of performance, two platforms that take on the body's blueprint. Rivers are where macro- and microcosmic waters chaotically converse, where bodies of water implunge.

"Going Glacial," my second chapter, explores three early modern Arctic narratives shaped by ice: George Best's *A True Discourse* (1578), John Davis's *The Worldes Hydrographical Discription* (1595), and Thomas Ellis's *A True Report* (1578). As explorers search for the Northwest Passage, they discover ice's monstrosity, but also its wondrous feelings and its sounds. Glaciers are networks of human and nonhuman things capable of freezing, thawing, and reassembling in a process I call "going glacial." Ice mingles in its "glacis" verb; its glassy surface conforms to a glaciality that distorts subject-object distinctions; speaks to desires for colder air and conditioning; thinks of transactions in addition to commercial frost fairs; transports bodies into frosty mixtures of material becomings that evince the passages of interaction; and sculpts texts, dreams, and desires that exist between the fleeting and the formidable. All to various effects: Best's multisensorium of skin-to-skin contact leaves him unimpressed, and although it is a powerful example of glaciated composition, Ellis's illustration is a road map of relationships not taken; it is Davis whose encounter with ice reconceives his attitudes and allows him to imagine a different kind of desirable being-with the ice world. Similarly attending to the ways early modern travelers participated in this congealing process of creation—but also confronting the inability of others, like the Inuit, to do so—paradoxically foments cold ways to reconceive our own relationships with the retreating icescapes at the moment and the vanishing ones (we are told) in future. In endless day and night, and sometimes nightmare, glaciers lead us to an experiment in oneiric composition: glaciers are good matter with which to dream.

"Making (It) Rain," my third chapter, follows the living matter of rain as it plunges things into precipitous intimacy, constituting acts of violence as well as pleasure that wash away the dusty impermeability between humans and nonhumans. Rain disorders ways of relating climate and culture—epistemologically (such as forecasting), ontologically (skin as shelter), ethically (drowned in deluge)—and, in turn, affords new ways of narrating our relationships with the showering world. Employing aleatory dynamics as a bridge between times, this chapter puts early modern and posthumanist theories of weather into stirring conversation, cohabiting the fall (or *clinamen*, "swerve") of rainwater to describe water's "cascade" effect: a pluvial power that collects and disbands beings via accidental collisions, errant desires, surprising in- and declinations. Explicitly tackling debates over the hydrological cycle that gained strength during the mid- to late seventeenth century—along with representations of rainwater as insalubrious and parasitical bad "seeds," beliefs long-disseminated through medicine and meteorology—I argue that William Shakespeare's rain song, *Twelfth Night*, and several monsoonal narratives by members of the English East India Company challenge the circular model of water's movement, reconfiguring it instead as a spiraling "whirligig" of unpredictable relationality. These writers investigate the possibility of inorganic life outside of its metaphorical fertility and agricultural context, or a life of the "it" in the phrase "it rains." They illustrate that whenever "it" rains, we may remake our coimplication with wet weather, recomposing our shared selves in cascading collaboration, fellowships that may weather catastrophes together through postsustainable times.

My fourth chapter, "Mucking Up," inhabits the New England swamps during one of the bloodiest conflicts in North American history: King Philip's War (1675–76) waged between the United Colonies and indigenous tribes. William Hubbard's description of the conflict, *A Narrative of the Troubles with the Indians in New-England* (1677), imagines swamps as sticky networks of non/human things in *quaking* proximity. Swamps materialize and exacerbate Puritan fears about things that bog the body down or invade it. Hubbard renders Puritans as pure, enclosed, firm, and human, while Indian bodies are invisible, toxic, fluid, and animalistic. This chapter takes on most explicitly the violent consequences of an ideology that relies upon utter nonhuman and human divisibility, one that militates against mucoid beings who "mushroom" and spontaneously generate in the wetlands, and that culminates, tragically, in scours such as the Great Swamp Fight of 1675. Swamps demand that we pay attention to how some actors distribute (or manipulate) agency to the detriment of others. I eventually drop us in the Slough of Respond, an ethical as well as spatial place that reveals the human's coextensiveness with the swamp things—with everything—of the world. Here we linger in the slow stickiness of intimacy. Sinking into the thick of things is a way to confound present-day models of separation through ontological confusion, to get closer to the matter at hand, to listen to the calls of humans and nonhumans, to be, in that word, *responsive*: the elemental shiver behind this entire book.

CHAPTER 1

Becoming Wa/l/ter

Why should a schoolmaster deny that which even the old mythmakers acknowledge? Love flows deep in rivers.

—Amitav Ghosh, *The Hungry Tide*

Should I of Water write, but what it is,
I should be drowned in my Theames Abysse:
And therefore I'le but dabble, wade, and wash,
And here and there both give, and take a dash.
. . . But Water, where it comes, it overcomes.

—John Taylor, *Drinke and Welcome* (1637)

On July 3, 2015, Venezuelan president Nicholás Maduro was forced to declare a state of emergency: flooding in the states of Apure, Táchira, and Barinas, triggered by two weeks of heavy rains, had burst the Arauca and Sarare rivers from their banks.[1] Over forty thousand people were affected in Apure, turning towns like Guasdualito into liquid labyrinths, damaging businesses, and breeding homelessness. Maduro's government acted swiftly—evacuating residents, delivering supplies, and providing health care—and the rivers fortunately began to fall on July 5. The floods in Apure were not nearly as bad as those in 2010, a disaster that affected 1.5 million in three states (including the capital, Caracas, where then president Hugo Chávez opened the presidential palace to refugee families and encouraged other government officials to do so), relocating over thirty thousand to temporary government shelters, and killing over twenty. But on the same day that Guasdualito's ten-foot-high floodwaters receded to a more negotiable three feet, July 8, the Boconó River in the northern state of Trujillo overcame the town named after it following four days of rain, affecting at least 250 families. The rise and fall of waters, week by week, show the illusion of any river's stability, from Global North to South: drifting far away from their images of timelessness and mythic "oneness," rivers advance the ravages of floodtimes and the uneven distribution of "relief" (depending on one's definition); they run through a palace's revolving doors. Venezuela's vast underground reserves of oil— rivers estimated at the beginning of 2014 to contain nearly three hundred billion barrels—have incited nationwide protests over economic inequality and threaten to displace further the country's indigenous populations. If it is hard to meditate on a river, let alone describe its shifting flows, it seems just as, if not more, difficult to love one.

River of Deceit

In the spring of 1595 another riverine emergency occurred in the region, this time on a delta of the Orinoco farther south and to the east. About midway through the *Discoverie of Guiana* (1596), Walter Ralegh (ca. 1554–1618) finishes retelling the "proceedings past and purposed" of his Spanish predecessors and begins to describe his own journey.[2] Soon lost at an aquatic intersection, the narrative takes a series of terrifying wrong turns. Ralegh had been disoriented before; even with the aid of native pilots he frequently gets lost in the rivers of Guiana. It was a wet trip overall. "[B]eing al driuen to lie in the raine" and "with the weete clothes of so many men thrust together," his situation was more "vnsauory" than "any prison in England" (10). But never had he encountered a liquid landscape as meandering as this one. An Arwacan guide promises to bring Ralegh and his company to the great Orinoco River, only to forget the route. "[H]e had not seene it in twelue yeeres before" (46). The fear is palpable. Ralegh recounts their close call:

> [A]nd if God had not sent vs another helpe, we might haue wandred a
> whole yeere in that laborinth of riuers, ere we had found any way, either
> out or in, especiallie after we were past the ebbing and flowing, which
> was in fower daies: for I know all the earth doth not yeeld the like conflu-
> ence of streames and branches, the one crossing the other so many times,
> and all so faire and large, and so like one to another, as no man can tell
> which to take: and if we went by the Sun or compasse hoping thereby to
> go directly one way or other, yet that waie we were also caried in a circle

amongst multitudes of Ilands, and euery Iland so bordered with high trees, as no man could see any further than the bredth of the river, or length of the breach. (46)

Ralegh loses his readers in the labyrinthine prose of the *Discoverie*, situating himself within the turbulent connections between "confluences" and "crossings." Ways "out" are simultaneously ways "in." The "ebbing" (withdrawing) water is also "flowing" (increasing). Enter Ralegh, the human, into the middle of deltaic things in flow. Although these endless intersections beg a direction to take, "no man can tell" which direction to go. Instruments are ineffective, sight is limited, and the traveler endlessly circulates around self-repeating island "multitudes." This hapless spot of multiplicity would not seem ideal for an assuring English explorer like Ralegh who promises repeatedly to lead his readers and country to the promised gold of El Dorado. It stymies the progress of English imperialism as well as his golden dreams. It seems there is only fruitless labor in this "laborinth." Ralegh is Theseus without Ariadne, aimless and antiheroic, utterly and hopelessly lost. Carried away by his artful language, bested by the environment, he and his voyage fail. It is Ralegh versus *guiana*—an Amerindian word for "land of water"—and *water* wins.

We might read his near-death experience as ecopoetic irony. According to the famous apocryphal story, Ralegh's career began with water: he entered the English court in the early 1580s after spreading his cloak over a "plashy place"—a puddle—in front of Elizabeth I.[3] Born into a humble household, his bountiful energy and dashing good looks allowed him to rise quickly in society. As a soldier, he distinguished himself in France and Ireland; as a budding poet, he introduced Edmund Spenser to the court; as an adventurer, he sponsored the voyages to Roanoke (North Carolina) in the mid-1580s and embarked on one of the first voyages to the Northwest Passage in 1578–79 with his half brother, Sir Humphrey Gilbert (1537–83). His ship played a pivotal role against the Spanish Armada in 1588. The epitomic "Renaissance man," his fortunes fell in the early 1590s when he secretly married Elizabeth Throckmorton, the queen's lady-in-waiting, and was thrown into the Tower of London. Thus Ralegh's description of his Guianan voyage in the spring of 1595 is typically seen as written for an audience of one, a story of a disgraced courtier in search of royal

forgiveness. But there were multiple reasons for going: to plot a route
to El Dorado and snatch its fabled gold for England; to cast a preemp-
tive strike against Hapsburg Spain and establish an English geopolitical
presence; to regain his standing at court; and to satisfy his own curiosity for new lands. We might now call the voyage a "publicity stunt." And
rightly so: the *Discoverie*'s title page promises to depict all that was "performed" (i). "Guiana," according to historian Benjamin Schmidt, "took on
a distinctive meaning for Ralegh. It served as an extension of the court,
a stage on which to perform knightly actions and seek redemption from
the queen."[4] Ralegh returned in the fall of 1595. Although he did not
discover El Dorado, the *Discoverie* was a stupendous success when it was
published in 1596, and multiple translations quickly followed. By initiat-
ing a "wholly new vehicle for travel literature," in Schmidt's estimation,

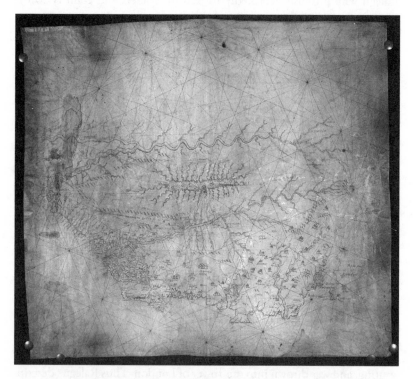

A map of Guyana, with the courses of the Orinoco and the Marañon, or Amazon; drawn about
1595 by Sir W. Raleigh, on vellum. Copyright the British Library Board; all rights reserved.
023961 Add. 17940 A.

his narrative helped him regain favor at home.[5] Ralegh continued to campaign against the Spanish until Elizabeth's death in 1603. James I imprisoned him in the Tower on treason charges the same year. Released in 1616 to undertake one final voyage to the "land of water," Ralegh not only returned empty-handed, but he had engaged the Spanish against James's express orders. He was beheaded in 1618.

"Is it unreasonable to wonder," as C. A. Patrides did, "whether Ralegh ever existed?"[6] If we buy into his larger-than-life legacy, *no*. But when we resist casting him as a hero of mythic transcendence, we glimpse a man bound to a more material place instead: the "plashy place" of puddles and G/g/uiana. Ralegh is haunted by waters of disaster. Few would argue against this unfortunate fact: the Guianan rivers did not deliver gold, and a puddle invited him into a courtly world that eventually ordered his death. Ralegh drafted a map of Guiana upon his return to England. According to Charles Nicholl, in the middle of this splotchy, ink-spilled, and liquefied labyrinth is a Minotaur-like "creature." Dead center is the monstrous Lake Manoa, the home of El Dorado: "There is no doubt about it. The lake at the center of Ralegh's Guiana chart is quite unequivocally something animate. It looks like a monster, a creepy-crawly, some nightmare *cucaracha*."[7] While the creepy amoeba of water plagues Ralegh, I think there is a more pernicious thing crawling around Nicholl's summation: the persistent theme of failure in the *Discoverie*'s scholarship. Critical reception tends to center on the voyage's catastrophes and offers its meet "helpe" to salvage something of significance. Although he did not find the gold, Ralegh's historical defenders often recuperate his failure in terms of his legacy. In the mid-twentieth century D. B. Quinn designated Ralegh's arrival in Guiana as the first step toward the British Empire, for example.[8] Contemporary critics saw the *Discoverie* as a fabulous story that led readers astray. In his *History of England* (1754–61), David Hume said the tale was "full of the grossest and most palpable lies, that were ever attempted to be imposed on the credulity of mankind [*sic*]."[9] Literary critics versed in poststructuralist schools of thought, however, have regarded Ralegh's slippery language as an asset. Less interested in the difference between "lies" and "fiction" (we will see), they read him as a paradigmatic self-fashioner, an early literary protagonist and a symbol of subjectivity, or a manipulator of linguistic-economic credit.[10] Whether in history or criticism, Ralegh's gaps take center stage. We are reminded of the *failure* to find El Dorado, to line up signifier and signified, to sustain a stable identity for the English. The *Discoverie*, in a phrase, is a come down: a "catastrophe," from the Greek *kata-* ("down") and *strophe* ("turning"), a "sudden turning" or a "turning down" that indicates the denouement of classical Greek tragedy. The curtain falls on his wet stage.

I think this critical recuperation of Ralegh's failures betrays our own desires to exit the wet "laborinth" and straighten out our relationships with an increasingly unpredictable world. Likewise, if water's amoebic agency is always configured against the human intruder, it explains why antagonistic language is so prevalent and why "creature[s] in the map" can transform seamlessly into projections of human psychology. The valorization of destination (telos) and the dismissal of errancy as determiners of "success" (former) and "failure" (latter) have run their course. More errancy is required; less mastery. Failure, according to Bruno Latour, uncovers the modernist tendency of "blackboxing," "the way scientific and technical work is made invisible by its own success." "Paradoxically," he continues, "the more science and technology succeed, the more opaque and obscure they become."[11] Levee breaks, for example, are not failures in the technocratic sense; they open black boxes (like dams) and allow us to explore a river-world's inner complexities. Watery errors disclose the "invisible" operators that had been hidden from view but have always been working with and upon us. When Andrew Pickering describes the "mangle" as a "decentered and open-ended becoming of the human and the nonhuman, a 'dance of agency,'" he uses the example of the recalcitrant Mississippi, a river that repeatedly deviates from the course laid down for it by the Army Corps of Engineers.[12] New Orleans, he proposes, should simply be "let . . . go."[13] I am perturbed by Pickering's advice. The bursts of rivers and breaches of literary record, the complexities of technology and narrativity discussed so far—Venezuelan water words—are actually opportunities for us to reconceive waterscapes as networks of interdependent things (such as silt, islands, concrete, cities, and so forth). If disasters like straying streams and the submergence of communities can be avoided (and they should), the intricacies of unrest—the turmoil of class and race—should be amplified, never quieted nor dis-placed. The breaks are lessons in failure from which to learn. The "length of the breach" Ralegh bemoans is precisely the "breach" that divides human from nonhuman as well as other humans. The valiant call to plug the hole with English (and others') dead—once more unto the breach—only maintains the separation between nature and culture because it assumes that the two opposing sides are ontologically separate. Once the crisis is averted, once the gulf is sutured, once efficiency is restored, the box closes, science seals itself from the becoming-water process once more: at least until the next time the hydraulic machine *surprisingly* splits. (It will.) "Water, where it comes, it overcomes."

I believe Ralegh can help us rediscover the human's co-constitutiveness with watery things in more productive, even desirable, ways. It is urgent to wonder how we coexist with waterscapes. "The trick" of cohabiting the "mangle," Pickering says, "is to let go of attachments and to be as fluid as the flow."[14] I am not certain that this quasi-religious pronouncement, in a phrase, holds water: it is precisely *because* of wet attachments that we are allowed to roam with and through fluidity, and not all beings are at equal liberty to do so (due to reasons, for instance, of socioeconomic status). Such complications of going with the flow demand that we hold on and *not* let go, that we rethink our current narratives. Or perhaps we should return to older ones. Simply put: the *Discoverie* shows us that there is no way "out" of the disorienting waterscape. But instead of intensifying our anxiety, it implores us to linger in its labyrinths some more. We are "in" and "out" of a deltaic realty at once, caught in the midst and middles of action. I advise an alternative to the perdurable tropes of catastrophe, failure, and monstrosity that characterize the *Discoverie*'s critical reception and our own ecodisastrous era. So let us turn down the labyrinth of rivers, for there are other actors on the stage, there is more to be "performed." Ralegh is not the principal playwright, just one actor of many in the watery drama that unfolds. Do not drop the curtain of catastrophe so hastily: if Ralegh was a "pilo[t] of delusion" he was made one by being diluted (*dilut-*, "washed away, dissolved"),[15] proving that the true illusion is positing a way "out" of water. He proposes we use our delusion (*ludere*, "to play"), rather, in transcorporeal pursuits.

Becoming Wa/l/ter

Ralegh was always drawn to water. He grew up in the West Country of England, in Devon, bordering the English Channel, near the slinking Exe. We may still walk, as he did, from Hayes Wood to the sea.[16] He lived in Durham House in London midlife, his study facing the Thames, and later, during his imprisonment in the Tower from 1603 to 1616, he saw the river from a different point of view. He is the "Ocean" in love with his "Cynthia," the sometime "Shepherd of the Ocean" so-called by Spenser, a passionate man on a "plashy" pilgrimage, gone off "[t]o seeke for moysture."[17] In short, Ralegh could not stop thinking with water. He surely thought about Guiana as he described the great rivers of antiquity in his *History of the World* (1614), maybe pausing now and then to remember the river garden he planted around his house, Sherborne Castle, on the Yeo. He had an intimate relationship with waterscapes both close to home and abroad. A fastidious gardener, he owned approximately fourteen thousand acres of land. Dotting the landscape were red cedars grown from seeds supposedly brought back from Virginia. He cleared and planted Black Marsh, for instance, spending much time and money, according to Sir John Harington, "drawing the river through rocks into his garden."[18] Listed among his last possessions is a "description of the river Orenoque."[19] Moving rocks by hand, drawing water, gardening: Ralegh understands the confluence of nature and culture firsthand. He is pleasured, not just haunted, by waters: the "failed" aquaman within Nicholl's map is also the dreamer of rivers.

True to Ralegh's performative nature, there are multiple selves he may take on. In what follows I wish to avoid reading water as a metaphor for "fluid" identity, however. One of the most notable studies of Ralegh's selves is by Stephen Greenblatt, who calls the first Guiana voyage "theatricalism in action," a "calculated performance" of propaganda that displays Ralegh's powers of self-fashioning and self-dramatization.[20] Ralegh thought about his body as watery far before it became common knowledge that the human body is made up of 60 percent water on average. Here lies one whose name was writ in water: "Walter" became "Water" primarily for linguistic reasons, a moniker derived from his broad Devonshire vowels. It was also his queen's personal term of endearment: the rival courtier Christopher Hatton once sent an empty bucket to Elizabeth to show his displeasure.[21] Ralegh's wateriness did not stop at the borders of the body, though. He had a blue thumb as well as a green one. He even wrote about the water-body in the *History*, comparing mankind to a watery network: the "bloud, which disperseth it selfe by the branches of veines through all the bodie, may be resembled to those waters, which are carried by brookes and riuers ouer all the earth."[22] Various "waters" converge and "dispers[e]" in Ralegh's sinuous veins. Ralegh references the geohumoralism of his day as well as an antique metaphor for the human body (as discussed in the introduction). The "spleene stones" he found decades earlier in Guiana, for example, supposedly cured one's gallstones and remedied a humoral imbalance of spleen (choler) (29). But he could also push this classical trope further, theorizing water's agency via his environmental embodiment; mere "resembl[ance]" and the "likeness" of simile cannot compass Wa/l/ter. His legendary love of tobacco, his experiments in biotropic drugs, and his connections to chemist-occultists like Thomas Hariot (ca. 1560–1621), John Dee (1527–1608), and Henry Percy (1564–1632), "The Wizard Earl" of Northumberland, reveal a keen interest in the powers of matter.[23] Besides the "Renaissance man," Wa/l/ter Ralegh is the more-than-human, the "Renaissance *post*human" in flow.

In this chapter, I trace the *Discoverie*'s living rivers and the powerful acts they perform. Ralegh's failure is less an instantiation of aquatic mission impossible than it is a reminder that humans and nonhumans cooperatively engage in hydrosocial production. Liquid forcefully attracts Ralegh: waterfalls, storms, and the motion of tides saturate everything. Solid gold melts in the native furnace; even the golden man ("El Dorado") must dive into the lake to wash the precious dust from his skin. Water reworks boundaries as much as it bounds; it territorializes as it deterritorializes. Ralegh's riverscape is a place of unlimited horizons that always secretes new paths and new connections. Its shores constitute a capillary network where ecoregions (water-land) fortuitously meet and mutually transform, jetting various actants in endless directions. Water is more than "something animate," in Nicholl's words, as if animated from *without*;[24] it has its own affective agency *within* instead. Rivers announce the flow of immanence in their very form. Although rivers carry Ralegh to alternate modes of being in the environment, his unlimited movement through the riverscape meets certain impediments: cartographic moments of inertia; the orientating gaze of the empirical naturalist; barges immured in mud. But by cohabiting the riverscape's flows of in/constant speed, new assemblages always arrive. A map cannot wholly enlimn a liquid landscape; things

gaze back; water touches and is touched. In other words, Ralegh's desire
to dwell in the riverscape is relative to his desire to dissolve in it. As much
as he vows to know the riverscape and move through it, he is constantly
moved by its matter-flows. His fluidic reality opens up new possibilities even in the narrative's most authoritative moments. At the same time,
however, we must confront the human and nonhuman beings who are
unable (or unwilling) to participate in Ralegh's water-travel: kidnapped
natives, Amazons, and Acephali all exist precariously within a feminized
landscape. While postcolonial and feminist critics have focused on these
voices in the narrative, I contribute to the conversation about the "romance
of the new world" through the lenses of ecological imperialism and environmental justice.[25] The *Discoverie*'s unsettling ethical dilemmas ask us
to consider how the coursing and conjoined lives of humans and nonhumans who do not freely flow can be made to flow freely once more.

I will pilot us to three destinations. (1) The Guianan riverscape is a
fluid network of human and nonhuman actants whose material becomings can be both catastrophic and desirable. The *Discoverie* is a meditation
on how humans are always-already flowing with the nonhuman waterscape. (2) Ralegh's narrative demonstrates not just how "Walter" becomes
"Wa/l/ter," but also how rivers and imagination influence ("flow into")
one another. The riverscape infuses Ralegh's text, thereby configuring his
language as liquid and mobile. "Liquid narrativity" defines Ralegh's rhetorical strategy of deferral, ambiguity, and slippery promises, eventually
approaching a kind of authorial alchemy. Ralegh's ecotome accentuates
circulation: how water enables stories (the *flow* of words) as well as bodies (the *flows* of consanguinity). His hydrohumoral interests do not just
predate the "correct" physiological discoveries later made by science (William Harvey's anatomical explorations), but highlight a matter-phorical
process that plunges the world into words. What is more, Ralegh's cartographic inklings theorize the way water writes, how rivers shape (-*scape*)
textual and fleshy bodies. The *Discoverie* is a compositionist credo, an
aquatic assemblage in itself. Thus his narrative demonstrates how the subject writes about water *and* how water writes the subject, confusing these
subject-object categories and disorienting our anthropocentric perspectives. (3) By cohabiting the riverscape, Ralegh compels us to think on
the inequalities of habitation. Yet his imperial motives may lead us to a

posthumanist ethics that resists precolonial or prelapsarian nostalgia. My hope is that by exploring the inner complexities of the early modern riverscape, we may better understand (and even improve) our fluvial relationships at present: that once we understand his rhea-toric to be a material effect wrought by touching water—never a mere metaphor—it may influence us.

Current Change

The search for El Dorado is a search for water routes. Approaching Trinidad, Ralegh notes, "my selfe coasted it in my barge close abord the shore and landed in euery Coue, the better to know the iland" (2). Once closer, he begins his geographical explorations outside Port of Spain: "I left the shippes and kept by the shore, the better to come to speach with some of the inhabitantes, and also to vnderstand the riuers, watring places and portes" (2). In the opening lines of the narrative, Ralegh desires to gain ground in a watery landscape. He resembles a fastidious naturalist and hydrographer, noting the valuable pitch for his ships as well as the delicious oysters from mangrove trees; referencing Pliny and André de Thévet, he examines "plante[s] verye straunge" (3). These empirical moments serve to ground him in the center of the environment. Ralegh's ecological research is the study of ecology from his subjective point of view; he is a knowing, and well-read, narrator.[26] But his reorienting strategies quickly slip away from him. He reminds his readers too often that his company is threatened by hostile nature: "the weather being extreame hot, the riuer bordered with verie high trees that kept away the aire, and the currant against vs euery daie stronger than other" (53). They are imperiled even exiting the riverscape downstream: "All the night it was stormie and darke, and full of thunder and great showers, so as we were driuen to keepe close by the bankes in our small boats, being all heartely afraid both of the billowe, and terrible Current of the riuer" (105). Not only is their mission unsuccessful, they barely make an exit: "To speake of what past homeward were tedious . . . we will leaue all those to the generall mappe . . . for I protest before God, that wee were in a most desperate estate" (106). Even the "mappe['s]" promise of orientation falls short in these moments of terrifying "tedious[ness]": that "*Chart*" must be drawn up in a drier and more secure location to be truly accurate. From beginning to end,

blue in tooth and claw through-and-through, the riverscape threatens to
drown Ralegh and his men.

Stuck in an antagonistic relationship with water, Ralegh must forever
fight his way to El Dorado. He resultantly recounts numerous episodes in
which he finds himself stranded on the journey upriver. Setting off down
the Capuri, for example, is impossible: "but they [his captains] laboured
in vain, for neither could they turne it vp altogither so farre to the east,
neither did the flood continue so long, but the water fell ere they coulde
haue passed the sands, as we after founde by a second experience" (43).
Stuck in the sands, Ralegh fears the worst. Fashioning even smaller boats
from larger ones, he decides to measure the depths:

> I sent *Io. Douglas* againe in my long barge, as well to releeue him as also
> to make a perfect search in the bottom of that baie: For it hath beene
> held for infallible that whatsoeuer ship or bote shall fall therein, can neuer
> dessemboque againe, by reason of the violent currant which setteth into
> the said bay, as also for that the brize and easterlie wind bloweth directlie
> into the same. (44)

Even his tedious work of charting water is of no use at this moment.
The company simply wants to get going. Douglas eventually finds several
"goodly entrances" for the diminutive fleet, but the watery surroundings
have irrevocably unmoored his command (44). No ship can ever "des-
semboque" from the abysmal bay, and this is an "infallib[ility]" that even
Ralegh will not question. Seeking knowledge at the banks of the Capuri
is different from his earlier attempts to confine his environment epistemologically; here, Ralegh must obey the water and winds that shift the
sands. In short, he discovers how water resists objectification by human
gaze and gauge, its essence escaping him the more he scientifically squeezes.
Water takes Ralegh places against his will, or it impedes his progress to
points elsewhere. Sounding an endlessly shifting riverscape reconfigures
knowledge as similarly shifty: there can never be a "perfect search" so long
as water constantly moves and shapes the environment. Just as river floors
accumulate and shed material layers, watery knowledge, once discovered,
is already on the move. Thus Ralegh's attempts to plumb the depths
expose a pervious but nonetheless perpetual riverscape. His soundings

are without stable bottom or end. Guiana is a place that may be measured but never completely understood; it is truly un/fathomable. The
Discoverie's emphasis therefore shifts from the knowledgeable explorer
(Ralegh) to the unknowable substance (water). Rivers possess their own
mysterious dynamism that Ralegh cannot master, only probe, cohabit,
and feel.

"[T]he currant against vs." The "terrible Current." The "violent currant." Ralegh understands that water possesses its own physical force, and
the frequency with which he notes the impossibly knowable and navigable flows of the Guianan riverscape divulges the *Discoverie*'s obsession
with water's liveliness. Working *with* water and its dynamic permutations,
not just against it, he enters a prepositional relationship that obtains motility. Entered and entranced, he might battle upstream at times, but he also
goes with the matter-flows of water to constantly create new assemblages
with the riverscape, those "goodlie branches" they pass through "[e]uerie
daie" (53). Despite the danger involved, these ever-burgeoning routes
through Guiana may actually be desired. Ralegh's desire for interminable
connections with the riverscape and for an endpoint at El Dorado seems
contradictory, however. In a poem probably written before 1602, "A Poesie
to prove affection is not love," he equates the goal of desire with the death
of desire:

> Desire himselfe runnes out of breath,
> And getting, doth but gaine his death:
> Desire, nor reason hath, nor rest,
> And blinde doth sildome chuse the best,
> Desire attain'd is not desire,
> But as the sinders of the fire.[27]

According to Ralegh, desire remains desire as long as it never attains its
object. It seems, then, that to reach El Dorado would spell "death": at
least the death of the desire for the fluvial that propels his entire narrative.
But Ralegh's desire in the *Discoverie* is constituted, and given life, by the
riverscape's lively matter-flows. Desire is immanent in the riverscape; desire
is movement. As Deleuze and Guattari describe it, "desire no longer lacks
anything but fills itself and constructs its own field of immanence."[28]

Motility without a motive: the flow of water moves Ralegh into a state of constant connectivity with the environment. His desire likewise flows: "Everything is allowed: all that counts is for pleasure to be the flow of desire itself, Immanence, instead of . . . internal lack, higher transcendence, and apparent exteriority."[29] Whether or not the golden city actually exists, or whether or not he reaches it, is therefore beside the point; as long as the riverscape opens up new possibilities and new desires in its capillaries Ralegh will toil terribly, pleasurably. He keeps moving, desiring, becoming, but never at a *lack* for material connections. He keeps on "getting" without fulfillment; he does not stop "getting" wet.

To deliquesce is to delight. If Walter Ralegh is the weary English discoverer lost in water, desiring some kind of orientation through knowledge, Wa/l/ter Ralegh is obsessed with water and abilities to dissolve the solid self in the "creeper-strangled, monster-bloated, erotically lubricated, filmy, floating world."[30] The riverscape's aleatory twists and turns are fonts of possibility. Wa/l/ter illuminates the material connections to be had between humans and living water once attention shifts from the individual (the anthropocentric narrator) onto aquatic assemblages of actants. Appropriately, Ralegh is most watery when drinking. His captains "garoused" of the natives' wine "till they were reasonable pleasant" (64). Ralegh himself often resists drinking with the natives—they are notorious drunkards, supposedly—but late in the narrative he eventually relents. In the town of Winicapora he meets the chief who promises to lead him up the mountain Wacarima:

> But when wee came in first to the house of the saide *Timitwara*, beeing vppon one of their feast daies, we founde them all as drunke as beggers, and the pottes walking from one to another without rest: we that were weary, and hotte with marching, were glad of the plenty, though a small quantitie satisfied vs, their drinke beeing very strong and heady, and so rested our selues awhile. (102–3)

Ralegh's repast is notable for his curious grammatical phrase "pottes walking." While the phrase technically means the passing of a pot from one guest to another, Ralegh hints at something agentic about the objects that participate in the drinking experience. Ingestion is one of the most

apparent forms of non/human sousing.[31] Drinking the wine of Winicapora does similar work: pot, water, alcohol, and Ralegh's body all aquat-
ically assemble in the drinking house. Alcohol is the key active ingredient
in water that affects Ralegh, most likely, but "walking" pots also play a
role. If a jealous courtier had previously likened him to an empty bucket,
he *is* one here: Wa/l/ter Ralegh, an ever-walking pot continually filled by
the walking waters of Guiana that always enter and affect his permeable
body. Ralegh's "heady" anecdote reveals how aquatic assemblages in the
riverscape are never "rested" but are always at work.

If ritualized drinking blurs the separation between a walking pot and
Ralegh—thus challenging the boundaries of the human—another thirsty
episode demonstrates the potential and possibility of flowing with water.
For most of the narrative's first half, Ralegh reflects on his Spanish predecessor—and now captive—Antonio de Berrío, noting the numerous
mistakes his prisoner made in his quest for El Dorado. One particularly grievous error occurred at the red marsh of Amapaia. "[D]rinking
thereof," the Spanish and their horses "were infected with a greeuous kind
of flux" (32). Berrío's company is decimated, and Ralegh uses the Spaniard's drinking problem to shore up his advantage as a narrator. Unlike
Ralegh, Berrío's strategy to map and master the riverscape is "vtterlie
vnlearned": unable to tell "the east from the west" or to have any intel-
ligible "discourse" with the inhabitants; and unaware, inexcusably, of any
river's name (34). Dependent on his Indian interpreters—the old, the
traveled, and the powerful chieftains of provinces and towns—Ralegh
assures his readers that he, unlike Berrío, can make these potent waters
potable:

> I demanded of those in *Guiana* that had trauelled *Amapaia* how they
> liued with that tawnie or red water when they trauelled thither, and they
> told me that after the *Sun* was neere the middle of the skie, they vsed to
> fill their pots and pitchers with that water, but either before that time, or
> towards the setting of the *Sun* it was dangerous to drinke of, and in the
> night strong poison. I learned also of diuers other riuers of that nature
> among them which were also (while the *Sun* was in the *Meridian*) verie
> safe to drink, and in the morning, euening, and night, woonderfull dan-
> gerous and infectiue. (32–33)

The red waters do more than implicitly assert Ralegh's dominance over his Spanish rival and the antagonistic environment, however. Amapaia is a powerful example of living water. As an un/healthy tide harboring bogs and mud—elemental cojoining of earth and water—the red marsh is the most likely part of the riverscape to birth interstitial beings. The *pharmakon*-like fen is a place of non/human "discourse": water, serpents, sickening bacteria, red silt, and parched explorers' intestines are brought together. As an ingestible actant, fluctuating water puts the human in flux, either rejuvenating or debilitating its drinkers. Drinking the red water moves the walking pot of Wa/l/ter Ralegh once more, but this time the red water possesses even more agitation. Ralegh notes that only "while the *Sun* was in the *Meridian*" could he drink the water, a significant time to slake safely: the exact middle of the day. Likewise, Ralegh is perpetually "in the *Meridian*" whenever he imbibes the red water. Thus to be "in the *Meridian*" is to be plateauing, caught in the middle of constantly becoming-water. Even if he appears to be going either up- or downriver, the current never moves unidirectionally. By drinking in the middle, Ralegh intimates how aquatic assemblages—of any color—always have the potential to accrue, reflow, and retouch. And acting somewhat differently from Timitwara's wine, the red marsh surfaces multiple pairings of desire. The light of the sun is a vibrant form of inorganic life, transforming the waters from "dangerous" to "safe," illuminating the "flux" that is the red water. Importantly, the connection between water and sun suggests that water might have desires for the sun and other non/human actants. While Ralegh is, once again, part of an ecological process of "flux" regardless of his incomplete understanding and indefinite destination, his anthropocentric decentering in the marsh insinuates a mutual desire to touch and be touched by the riverscape that is not dependent upon his exclusive powers of observation. All water and its actants are perpetually "in the *Meridian*" of this synergetic activity, caught up in the "flux" of becoming.

The episode at Amapaia importantly precedes Ralegh's first descriptive portraits of the Guianan riverscape. Henceforth Ralegh's narrative opens up to nonhuman desires and nonhuman perspectives as well, his entanglement with the "fenny and boggie ground" leading him to witness the riverscape as a meshwork of co-constitutive actants. Consequently, he begins to draw pictures for his readers that foreground both hostile and desirable material connections. Cohabiting the liquid landscape puts Ralegh in full flow; water leads him to new vistas and new worlds, even if he must row against its routes. Although he and his men seldom lack sustenance in their abundant surroundings, Ralegh tells of another near-disastrous moment in which they almost starve on the Amana River.[32] Their problem is compounded by the fact that their unreliable pilot promises their destination is "but a little farther" (56). Finally arriving at the Arwacan town shortly after midnight, and rejuvenated by the victuals of the town, including "Indian drinke" (57), Ralegh continues down the unknown river. Now the riverscape appears beautiful:

> On both sides of this riuer, we passed the most beautifull countrie that euer mine eies beheld: and whereas all that we had seen before was nothing but woods, prickles, buses, and thornes, heere we beheld plaines of twenty miles in length, the grasse short and greene, and in diuers parts groues of trees by themselves, as if they had been by all the art and labour in the world so made of purpose: and stil as we rowed, the Deere came downe feeding by the waters side, as if they had beene vsed to a keepers call. (57)

Ralegh is shocked at the shift from aquatic wilderness to pastoral plenty. Anthropologist Neil Whitehead helps clarify Ralegh's confusion over the "made," explaining that "landscape features in Amazonia are often far from 'natural,' being a result of the conscious ecological management of flora and fauna by the indigenous population over many centuries."[33] But Ralegh's astonishment reveals more than a missed chance at native appreciation. While his full stomach undoubtedly contributes to his sudden shift in perception, the riverscape's menagerie of natural things has a transformative effect: "whereas . . . [he] had seen before" a foreboding shoreline, the riverscape is shockingly inviting. It extends itself to him through his labor as he works upstream. More and more of its beauty appears as they "ro[w]." Although Ralegh appears to have found a sculpted garden in the middle of the wilderness, the difference between nonhuman and human forces is unclear. He is not so much startled by the fact that nature could produce something so artistic—or the opposite, that humans could produce something so natural—but that the two realms are indistinguishable.

"[M]ade of purpose" is a purposeless statement if both art (labor) and nature (riverscape) are already one and the same. Thus this seemingly cultivated shoreline inundates lines between nature and culture rather than enforces them. In turn, Ralegh's description shows him to be more open to water's impressions. He avoids outright comparison to an Edenic landscape, thereby avoiding a prelapsarian nostalgia that would render the riverscape and the natives' ecological consciousness static and timeless.

Ralegh's first foray into the "beautifull countrie" invokes a desire to dwell, and the narrative's flow appropriately slows down after this moment. Yet dwelling for Ralegh is not to idealize irrecoverable, glad-diluvial movements gone by. His desire appears paradoxical: a wish to anchor and dissolve at once in the matter-energy that is water, to exist always in water's confluence of fluxes. As such, Ralegh's desire to be *moved* actually explains his anchoring points in the riverscape. Shortly after his bankside vista, for instance, he secures his ship precisely at a point of turbulence: "the parting of three goodlie riuers" (63). A random decision, perhaps, but mooring at a site of lively matter-flows and intersections that constantly move is exactly what the possibilities of flowing with water afford. The liquid "laborinth" of Guiana therefore transforms—just like the prickly bushes and thorns above—from portentous catastrophe to sheer possibility of transformation. To dwell, then, is to dwell with speed. Water has speed in the obvious sense of flowing downriver, but also in the nomadic sense Deleuze and Guattari define: "Movement is extensive; speed is intensive."[34] Movement characterizes Ralegh as "one" stratified and territorialized organism, "*speed, on the contrary, constitutes the absolute character of a body whose irreducible parts (atoms) occupy or fill a smooth space in the manner of a vortex.*"[35] Water as matter-movement importantly deterritorializes Ralegh into smooth spaces of becoming even when he seems to be at his most immobile. The riverscape, and he, will not stay still. Like the shoreline's hybridity of earth-water, Wa/l/ter and his men slip through the riverscape with speed, simultaneously liquefying and solidifying along with its various actants. The labyrinthine places of ecological multiplicity—streams, branches, "multitudes of Ilands"—are desirable places to cohabit because of their intensive flows. So are his more solid spots of anchoring. He lands "vpon a faire sand, where we found thousands of *Tortugas* egges, which are very wholsome meat, and greatly restoring, so as our men were now well filled and highlie contented both with the fare, and neerenes of the land of *Guiana* which appeered in sight" (63–64). Ralegh feasts on the sight of the riverscape as much as the actual items in it. "Sight" would seem to flow from the active subject to the passive riverscape, but the riverscape also looks back: the "neerenes of the land" energizes the viewer. "Sight" is shared as well as the meal. Seeing Guiana "well filled and highlie contented" satiates him as much, if not more, than the "fare" of eggs does. Ralegh beholds Guiana, and, in doing so, feels "greatly restor[ed]." He is both beheld by the "land" and beholden to it.

The mobile waterscape initiates a river change in Ralegh. Things look different after acting upon him. Intriguingly, he finds watery bodies like himself at these spots of confluence. Even though he may be said to put a face on nature, it is not to grant the supposedly lifeless matter of the riverscape an exclusively human agency. Rather, as he faces the landscape he also sees his co-constitutive relationship reflected back at him as a material image. When he dwells in the particularly streamy town of Toparimaca, for example, he encounters his watery side face to face: "This seate of this towne . . . was very pleasant, standing on a little hill, in an excellent prospect, with goodly gardens a mile compasse round about it, and two very faire and large ponds of excellent fish adioyning" (66–67). The town exists in a similar site of "coueted" nature-culture confluence (68)— ponds, gardens, and fish—that he visits shortly thereafter near Putapayma. It is the people of the town, nevertheless, who are the most notable: "In that place I sawe very aged people, that we might perceiue all their sinewes and veines without any flesh, and but euen as a case couered onely with skin" (67). Like Ralegh's reference to bloodstreams in the *History*, human and nonhuman veins of water are vivified in Toparimaca. These natives beyond conceivable age might represent a temporal disjunction Ralegh laments (an antediluvian Eden), or personify the ageless rivers, or perhaps both. More than anthropomorphic marvels, however, the water people embody the hybridity of human veins and nonhuman streams that compose Wa/l/ter Ralegh as well. His surroundings reflect back at him his desire to touch water, and yet the strangely human face of the riverscape reveals how the human and nonhuman are always-already in assemblage. Thus Ralegh's "excellent prospect" (view) of the town and its inhabitants materializes the connections between skin and water. Such a "prospect" makes transparent the vibrant reality of all things in the riverscape: lives of touch and flow.

Drawing Water

Ralegh's use of "prospect" highlights the common definition of "a view"—such as the view of Toparimaca—but it also attests to the agency of living water. Etymologically combining both the root *pro-* ("forward") and *specere* ("to look"), there were two basic meanings of the "prospect" available to early modern writers: (1) a phenomenological concept of facing forward, involving the physical senses; and (2) a temporal term of futurity and anticipation.[36] As a noun, the "prospect" simply could be that which faces forward, the relative senses of such, or the view itself. Crucially, by the mid-sixteenth century "prospect" also denoted an action: *to* face forward, *to* situate. The act of prospecting thus developed coextensively with the literal exploration of geographical spaces: spaces full, no less, of rich metallic prospects like Guiana. In addition to the sensory and active idea of prospecting, the idea of "looking forward" is a spatial activity (to look into the distance) as well as a temporal one (to look into a distant future). A "prospect" is *a* look and to "prospect" is *to* look forward across space and time, and sometimes all at once. The "excellent prospect" at Toparimaca therefore alludes to the power of water to "prospect" Ralegh in new directions: an interaction he anticipates, or "looks forward to" in the indefinite future. What is more, by utilizing the active meaning of the word "prospect," he unleashes the liveliness of water that runs across all of the senses and is not simply *seen*. In addition to the riverscape's profound visual affect, it is *felt* as water on skin and currents under barges, *heard* in calamitous rainstorms and waterfalls, *tasted* in heady wine and meridian springs, and even *smelled* in fresh breezes. Early in the narrative Ralegh admits that writing about his surroundings is a dull endeavor, that true pleasure resides in firsthand experience: "[Berrío] passed by the mouths of many great riuers, which fell into Orenoque both from the north and south, which I forbeare to name for tediousness, and bicause they are more pleasing in describing than reading" (33). Yet we have seen how the pleasure of becoming washes away Ralegh's logic the longer he dwells in the riverscape's flows. These sights are indeed pleasurable to describe and to read, but there is more pleasure to be had in feeling the multisensory waters. Water saturates everything. Ralegh cannot stop moving and being moved—in all senses of the word—by fluvial things. "[W]e passed the most beautifull countrie that euer mine eies beheld . . . and stil . . . we rowed." Prospected by native guides and the riverscape itself, the near-end of his journey contains Guiana's most sensational places that push the *Discoverie* past any preconceived limitations.

Water's most moving moments are predictably at its most forceful locations: waterfalls. These sonorous places are areas of aleatory phenomenology, settings where the entire body becomes a tingling palate of sensation exposed to infinite affect. Always prevented from his golden goal, and shortly after leaving Toparimaca, Ralegh reaches a stream so powerful that he is forced to journey by land. One half of his party goes on a political reconnaissance mission to enlist guides and scout the nearby towns. Ralegh meanwhile departs on a sightseeing tour. Distracted from his mission, he purposefully marches overland to view the Caroli's waterfalls and the adjoining plains of Canuri. The view of the riverscape is breathtaking:

> When we ronne to the tops of the first hils of the plaines adioyning to the riuer, we behelde that wonderfull breach of waters, which ranne downe *Caroli*: and might from that mountaine see the riuer how it ran in three parts, aboue twentie miles of, and there appeared some ten or twelue ouerfals in sight, euery one as high ouer the other as a Church tower, which fell with that fury, that the rebound of the waters made it seeme, as if it had beene all couered ouer with a great shower of rayne: and in some places we tooke it at the first for a smoke that had risen ouer some great towne. (81)

Not just one "ouerfal[l]," but "ten or twelue," in all their "fury," crash together. The sight must have been stupendous. There is no doubt that Ralegh found this furious confluence of water affective: water is pure plummet in repeat, the "breach" a telltale sign of water's torrential force bursting over the brink. Collisional water is clearly the point of fixation here; his reference to church towers is devoid of religious significance, transcendental rumination, any "craving," as Simon Schama, one of his more empathetic readers says, "to find in nature a consolation for our mortality."[37] Even the presumed town is minimized: the water seems to be flowing and falling into the town below, a magnificent image of how water's energetic flows bridge and enliven nature-cultures.

The Caroli's "wonderfull" water enacts a somatic effect analogous to Stephen Greenblatt's description of wonder: "The expression of wonder stands for all that cannot be understood, that can scarcely be believed. It calls attention to the problem of credibility and at the same time insists upon the undeniability, the exigency of the experience."[38] Wonder, indeed, makes it difficult for Ralegh to connect heart and mind. Yet if "the experience of wonder continually reminds us that our grasp of the word is incomplete," as Greenblatt continues, how Ralegh understands "incompletion" is crucial.[39] For Ralegh, the wonders of Caroli do not so much frustrate his attempts at completion—immobilizing his powers of knowledge, or bodily "oneness"—but show his exigent desire for constant becomings with his surroundings. Gaps mark spaces to inhabit, not sites to deplore out of lack. Since a "breach of waters" is also a literal breach, or opening, Ralegh shows his watery self to be an open place of connectivity with water that reciprocally opens him to new possibilities. This "breach" is similar to the "breach" Ralegh experienced earlier in the labyrinth (which is too quickly defined as a divide). Like the rushing water at the top of the falls, he is always on the brink of new assemblages. Ralegh enters, like water, new worlds below. The "rebound of the waters" catches his attention above all because to rebound is to interact (bounce off of) something else. Rebounding water mirrors his passionate desire for aquatic connections, for water that touches and is touched. Water constantly swerves, hits, and moves again at Caroli, the exact kind of vibrant ecological activity that defines the Guianan riverscape in general: atomistic veering akin to the liquescent poet Lucretius (first century BCE), a Roman writer Ralegh might have read as an amateur translator of Epicurus, rendering the *fall* of waterfalls more awhirl than straight, lines imagined in a vortical manner, an eddy in descent.

The water of the next, and final, waterfall Ralegh sees at Winicapora is even more magnificent. Traveling down the Cararoopana and observing "many goodly Ilandes" (101), Ralegh once again wanders through the riverscape, this time distracted by rumors of a strange crystal mountain:

[T]o which in trueth for the length of the way, and the euill season of the yeare, I was not able to march, nor abide any longer vpon the iourney: we saw it a farre off and it appeared like a white Church towre of an exceeding height: There falleth ouer it a mightie riuer which toucheth no parte of the side of the mountaine, but rusheth ouer the toppe of it, and falleth to the grounde with a terrible noyse and clamor, as if 1000 great belles were knockt against another. I thinke there is not in the worlde so straunge an ouerfall, nor so wonderfull to beholde. (101–2)

Here Ralegh uses the familiar tropes of church tower, wonderment, and strangeness he employed at Caroli. Yet his emphasis on sound in his description stands out. Although "not able to march" directly to the water, Ralegh can still feel water via its "terrible noyse and clamor" akin to the sound of "1000 great belles." His previous river soundings demonstrated water's illimitable depths: an imperious gaze could not objectify the riverscape. At Winicapora Ralegh discovers how water sounds him. As if tasted on his tongue or dripped onto his skin, water touches: its sound waves penetrate his ears and barrel into his body. Watery noise acts as a parasitic "third" that instigates "relations with relations" and disrupts the human's one-way relations to things.[40] Waterfall racket: in its noisy interference, the sound of falling water introduces new embodied material relations with/in the riverscape. Ralegh can enter watery assemblages and not even get soaked; the water comes to him in mists and waves that travel through the humid air in the "euill season" of tropical heat. Standing there, sweating, in a bewildered state of wet reciprocity and porosity, he is closer to wetness than he thinks: even if water "wonderfull to beholde" cannot be reached by a long "march," even if it appears that water and rock "toucheth no[t]," the river's "rus[h]" is actively intimate, and intimately affective, with these participants in its proximity, no matter how "farre off" they may be.

Ralegh's aqueous encounters with the Caroli and Winicapora waterfalls are more attuned to desire than ever before. His reaction to the Caroli falls, in particular, is touching: "For mine owne part I was well perswaded from thence to have returned, being a very ill footeman, but the rest were all so desirous to go neere the said straunge thunder of waters, as they drew mee on by little and little, till we came into the next valley, where

we might better discern the same" (81–82). Ralegh believes he is unfit
to continue—he cannot be both an "ill footeman" and a water-man at
once—and it appears that he has seen enough. His company must force
their reluctant leader to continue. What exactly prospected Ralegh to the
next valley, what "drew" him "little and little," seems inconclusive. Ralegh's
indefinite "they" could mean either the clamor of the falls, his men, or
both. The "straunge thunder of *waters*" (emphasis added) might just as
well draw him due to his ambiguous phrasing. And the thunderous waters
of Winicapora do just that: in a remarkable phrase, Ralegh lays bare the
process of becoming-Wa/l/ter for us: the alluring agency ("drew") of water
that redefines the human ("mee") as a body of water in prepositional travel
("on"). Across impassable distances and impossible hardships, Ralegh is
inextricably drawn to and by the wonders of water. Urged ever onward
by the vibrancy of waterfalls, the view that appears to Ralegh around the
Caroli's bend is his ecopoetical masterpiece:

> I neuer saw a more beawtifull country, nor more liuely prospectes, hils
> so raised heere and there ouer the vallies, the riuer winding into diuerse
> braunches, the plaines adioyning without bush or stubble, all faire greene
> grasse, the ground of hard sand easy to march on, eyther for horse or
> foote, the deare crossing in euery path, the birds towardes the euening
> singing on euery tree with a thousand several tunes, cranes and herons of
> white, crimson, and carnation pearching on the riuers side, the ayre fresh
> with a gentle easterlie wind, and euery stone that we stooped to take vp,
> promised eyther golde or siluer by his complexion. (82)

Water prospects Ralegh toward the best "prospectes" he has seen so far, a
"liuely" country that trumps his earlier shoreline experience with the deer
led by "a keepers call." Added to water's pulsating noise are now other
nonhuman vibrations like birdsongs of "thousand several tunes." He even
smells the "fresh" air mingled with the waterfall's mist. This "liuely" riverside at Caroli is a remarkable example of the living riverscape: all things
connect and adjoin in "diuerse braunches" with the possibility to meet
and transform like the deer that intersect "euery path." Notably, if Ralegh
describes Arcadia on the Caroli he does not place himself at its center. The
plains of Caroli encompass the desirable ecological connections available

everywhere in the narrative, connections that flowing nonhuman actants make as well as humans: the "gentle" wind touches Ralegh in its course heading in the rough direction (east to west) upriver to El Dorado; stones "promis[e]" the way to the golden city if only touched. It is here, near ("on") the falls, that Wa/l/ter Ralegh best articulates Guiana's riverscapes of desire: networks of coimplicated things that crash, connect, and create. And we have not ceased to coexist with them. The ways are "diuerse" and the results unpredictable. Guianan waters are without rest. The *Discoverie* beckons us, "little and little," to acknowledge the historical failures that haunt riverscapes. It also asks us to rediscover the desires—even those of nonhuman things—that prolong them, that provide hope, and that may help us imagine future prospects in which non/human bodies of water mutually benefit. *And still we row.*

Water Writes

Underscoring the ecomaterial connections with the riverscape seems at odds with Ralegh's overall mission to acquire El Dorado's gold. Back goes the search to solid ground; even if his watery becomings bespeak an immanent relationship with the riverscape, he must ultimately address the *Discoverie*'s problem of verifiability. But the search for gold runs parallel to his liquid excursions: a refiner's basket suddenly appears after the liquid labyrinth; the "precious stones" of the Caroli and the "Diamondes" of the Winicapora catch his eye. Concerning the latter, for instance,

> *Berreo* tolde mee that it hath Diamondes and other precious stones on it,
> and that they shined very farre off: but what it hath I knowe not, neyther
> durst he or any of his men ascende to the toppe of the saide mountaine,
> those people adioyning beeing his enemies (as they were) and the way to
> it so impassible. (102)

Precious solid objects are close but always just beyond reach. Indeed, most of Ralegh's aquatic portraits surround his most passionate promises to achieve the Guianan gold that always seems to shine "very farre off." Solid objects turn liquid; minerals have flow; "rocks of a blew metalline colour" bleed into rivers (69). As Ralegh learns how the Epuremei people work with gold—"not seuered from the stone" but gathered from Lake

Manoa, mingled with copper, melted, and then poured into moulds to make "plates and Images" (96)—he witnesses gold's liquidity, even if secondhand. Metallurgy is the nomad's art. But if gold has movement, it moves *away* from him. Theorize all he wants about the flow of mineral gold, Ralegh's investors still demanded wealthy returns. He only has the words of the *Discoverie*, whereas Berrío "dispatched his Campmaster for Spaine with all that he had gathered, therewith to leuy soldiers, and by the shew thereof to draw others to the loue of the enterprize" (41). The previous explorers of Guiana brought back numerous signs of proof as well. On his deathbed, Johannes Martines (Juan Martin de Albujar) produced beads of gold from El Dorado, the sole pieces of the city's elusive treasure that he managed to protect from thieves. Domingo de Vera, taking possession of Guiana on Berrío's behalf, brought back "diuers rarities which he carried to the *Spanish* king" and that were displayed in Seville to public amazement (25). Ralegh, however, brings hardly anything back. He sends his benefactors, Charles Howard (1536–1624) and Robert Cecil (1563–1612), two golden images he obtained from the Epuremei, "more to shew the manner of them, then for the value" (96). He tested a small quantity of Guianan ore, publicly believed to be fool's gold, which he assured his readers to be real in the *Discoverie*'s prefatory materials. Multiple assayers "made manie trialls" that proved auspicious (xii). This quantity might be the same "oare" he additionally sent to his patrons, promising that "wee tried them to be no *Marquesite*, and therefore such as the Spaniards call *El Madre del oro*, which is an vndoubted assurance of the generall abundance" (96, 97). When the ore is proven priceless, Ralegh pulls out the excuses for not pocketing any: primarily, that he "had neither tyme, nor men, nor instruments fitte to labour" (xii). He dispels rumors that he hid in Cornwall during the voyage, bought the gold ore in Barbary, and even served the Spanish king. "I hope the better sort will judge me by themselves, & that the way of deceipt, is not the way of honor or good opinion" (xiii). With only promises of a "generall abundance" in such scandalous times, with doubtful and "doubted" signs, Ralegh could hardly expect, like Berrío, to "draw others to the loue of the enterprize."

Ralegh's solution, in fact, is the solution that is all around him: *water*. The infinite possibilities of the riverscape he witnesses—its unfathomable depths, wonderful attractiveness, and oozing pathways—affords the *Discoverie*'s language a liquidity that is useful to a writer like him who needs, first, to explain away his empty-handed expedition and, second, to recruit potential Guianan investors. His language has more than a metaphorical "flow" to it. In his study of the riverine in Renaissance literature, Wyman H. Herendeen argues that "the river . . . is inseparable from the shaping art of language," that it "challenges our epistemological concepts, our language and understanding. It forces us to work toward ordering concepts, and yet it defies them." The river erodes discrete divisions and definitions; it swaps them, like silt, for "only space unfolding."[41] Rivulets of words, language on a run/nel: "Guiana" is where riverscape and text intermesh to create liquid narrativity. Watery writing is thus Ralegh's precise methodology in the *Discoverie*, a discourse in which matter-phors are magnified, in which the bonds between language and water, material and metaphor, are accented. His writing shows that the truly "impassible" route to take is the one that tries to sever these terms. Like the dangerous road to the top of Winicapora falls, the binaries are impossible to maintain. Water saturates both his words and his body. Ralegh seizes upon rivers' twists and turns in order to maintain the impossible verifiability of his account. Wa/l/ter's agency "drew [him] on" before. Now, he draws others "on" through his newfound attraction. To put liquid narrativity in terms of his "Poesy," watery language keeps desire from "runn[ing] out of breath." Or to put it in the wet words of another poetical water-man, the self-proclaimed "Water Poet" John Taylor, to take a "dash," or drink, of water is also to "dabble" in the dashes—like that—of script. "Should I of Water write" would mean to write the "I" that is additionally watery, the more-than-"I," the "Abysse" of self that is always awash.[42]

Ralegh's watery language serves an important strategic purpose. Greeting his readers as fellow questers for El Dorado, Ralegh treats them as potential capital investors who, like him, want to reach, and profit from, the promised golden end of his unfinished story. Ralegh can only imagine the gold as a future rather than present prospect "very farre off." Repeatedly in the *Discoverie* the natives guarantee Ralegh a larger prize farther ahead: "[I]f wee entred the lande over the mountaines of *Curaa*, wee should satisfie our selues with golde and all other good things" (80). But this satisfaction remains endlessly deferred to an indefinite future: it is a prospect that can never be realized. The mountains resemble nuggets of golden ore: "[W]e sawe al the hils with stones of the cullor of Gold and siluer" (97), Ralegh observes, but these gold and silver mountains remain on a distant horizon that he never reaches. When "a Spaniard of the *Caracas*" convinces him that one such stone "was *El Madre deloro*, and that the mine was farther in the grounde" (83), Ralegh moves on. Digging the mine would be the obvious choice in an effort to authenticate his report. Ralegh, however, speaks promises instead: "But it shall bee found a weak pollicie in mee, eyhter to betray my selfe, or my Countrey with imaginations . . . were I not assured that the sunne couereth not so much riches in any part of the earth" (83). "[I]maginations" do not produce riches, but neither does he. Rather than attempting to close the ambiguous gap of language in his narrative between words (his report) and things (the gold), he keeps it open. He always aims for El Dorado, the mother lode ("*El madre deloro*"), rather than small profit. Indeed, he assures his readers that he could have brought back plentiful, but not extraordinary, stores of gold "if I had not shot at another marke, than present profit" (60).

Ralegh inundates his readers with slippery promises from the very first line of the dedicatory epistle. "For your Honors many Honorable and friendlie parts, I have hitherto only returned promises" (iii). Ralegh is acutely aware of the predicament facing him, therefore it is interesting that he concludes the *Discoverie* by extending his promise once more to his readership: "For the rest, which my selfe haue seen I will promise these things that follow and knowe to be true" (111). Ralegh heaps "promises" upon more "promises." Whoever accepts Ralegh's offer and then journeys to Guiana will find there "more rich and bewtifull cities, more temples adorned with golden Images, more sepulchers filled with treasure, then either *Cortez* found in *Mexico*, or *Pazzarro* in *Peru*" (111). In fact, his repetition of "more" bespeaks his supplementary intent. "More" conspicuously rhymes with the absent *ore* of his obsession. Ominously, he offers his own life as collateral in "To the Reader": "I wilbe contented to lose her highnes fauour and good opinion for euer, and my life withall, if the same be not found rather to exceed, then to equall whatsoeuer is in this discourse promised or declared" (xv). Promises have lives at stake, and Ralegh continually upped the ante until breaking his "discourse promised," and dying for it, twenty years later.

As the m/ore conflation suggests, Ralegh is able to weave the economic and the linguistic together in order to suspend his deferred promises indefinitely. New economic theorists and critics have explored the homologous relationship between gold and language to point out Ralegh's liquid linguistic economies. William N. West, for example, describes the credit Ralegh seeks as analogous to the early modern shift from gold as an autonomous signifier of value (a bullionist perspective) to gold as a representation of value, an absent elsewhere (a financial form of credit).[43] Mary C. Fuller considers El Dorado as the anchoring yet perpetually deferred referent in Ralegh's economic and linguistic fantasies. His expedition, she argues, is the search for a golden referent of language. When words might be tried against things, he refrains from creating a true report of Guiana and gestures instead toward language itself: "What appears to be a turn away from language into 'the concrete and everlasting world' dissolves into multiple references back into the order of language."[44] The liquidity of money coterminous with the liquidity of language these critics suggest significantly points to the *Discoverie*'s watery language that similarly refuses to close the gap between signs and their referents. Better yet, the movement away from the "concrete and everlasting world" that interests new economic critics can exceed the linguistic and economical. The "turn" also reflects the ways in which the aquatic environment veers the subject (the *virer* of *viron*). Riverscapes are sites of simultaneous siltation and erosion. True, language dissolves back into the labile structures of language, yet this language is also a form of *fluency* inseparable from the Guianan rivers that challenge the very idea of concreteness.

Far from a "weak pollicie," liquid narrativity keeps the ambiguous gap open between language and truth and allows Ralegh's and his readers' imaginations to profit creatively and, he hopes, financially. The "*Chart of discouerie*" (53) models his preference for uncertainty over absolute knowledge. He promises a map of Guiana that cannot, contrary to its function, be used; he charges Cecil, his political sponsor, with keeping a secret: "[Y]our Lordship shall receive in a large Chart or Map, which I haue not yet finished, and which I shall most humbly pray your Lordship to secret, and not to suffer it to passe your own hands" (26). Rivers are important in Guiana, but none so much as the Caroni regarded as the entrance to El Dorado. Significantly, the Caroni is the only river not mentioned on the map. Far from betraying Ralegh's reconnaissance anxieties, the absence of the Caroni on the map serves yet again to signal the gap between words and things Ralegh exploits, or, in this cartographical example, lines and things. The Caroni's absence stands in for something which is supposedly there in the Guianan jungle, but only on the condition that the reader credits Ralegh with its route. The unfinished map must remain just that: "not yet finished." Wa/l/ter Ralegh had gone along with the matter-flows of water the year before; now, in his hydrographic chart, he urges his readers to go along with him.

Re-turning into the liquid labyrinth, then, these intersections become places of narrative possibility rather than helplessness. Ralegh's streamy recollections, and the *Discoverie* in general, orientate the reader in the direction of disorientation: just in time for Ralegh to extend his hand and guide the reader to the destination of his choice, which is always just inches short of the Manoan riches. Ralegh loses his readers in order to bring them back out and follow him on successive enterprises. Failure, deferral, and disorientation are advantageous directions to take for one who employs the liquidity of water to keep his narrative flowing. In fact, he foresees his readers' responses. He treats his crew essentially like the readers of his narrative. None will continue to El Dorado, physically or in the imagination, "had we not perswaded all the companie that it was but onlie one daies worke more to attaine the lande where we should be releeued of all we wanted, and if we returned that we were sure to starue by the way, and the world would laugh vs to scorne" (54). Ralegh pushes his crew, and his readers, to persevere with only "one daies" more effort—albeit repeatedly—against the scorn of the unbelieving "world." To the crewman who cannot see any farther across the breadth of one river in the "laborinth of riuers," he offers his leadership. To the reader who cannot breach the similar gulf of skepticism in the narrative, he offers fellowship via his credible report of Guianan gold. Both offers operate on the clause of an indefinitely deferred gold: a contract written on, in, and with water.

Water rises higher and flows fiercer in the narrative, constantly washing the gold just beyond Ralegh's reach: "And to say the truth all the branches and small riuers which fell into the Orenoque were raised with such speed, as if wee waded them ouer the shooes in the morning outward, we were couered to the shoulders homewarde the very same daie" (60). Ralegh's predictable near misses transform his narrative into a kind of textual alchemy, a format that is far from mere coincidence; fittingly, it is immediately after he regains his bearings at the labyrinthine intersections that Ralegh finds the tools of the trade. He espies four canoes coming downriver, two of which run ashore after he gives chase. One of the canoes is loaded with bread, while the other contains three Spaniards: "[W]ho hauing heard of the defeat of their gouernour in *Trinedado*, and that we purposed to enter *Guiana*, came away in those *Canoas*: one of them was a *Cauallero*, as the Captaine of the *Arwacas* after told vs, another a soldier, and the third a refiner" (58). Inspecting the bushes by the abandoned canoes, Ralegh makes a fascinating discovery: "I saw an Indian basket hidden, which was the refiners basket, for I found in it, his quicksiluer, saltpeter, and diuerse things for the triall of mettals, and also the dust of such ore as he had refined, but in those *Canoas* which escaped there was a good quantity of ore and gold" (59). Inexplicably, Ralegh knows the contents of the lost canoe but does not pursue. Fuller notes that the canoe chase "typifies the scene of discovery" in the narrative, an example of the simultaneous search for the referent and the desire for distance between words and things.[45] But the other metals Ralegh discovers should not be overlooked, especially because alchemy was a subject he knew intimately. Elizabeth sponsored alchemical experimentation and mineral works in the latter part of her reign. It was during this time that Ralegh developed a reputation as a "chymist," his library containing seventeen works on chemistry and medicine. According to the biographer John Aubrey (1626–97), he "studied most in his sea voyages, where he carried always a trunk of books along with him."[46] John Hester (d. 1592) dedicated a book of medicines to him under the pseudonym, no less, of the Renaissance polymath Paracelsus (1493–1541). His close circle included alchemical dabblers: Percy, Hariot, and Lawrence Keymis (ca. 1565–1618), one of his captains. After his return, Ralegh brewed a "Balsam of Guiana" with famous powers (that allegedly cured Queen Anne's fever), and he continued to concoct alchemical cure-alls in the Tower throughout his imprisonment.[47]

Although it is humorous to imagine Ralegh brushing up on his alchemy during the long voyage of 1595, his chemical background is of greater importance. The refiner's quicksilver combines his arcane interests with his liquid narrativity, thereby transforming him into a kind of alchemical author. Alchemy depends on obscurity and deferred knowledge passed down from master to apprentice. Lee Patterson's work on alchemy in Chaucerian contexts defines this knowledge as a "negative knowledge" or "the 'logic of the supplement.'"[48] In short, instead of closing the gap between word and thing, language and truth, alchemy operates on multiplication, substitution, and excess; as a result, meaning is always in motion: "the disclosure of an original meaning becomes the multiplication of meanings; as each signified is revealed to be only another signifier, the act of revelation becomes itself a concealment."[49] To speak the truth of alchemy would deprive it of its efficacy. Hence, the truth becomes unsayable. Moreover, alchemical writers often promise to clarify the obscurities or failures of other alchemists. Lastly, alchemy markedly affects concepts of self-representation since it pushes the practitioner to near-theatrical heights. As a result, the endlessly multiplied revelations (concealments) turn into acts of *self*-revelation. The experimenter's self—the Yeoman, in Patterson's case—is left equally in motion, unmoored, "his language multiplying itself—proliferating uncontrollably—yet never finally grasping the essence it seeks. The more he talks about the self that so fascinates him, the more dispersed it becomes, leaving him a cipher, an absence, a desire—a being who seeks rather than an object sought."[50] The *Discoverie* is a striking analogue to the Chaucerian example. To reach El Dorado would effectively immobilize his narrative; hence, the truth of the matter must be unknowable. Ralegh's pronouncements of superior knowledge and his derision of previous explorers parallel the competitive nature of alchemists. His mention of the "triall of mettals" in the riverside brush symbolizes the transmutation of his narrative into the narrative gold of El Dorado and the approval of the reading public. Just as the Yeoman, Ralegh's trademark performativity and desire for gold certainly categorize him as a "being who seeks" across the Guianan landscape. Perhaps unlike the Yeoman, however, Ralegh revels in this self-mobility, using it to his advantage as he pursues an "object [infinitely] sought." Understanding Ralegh's watery language as an alchemical discourse—with its inherent multiplicities, translations, supplements, and ambiguous gaps—reveals his intent to layer language upon language, promise upon promise, in the hope of attracting future investors to his Guianan enterprise. Like the coiling confluences of the riverscape, mercury and its "diuerse things" drive the narrative's boundless diversities and multiplications of meaning. Alchemy's liquid knowledge encourages the narrative's liquid language, and the truth keeps on slipping.

Water Drawing

It could be argued at this point that liquid narrativity runs the risk of centering Ralegh in the riverscape, transforming him into a masterful alchemist or a too-human author who writes alone: a laborer in the "laborinth" who will not brook collaboration. By equating the multiplicity of language with the *Discoverie*'s "multitudes of Ilands" and interminable flows of water, Ralegh indeed writes water to his advantage. But water's work is "not yet finished." Water enables Ralegh's watery writing. As much as alchemy describes the self and language perpetually in motion, these authorial formulations should be reconceived as fluidic selves within larger non/human wet labs and networks of labor. If liquid narrativity instantiates a broad semiotic breakdown of language, it also amplifies Ralegh's ecopoetical process *with* water. We have seen how Wa/l/ter Ralegh resists the metaphorical fluidity of identity through his material and embodied becomings, and how Ralegh's composition illustrates more than just the metaphorical fluidity of language that poststructuralism takes for granted since it draws on the Guianan riverscape in order to draw others on. In its genesis from the riverscape, water writes the *Discoverie* into an ecocompositionist manifesto. Admittedly, Ralegh's legacy as a (or *the*) "Renaissance man" overshadows the agency of water. As I previously mentioned, critical praise is often reserved for his fluid identity and self-fashioning, often draining the materiality of water as a result. Schmidt's bibliographic work, for instance, describes Ralegh's genres as "active," meaning that they invite different processes of reading: "It is not simply that the *Discovery of Guiana* streams its words along in a forceful rush of prose—the result, no doubt, of Ralegh's kinetic literary style and his imperative call (in this case) to colonial action." Even with the "thrust of Ralegh's prose" that "convey[s] the audience headlong" into subsequent passages, Schmidt focuses on the broader interplay between content and form.[51] How all the specific actants involved—human and nonhuman—guide the flow of form remains unexplored. Shannon Miller argues that Ralegh's influential circle of patronage constitutes a system of production. Addressing the *Discoverie*'s stream-like composition, and effectively decentering Ralegh, she intriguingly returns to the literal meaning of "influence" (*influere*, "to flow in") to show how "the 'flow-in' of other streams builds an ever-changing, ever-shifting inundation, allowing for the multiple influxes that necessarily comprise the artistic or intellectual project."[52] Miller's study importantly describes a liquid process of narrative influence. Consequently, watery influence does not just decenter Ralegh and the typical sites of power relations (like the new historical approaches to which Miller responds) but also applies to any investment in core meaning of the *Discoverie*. Truth is equally unmoored by "flows-in" and "flows-out" of influence, and Ralegh was highly aware of the liquidity of language in this regard. Both these readings of Ralegh's compositional process, however, would benefit by including not only his personal circle of human patrons but also water's influential flows that decenter the subject and "convey" writer and reader "headlong" through the riverscape.

In order to experience writing (with) water in all its freshet-fullness, we need to refresh our view of the "*Chart* of discouerie." Ralegh as humanist explorer cannot fully draw the route to El Dorado for the primary reason that he could not realistically reach the city. Nor could he possibly visit all the innumerable waterways of Guiana during his brief mission. Hence his chart's "not yet finished" areas: the terra and aqua incognita of the chart is the place for the imagination to inhabit. The chart keeps these imaginative routes flowing by visualizing the living riverscape: "[h]ow all these riuers crosse and encounter, how the countrie lieth and is bordred, the passage of *Cemenes*, and of *Berreo*, mine owne discouerie, and the way that I entred, with all the rest of the nations and riuers" (26). Ralegh's chart importantly coinvents with the riverscape it attempts to display. The "passage[s]" of explorers intersect as "riuers crosse." Nonhuman and human "encounter" on the chart just as Ralegh does in the riverscape. Like the "deare crossing in euery path" of Caroli falls, the chart's hydrographical points, lines, and curves vivify the riverscape's bustling interweavements and nature-culture crossings. Exemplifying the inventiveness shared with an agentic riverscape, the chart breaches the borders of humanism to embrace posthuman possibilities. Remember that the waters "drew mee on": if Ralegh had *drawn* water for his own purposes earlier, here the self of Ralegh is *drawn* by water, the act and art of drawing a dual instantiation of attraction and composition. Thus living water draws him on (moves him), allows him to draw others to his enterprise through liquid narrativity (persuades them), and now collaborates with the human to draw a map. The map is like a mirror in which Ralegh sees his unfinished watery self. The human, as (the) chart, is always "not yet finished," ever-incomplete. The chart's lines and points are seemingly indelible: note the topographical traces of already-imprinted footpaths, connections made, borders sunk in, a country that "lieth" still (26). Yet the map is topological as much as it is topographical. These water lines are really vectoral becomings that advance new points of encounter with things yet to be encountered, those that refuse to "lieth" there, immobilized. The chart constantly flows with water, bringing these unpredictable points into enfolded contacts and percolating change. The gray area is not a gap that seeks human imagination and inventiveness to fill it; rather, it signifies the desirable insolvability of water. Rivers cannot be plumbed or fully known, but they can surely draw and move the watery explorer to new possibilities. Un/charted: the "not yet finished" chart is thus a site of possibility with "not yet finished" material connections. Water ensures that terra-aqua incognita will never be wholly territorialized, even on the literal page that sometimes ensnares its ambit. Ink spills over the "bordered" segments; it *runs* everywhere; it may dry but it continually has speed of its own. Just as rivers spilled into Ralegh's language and prospected him to new horizons, writing resists stratification in its very medium. Like the slippery shoreline of water and earth, the chart's various actors—ink, paper, and hand—forge a coauthorial network. Meaning flows in collaboration with inky non/human hands. If there is room for error in Ralegh's authoritative chart, then, it is infinite space to be explored, cohabited, and desired. The "not yet finished" chart of the *Discoverie* manifests Ralegh's necessarily "not yet finished" desire to connect with the living riverscape. Rather than looking at the "*Chart* of discouerie" for traceable, plottable points, the chart should be read for endless directions—onward prepositions—instead. Reconfiguring water— and its graphic vehicle, ink—as endlessly inventive routes characterizes Ralegh's unique contribution to non/human cartography as much as his fluctuating narrative of watery words and, finally, his desire to cohabit the Guianan waterscape's bottomless riverbeds of connectivity. The creature in this map of relationships is, and has always been, the living creature of water.

Water Rights

A map may also speak of conquest, of course, especially when its lines force non/human bodies into discrete areas. Some creatures raise the objections of ecojustice. Although Ralegh theorizes the writing of water in the *Discoverie*, he is far from an environmental crusader. He is in Guiana, ultimately, to promote English enterprise. The waterscape is an untapped land of abundance: "Brasill woode," "berries," "Cotten," "sylke," "*Balsamum*" (113). Gold is the priority, for "[w]here there is store of gold, it is in effect nedeles to remember other commodities for trade" (113). As we saw earlier, plumbing the waterways for precise measurements is an impossible feat. Mapping the water routes is an easier way for him to orient himself in a slippery riverscape. While his technical work is necessary, charting the "*Chart* of discouerie" proves monotonous. As Ralegh and his men travel, they make sure to chart every river: "Euerie daie we passed by goodlie branches of riuers . . . but those I leaue to the description in the *Chart* of discouerie, where euerie one shall be named with his rising and descent" (53). If water cannot be made knowable via depth-soundings, another useful technique is to name it. Coming out of the "laborinth," for example, demands a colonizing approach: "But this it chanced that entring into a riuer, (which bicause it had no name we called the riuer of the *Red crosse*, our selues being the first *Christians* that euer cam therein)" (47). The choice is highly symbolic, referencing Edmund Spenser's (1552/53–99) Red Crosse Knight from *The Faerie Queene* (1590/96), the Protestant hero St. George of England, and even the religious sect of Rosicrucians at once. George Chapman's poem composed shortly after Ralegh's voyage, "De Guiana, Carmen Epicum" (1596), anticipates England's grand course: "*Riches*, and *Conquest*, and *Renowme* I sing."[53] In spite of his relationship with water built upon open-ended processes and desires of becoming, Ralegh's empirical and imperial forays into the riverscape also demonstrate his wish to limn the waters, mark their boundaries, and understand their recalcitrant flows. Encounters like these are acts of territorialization, desires for domination, and attempts to harden Guiana's matter-flows into hierarchies of knowledge. A squiggly line is drawn on the "*Chart* of discouerie"; an unknowable river gets a name "*Red crosse*"; the company moves on: a colonial methodology so often repeated that it, too, seems "not yet finished." This progression demands further exploration if it is to be refuted.

Ralegh's liquid body and narrativity on the River of the Red Cross—coded as male, English, and Protestant—necessarily raise questions of environmental justice, the remonstrations of Guianan river-bodies that do not want to go with the flow in a specified direction, or are prevented from doing so along a route of their choice. Becoming-water flows unevenly. The efflorescence seen earlier on the banks of the Caroli where nature and culture intersect—the "beawtifull country, nor more liuely prospectes"—resembles a paradise of symmetrical relations. The *Discoverie*'s "discourse" between heterogeneous human and nonhuman characters is much more complex, however, and oftentimes asymmetrically enforced. Not all beings share the same "liuely prospectes." Guiana's living waters struggle to erase all hierarchical divisions, and special actants may use insurmountable ontological difference to their advantage, shoring up indissoluble breaches between the human and the nonhuman as well as human from human. Ralegh's colonial injunction is the most obvious example: "it is in effect nedeles to remember" anything other than the gold he promises, even if this means—purposefully or not—neglecting the ethical dilemmas of ecoimperialism. His pact is simple enough: the English acquire riches and the Guianans are freed from Spanish oppression. The contract is supposedly beneficial to both, despite the fact that the natives lose one master only to gain another:

> I made them vnderstand that I was the seruant of a Queene, who was the great *Casique* of the north, and a virgin, and had more *Casiqui* under her than there were trees in their iland: that she was an enemy to the *Castellani* in respect of their tyrannie and oppression, and that she deliuered all such nations about her, as were by them oppressed; and hauing freed all the coast of the northern world from their seruitude, had sent me to free them also, and withal to defend the countrey of *Guiana* from their inuasion and conquest. (8–9)

Always one to offer promises, Ralegh offers the hope of redemption. The irony is obvious: in order to liberate the Guianans, England must invade their territories. Ralegh's ethnographical reconnaissance is sparse. While he has a general idea of the multiculturalism of Guiana—he is aware of domestic conflicts, for instance—its diverse peoples are assumed to be a willing conglomeration: "The countrey is alreadie discouered, many nations won to her Maiesties loue and obedience" (118). Likening himself to an English Columbus—"The west Indies were first offered her Maiesties Grandfather by *Columbus* a straunger, in whome there might be doubt of deceipt" (117)—Ralegh picks up where the legendary explorer left off. He is discovering a country already "discouered." His task, then, is to show others what they have been missing. Everything is ripe for English conquest: the people are pacified, the minerals are ready for removal, the Spanish are retreating. Guiana is *rich* for the taking.

Yet few besides the English would approve of these "prospectes." Once again, "doubt" and "deceipt" are meant to encourage colonial investors, though only Elizabeth could give the final go-ahead. The amicable Guianan–English relations he describes must be taken at his word. Ralegh assures his readers that an English settlement, once attempted, will last. "[K]eeping one good fort, or building one towne of strength, the whole Empyre is guarded" (117). He surveys the waterscape not just to map the way to El Dorado, but also to suggest where a "defensible" fortress might be built in order to prevent any plots against the proposed English colony in the future (115). Nearby rivers, deltas, and mountains are useful allies in this martial sense. Moreover, he hopes that the amount of geographic detail he provides will amount to a better route for invasion, "*an easier way to inuade the best parts therof, then by the common course*" (vi). The sea towns and islands are "*anatomized*" and "*by what meanes they may be beste inuaded, as farre as any meane Iudgement can comprehend*" (ix). This guarantee of English security dovetails into his earlier promises of gold. Colonial and financial incentives intersect; both results are deferred: dig a mine *here* and riches will appear, build a colony *there* and the English will come. But he must explain why he did not invade when he knew the strengths and weaknesses of Guiana. Upon deliberation, he found it "verie euill counsell to haue attempted it at that time" (95). His logic is deplorable for its ethical maneuvering:

> but as yet our desier of gold, or our purpose of inuasion is not known vnto those of the Empire: and it is likely that if her maiestie vndertake the enterprize, they will rather submit themselues to her obedience then

to the Spanyards, of whose cruelty both themselues and the borderers
haue alreadie tasted: and therfore til I had known her maiesties pleasure,
I woulde rather haue lost the sacke of one or two townes (although they
might haue been very profitable) then to haue defaced or endaungered
the future hope of so many millions, and the great good, and rich trade
which England maie bee possessed off thereby. (95)

Ralegh's general assurance is double-dealing. He lists yet another reason
why the Guianan gold could not be brought back to England: to begin
mining or to ransom local chieftains would divulge ("defac[e]") the secret
nature of the enterprise. If the "desire of golde will aunswere many obiections" (95), it is a desire he must bury deep within himself. But negotiations cannot truly take place if only one party is aware of the terms. No
matter: gold trumps everything. The "desire of golde" goes hand-in-hand
with his assurance of successful colonialization. The choice *not* to invade,
in other words, is done for commercial rather than ethical reasons. Liberation is on the agenda as long as it turns a profit. The "hope of so many
millions" is monetary millions; Ralegh does not refer to the riverscape's
nonhuman and human populations here, regardless of our inclination to
read it this way at first glance. "They" hope to live. Ralegh hopes for gold.
His true motives could not be clearer: the "desier of gold, or our purpose of inuasion." His desire for gold *is* invasive because it is inherently
a desire *to* invade, to "sacke and spoyle them" (95). The "or" equates the
two clauses. But by couching his desire in terms of rescue—he is an action
hero who prevents a massacre at the hands of the Spanish—Ralegh saves
face and the *face* of the English enterprise.

Or so he thinks: the lives he has "endaungered" by his actions encap-
sulate the difficulty of conjoining Ralegh's two desires—becoming watery,
accruing gold—under the banner of environmental justice. Topiawari tells
him in confidence that the "*Epuremei* [a rival tribe] woulde inuade him,
and destroye all the remayne of his people and friendes, if hee shoulde
any way eyther guide vs or assist vs against them" (93). Likewise, the
Spanish "woulde be nowe more vehement when they shoulde vnderstand
of his conference with the English" (93). Ralegh's promises have dangerous political consequences he does not fully understand. The inhabitants

of the riverscape are put at risk. Read this way, the *Discoverie*'s memorable line about Guiana's virginity deflects the riverscape's present dangers away from his voyage:

> To conclude, *Guiana* is a Countrey that hath yet her Maydenhead, neuer sackt, turned, nor wrought, the face of the earth hath not beene torne, nor the vertue and salt of the soyle spent by manurance, the graues haue not beene opened for gold, the mines not broken with sledges, nor their Images puld down out of their temples. It hath neuer been entred by any armie of strength, and neuer conquered or possesed by any Christian Prince. (115)

More idealistic than realistic, Ralegh's vision of trouble-free invasion is wishful thinking. Of course, one could quickly point out his hypocrisy on multiple levels: this is the same author, for instance, who rifles mountains for their supposed gold. The passage is notable more for its ironies, though; instead of simply demonstrating his artfulness, he translates the stakes of environmental justice into idyllic terms. He describes a landscape that can be "entred" and still retain its "Maydenhead"—the gendered language of rape uncomfortably lingers, even so—a generative space that is fecund without "manurance." "To conclude," Ralegh slips into reverie, but I am not convinced that he dreams of a water-land of unspoiled essences. If there is anyone who should know that nothing is untouched, it is he; he who saw parks on the riverbanks, felt sound waves of waterfalls, and drank the red water of Amapaia. Guiana is elemental mixture in extreme, not a taxonomic Eden where every thing has a name and a place. And invoking nostalgia, the classical trope of the Golden Age, overlooks the fact it was a period, according to Ovid, in which both gold and travel were undiscovered: "The fertile earth as yet was free, untouched of spade or plough; / And yet it yielded of itself of everything enough."[54] Ralegh will put an end to this age; he will personally bring the "sledges." Or perhaps the gendering of "Countrey" is an allusion to his patchy relationship with Elizabeth, the passage evoking "interplay between . . . romance and colonial discourse."[55] To be sure, Ralegh's reference to "Maydenhead" is misogynistic imperialism at work, pitting an active masculine force against a passive feminine nature. Rather than reading his reverie for its blind spots or for its willful manipulation of his audience, however, I suggest we take a closer look at how he perceives the environmental effects of his conquest. Guiana is not a prelapsarian paradise he preserves: it is a precarious ecology he violates, and his pleasurable experiences come with a price. My proposition is not in Ralegh's defense, nor is it meant to attribute blame. (If he bemoaned his conflicting desires outright, we could hardly exonerate him.) Instead, we are implored to take up the ethical issues Ralegh leaves behind. When he confronts the real impact his expedition makes on the riverscape and its peoples, he spins his encroachment in a positive light. He speaks of his own infiltration chastely. The Spanish are the sole European injurious party. Not only do they buy women and children from the cannibals and sell them for a profit—among other horrors—but they also take the natives' "wiues . . . and daughters daily, and vs[e] them for the satisfying of their owne lusts" (61). The English are in direct contrast to the Spanish "who tyrannize ouer them in all things" (61). Ralegh commands his men never to touch, even "offer to touch," any of the wives and daughters:

> I protest before the maiestie of the liuing God, that I neither know nor beleeue, that any of our companie one or other, by violence or otherwise, euer knew any of their women, and yet we saw many hundreds, and had many in our power, and of those very yoong, and excellently fauored, which came among vs without deceit, starke naked. Nothing got vs more loue among them than this vsage. (61)

Chaste conquest is an appropriate strategy to maintain the "Maydenhead" of Guiana. The English have desires, at least for the "very yoong" and "excellently fauored," but their greater self-control separates them even further from their licentious Spanish rivals. These women are treated similarly to the land. He also prohibits his men to take up a "*Pina* [pineapple], or a *Potato* roote, without giuing them contentment" (61). Women and fruit entwine; he forbids both to be plucked. And while no one is perfect—Ralegh confesses that "the meaner sort from spoile and stealing . . . in all I could not preuent" (61)—the English are generally admired for their discipline. Yet English virtue is based upon colonial progress, nonetheless.

Ralegh's environmental ethics serve a strategic purpose. The natives' fair treatment "drew them to admire hir Maiestie" (61). The English still use the women to gain favor and ultimately use the land. The "vsage" of Guiana's "Maydenhead"—and by extension, the maidens'—is both politically motivated and chastely performed. The Spanish policy depended upon "violence or otherwise." Ralegh's purer motives are "without deceit, starke naked," leaving no one to object.

His kidnapped native pilots certainly could; after exiting the River of the Red Cross, their navigator, a native man they renamed Ferdinando, enters a village to gather information and victuals for Ralegh and his men. He took his brother along with him, and the natives "offred to lay hands on them, purposing to haue slaine them both, yeelding for reason that this Indian of ours had brought a strange nation into their territorie to spoyle and destroy them" (47). Ralegh has led these men to their deaths. A chase ensues; in the fracas, Ralegh takes action: "[W]e set hands on one of them that was next vs, a very old man, and brought him into the barge, assuring him that if we had not our Pilot againe, we would presently cut off his head" (47). His oath fortunately did not need to be put to the test. The two men escape and return to the barge. "[B]ut our good hap was, that we kept the other old Indian, which we handfasted to redeeme our Pilot withall" (48). Because of his old age, the handcuffed captive presumably knows the waterways better than Ferdinando. (He does not.) Ralegh grows impatient with "[o]ur old Pilot of the *Ciawani*" (55). Though he leads them to their place of refreshment and, on the following day, "the most beautifull countrie that euer mine eies beheld," the old helmsman is under the gun. "At the last we determined to hang the Pilot; and if we had well knowen the way backe againe by night, he had surely gone, but our own necessities pleaded sufficiently for his safetie" (56). At such moments of selfishness—Ralegh's own "necessities" take priority—interdependence is clearly not the nature of relations, it is a choice. Not all bodies on the river roll on desirably; some are "handfasted." Ralegh states in the dedication that he "*could haue laid hands and ransomed many of the kings and* Cassiqui *of the Country*" (x) but decided against it for fear of jeopardizing English–Guianan relations and the sums of gold to be exchanged. Yet he does lay "*hands*," as he must: the "desire of golde" depends on it.

Ralegh's hands "*laid*" upon these native bodies are mere footnotes within his greater golden cause. Like the transparent residents he meets at Toparimaca, the old "Pilot" simply disappears back into the riverscape where he belongs. The *Discoverie* is an economical rather than an ethnographical narrative; native bodies are often rendered invisible. Although the "Pilot" and others are lost, there exist more enduring intercultural relations, moments that initiate stories "not yet finished." Topiawari "freely gaue me his onelie sonne to take with me into England" (95). Cayoworaco, given the name "Iwiakanarie Gualtero" by the Spanish (a term for "Walter Ralegh"), spent time with Ralegh in the Tower before returning to Arromaia to rule again in the early 1600s.[56] Cayoworaco could have shared Ralegh's desire to travel as well as his name; he is the one who famously tells Ralegh about the Ewaipanoma (Acephali), the headless men "written of by *Maundeuile*" who ravage his father's country: "[B]ut it was not my chaunce to heare of them til I was come away, and if I had but spoken one word of it while I was there, I might haue brought one of them with me to put the matter out of doubt" (86). Cayoworaco's careful silence reveals his own strategy to keep moving, to become liquid, perhaps, to chart his discovery of England. In the same paragraph, we learn of Francis Sparry and Hugh Goodwin, two English boys left behind—or who volunteered to stay—in the waterscape: the former was meant to "describe [the] cuntrey with his pen" and the latter "to learne the language" (96). (The Spanish capture Sparry, unfortunately, and jaguars catch Goodwin.) Such cross-cultural exchanges loosen, even if slightly, the "handfasted"-ness of others. Ralegh is not the only one unleashed. Becoming watery can be a shared process, even if it is left to the imagination. There are more "obiections" to come: as Cayoworaco's comment about the headless men suggests, creatures roam off Ralegh's map of relationships. A shipwrecked Dutch sailor, Lourens Lourenszoon, supposedly witnessed the capture, torture, and execution of an Acephali in 1623.[57] Ralegh has a kinder, gentler, monster-grabbing hand; he "might haue brought one of them" back. We are left to wonder if these men—hybrids like himself—would have had the urge for flowing like him. The Amazons are treated similarly: escaping capture but not his interest, subjugated in future if not in present. Ralegh "was very desirous to vnderstand the truth of those warlike women," which he receives from a "*Casique* or Lord of people" (27, 28). He then proceeds to correct the lord by informing him, for instance, that Amazons do not cut off their right "dug." Although Ralegh never encounters either group, he makes good "vsage" of these imaginary inhabitants. Like the other Guianans, the Amazons will submit to English rule:

> And where the south border of *Guiana* reacheth to the Dominion and Empire of the *Amazones*, those women shall heereby heare the name of a virgin, which is not onely able to defend her owne territories and her neighbours, but also to inuade and conquere so great Empyres and so farre remoued. (120)

The Amazonian empire translates into an English one; the "warlike women" get a new queen: Elizabeth I. The same holds for the headless men of John Mandeville's *Book of Marvels and Travels* (ca. 1356). Ralegh becomes the new author of the marvelous, a new Mandeville, and the disunited populations will finally get a new head: the queen. By pushing the Acephali and Amazons outside the margins, Ralegh silences them and their desires by policing the borders of becoming.

Even if his colonial motives conflict with his chaste desires for the environment, Ralegh remains a self-confident invader. True to the riverscape's living waters, however, Guiana's "Maydenhead" is not so easily taken. He might assume he is the one who penetrates—to follow the passage's sexual metaphor—but he is constantly reminded that he is being penetrated. As I have shown above, the dangers of the waterscape are well understood. The interpenetration of the riverscape is not always safe to experience. But when the riverscape strikes back, Ralegh learns his lesson at the expense of another. Immediately after his eye-opening experience on the Amana River, Ralegh tells of an unfortunate accident:

> Vpon this riuer there were great store of fowle, and of many sorts: we saw in it diuers sorts of strange fishes, and of maruellous bignes, but for *Lagartos* it exceeded, for there were thousands of those vglie serpents, and the people call it for the abundance of them the river of *Lagartos*, in their language. I had a *Negro* a very proper yoong fellow, that leaping out of the *Galley* to swim in the mouth of this riuer, was in all our sights taken and deuoured with one of these *Lagartos*. (57–58)

Though a "*Negro*" is not listed in the ship records, whether or not this incident is spurious is beside the point.[58] The one person who succumbs to the entangling environment is the sole black body in the company. The river is going to get you: the dangerous incorporation of the human body into the riverscape via the maws of "*Lagartos*" (alligators) reminds Ralegh of the nonhuman's powerful agency. But it also foregrounds the questions of environmental justice Ralegh avoids: why *specific* bodies, and their attendant stories, are absent from the narrative. While the "*Negro*['s]" desire for the waterscape literally consumes him (as it will Ralegh), he is significantly *not* Ralegh. This scene raises more questions than it answers about creating livable lives for both humans ("a *Negro*" and Ralegh) as well as nonhumans (the Amana, alligators), who encroaches upon whom, and whose desires take priority. Ralegh's most aesthetic descriptions of the riverscape impinge on his narrative's most troubling moments: "a *Negro*['s]" death, kidnapped pilots, dark bodies erased from the map, the colonial "way of deceipt." Such discrepancies compel us to think of the *Discoverie* in ethical terms. Ralegh's quest leaves us with questions we should not, and cannot, avoid: above all, to wrestle with the idea that if the "desire of golde will aunswere many obiections," whose "obiections" are suppressed, why, and at what cost.

Ultimately, Ralegh knows a chaste penetration of Guiana is untenable. He always leaves a physical mark. At the end of the *Discoverie* he turns defensive, reiterating a local prophecy in order to justify England's imperial desires. Ostensibly, a future expedition would free the oppressed Guianans from the Spanish, Ralegh's ideal situation, since it would return him to the riverscape without having to vindicate his "desire of golde":

> [T]here was found among prophecies in *Peru* (at such time as the Empyre was reduced to the Spanish obedience) in their chiefest temples, amongst diuers others which foreshewed the losse of the said Empyre, that from *Inglatierra* those *Ingas* shoulde be againe in time to come restored, and deliuered from the seruitude of the said Conquerors. (119)

The prophecy not only hands Guiana over to the English, but it conveniently thwarts the Spanish as well. Their best imperial defense has been waiting for them in their future home all along. Ralegh need not give any more reasons for a chaste conquest. The narrative concludes, finally, with a simple choice: "eyther defend it, and hold it as tributary, or conquere and keepe it as Empresse of the same. For whatsoeuer Prince shall possesse it, shall be greatest" (120). *"Inglatierra"* (England) overtakes *guiana* ("land of water"). Only from a more solid (terrestrial) foundation may a colony be built. The English are next in line in a trajectory of empires that leads from the Incas, to the Spanish, and finally to themselves. The Incas are "restored" and "deliuered" just in time to be supplanted by their English restorers. Conveniently for the English, the ancient prophecy is a self-fulfilling one. The ecological future of Guiana is degradation. Deliverance: mountains removed; rivers choked with commerce; natives displaced; coastlines civilized; "the reliefe we found by killing some store of [foule and fish] with our fouling peeces" (54). Ralegh does not think on environmental destruction or accountability. He need not: ecoimperialism simply goes on. The inhabitants either assimilate or perish. Ultimately, Ralegh proves that a chaste conquest is impossible *not* because a pure and virginal nature is a fantasy, but because the idea of human separation from any riverscape (any -scape) is a delusion. In the end, Ralegh cannot have his water without making contact; he cannot enter Guiana without creating ripples. As we have seen, colonial contact profoundly altered the riverscape. Environmental justice demands more than the human making a lesser impact on its surroundings, more than smarter "vsage" of rivers' resources, more than becoming stricter "keepers" of them. A posthumanist ethics requires hearing the call of fluvial things and responding to them. Of living enmeshed with *living* riverscapes. Of living more-than-human. More.

Water Martyr

In 1844, Henry David Thoreau published an essay on "Sir Walter Raleigh" in order to awaken American heroism: "If an English Plutarch were to be written, Raleigh would be the best Greek or Roman among them all."[59] What sets Ralegh apart is his "nature": "He seems to have had, not a profounder or grander, but, so to speak, more, nature, than other men."[60] By "nature," Thoreau explicitly means Ralegh's combination of martial rigor and genteel behavior—a mien that somehow came "naturally" to knighthood—but he also points implicitly to Ralegh's material connections with the natural world. The blue blood of Ralegh that Thoreau details is the bluest of all: blue by fact of being conjoined with blue waters. Wa/l/ter Ralegh has "more nature" because he desires more water, more movement, more and more. And his riverscape of desire has not been lost on his readers. Robert Schomburgk, one of the *Discoverie*'s first editors, wistfully describes the narrative's imaginative longevity in the preface of his 1848 edition: "Every page, nay almost every sentence, awakened past recollections, and I felt in imagination transported once more into the midst of the stupendous scenery of the Tropics. . . . I explored in 1841 that wondrous delta of the Orinoco."[61] Visiting Ralegh's text prompts Schomburgk's revisitation to Guiana in his imagination. Nicholl literally follows Ralegh's footsteps in his book. A tribute to Elizabethan heroism or not, the *Discoverie* assembles "more . . . natur[al]" bodies flowing as the lifeblood of landscapes: "walking" waters, potable marshes, translucent skin, animate ink.

"We have not another such head to be cut off!"[62] Ralegh's blood must run its natural course, alas. Relegated to a haunting narrative of failure, error, and incredible lies, his ecotheorization of living waters culminates at the final scene of execution. In his opening letter to the readers, Ralegh spoke of the voyage dryly: "I am not so much in loue with these long voiages, as to deuise, thereby to cozen my selfe, to lie hard, to fare worse, to be subiected to perils, to diseases, to ill sauours, to be parched and withered, and withall to sustaine the care and labour of such an enterprize" (xiii). A desiccated *Discoverie*. But as we have seen, his adventure was sheer liquefaction. Those present at his execution in 1618 discovered the symbiosis of human blood and watery flows firsthand. Far from being "parched and withered," one anonymous witness noted that Ralegh's "large Effusion of Blood, which proceeded from his Veins, Amazd the Spectators, who Conjectured that he had stock enough of Nature to have survived many Years."[63] "More nature" proves to be not "enough" in the end. And yet, perhaps this person had read the *Discoverie*, perhaps even associated him- or herself with Wa/l/ter's desire for diluvial places. The spectator's language transforms the scaffold into another riverscape, albeit a grisly one. Trauma and desire for perpetuity conjoin; bloodstreams yearn for another drop. Effusive like his language, Ralegh's blood spills over: some tumbles over stone, jetting in rivers around the cobbles; some meets with dust, coagulating into little lakes and "plashy" ponds; some may even join with the Thames, moving "on" (eventually) into Guiana after a rainfall.

Ralegh's "martyrdom," as it is usually conceived, need not be religious; nor need it privilege the human and its heroic masculinity: *martur* in Greek means "witness." In the execution, we witness our own watery selves on the stage-scaffold. The ghastly scene of Ralegh's supernaturally flowing blood is a torrential ecology of the passions; a sanguine, passionate man like Wa/l/ter appropriately makes waves. Ralegh's death parallels Gail Kern Paster's reading of Amavia's in *The Faerie Queene*: "Thus insanguinated, the ground expresses human blood's analogical relation to rivers and streams; it recalls blood's place in bodily topography as the body's liquid source of nourishment as well as its current of feeling and consciousness."[64] And his intensifies it: both "analogical" and geographical, material and metaphorical, becoming the riverscape disrupts inside and outside configurations of human and nonhuman embodiment. By his "relation to rivers and streams," Ralegh is G/g/uiana; as are we all, all of us bodies of water of some kind. Witnessing his roving blood, we understand that the scaffold need not be our final destination. The *Discoverie* depicts a riverscape of ecomaterial things in constant and creative co-constitutiveness. Exploring Guiana deepens our material, "hands on" interactions with the *guiana* of today. Ralegh demonstrates the pleasures of dis/solution, the joys of cohabiting a river's unfathomable uncertainties. He also points us to the "breaches" that may harmfully separate non/human things; these watery beings solicit a new ethics from us. A "conference" need not be interrogational, but a parliament, an assembly, a home, a "confluence of streames and branches."[65] Ralegh confers with the natives, but he has been in Guiana's swirling "conference" of diverse things all along. He was not *only* haunted by waters; neither should we be. Catastrophes are possible, and do happen, but the shores of any riverscape offer endless departures to new assemblages with the world. This is a capability too often barricaded by the failures of technology, hopes for the tropical Edens of sustainability, and faith in the salvific sovereign. Replying to the hot-headed Hatton, Elizabeth demanded that "there *shall* be no more destruction by water."[66] The sovereign's wish to be the exception will not work. What is crucial to remember is that the scaffold can always become the "prospect," "*a painful pilgrimage*" a voyage of "contentment" (v). A point of termination becomes a way of facing a different horizon, of having a future. Ecology reconceived in our shared deluge unleashes the potential of water's living matter-flows: a potential that never runs its course, within and without us. Like the "*Chart* of discouerie," our fluvial bodies and stories are truly "not yet finished."

CHAPTER 2

Going Glacial

For some people, what they are is not finished at the skin, but continues with the reach of the senses out into the land. . . . The land gets inside us; and we must decide one way or another what this means, what we will do about it.

—Barry Lopez, *Arctic Dreams*

Cold is so barren a subject.

—Robert Boyle, *New Experiments and Observations Touching Cold* (1665)

On August 5, 2010, an ice sheet one hundred square miles in size calved from the Petermann Glacier in Greenland. Heading through Nares Strait, it threatened to enter the Atlantic Ocean and eventually strike urban areas. It fortunately did not; but what this wandering chunk of matter did accomplish, unfortunately, was to condemn human civilization to an inevitable collision course with the icescape. (A fifty-square-mile piece broke off two years later.) On February 25, 2015, a new record for the lowest maximum winter extent of Arctic ice was set at 5.61 million square miles. A different fear—cities' submergence through rising sea levels—worsened. In September 2008, the MV *Camilla Desgagnés* became the first commercial ship to sail through the Northwest Passage, and it did so, moreover, almost entirely unobstructed. (The *Beluga Fraternity* and the *Beluga Foresight* crossed the Northeast Passage in 2009.) At this current pace of climate change, scientists predict an ice-free passage by midcentury.[1] While they may be welcomed by some parties for liquefying capital assets even further, these rates and routes of exchange present a series of bio- and cryopolitical predicaments: in particular, which nations and ethnic groups own the lanes and land, along with the oil, gas, and mineral resources yet to be discovered underneath the ice. Such scares accumulate evidence for climate change like a runaway snowball rolling downhill. Bill McKibben, founder of the global warming watchdog 350.org, seizes upon these historic events and international fears, arguing that the passages' dissolution forces us to see "how profoundly we've altered the only place we've ever known."[2] If the Petermann incident, for example, illustrates ice's transgressive vitality, in McKibben's view it is the human who terrorizes the ice: "We need now to understand the world we've created, and consider—urgently—how to live in it."[3] Cold heaven beside you: we watch as northeastern and northwestern worlds implode on icy eves of destruction.

Arctic Counsel

It seems that the human has moved to the center of the Arctic Circle, a circumference that it alone has "created." The northwestern Atlantic has hardly been an unpopulated region historically, after all. The Norse colonized Greenland centuries before Columbus; Iceland was a commercial hub for the English beginning in the early fifteenth century; and, starting in the first half of the sixteenth century, the French and Portuguese competed in the fishing industry off Newfoundland.[4] Indigenous peoples like the Eskimo-Inuit, of course, had been living in the area before the Europeans arrived. But these histories are stiffly anthropo- as well as Euro-centric; narrating ice from the human point of view risks territorializing ice all over again.[5] If Bruno Latour's actor-network theory helps deterritorialize landscapes and disperse its agents, it is fitting that his landmark text, *We Have Never Been Modern*, opens in a cold place. The ozone layer crisis over Antarctica, Latour argues, exemplifies the "proliferation of hybrids" shunned by modernity, which translates agentic ice into an objectified, even if dangerous, substance.[6] Humans exist in an icescape that they must master, exploit, or escape. The (still) lost expedition of John Franklin that left England in 1845 and the contested American claims for the pole in 1908–9 are stand-ins for masculine heroism and colonialist fortitude that continue to intrigue.[7] Somehow pristine and pure in its violence, and barely able to sustain life, icescapes are barren and inhospitable places where the only things alive are invasive or on the brink of collapse, and where, consequently, indigenous cultures risk being "frozen" into static histories of survival amidst trackless waste, caught in ideologies of "whiteness" such as Hanns Hörbiger's 1913 *Welteislehre* ("World Ice Theory") that justified the racial superiority of cooler Aryan temperaments.[8] Ice and humans are not only autonomous things-in-themselves, but indefatigably opposed as well. The poles of nature and culture, like the North and South Poles, stand stolidly apart; polar-ization sets in; cold wars are waged with no surrender in snow-blinded sight.

So many wars. Conflicts that pose human sovereignty as the answer (of which "saving" the world is a part) only exacerbate the onto-epistemological problem of divide-and-conquer that plagues the Arctic. Conflicts against ice at the northernmost geographical *end* of the world freeze political action into modes that necessitate anthropocentric causes and solutions to climate change: the stakes being, no less, the apocalyptic *end* of the world. A frosty poet once prophesized: "Some say the world will end in fire, / Some say in ice."[9] Global warming, indeed, supplies enough "to perish twice": with almost the entire world's ice locked precariously at the ends of the earth, it is not hard to think of ice and global ends, death by water lukewarm or cold. Or, harder, to think of nuclear winter, another kind of end by fire (first) and ice (later). Admiral James G. Stavridis of the U.S. Navy warned in 2010 of an "icy slope toward a zone of competition, or worse, a zone of conflict" thickening up north.[10] The newly identified "Anthropocene" takes the present geologic time, the Holocence, hostage, puts the human at icebreakers' helms, slides us into one-way catastrophe: the slippery "slope" of change known as "climate" (Greek *klima* "slope, zone" from *klinein* "to slope"). Another poet of winter, William Shakespeare, created the word "climate" for his play *The Winter's Tale* (1609–11) to meditate on what stories may come: "Merry or sad shall't be?" (2.1.25).[11] Ice's transnational attention to *ends* centers around what steampunk author Jean-Christophe Valtat calls the "poletics" that ultimately ruin the "Pearl of the Arctic," the fantastical New Venice of his novel.[12] As commerce expands and neoliberal colonization spreads—Russian Federation submarines planted a flag on the seabed under the North Pole in August 2007—the difficulties of establishing international law or treaty in an area that is neither land nor water, and whose terms do not translate easily to the presence of native populations, only intensify. The express mission of the Arctic Council, formed in 1996 and comprised of eight nations and several indigenous groups, is to preemptively tackle these issues. The problem is, as Mick Smith points out, that all these interactions are defined in terms of human-serving sovereignty that reframes ice as a redeemable object worthy to be rescued;[13] as a site of political negotiation, the terms of negotiation need to be themselves renegotiated to rid us of the salvific impulse.[14] This is not to say that humans do not have real consequences for which they must be held responsible. (I do not mean to invalidate McKibben's and other activists' concerns.) But if these "poletical" incidents illustrate ice's vitality, within sovereign modes this agency translates to humans' industrial might, humans who have engineered their own end through fossil-fueled climate change. The deep-historical ages of ice concede to the universal fact that ice needs human aegis; debates about ice's future are reserved for international councils who may or may not offer protection. Thus the language used to "preserve" the ice, even if it means granting "endangered species" statuses of various levels, needs to be crucially reexamined.[15] Even when rendered a "species," for example, ice's agency melts away, the chill of unknown causality avoided, the end of the world prevented, humans saved from an icy end by saving the ice (from themselves) that once was disappearing or had nostalgically disappeared. All of my reporting from the war zone, I admit—unlike the South Pole where demilitarized "Science" undersigns an international treaty—must seem like cold comfort for world change, cold cynicism about a peace that can never be ensured. I believe that as long as this logic of Arctic anthropocentricity predominates, we will be stuck in a causal mode of tragic apocalypse—preventive measures must be taken *or else*—while not addressing the larger question of ice's material agency and the opportunities it affords to rethink our pole positions with ice, where it is taking us, and how to reimagine and provide for habitable coexistence for as many beings as possible. But I also believe that there are new kinds of negotiation to be found in what is predicted to be one of the world's most negotiable passageways, the Northwest Passage, and that its earliest traversers can show us how to rewrite our cold co-constitution.

By approaching ice in a refusal of sovereignty, I realize that I am on a slippery ethical slope of my own. Yet we may renegotiate terms to end the (human) sovereign and (nonhuman) subjugated world—and create new ice worlds of hyperpotential—through greater intimacy with our polar appositeness. Fear does not have to be the only motivation to act: love may help us do so.[16] Maybe an end to the modernist, bifurcated, and bi-polar world is not as cataclysmic as it is supposed to be. I will not be advocating an apathetic approach in the face of the cold truth, however; on the contrary, this chapter is a call to reconsider what we mean by the "end of the world" and the things—icebergs and many others—that presage a warming world and thus an implicit teleological end to it. Timothy Morton describes "hyperobjects" as "things that are massively distributed in time and space relative to humans" that announce the end of the world: for him, the world as we know it—as a bounded environment with interiors and exteriors—augurs "the end of modernity," "*the end of teleology*."[17] In its stead, we have the ecology that *is* intimacy, care for and with the strange stranger, an ethical injunction that is conjunction: "to swear allegiance to coexistence with nonhumans without a world."[18] The hyperobjective image he uses to announce the end of ends (and that graces his book's cover) is apt: the iceberg, that which constitutes a "*being-quake*" when it collides with modernity's epistemological and ontological grounds.[19] This shivering and shattering form of being-with-others is the treaty I wish to broker, the icy materiality I am after here, the truly *hyper-* material. Those who lived in the extreme north were "hyperborean" to the ancient Greeks (*hyper-* means "over, beyond" and *boreas* "north wind"), just over the horizon. Our uncertain futures now are just "beyond" the horizon as well. What the early explorers described as "troublesome neighbours" remind us that the end is nigh in a different way: that we exist because of our relationship to ice, by being "nigh" to the icy ocean;[20] their writings rewrite and relay subject-object reconstitutions, precarious through and through, because written in and by ice. This proximity reflects a cold af/front of touch rather than a circle of separation, and its freezing nature-culture fusings can still be gauged: the "polar vortex" of winter 2014–15 that swept across North America, crawling out of its prescribed circle; ice "shoves"; "bleeding" glaciers. To feel (even if that means to anthropomorphize) the weight at the ends of the world, to be responsive to the touch, and to compose messages back: this is a harder ecological thought about ice than the famous transcendentalist maxim that "[i]ce is an interesting subject for contemplation."[21] Ice is more immanent and urgent than that: it is an ordered vortex of instability (water molecules arrange into im/permanent hexagonals); a cold breath of enlarging breadth (ice floats because water inconceivably expands below 39°F); a call not to transcend or move beyond the human but to redefine it along crisp lines. At the same time, ice manages to withhold its secrets: the still-unknown physics behind ice's slipperiness emphasizes the magic of its elemental matter, making the conversation a little less one-sided as we hit the slopes with ice bodies, as we come into catastrophes and loves. What we need, then, is a dissolution of the end of the "world" as we know it, not a solution to climate change (which is impossible), but an expansion of the list of actors involved so that "human-glacier relations are influenced by more than just climate and greenhouse gasses."[22] Ice announces our hyperbo-*reality* with which we must come to terms: hyperobjects of uncertain intimacy and futures, boreal becomings that begin beginnings from ends, like an icicle's slow drip.

Chatter

So many sounds. One way to enhance awareness of our enmeshment with hyperboreal beings—and the method I mainly appropriate here—is by listening to them; never the lands of silence, an icescape's sounds are where the breakdown between alive and dead material occurs, where mere similes ("like") cannot hold up for long, and where living creatures loom instead. My task ahead is to follow ice's indecipherable and extralinguistic noise and the literary ways they were marked in pictures and words, straining for the crypto- of the cryo-, even if it presages illegibility: a chattering Arctic admixture I call "icespeak," a raw rhizomatic and Latourian ar/c/ticulation of non/human assemblages undergoing translation, an eventful doubling of content and expression that amplifies geological stratum and their de/territorializing dialogues.[23] I find myself akin to Fran-çois Rabelais's (ca. 1494–1553) character Pantagruel, who, upon hearing unidentifiable voices in the icescape, is informed by the captain of the ship that a battle took place on the edge of the frozen sea. The noises are trapped in ice; when the crystals are brought onboard, their vociferousness is released with the slightest touch: "When we warmed them a little between our hands, they melted like snow, and we actually heard them, though we did not understand them, for they were in a barbarous language."[24] For the traveler-poet Gretel Ehrlich, ice is an unsolvable mystery: "So much in a glacier, like so much in a brain, is hidden, we don't know what a thought or a mass of ice is saying, or why it moves."[25] Renouncing the name of war and of complete understanding, I raise a motion to clutch ice in our hands in an effort to listen, to embrace, and to become more intimate. Almost every traveler who passes through the cryosphere (including the attentive ecotourist of today) is astonished by its sounds. George Weymouth (ca. 1585 – ca. 1612) found "the noyse of a great quantity of ice . . . very loathsome to be heard" in 1602, and as loud "as though it had beene a thunder clappe."[26] The American nature writer Barry Lopez is a rapt auditor. For him, the northern landscape is inseparable from the imagination: "It is easy to underestimate the power of a long-term association with the land . . . with the span of it in memory and imagination, how it fills . . . one's dreams."[27] We would benefit from an icy ecopoesis in which place and psyche are always entwined, a bustling "country of the mind" that extends Lopez's Arctic dreams, nearly three decades later, into a more melted world, and allows us to dream better as a result.[28] Icespeak bridges the early modern era with our own because its noisy broadcasts of both dreams and nightmares manifest the transhistorical transmissions that coldness emits: imagine a resounding land bridge across times whose commuters pass back and forth across opening-closing passages of page and place, chasing the generativeness of the gelid, the materiality of cold, to a prime source that cannot be accessed, only sensibly pursued, an age of algidity whose cracks and fissures are not the crevasses of chronology but a crystalline latticework of thin and thick lines that connect to other times. Voice is an icefield of embodied material impacts: compo-, trans-, and cryocorporeal signals, transferals that transform, cool vibrations.

Still, the "barbarous language" can too easily convert into a halting impasse. Ships do sink, ending lives onboard. The response could be like that of seventeenth-century Irish natural philosopher Robert Boyle's *New Experiments and Observations Touching Cold* (1665), in which the touch of cold was repulsive, even if his experiments into the agential substance behind cold, the legendary *primum frigidum*, were "promiscuous" (from Latin *miscere* "to mix").[29] Thus the question is not how we misinterpret what ice is saying, but why we do not want to hear (or re/mix) it at all. If the modernist view of nature, according to Latour, demarcates who can and cannot discuss as well as what can be discussed, our narratives about the physical world are certainly susceptible to this question. To rob ice of its voice is a violent act of silencing. This is the albatross we must bear. We choose, that is, to listen: here the gap between alienated subject (vocalizing human) and object (mute nonhuman landscape) freezes over. Anthropologist Julie Cruikshank argues in *Do Glaciers Listen?* that there is no distinction between changing biophysical worlds and changing social worlds; citing Latour's work against the moderns' "Great Divide," she believes glaciers are key actors that negotiate science, history, and politics, creating "natural-cultural histories" that encompass environmental change, human encounters, and local knowledge. These convergences are not without conflict; they leave behind "stubborn particulars of voice" and "entangled narratives" for postcolonial ecologists, like her, to trace.[30] Glaciers are "sentient landscapes in perpetual motion," according to Cruikshank, that "engage all the senses."[31] But glaciers not only listen, we will discover, they speak, they feel. Furthermore, what can be known of a thing or object is not limited to the human's sensory interactions with it; just as we should not define the real by what is or is not audible at a given time, icespeak exceeds the merely symbolic or representational, bursting voice's organic and animalistic (especially mammalian) boundaries. Others herein welcome the chilly sound/waves unfurling like icy fingers that quaked them to their cores of being and knowing, offering remarkable contrasts to Boyle's shunned (though integral) tactility of contact. We will hear in their chattering experiments and "promiscuous" labs on- and off-ship touching conversations that convert, that change the "subject" of cold from "barren[ness]" to garrulous plenty, that change the subject (the "cold" human) by virtual becoming icy through the virtue (thing-power) of ice. In other words, the question of whether or not glaciers speak is an ethical one; observing the touching experiments below and their different degrees of reply—witnessing the ramifications, even, of turning willingly away from the vociferous happening that ice *is*—enlarges our vocabularies and advances pellucid lessons for us in how to be keener conversationalists.

Cold Terms

I choose to chase the cold in the early modern English imagination, not to come in from it. Icy intimacy—"colde tearme[s]" of enmeshment, if not always endearment, to borrow from John Taylor's broadside about "the Frozen Age" (the bitterly cold winter of 1620)—is what the English knew intimately.[32] For those who lived during the Little Ice Age (ca. 1300–1850), ice was a menacing creature: glaciers on the continent advanced into towns; crops failed; and rivers froze repeatedly, like the Thames in 1608, 1609, 1620 (and so on); a "gnashing age of Snow and Ice," Taylor retells, a "time when men wore liquor'd bootes." Amusing "frost fairs" spontaneously appeared on the Thames in the sixteenth and seventeenth centuries, but it can be said that the Tudor-era citizens of London onward who suffered the cold were far from Boston's "Ice King," Frederick Tudor, who was able to capitalize on the cold in the nineteenth century. The cold was something to be endured or, at best, temporarily utilized for entertainment, not something actively sought. And citizens abided differently; as Alvin Snider's survey of the 1684 "neo-boreal trend" makes clear, poets and pamphleteers responded widely to the phenomenon of the frozen river: focusing on cold's effects on bodies (like hypothermia), the economic hardships of watermen, the vulnerability of the poor, and moralizing providentialism that attributed the metropolis's chill to endemic political ills. Yet despite its recrudescent presence, one that would only widen the range of geohumoralist studies—accentuating the central climate-culture principle "that embodiment is a dynamic process . . . an unsettled relation of balance and imbalance with surrounding conditions"[33]—early modern ecocriticism is relatively silent about ice's ecomaterial touch. The question, then, is not only why we have historically "forgotten" cold parts of the world, as Mary C. Fuller, who is perhaps the most prolific early modern scholar of the northwest, asks,[34] but also, and more importantly, what work the northern icescape did in the early modern English imagination—past the realms of cultural studies (such as English–Russian contact), historiography (how experience was legibly compiled), cartography (the production of space)—and what it can do in ours.[35] Like Thomas Dekker (ca. 1572 – ca. 1632) and John Webster's (ca. 1580 – ca. 1632) collaborative play *Northward, Ho!* (1605), which ventures just barely north of London, critical examinations only go so far spatially as well as temporally: romantic studies on up predominate.[36] When ice is vocalized, it typically becomes a network of predominantly human commerce and activity. Joseph P. Ward, for instance, examines how the frozen Thames was "tamed" multiple times in the seventeenth century: "Londoners used their frozen river as a symbolic field that lent itself to interpretations of the social health of both the metropolis and the wider region."[37] The carnivalesque atmosphere has a human ringleader; reading this river this way suggests economic ephemerality, short-lived collaborations with certain humans and nonhumans admitted to the circus. River ice should make the "social" more frivolous, not less, through its elemental metamorphosis.

In what is ahead I reveal a rimy early modern English imagination at work, a true Arcticology of north. Like the young Orlando in Virginia Woolf's novel of the same name (1928), who espies an apple seller in "suspended animation" under the Thames ice—spectacles King James "liked to look upon"—and who overhears, at the same time, "Admirals . . . up and down the narrow pathways, glass in hand, sweeping the horizon and telling stories of the north-west passage," the English of the frozen age were captivated by ice at home but could also be propelled by it abroad.[38] The north was supposedly reserved for dearth and death, yet they traded the "barren" for the vivacious, found Arctic actants of attraction, witnessed the brisk bustle through Orlando's eyes: "nothing could exceed the brilliancy and gaiety of the scene by day."[39] Travelers seeking the Northwest Passage discovered vociferous stuff: ice acts, carves worlds, builds weather systems, emits creaturely noises, defies logic of land and water, mystifies with its multiplicity of bergs, reveals that marvelous state of melting and congealing matter at once. Classical and medieval traditions told of pygmies, unicorns (narwhales), and white bears; endless days and nights; the North Pole, a giant mountain surrounded by a whirlpool that drained into the earth; another mountain made of iron that enticed compass needles. The maps of Gerardus Mercator (1512–94), along with the fabulous tales of the Zeno brothers (ca. 1326 – ca. 1403) and Nicholas of Lynn (fl. 1360), added to this imaginative geography. For these earliest explorers, cartographers, and writers, the icescape possessed an incredible energy. The Greeks believed that the Arctic was inhabitable; theories of a temperate climate were hard to disprove: "Arctic" comes from Arktikós, "the land of the bear," a reference to the constellation in which the North Star is found, Ursus Major, the Great Bear.[40] As a guiding force in the northern sky, the star and its directionality gathers non/human actors into vast constellations like so many stars, maps as movable as the magnetic north. The early modern English intended the Arctic to be a valuable stopping point en route to a lively and exotic Cathay; but in their passages north by northwest they discovered a living and alluring icescape in the frigid zone, skating across skeins that concealed their contents more than they revealed.

Going Glacial

This chapter will be slow, but I hope it slowly, like a glacier, does some work. Touching cold, I propose a frosty thought experiment of my own: to speak for, with, and through ice in order to recognize our complex coimplication with it, cryocompositionism in this case functioning as a reminder of how we slowly compose with and are composed by the icy world. Realizing the desires in these wintry connections, we may reimagine or reorient new futures, collectives, and joys. Try to perceive this north about which I dream. (1) In their persistent attempts to discover the Northwest Passage, the English distinguished themselves as tireless conversationalists with ice, articulate with its articulation and "stubborn particulars of voice." There was always ice on the horizon from the first explorers forward, and the narrators I describe were good listeners, feelers, and sometimes lovers. Three English travel narratives serve as onto-ecological points of embarkation: George Best's *A True Discourse* (1578); John Davis's *The Worldes Hydrographical Discription* (1595); and Thomas Ellis's *A True Report* (1578). (2) The early modern Arctic redefines the relationship between humans and ice, configuring them not as impervious antagonists, but as co-constitutive, sensual bodies constantly interacting in a process I call "going glacial." In its etymology, the touching cold of (a) "glacier" thaws the ontological rigidity regarding ice, scratches (even effaces) the human subject. All three Boyleian labs, Best's especially, show what happens when "stubborn" barriers are put between cold things, separating humans from nonhumans as well as other humans. (3) In their errancy, these early explorers found northwest passages: not the singular Passage dismissible as legend, but as proliferating passages of non/human bodies that pass in and through each other into unpredictable assemblages; a multiplicity of middle passages without endpoint; a whirlpool of sensations and commingling without completion. By navigating these troubled spaces (passages), they produced texts (passages) that overlap what are now defined as the "hard" and "soft" sciences. Their climatological treatises arrive at a useful interdisciplinary point for us right now as we create our own passages in response to a warming world; it is not anachronistic to think through climatic complexities like global warming—a world with or without ice—alongside these writers who, like us, found themselves sliding into uncertain futures. Just as some of these authors realized their observational methods to be too detached, their worldviews to be too delimited, their bleak bodies and minds warming up to the cold, my hope is that these early modern forays into frost will alter our imaginations as well, sponsor new shapes of intimacy across ice's translucent sluices. To become converted by, and converts to, the cold: if I have an Arctic dream of my own, that is it.

Slip

The textbook scientific definition of glaciers might regard them as "living" bodies of ice due to their trademark characteristic of movement— up to a meter a day—as well as their ability to sustain organic life forms such as worms, plants, and algae; or, more exactly: "a glacier is a natural body of ice, originating on land, and undergoing movement that transports ice from an area of accumulation to an area of disposal. . . . Glaciers are dynamic entities engaged in accumulating, transporting, and disposing of ice."[41] Glacier ice, like all ice, is a type of rock. (Rock is defined as that which is made of one or more crystallized minerals; ice is a mineral.) Glaciers are paradoxically flowing rivers of rock: as they accumulate the snowy particles of sediment, they become sedimentary rock in the process of aggregation, and they even become metamorphic rock as heat, stress, and recrystallization occur. The idea of "living" ice comes from this observable process of material transformation and transportation. As glaciers carry a "budget" from an accumulation area to a wastage area, they leave material leftovers called till, glaciofluvial outwash, and loess units. A number of actions have taken place: ablation (melting), calving, erosion, abrasion, and plucking. Not all ice is glacial, however. Glaciers move, and are defined by, these internal adjustments; technically, falling ice is not a glacier, and neither is sea ice. Although the most recognizable type of glacier is the valley variety, coastal glaciers produce icebergs, ice shelves, or both. Most glacial activity is unseen because it takes place in Antarctica and Greenland, the only two places where ice sheets, a type of glacier, still exist in Ice Age dimensions. Alaska, Canada, South America, and the mountain ranges of south central Asia yield the most glacial ice easily visible. They promise to be reliable timekeepers: ice cores contain up to eight hundred thousand years' worth of climate data. (A 1.5-million-year-old sheet was found in 2013.) With about 68 percent of the planet's total freshwater locked within icecaps and glaciers, they provide drinking water; reflecting sunlight, thereby regulating temperatures, they influence global weather patterns. In short, we should be aware of glacial activity every day, past and present: glaciers covered 32 percent of the land in the last Ice Age, and the remaining 10 or 11 percent pulling steadily back affects us still.

Even though modern scientific discourse envisions glaciers as sites of transformation, history, and flow, *living* ice is different from the metaphorical life that science grants it. Movement does not always equal liveliness. The etymology of "glacier," however, helps us understand ice's agency. "Glacier" as a noun for "ice" in early modern English is unrecorded. The "glacier" we think of now ("a river of ice") was not coined until the mid-eighteenth century.[42] Thus the meanings we most commonly associate with the adjective "glacial," such as "of a glacial time period" and "of a slow process," did not appear until the mid-twentieth century. Yet early moderns used "glace" in its Latin meaning of "ice" (*glaciēs*). Circa 1400–1450, to be "on a glace" was "to be frozen." A "glacis," a gently sloping bank used as a fortification (ca. 1270), closely resembles a glacier's appearance. The earliest use of "glacial" relative to iciness is from 1656: "Full of, or having the nature of, ice; cold, icy, freezing." And "glaciate," "to freeze," appeared in 1623. Clearly, the English had *glaciēs* on their minds whenever they imagined something cold or formidable. From 1400 onward there was also a verb form available in French. The Old French words "glacer, glacier, glacher" ("to glide, slip") came from the Latin *glacicāre* ("to slip, slide"). "Glacer" could be an intransitive verb, "to glance, glide; to move lightly or quickly," especially regarding weapons: "to glance off, to slip, to fail in giving a direct blow; also, to glide, pass easily through." Intriguingly, "glacer" could be a transitive verb as well: "to cause to glide or slip," as when Randle Cotgrave (d. 1634) writes in his 1611 French and English dictionary, "*Glacer vn mot*, to insert, put, thrust or foist a word into a writing." In time, the French noun "glacis" (first recorded in the sixteenth century) came to designate "a place made slipperie by wet lately

fallen and frozen on." Thus the Latin noun *glaciēs* ("ice") had merged with
the verb *glacicāre* ("to slip") to describe what we would now call a "glacier"
in English. Astonishingly, a glacier does what the Old French word "glacier" denotes, the action of *glacicāre*. To make a long etymological lesson
on cold terms simpler: ice is slippery *and* it slips.

The early modern English rarely used "glacier" instead of "ice" (and its
multiple spellings) when writing about the icescape. But Best, for example, one of the most influential Arcticologists at the time, was able to
congeal them: "we thought these places might only deserve the name of
Mare Glaciale, and be called the Isie Sea."[43] The English were able to hit
upon the multivalent meanings of "glacier" when describing ice. It is therefore viable to speak of early modern "glaciality" since ice and glacier perform the same theoretical work in these narratives. Like the *glaciēs* (noun)
side of ice, ice in the early modern lexicon indicates cold material, slippery
slopes of contact, and places where things glide, glance, and pass through.
And like the *glacicāre* (verb) potential of ice, ice slides and causes things
to slide. If modern science and early modernity seem incongruous, then,
the etymology of "glacier" helps us apprehend the agency of living ice and
furthermore shows how modern and early modern icescapes may mutually imbue one another. The action inherent to "glacier" shifts the focus
away from knowable glacial geography to a more theoretical engagement
with geo- (or hydro-)philosophy. A glacier's internal dynamism is really an
aspect of its a-lively, creaturely, and desiring attributes; it carries, disperses,
and distributes human and nonhuman bodies in its icy trajectories. *Living*
ice, never figuratively "living" ice, conjoins the separate fields of glacial
geology (the work being done by glaciers) and glaciology (the study of
glaciers). To study a glacier is always to study its work that is never done.

In their unflagging determination and sheer number of attempts, the
English were apt observers of the glacial process. Beginning with John
Cabot's (ca. 1451–98) trip to Newfoundland under Henry VII in 1497,
by Elizabeth I's reign the English obsession with the northwest was un-
matched.[44] The reasons to reach Cathay were political as well as economical; arriving later than their wealthier European neighbors in the
affairs of global trade and overseas settlement, English feelings of inferi-
ority were also responsible. The magus John Dee claimed that the English
rightfully deserved the area, being as they were the inheritors of King

Arthur's legendary conquest of the northern ocean.[45] This passage, so they thought, would finally make the country a global colonial power. It was also hoped that the ethnographic information gained would complement their imperial ambitions by settling an age-old geohumoral dispute: in order to validate their claims of ethnic superiority over peoples of the frigid zone—like the barbarous "Scythians," a catchword for northern folk—the English had to prove themselves to be the exception to the Hippocratic rule that northern regions generated dull minds; thus cold/er weather actually warmed their lingering anxieties of identity: "the fear remained that England had a tenuous hold on its temperate weather."[46] Many English writers in reaction pointed out that the most demanding seafaring in the world was through the monstrous icescapes of the north. The Arctic was the perfect proving ground for the stalwart English, as in Best's opinion: "the adventure the more hard the more honorable. . . . [T]he Englishman deserveth chiefe honour above any other" (20). Englishness itself was oddly bound up with the ice that stupefied everyone. Indeed, these "invincible mindes of our Englishe nation" had never encountered anything like the hazards of the icescape (19). While the Thames had made London a cryopolis (above), making icy "heapes in some places," as one onlooker wrote in the winter of 1621, "that yt lies like rockes and mountaines and hath a straunge and hideous aspect,"[47] the explorers who made first contact fifty years previously struggled over fathoming icebergs' scale, transport, and transmutation in ways without nautical precedent and for which they could not prepare. Contemporary manuals, in fact, guaranteed an unsurprising and unencumbered trip, like William Bourne's (ca. 1535–82) *A Regiment for the Sea* (originally published 1574), whose newly expanded 1580 edition added a "hidrographicall discourse to goe vnto Cattay" that described an ice-free open sea route directly north over the pole. (Succinctly: "the great salt sea neuer freezeth.")[48] Then as now, glaciers produce icebergs and ice shelves in the parts of Greenland these authors visited. The East and West Greenland Currents carry icebergs calved from glaciers, floes of shore ice set adrift in summer, and year-round ice torn loose from farther north. Propelled by unpredictable winds and currents, and shrouded in fog, sea ice was notoriously treacherous. The search for the legendary Northwest Passage, it might be said, was a search for the way out of an inimical icescape. Here the English appear to circle back to the same Nares Strait where this chapter began, in antagonism, the start of the worst journeys of the world being set down in writing.

Yet in describing ice's incredible monstrosity, English explorers' baffled expressions also noted ice's express potential to create. There is a seduction, they discovered, in glacial alluviation. Authors flowed with and through these icy stripes, often describing desire and disaster on the same page. Slipping with icy matter-flows is what "going glacial" is all about. Gilles Deleuze and Félix Guattari were right to call the body without organs "that glacial reality."[49] Both a solid and a liquid at once, glaciers are interstitial places. What early moderns such as Best called "*Mare Congelatum*" (as well as *Glaciale*) is really the congealed sea (34): to "congeal" literally means "freeze together." Yet to freeze is not always to stop; it also means to accelerate;[50] it challenges tropes of stasis and expands beyond the metaphorical valences of "frozen" in order to accentuate the "speed" of slowness, of freezing, reconceiving it as a hyper- and hypoactive becoming-cold that stresses intimate interactions between human and nonhuman bodies that, in turn, cracks open their ontological limits.[51] Though frozen, things incredibly move; they flow, harden, dissolve, and then congeal with other substances. The corpse of Hugh Willoughby (d. 1554), one of the earliest voyagers to the northeast, highlighted a northwest passenger's worst fear: to be frozen to death. The Venetian ambassador in England, Giovani Michiel, wrote in 1555 that he and his men were found "in various postures, like statues" with "some of them seated in the act of writing, pen still in hand."[52] But others felt movement in ice's seeming immobility, entered the icescape's mix of human and nonhuman things, harnessed feedback loops and flows of sedimented bodies that fuse with one another as they move with intensity. Ice *is* matter-flows, and, while catastrophic at times—a monstrous hull-piercer—it also slips up bodies and cleaves cryophilic desires. Before I turn to my first primary source indelibly shaped by glaciers' flowing touch of *primum frigidum*, I need to say a bit more about how and why the ice-English went northwesterly in the first place.

The Icemen Cometh

The English moved slowly into the Arctic. Pope Alexander VI's edict of 1493 partitioned the world between Spain and Portugal: Spain had Columbus's New World and Portugal the southern and eastern parts of the globe. An imprecise longitudinal line divided the claims off the Cape Verde islands. Technically, the slivers of the Arctic Atlantic—Newfoundland, Labrador, and Greenland—were Portuguese since they fell east of this line. Although the French encroached on these rights to North America between 1520 and 1540, the English were hesitant competitors. John Cabot's 1497 voyage claimed his "Newe Found Islande" for England. His son Sebastian's (ca. 1481–1557) voyage of 1508 might have been imaginary. Bristol merchants made another attempt in 1527, but they turned south to the Caribbean after encountering icebergs. Mary I avoided conflict with Spain during her reign by moving the expeditions from the west to the northeast. The 1553 search for the Northeast Passage through the north of Norway was calamitous: Willoughby's frigid fate was just mentioned; Richard Chancellor (d. 1556) reached the Russian coast and was able to salvage the English efforts by establishing trade relations with Ivan IV's court in Moscow. The Muscovy Company opened a profitable trade. Explorers failed in subsequent years to push farther east, bringing back only tales of defeat. With Elizabeth's accession in 1558, foreign policy changed. By allowing negotiations with Spain to dwindle, hopes for the Northeast Passage were gradually abandoned. In the second half of the sixteenth century, the English renewed their search northwest. The route made sense; the eastern route to Cathay navigated by Ferdinand Magellan (ca. 1480–1521) was too long and the Northeast Passage too dangerous. Into this climate entered Martin Frobisher (ca. 1535–94), an uneducated pirate turned navy officer who sought riches and fame in northern climes. Major players backed Frobisher's three voyages to modern-day Baffin Island from 1576 to 1578: Humphrey Gilbert, explorer and author of *A Discourse of a Discouerie for a New Passage to Cataia* (written in 1566 and published a decade later), promoted the idea in court; Dee, the mystical polymath, invented nautical instruments and provided the maps and navigation techniques; and Michael Lok (ca. 1532 – ca. 1622), the London agent for the Muscovy Company, supplied money and stockholder support. Not much is known about Frobisher. He made a name for himself raiding Portuguese Africa at the age of seventeen. As an occasional privateer, he must have surely been intrigued by the thought of wealth, fame, and adventure in the northwest. As his poem states in support of Gilbert's voyage to Newfoundland in 1583,

A pleasant ayre, a sweete and firtell soile,
A certain gaine, a never dying praise:
An easie passage, voide of loathsome toil,
Found out by some, and knowen to me the waies.
All this is there, then who will refraine to trie:
That loves to live abroad, or dreades to die.[53]

Frobisher's vision of "firtell" Arctic lands echoes contemporary claims of
a habitable north. His poem captures a desire for the land while recognizing its dangers. Gilbert did not "refraine to trie," but he did not return
either. Without a doubt, voyaging to the northwest was a risky venture
with lives at stake.

Frobisher's three voyages to modern-day Baffin Island were far from
"easie." Storms and ice harassed his first attempt in the summer of 1576,
as they would invariably thereafter. With only apocryphal knowledge of
the area, he sighted two forelands north of Labrador, believing the strait
between them to be the Northwest Passage. While surveying this "channel" he aptly named "Frobisher's Streytes," several Inuit approached the
ships and began to trade. Five English scouts disappeared. Two days passed
without word. Fearing cannibalism and the onset of snowier weather,
Frobisher seized an Inuit man in retaliation—kayak and all—taking him
and several tokens of possession back to England, including a black stone
that was "proven" to contain gold shortly thereafter in London. Speculation was enough for a second voyage in 1577, but this trip only produced
worse relations with the natives. An intended hostage exchange escalated
already-tense English–Inuit relations. Frobisher managed to interrogate a
native about the five sailors; when he discovered stray bones, his suspi-
cions of cannibalism were confirmed. So began the skirmish at "Bloudy
Point": five or six Inuit were killed, an English solider seriously wounded
(Frobisher was wounded "in the buttock with an arrow," says Best, 131);
an Inuit man and woman along with her infant son were taken prisoner.
Frobisher addressed a letter to the marooned five, but it was unanswered.
Dissatisfied, he departed for England with his three captives and two hundred tons of rock. Although Elizabeth was pleased with her new claims
to "Meta Incognita," as it was called, the young joint-stock Company
of Cathay was in dire straits. And when dubious assayers pronounced

conflicting assessments of the ore's worth, investors' skepticism grew. Nevertheless, in 1578 a fleet of record size disembarked with orders to colonize the area. A huge storm separated the ships. Frobisher lost valuable time in the "Mistaken Streytes" (Hudson Strait) until he realized his error and eventually regrouped at the Countess of Warwick's Island. Mining began, but unbearable weather, the waning summer, and low morale forced Frobisher's return. He hurriedly erected an unmanned watchtower—England's first structure in America, mainly to harbor the men missing for two years now—before heading home with one thousand tons of worthless rock. Litigation, scandal, and insolvency beset the principal venturers over the following years. Frobisher died fighting the Spanish in 1594; he claimed, or at least others claimed for him, that the "Mistaken Streytes" was the passage to Cathay. The "passages" from 1576 to 1578 had produced only "loathsome toil." If anything, Frobisher perpetuated the geographical interest in the region, and later expeditions by Henry Hudson (d. 1611) and William Baffin (ca. 1584–1621) helped establish future profits (in fur) for the English in the Arctic, a feat that Thomas Churchyard's (ca. 1523–1604) *Prayse* predicted in 1578: "[H]ee hath broken the Ice, explained the passage and opened the Port of present commoditie and gaine."[54] By 1635, Luke Foxe (1586–1635) was able to publish a massive collection of northwest travel literature, *North-west Fox*, a "Child of mine, begot in the North-west's cold Clime (where they breed no Schollers)," and that culminated, coincidentally, in his own narrative.[55] Much was begotten and bred from the boreal burgeoning of 1576–78. But Frobisher's main legacy to "Schollers" has been monetary.[56] There is more to be "gaine[d]" than his ersatz gold, I think, more pleasures than the pecuniary affords.

Freezing Ice: Best

Several members of Frobisher's company produced narratives immediately after the 1576–78 voyages, the first being Dionyse Settle's *A True Reporte* (1577), an account of the second voyage that was quickly translated. The most widely known compendium of all three voyages is Best's *A True Discourse* published a year later. Best (ca. 1555–84) was lieutenant on the *Ayde* during the second voyage of 1577 and captain of the *Anne Frances* during the third trip of 1578. The *Discourse* includes a lengthy preface that explains the general advantages of English explorers over their Spanish and Portuguese rivals, exalts the gifts of modern navigational methods and instruments, and defends the existence of the Northeast Passage. Best encourages his countrymen to go further in the direction of Frobisher, who "dissolved the long doubt of the passage which we seeke to find to the rich countrey of Cataya" (242). He objects to those who find Meta Incognita inhospitable, arguing not only for a passage to Cathay but for a temperate and livable north fit for English habitation as well. Frobisher's voyages climatologically confirm "all partes of the worlde to be habitable" (43). According to Best, the strength of the sun is determined by its "angle" and "continuance" (48), which explains why "in such reasons, over which the sun riseth lower (as in regions extended towardes eyther pole)" sunlight "maketh there unequall angles, but the sunne continueth longer, and maketh longer days," thereby providing "[g]reat heat" that could border on discomfort (63, 250). Best complains of warm blasts of air at one point, "as though we were entred some . . . hote-house" (251). The Arctic, he asserts, can grow riches just like the equatorial countries lining the torrid zone to the south. (Tropical heat was believed to generate valuable metals.) "A generall briefe description of the countrey, and condition of the people, which are found in 'Meta Incognita'" lists the valuable northern commodities in an effort to attract, primarily, the company's disgruntled investors (280). On their way back to England, they discover an island teeming with wildlife in the "same mistaken straites," the most "fruitful" tract they have discovered so far (245). After the voyage they pass by another imaginary island off the map, the island of Busse: "a great ilande in the latitude of [erased] degrees, which was never yet founde before, and sayled three dayes alongst the coast, the land seeming to be fruiteful, full of woods, and a champain countrie" (280). This boreal Bower of Bliss, although erased, supports Best's general conclusion that the Arctic is habitable, fecund, and exploitable:

> To conclude, I finde all the countrie nothing that may be to delite in, either of pleasure or of accompte, only the shewe of mine, bothe of golde, silver, steele, yron and blacke leade, with divers preaty stones, as blewe saphire, very perfect, and others, whereof we founde great plentie, maye give encouragement for men to seeke thyther. (288)

Taking the "delite" of the company to heart, Best furnishes his readers and embittered investors with the "shewe" of the region, a strategic move that essentially decreases the risk of a poor return, configuring the veritable dangers of the icescape as surmountable setbacks (if that).

Best's *Discourse* invokes the argument for English dauntlessness, placing the intact body at the center of an adverse environment they must tame, one that threatens to fracture them into pieces by shipwreck, cannibalism, or both. He opens with a promise to set forth "[h]ow a pilot may deale, being environed wyth mountaines of ise in the frosen sea" (15). Like many of his peers, "environed" (sometimes "compassed") is less of a navigational term and more of a terrifying state to be in while sailing through unmapped and unmappable routes: "environed" means to be both surrounded and turned (*virer*), stuck to a certain circuit, a wish to flee from the center of icy relations as the glassy walls of ice draw closer. He amplifies the enormity of the icescape; in his account of the first voyage, for example, Best notes the treacherous intermingling of ice and land. Off of Friseland, an imaginary island believed to be east of the Passage and hence a guiding point for many explorers—and sometimes spelled "Frizeland," which makes one wonder if the location was actually ice, compounded "freeze-land," as every iceberg is—they see "high ragged roks all along by the coast, and some of the ilands of ise were nere yt of such heigth as the clowds hanged about the tops of them" (81). The icebergs are so large they resemble landmasses with their own weather systems. Usually a place of gigantic impediments like these ice-mountains would not be greeted by someone navigating uncharted waters. In his preface, however, Best states that the English feats surpass those of Hercules and Alexander, both of whom falsely believed to have reached the western and eastern limits of the world (respectively). As a result, he transforms Frobisher into an epic figure pushing through the formidable ice: "We were forced manye tymes to stemme and strike great rockes of ise, and so as it were make way through mightye mountaines" (235). Frobisher almost single-handedly prevents his ship the *Gabriel* from sinking during a storm. Likewise, the natives that the English encounter become devious cannibals. The icescape's alleged gold comes with the risk of being devoured, especially by the second voyage: "For they knew ful wel, that the beste cheare the countrey coulde yeelde them, was golden rockes and stones, a harde foode to live withall, and the people more readie to eate them, than to give them wherewithall to eate" (132). By making statements that pit an annihilating icescape against reliable English fortitude, Best's *Discourse* makes a grand attempt to sway popular opinion about an ungovernable north and establish Frobisher as an Arctic action hero.

Best regularly establishes corporeal and ethnographic boundaries in his icescape: English versus ice, cannibals, and storms. The nonhuman ice particularly threatens them since it environs at all times. In their almost compulsive descriptions of ice, however, English crewmen allude to its creatureliness; it is not simply a floating, submissive substance, but something that actively *drives*: "fleting and driving with the wyndes and tydes and streams" (82). Frobisher's only recourse is to move on due to "being greatly endangered with the driving ise alongst the coast" (126). The ice, in league with the winds and tides, propels them as much as they drive through it. But Best intimates the harrowing togetherness of the icescape in these moments merely to shut down its possibilities, even if the English taste the "sweet and holesome water" of dissolved ice to prove its origins from fresh instead of salt water (235). He militates against the thought of mingling with the icescape even at his lowest points. The men debate suicide on the third voyage: "And againe some were so fast shut up and compassed in amongst an infinite number of great countreys and ilands of ise, that they were fayne to submit themselves and their ships to the mercie of the unmercifull ise" (236–37). To submit to ice is a scary prospect for Best, for it means certain death: an "unmercifull" foe can know no "mercie." Members of the company consider jumping ship and taking their chances with "those ravenous, bloudye, and man-eating people" rather than sink (242). One cannot embrace the maws of this Arctic monster. According to Best, when faced with binary breakdowns between ice and human, English and native, the only option is to enter an icescape of pure destruction and retrieve the consumables (commodities) before being literally consumed by the frozen hungry tide and its "ravenous" peoples. Protecting the body was paramount; in probably his most in/famous remarks, Best argues that skin color does not derive from climate but from infection: how else could the Inuit be dark, or a child born from an Ethiopian father and white mother? "[T]his blacknesse proceedeth of some naturall infection of the first inhabitants of that countrey, and so all the whole progenie of them descended are still poluted with the same blot of infection" (54–55). Although Noah's son "Cham" (Ham) is identified as the origin of "this blacknesse," Best's racial remarks expose his fears of a white and black icescape that will infiltrate the exposed English body, incurably changing its identity and composition. Like a pilot keeping watch at night in icy seas, they must always be on guard against "infection."

Even though they collaborate in the icescape, when Englishman and ice meet they seldom interfuse. The "driving" ice carries the English; oftentimes they fasten onto icebergs with makeshift grappling hooks in order to ride their momentum through the sea ice. (Since icebergs follow underwater currents, they are natural icebreakers.) Or the men fasten the nose of the ship to icebergs and use the wind to break through. Yet working together seems to put most of the work in human hands; a marginal note reads: "Extremitie causeth men to devise new arts and remedies" (253). Ice threatens; man invents. The English hack their way through the ice. The ice does not open up new perspectives because an unbreachable cryo-ontological fissure still exists between them. Even when beautiful prospects come into view, the visions are mired in conflict: "And having by this means at length put their enemies to flight, occupied the cleere place for a prettie season, among sundry mountaynes and Alpes of ise" (253–54). Broken "prett[ily]" before them, ice remains "enemies" for the English to battle. When the ice cannot be defeated, Best employs a different strategy to know his enemy and thus distance himself from it. One iceberg appears to be "sixty-five fadome above water, which for a kind of similitude was called Salomons porch. Some think those ilands eight times so muche under water as they are above, by-cause of their monstrous weight" (254). He was right: icebergs are not mirror images below water. Arctic explorers were just beginning to realize the spatial dimensions of floating ice. ("Salomons porch" is a unique likeness: Best is probably envisioning a colonnaded section of the Second Temple in Jerusalem.) The unknown must be made familiar in order to deactivate its power. In both name and measurement, the "porch" moors the company with a degree of certainty, perhaps even appropriates the biblical king's wisdom (so Best believes) for the proper mathematical judgment of towering ice forms and "[h]ow a pilot may deale" with them. This knowledge bolsters the separation between the observing human subject and the observable inhuman object, despite their bodies being physically attached to the ice-island's "monstrous weight."

Nose-to-nose with ice, it is difficult to tell who or what drives whom. "Driving" ice challenges the *Discourse*'s built-in subject-object differentiation. Ice acts upon Frobisher's men as much as they latch onto it. Best cannot ignore the fact that monstrous matter always surrounds them, touches them, and invades their fragile anthropocentricity. To put it another way: the ice gets inside him, and Best must decide what he will do about it. A stirring moment in the third voyage puts pressure on Best's efforts to evacuate the icescape from his company's bodies. Every commentator describes the Bear Sound storm in early July that dispersed and nearly destroyed the fleet. He relates the company's terror:

> And albeit, by reason of the fleeting ise, whych were dispersed heere almost the whole sea over, they were broughte manye times to the extreamest poynte of perill, mountaynes of ise tenne thousande tymes scaping them scarce one ynch, whiche to have stricken, had bin theyr presente destruction, considering the swifte course and way of the shippes, and the unwildynesse of them to stay and turne as a man would wish. Yet they esteemed it their better safetie, with such perill to seeke searoome, than without hope of ever getting libertie, to lie striving against the streame, and beating amongst the isie mountaines, whose hugenesse, and monstrous greatnesse was suche, that no man woulde credite, but such as to their paynes sawe and felt it. (238)

This chilling scene is an example of the company's physical fragility. Indeed, the English narrowly dodged their demise, and for over a week afterward Frobisher led several crews aimlessly through the channel he called, in retrospect, the "Mistaken Streytes." But the storm also lays bare the weaknesses of Best's human-icescape division. The word "scaping" reflects the idea of English e-"scaping" their "perill," certainly, but it also points up the icescape's ability to *-scape* ("shape") things that any -scape in general possesses. The men, like the boats, are being shaped by their surroundings: ice is "scaping them." No matter what a man may "wish," the ice has its own wishes. The "unwildynesse" of ice "to stay and turne" characterizes a creature with its own unpredictable will. The men furiously beat back the ice with oars, "striving" to detach themselves from their enmeshment with "greatnesse." Best shuns the unpleasant touch of ice; as the men push off, he himself struggles to keep the ice from entering: "beating" begets more "beating" as the human seeks the prime position (first place) through physical violence (giving ice a beating).

Try as he may to fight the touching cold and freeze its invasive advance, the contact with ice on Bear Sound is a significant moment of commingling in Best's narrative that not only accommodates ice's agency but also snaps the human-nonhuman boundary altogether. He desires impossible e-"scaping" by gaining greater "searoome," but they are never at "libertie" to be autonomous. Ice has skin on Bear Sound, and the English feel its touch as it "scap[es]" them in a hypersensual, hyperborean way. In the end, Best's words cannot convey the attack of the ice, just the palpable sensations they "sawe and felt." The senses make the best witnesses; the ice has gotten under their skin. "[H]ugenesse" opens up an ecophenomenology that Best only reluctantly allows for: sensing sense with and through ice. "[M]onstrous" here is telling—of births (icebergs that keep coming) as well as warnings (from Latin *monere*, "warn")—and what it portends is that the human is always-already icy. Touching and being touched by ice in Bear Sound is a powerful moment of going glacial in the icescape. The storm illuminates the sentience of non/human skin; flesh and ice flow and congeal together, slough off and take on sense-bodies. These turbulent interstices of "unwildynesse" are what we should visit more often— in the sense of "insertion" ("glacer")—and let ourselves be glanced. Cryocritics are eager to meditate in the icescape, but to meditate *with* the feeling landscape is an entirely different sort of feeling for the field of cold studies. When Lopez writes that for some "what they are is not finished at the skin, but continues with the reach of the senses out into the land,"[57] the reverse holds true as well: the land reaches out, sensibly, into the human. Our shared skins are never finished. Pathways of sense-bodies burgeon to create new passages on "swifte course." We should inhabit these glacial sites of embodied potential and see where they lead, reach out and close that distance of "scarce one ynch," touch "hugenesse" with cold hands: there will be "paynes," but perhaps the "extreamest poynte of perill" can lead to points of pleasure, "fleeting" pain, instead of ice wished away.

Meditation with the ice is what Best does best; at first glance, he simply spends pages detailing the storm, "which did so wette thorowe oure poore marriners clothes, that he that hadde five or sixe shifte of apparell, had scarce one drie threede to his backe" (250). Enter mariners, freezing: repeatedly ice and snow pierce ships and bodies, "whiche [both] being leake, and sore brused . . . [are] lykely to be put into an yll harborough" (263). Upon closer inspection, however, the skin of ice looks appealing. Meditating on Best's icy scuffles uncovers the actual desires operating within them. Meanings proliferate when he hooks onto—thinks with and through— ice. Exerting its irrepressible influence despite Best's intentions, ice drives the company to desire the icescape. Immediately after his meeting with ice at "Salomon's porch," the glance of ice ushers in a new world of feeling:

But now I remember, I saw very strange wonders, men walking, running, leaping, and shoting upon the maine seas forty miles from any land, withoute any shippe or other vessell under them. Also I saw fresh rivers running amidst the salt sea a hundred myle from land, which if any man will not beleeve, let him know that many of our company lept out of their shippe uppon ilandes of ise. (254)

This moment is unlike any other in Best's narrative, for here he pleasurably invokes the "strange wonders" of the icescape. Still, Best's snapshot could be construed as a moment of colonization, a precursor to the vilified baby seal clubber of the present day: "and with their calivers did kill great ceales," he continues, "whiche use to lye and sleepe upon the ise" (254). It is an expected portrait; Frobisher was instructed on the third voyage to build and provide for a settlement of one hundred men. What Best is looking for are signs of domestication, not recreation: "this ise melting at the top by reflexion of the sun, came down in sundrye streams, whyche, uniting togither, made a prettie brooke able to drive a mill" (254). Sights like this would have been welcomed by these members destined to winter until the next year. The Arctic colony was never built, but Captain Edward Fenton constructed a small structure on the Countess of Warwick's Island as they prepared to leave. "[T]oyes," "pictures," and even "an oven [with] breade . . . baked therein" were left inside to "allure those brutish and uncivill [Inuit] to courtesie" (272). Following this narrative of possession and conversion, the English appear insensitive to the "strange wonders" around them. Brooks are "prettie" for future industry; seals "sleepe upon the ise" for meat and sport.

But Best surprises himself. "[N]ow I remember" catches him lost in his own Arctic reverie as he retells his story for publication, entranced by his own memories of encounter. The iceberg is an ecosystem explained scientifically—reflected sunlight heats accrued snow above that melts and flows to the sea below—but more importantly, the iceberg is an interstitial ecoregion that defies definition and becomes a wondrous place in description. Recounting the solid water that resembles land, Best cannot comprehend what he feels. His amazement comes from both the "strange" terrain of the water and his men's behavior when they observe it: "men walking, running, leaping, and shoting upon the maine seas." Participants in London's frost fairs might have shared in the sailors' thrill, as an anonymous poem from a century later relates, *Thamasis' Advice to the Painter, from Her Frigid Zone, or, Wonders upon the Water* (1684): "All things do move upon this Element, / As if on Terra ferma their feet went."[58] Walking on floating water, Best realizes his attachment, after all. Somehow this "strange" ice-land is desirable for these men; when water freezes, the idea of moving with and on water is made most manifest since it literally provides the aqua-"ferma" ground on which to walk. Like a proto-glaciologist, Best describes the iceberg's features. More like an ecomaterialist, he demonstrates going glacial: ice attracts his men, slips and glides them across its skin, calves new desires. Ice teaches one how to slip with living matterflows. Playing at "Salomons porch" is more than just the "shoting" (and shooting) of colonization, then, but a dialogue that peaks in icespeak. It is better to focus on those inexpressibly "strange wonders" that baffle Best. To read about ice's "wonders" is to put the reader in that mixture, the glancing insertion of the visit, but not solely to conquer or comprehend. Best is moved in all senses of the word by his remembrance, on the ice and in his mind. Englishmen on ice: the icy porch of sense-bodies invents new ways for thinking about human and nonhuman alliances. If the battle against ice in the July storm demonstrates ice's driving agency and its rejected assemblages with the human, the touching event at "Salomons porch" adds the element of desire to temper Best's antagonistic viewpoint. The ice is not beaten back, but is actually embraced. The *Discourse*

suddenly widens. Regardless of Best's intent to master the icescape—
to freeze ice flows in their tracks—we can see where ice unremittingly
punches holes in his hull of reason. Ice punches holes in ships, of course;
Fenton ingeniously plugged the *Judith*'s hull with beef during the Bear
Sound storm and stayed afloat. But Best proves that ice invents more than
a sinking feeling. Although done infrequently, explorers could nonetheless refuse to plug the hole of uncertainty and slip through it to feel the
"tacit ascendancy of the tactile" that ice demands.[59] When they did, they
found that these openings are focal points of desire, glacial passages that
could lead to chilling sensations and "strange wonders": it takes one step
off ship, a motion to leave the English vessel-nation behind, a leap of faith
from the front "porch" (the *oikos* of human households) onto the floating
element of thin ice, a new home.

The ice storm communicates the "unwildynesse" of reality that constantly asks what directions the English (and we) will take, whether to
"stay" or to "turne" with and into the stinging turbulence. Even for a
stalwart captain like Best, by the third voyage his rigid narrative methods
begin to thaw a little. He begins to get lost; he slips and loosens up; he
senses the marvelous in the ice around him. The first and second accounts
of Frobisher's ventures are rather straightforward in their tone. Over the
years Best feels the ice's pull, his brumal body makes re-turns, and his style
subsequently bends. His account of the third voyage, touched by the disorienting experience of the Bear Sound storm, effectively embraces the pleasures of glacial excursions. Stuck at an icy intersection of fluxes, the crew
mistakes their position:

> And truly it was wonderfull to heare and see the rushling and noyse that
> the tydes do make in thys place, with so violente a force that our shippes
> lying a hull, were turned sometimes rounde aboute even in a momente,
> after the manner of a whirlpool, and the noyse of the streame no lesse to
> be hearde a farre off, than the waterfall of London Bridge. (240)

Best relates the wonders of disorientation, presents himself like a Thames
waterman under the bridge dreaming. The noisy icescape transports them
into a sharp stupor: "it was wonderfull to hear and see" the "violente . . .
force" of the storm as it swirled ice and men. Its "noyse" was surely felt

as well: ice produces "rushling" sounds that reverberate, glance ("glacer"), bounce off bodies with a touch. Ice also slips in, enters the English body via sound-storm. As Best's ship is "turned . . . rounde aboute," the bodies onboard turn. Sound and body come together in a "wonderfull" conjunction. Once "turned" by the ice, these ice-bodies go glacial, extend out into the sound (and the Sound). To be caught in "the manner of a whirlpool" causes men to admire as well as to despair. Thus the reference to London Bridge, perhaps cited by Best as a mooring gesture of reference, ultimately falls short. Escaping mere metaphor, the sound of icy waters enters the men even if "hearde a farre off." The whirlpool disperses ontological categories by its dizzying power to disorient. Ice, men, and sound stick together in icespeak. They "shote" in the "sea-lung" of Pytheas of Massillia perhaps, the Greek traveler of antiquity who purportedly entered the thick-iced seas of "Thule" north of England in the fourth century BCE, "in which there was no longer any distinction of land or sea or air, but a mixture of the three."[60] The Arctic maelstrom is a dangerous place, but also a place of vertiginous bodies with potential. Ultimately, the "whirlpool" stands in for what the icescape has been all along: non/human bodies in a maelstrom of mixture, "Ultima Thule" of farthest north, a living and breathing icescape of indefinite borders, a mixed-elemental atmosphere.

Northwest Passages

Instead of discovering *the* Northwest Passage, explorers like Best stumbled upon sensorial passages almost by surprise. I am reminded of yet another passage, this one unfurled before us by Michel Serres: "It transports us, in fact, from one major body of knowledge to the opposite one through the North-West passage. In geography, the carillon of the hard sciences finally falls silent, when that of the human sciences is barely beginning. In this almost silent space lies the landscape."[61] For Serres, the Northwest Passage is less a physical location and more an interchange between the local and global, the geological and political, the human and the exact sciences. In this muddled and meddling landscape of wet and dry, geography actively transports; like ice that hardens, melts, and carves, nothing is constant here except fluctuation itself. Passages ceaselessly emerge; maps must continually be redrawn. The Northwest Passage

offers a way to think about being *between* (like a solid and a liquid, like
a poet and a scientist), about being endlessly connective, to not only ring
the bells of alarm—iceberg, dead ahead!—but also to strike up a carillon
call of collaboration between disciplines, beings. Peals never quiet in the
"almost silent" seascape: Best's icescapes of desire involve brief voyages
out into these meandering glacial passages that redefine the Passage as a
series of passages, of going glacial, a slippery "trip" sideways inconceivable
to an English navigator like Frobisher meant to locate, and profit from,
the mappable Northwest Passage. If the idea of inhabiting pluralizing
passages seems too abstract, Best's recurring image of the missing men is
a fascinating example (for us) of an invitation taken. In their first encounter with the Inuit in 1576, the English "had sundry conferences" with
them, trading toys for furs "and suche like" (73). Frobisher asked for directions to the Passage, but without a shared language, most conversations
were confusing. A native whom Frobisher enlisted as a guide was set ashore
with a small English reconnaissance party. What happens next is startling:
"After great curtesie and many meetings our mariners contrarie theyr cap-
taines dyrection began more easily to trust them and five of oure men
going ashoare were by them intercepted with theyr boate and were never
since hearde of this daye againe" (73). Investigating Best's greatest un-
solved mystery reveals that their absence is not a problem to be solved
but rather an avenue to be explored. The most methodological routes
prove to be those passages that carve through a mixed icescape. Frobisher
lamented the thought of voices—those of his forsaken men—trapped
in ice; he believed that they were out there, mixing, but that they could
no longer be heard. Noisy glaciers and unquiet souls intertwine with the
land, and the company's greatest fear was to be enveloped and silenced
by ice. Thus the real danger for Best is the deterritorialization of going
glacial, of becoming-ice. Like the men sliding on "Salomons porch," these
five inhabit the icescape's smooth spaces. (Not much is smoother than ice.)
To Best's disbelief, the sailors went for a walk, or glide, in the foggy labyrinth. He routinely advises against rambling into the unknown. Leaky
vessels require safe harbors, for example, but soundings are impossible:
"and before the next cast, ere you shall bee able to have your lead againe,
you shall be upon the toppe thereof, and come aground to your utter
confusion" (262). The icescape cannot be sounded, and yet the English

entered it time and time again in their efforts to understand it. There is little difference between rambling and navigating in an icescape that refuses to stay still. These men point to desire immanent in the icescape, demonstrate that the "utter confusion" of the icy labyrinth can be its most magnetic trait; accordingly, the insufferable Arctic fog noted frequently by explorers proves helpful. Its mists remystify the ontological relations between things; its thickness fills space with new creations.[62] An iceberg's trail through the labyrinth does not point the way out, only newer ways in, leaving in its wake the misty interchanges of mist, the moment when bodies dip below dew point.

It is a hard turn to make: to stay in the foggy ice labyrinth of confusion, in the fog of unknowing, the P/p/assage. I am not sure the five lost sailors ever finish haunting the *Discourse*; they clearly bother Best. But what the text is truly haunted by is the violence of white imperialism: when only the desires of a few are allowed, when beings *choose* to silence themselves (like the Inuit captive)—"for very choller and disdain, he bit his tong in twayne within his mouth" (74)—when hot-blooded tempers rampage through a cold climate. Best's theory of inheritable skin color through "infection" partly explains his fears of bodily penetration of becoming-Inuit as well as becoming-ice, that maybe Cham's curse is communicable and geohumoralism unreliable. European whiteness warps white icescape and dark inhabitants together, collapses them as contagion touched by "blackenesse." The fates of the first four Inuit in England allow us to see how violence can be directed at both humans and nonhumans at once. Not only did Frobisher jeopardize future relations with the natives of Baffin Bay, he also established an ethnological limitation to going glacial. The natives were meant to be signposts on the way to Cathay, their dark skins corroborating the closeness of tropical climes. The kidnapped kayaker of 1576—"[h]is cullor of skyn all over his body and face of a dark sallow, much like to the tawny Mores, or rather to the Tartar nation, whereof I think he was. His countenance sullen or churlish and sharp withal" (87)—died immediately after arriving in England. The three taken in 1577 did not fare much longer, though they became celebrities around the seaport of Bristol. The man demonstrated his hunting skills on the Avon River before succumbing to a lung infection brought on by broken ribs sustained during his capture. The child, sent for by the queen, died en route. The woman caught measles shortly after witnessing the man's burial, a ceremony put on by the English to prove to her that they buried rather than ate their dead. The English had intended for the man and woman to start a family. On board, the crew members eagerly waited for them to copulate: "Having now got a woman captive for the comfort of our man, we brought them both togither, and every man with silence desired to beholde the manner of their meeting and entertainment. . . . The woman spared not to do all necessarie things that apperteyned to a good huswife" (144–45). Yet Best clearly dehumanizes them, thereby disallowing (or suppressing) any hint of English voyeurism. He speaks of their barbarity at length, their crying "like the mowing of bulles" (129); as beasts "[t]hey live in caves of the earth and hunte for their dinners or praye, even as the beare or other wilde beastes do" (283). The woman was supposedly found licking her infant's wounds like a dog after the battle of "Bloudy Point";[63] the natives at first are mistaken for seals and, once onboard, eat raw fish. Since they were sometimes animals, cannibals, and eaters of uncooked flesh, Frobisher could kidnap and discriminate with a clear conscience. Fortunately, the threat he made in a letter to the lost men was not carried out; known for his violent temper, the captain guarantees genocide if his demands are not met: "Moreover, you may declare unto them, that if they deliver you not, I wyll not leave a manne alive in their countrey" (147). Disturbingly displaced when the mining of the land and the lives of its people intersect, these four Inuit bodies go glacial as well, but they do so by a foreign captain's orders and without their consent. The temperate English climate stops their flow; its warmth is their death sentence.

Icescapes call us to pay attention to these problematic entanglements: native bodies hoisted on deck, the meeting of bullets with flesh at "Bloudy Point." The ice-eddy is a vortex of change; for Best, its interchanges of peace are not given a chance. Yet the tumultuous "whirlpool" is not just his: going glacial can counter his unjust encounters by making a space for more tolerant kinds of intercultural relations and interactions in the interchange.[64] The *Discourse* is important, even useful, for the discourse of environmental ethics it avoids. We cannot know what the five men felt, what exactly drew them on, what "intercepted" them and earned their "trust." Likewise, we can only imagine what the four Inuit captives felt,

what "mournefull song . . . and Dirges" the woman sang and what story
the man told in unfamiliar tongues onboard the *Ayde* bound for England
(284). And here are better dreams: glaciality keeps *going*. Best's descriptions of the "strange wonders" on the iceberg and the skin-on-skin contact in Bear Sound's whirling storm demonstrate the icescape's potential
to challenge damaging human and nonhuman divisions while acknowledging the fragility of our coexistence, while remembering the histories
of violence that have broken the ice. It is the same "violente a force" as
well as shivering intimacy that Serres saw once in an open bergschrund:
"'If you curl up into a ball,' [his guide] said, 'if you defend yourself and
get dressed, the enemy will penetrate down to your liver: cold is more
invasive than you. No. Present yourself, uncover yourself, go toward it,
make it your friend; it'll respect you. Turn the *against* into a *for*.' Yet without going beyond the lethal limit."[65] Even the best men in the storm, "the
expertest mariners," as Best deems them, by exposing themselves to the
sound "began to marvell, thinking it a thing impossible" that they could
be so marveled, that they had not observed anything like it "than before
time they had observed" (240). They were "deceyve[d]," that is, by limits
they thought were impassable (240). The old maps need to be reconceived
for this prepositional change to happen; let us make room for voices re-
glossed in the glassy material, let us make new maps that ice affords. We
spiral still in the ice-whirl of race and specie/s relations.

Meta

For its sheer sensual power, Best's rumble in the whirlpool is his most
promising moment of ecomaterialism. He did not realize that he had
felt something extraordinary pass through him; had he been converted
("turned . . . aboute") enough by ice, his narrative might have been vastly
different. Nevertheless, Best narrates the marvels to be found when passing. The geographic Northwest Passage kept changing, of course: from
"Frobisher's Streytes," to the "Mistaken Streytes," to Hudson Strait. The
original name given to the icescape is telling: Elizabeth chose "Meta Incognita" (Unknown Limits). Arctic topography can never be fully mapped
or known, only felt and passed through, its layers observed and inhabited
like skin. Best describes Frobisher's amazement at this fact. After various cases are presented for returning home, Frobisher pushes north and

finds that "the land was not firme, as it was first supposed, but all broken ilandes in manner of an archipelagus; and so, with other secret intelligence to himselfe, he returned to the fleete" (274). The archipelago presents a topography of multiplicity unknown to Frobisher. The islands are both familiar and unfamiliar at once: "These broken landes and ilandes, being very many in number, do seeme to make there an archipelagus, which as they all differ in greatnesse, forme, and fashion one from another, so are they in goodnesse, couloure and soyle muche unlike" (281). These lands may be "broken," but they are somehow also connected in a network of bridges and pathways. Ice is constantly moving, forming, dissolving, and connecting. Ice-land is endless archipelagos, segments, and things set adrift. Contemporary maps could not encompass it. Best's map is commonly reproduced as an amusement, a juvenile effort exemplifying the era's misguided beliefs about the pole. I reexamine it here not to question

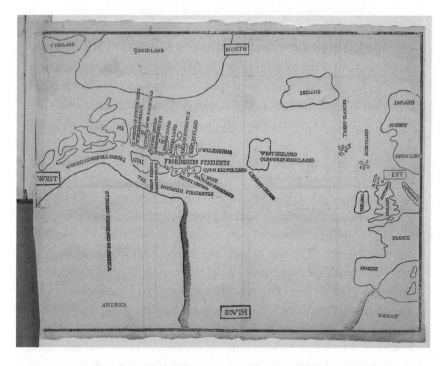

Meta Incognita, from George Best, *A True Discourse*, RB 14571, The Huntington Library, San Marino, California.

its reliability, but to check our own preference for order and our dependence on graphic authenticity, as if a polar positioning system is actually possible. This crisp chart indicates a place where land and icebergs, never discrete, intermix: where locations float, and appear to be, icebergs. The map discloses the untidiness of glacial reality: if "Meta Incognita" was originally the "Unknown Limits," there truly are no known limits to glaciality, just potential. "Meta" comes from Latin *meta* ("a pyramidal column used as a turning-post or winning-post; any turning point") and therefore designates a veering as much as a finishing point or line.[66] Best's map encourages us to keep redrawing maps of relations in the place that has not been, and cannot ever be, fully mapped: not to turn "home" for the "win" but to keep turning with the bergs to come, the iceberg-islands that drift on and off the map, to take deviating "Streytes," "Streights," and "Straightes" that refuse to run straight or eventually straighten, that endlessly stray.

Illimitable islands of multiplicity finally bring us back to the meshwork of dissolving and forming connections that the shifting "archipelagus" of ice represents: the slips and slides into the U/u/nknown, the act of going glacial. To think back, then, on Best's finest summation of his captain:

> And, as some of the company reported, he hath since confessed that, if it had not bin for the charge and care he had of the fleete and fraughted shippes, he both would and could have gone through the south sea, called Mare del Sur, and dissolved the long doubt of the passage which we seeke to find to the rich countrey of Cataya. (242)

The proof of the Northwest Passage is in the joys of dissolution one finds by passing through glacial passages. Frobisher does not "dissolv[e]" the "doubt" of the Passage: the Passage "dissolve[s]" him. Whether he sensed his own iciness, or realized that the Passage is a problem never solved, only a route cohabited, is hard to tell. But Best holds up the possibility in this moment of deferral that we, too, can be better explorers. His title page sends us "Northweast," fans in the direction/s of north-east-west all at once; it is a true *Discourse*, we might humbly add: a "running to and fro," a book with passages without ends, that documents the absence of telos at one of the world's "ends." We are marooned only from the perspective of the warm-blooded human surrounded by ice, the sport of kings, like the James of *Orlando*, who wrongly believes a "certain blueness about the lips hinted the truth": that the "old bumboat woman" with her fruit, and not he, has the touch of blue.[67] Once we roam from our anthropocentric vessel, we discover the pleasures of living ice, hear where boreal voices are not hijacked or muted. Touching its skin, it touches ours. This is a different "conference" between humans and nonhumans, a glacial assembly of non/human things speaking together, dreaming up "sundry" assemblages yet to come, taking the cryological turn. The Northwest Passage reminds us that passages still open, that non/human mixtures are always flowing down polar expressways—somewhere, everywhere—lingering in loves, negotiating the "lethal limits" of limits unknown.

Flipping Ice: Davis

One explorer who was less reluctant to pursue this alternate polar path that Best had opened (inadvertently or not) was John Davis (ca. 1550–1605). Like Frobisher, he was obsessed with the Northwest Passage; and like many of these early Arctic voyagers, not much is known about him. As a skilled navigator, his legacy includes the Davis Strait to the west of Greenland, a land he named "Desolation"; his lauded *Seamans Secrets* (1595); and the Davis Quadrant. His three northwest missions between 1585 and 1587 were mainly exploratory. (Frobisher's later voyages were primarily for "gold": the discovery of the Passage was secondary.) Convinced that the Passage lay farther north and west than Frobisher's findings, Davis pushed up the coast of Greenland until ice forced his retreat south. On his first two missions, he plotted regions far north and caught cod that furnished the expedition with a meager profit; on the third, he reached northeastern Baffin Island and explored the Hudson Strait. Without backers like Francis Walsingham (ca. 1532–90) after the third voyage, Davis joined a team in 1591 to find a route from the west (via Alaska). Although that objective was not met, he was credited with the discovery of the Falklands. *The Worldes Hydrographical Discription* appeared four years later, detailing his 1585–87 Arctic voyages. His hydrography is a series of approximately seven quasi-scientific answers against opponents' "objections" and "all impediments" to travel northwest, supplying evidence from his three personal voyages as a rebuttal. The *Discription*'s goals are both worldly and spiritual: to establish trade with India as well as to become better Christian proselytizers by means of Greenland's "perpetuall light."[68] The prospective benefits and enrichment are so delineated, Davis believes, that hearts could only melt for the opportunity to enter the cold: "it is impossible that any true English hart should be staied from willing contribution to the performance of this so excellent a discovery" (228). But he was unable to go toward the "light" later in life: after serving successfully with the Dutch in the East Indies, Davis became the chief pilot of the East India Company and was killed in a skirmish with pirates in 1605.

On the surface, Davis's hydrography seems unremarkable. His response to the first objection, that the Northwest Passage is nonexistent, resembles Best's strategy of deferral in the *Discourse*. The unfathomable passage that cannot be sounded verifies its existence by its very uncertainty. On his third and final voyage, Davis describes the natives in detail. As they row out to trade, he interprets their signs to mean that a larger sea lies farther off: "after I had sayled towards the West 40 leagues, I fel upon a great banke of yce: the winde being North and blew much, I was constrained to coast the same toward the South, not seeing any shore West from me, neither was there any yce towards the North, but a great sea, free, large, very salt and blew, and of an unsearcheable depth" (210). The "unsearchable" blue water (of the Hudson Strait) evokes the trope of the Northwest Passage as a searchable passage that is always elusive. Limitable in scope and limned by maps for future reference—so it was hoped—the Passage is nonetheless limitless. The Arctic is abysmal, bottomless, and forever uncertain. Davis finds this "depth" advantageous. Like Best's exoneration of Frobisher, Davis is candid about his retreat. He could have gone farther and dissolved the doubt once and for all: "by this last discovery it seemed most manifest that the passage was free and without impediment toward the North" (210). But a series of events forced him to return to England: Walsingham had died; the fishing fleet he had ordered to wait for his return abandoned him; and the Spanish Armada was soon to arrive. Davis seems to be yet one more explorer who adds ambiguous knowledge onto an already-ambiguous geography. His account of all three voyages simply widens the gap of uncertainty via deferral: language, linked with melted material, is purposefully meant to "run away." His words, wrought from personal experience, are enough. He even helped produce a globe, "the new map with the augmentation of the Indies" cited by Shakespeare (*Twelfth Night*, 3.2.66–68), puffing up his accomplishments as much as the skill of its maker, Emery Molyneux (d. 1598): "whereby he is now growne to a most exquisite perfection" (211). There is not much to be desired in his hydrography; the icescape is a cold, mute, and impersonal place that impedes his progress. Ice has little else to say, it seems.

What makes Davis's northern routes truly novel, though, is his ability to vacillate from scientific description to more curious explanation in his "objections," retaining the object-subject distinction in the former while reconceiving himself as quasi-subject in his cold laboratories in the latter. Francis Bacon (1561–1626) would later say in his greener-toned tome *Sylva Sylvarum* (1627), "Whosoever will be an enquirer into Nature let him resort to a conservatory of Snow or Ice."[69] Davis is caught between splitting body and mind, climate from "conservatory," in his literary labs. Consider the "objection" concerning the hypothesis that the seas may freeze; his hydrography espouses scientific analysis as much as geographical exploration. With his firsthand observations of northwestern ice as his lab materials, Davis is objectifying at first. Seawater, he declares, is impossible to freeze, simply proven, "by the experience of all that have ever travelled towards the North it is well knowne that the sea never fryseth" (217). But for those who are not so lucky to see it firsthand, he explains that ice is congealed fresh water that has been separated from saltwater by cold temperatures near rivers and shorelines: "And as the nature of heate with apt vessels devideth the pure spirit from his grosse partes by the coning practise of distillation: so doth the colde in these regions devide and congeale the fresh water from the salt" (217). Playing upon the "coning practise of distillation" and congealment, Davis's understanding of the icescape's dynamics is alchemical; his rationale simplifies the scientific matter of ice, defrosts the frozen sea of "*Mare Congelatum*," "for all yse in general beeing dissolved is very fresh water" (217). In other words, he offers a solution to the question of ice's solubility. Davis's argument is essentially the unmixing of mixture; he "devide[s]" the fresh water from the salt water in the same way that bodies in the icescape would divide according to the practice of modernist purification: a tidying, that is, which depends upon a veiled truth rather than proliferations of meanings. Analysis, in

Davis's case, arrests the possibility of understanding non/human mixture in cryocomposition. Regarding his hydrography's readership, he does not try to hide the idea of ice's "distillation," but instead uses this scientific knowledge as a way to simultaneously reveal and conceal the existence of the Northwest Passage he promises to have found but cannot prove. A true alchemist, he is loosening language and inhabiting deferral: touting his knowledge, perhaps, but not cohabiting glacial becomings.

Like several before and many after him, Davis notes the dangerously vertiginous ice that "environ[s]" and "compasse[s]" him: he confronts a "strange whirle-winde" in Gilbert Sound on the second voyage—"not for a puffe or blast, but continuall"—only to be followed by a "mighty masse of ice" that was "so bigge as that [they] knew not the limits thereof" and whose "contagious" and "grosse fogge" enfeebled his men (22, 24–25). The same ice that grounds his theory against frozen seawater possesses its own vitality. As he continues to analyze the ice of his second objection, it begins to swerve:

> [B]ut wee know that the sea dissolveth this yse with great speede, for in twentie four houres I have seene an ylande of yse turne up and downe, as the common phrase is, because it hath melted so fast under water that the heavier parte hath beene upwarde, which hath beene the cause of his so turning, for the heviest part of all things swiming is by nature down-wards, and therefore sith the sea is by his heate of power to dissolve yse, it is greatly against reason that the same should be frozen, so that the congealation of the seas can bee no hindrance to the execution of this passage. (217–18)

Flipping icebergs that "turne up and downe": this is ice in motion and with "speede," independent of the onlooker's gaze. Davis automatically turns to the scientific discourse he knows so well. Salt heats the heaviest, and thus the bottommost, part of the ice, causing it to flip. Performing a kind of cryospheric dance, the agents of the icescape—salt, water, ice—present a mystery to the explorer, their desires needing little (or nothing) to do with human ones in order to operate. Yet Davis quickly halts the flipping ice by translating the nonhuman event into an authorial perfor-mance of knowledge. He prefers explication over speculation, and the ice becomes a scientific "passage" upon the page to prove the viability of the larger Passage at softened and salted sea. His scientific mind has no interest in rambling out into the swerving world so close to him. Similar to Best's earlier attempts to barricade human bodies from nonhuman elements, Davis's erudition alienates him from his objectified matter of study. Arguing against another objection, soon after, that air in the cold regions is unendurable, Davis demonstrates how the icescape breathes. Metals are "concoct and molten in veines" in the mountains of Norway and Sweden. Arctic exhalations, by "pearcing the earth and the waters, and through both those natures breathing forth into the ayre, tempereth the quantitie thereof, making it tollerable" (220). If the earth breathes a hot metallic air and brings riches, Davis has effectively proven Greenland's temperate climate since "the extremities of elements consent with their next" (221). He launches into an intricate series of deductions "execut[ed]" with precision: salt, as the heating ingredient in water, produces coldness; the cold water interacts with the hot and thin vapors; this process results, finally, in a temperate climate. This is the good touch—copper and silver—not the bad touch of ice: "it plainely appeareth that the very breth of the yse is . . . the cause of this colde" and not the air (221). Davis's theories admit an Arctic vitality—breathing, heating, ore-bearing, and all of different qualifications—but not quite agency. Moreover, these substances exist in contradistinction to one another. His vitalism is comprehensible and replicable. For Davis, then, the expedition creates an identifiable, and observable, icescape that can be understood scientifically and plotted geographically. Any question left unanswered is directed upward to God: "divine providence . . . hath made nothing uncommunicable" (221). His trim epistemological lines stifle ontological exploration. Teleological truth, divine or worldly, is hierarchically organized just as the human scientist is superior to, and separate from, the icy matter at hand.

Communicate with the "common" phase transition of freezing he does, however: before proving his quasi-scientific theory about freshwater "distillation" derived from alchemical "practise," Davis must put real ice in his hand; he decides to conduct an onboard science experiment in the northwest. In order to test the hypothesis that a seventh of an iceberg is visible above water, ice comes on ship. Fascinatingly, Davis creates his own little cryosphere "by taking a peece of yse, and have put the same in a

vessell of salt water, and still have found the seventh part thereof to bee
above the water, into what forme soever I have reduced the same" (216–
17). Davis's experiment shores up the anthropocentricity of analysis; once
again, he demonstrates his reliance upon subject-centered modes of observation, similar to how Sophie Lemercier-Goddard, summoning Michel
Foucault's "panopticon" as "a kind of laboratory of power," has argued
that Best's *Discourse* serves as a political and propagandistic case study:
"rare voices are heard, revealing the Arctic to be a laboratory where English identities could be fashioned and tested."[70] These experimental identities that problematize English-Inuit differentiation, I would add, can also
be fashioned through speaking with those rarer, more nonhuman voices
that cannot be sealed, only ignored. In his "vessell" Davis mixes one piece
of ice with one part seawater, and the result is the universal scale of these
great "ylands of yse." Not only does he observe the activity within the
vessel, he also creates it by constructing his own little iceberg. Similar to
Best's analysis of "Salomons porch," measuring the frozen creature outside the ship evacuates ice's monstrosity. His "playne experience" assuages
his fears and those of his men; look and make sure to touch: this chunk
of ice is "nothing but snowe" (217). Davis effectively designs a miniature
ecosystem that he can monitor, manipulate, and disseminate to his readers and those more familiar with "wrested philosophical reasons" and "the
repetition of authorities" (216). He has a whole ice world in his hands.

Yet how easily this Arctic- and anthropocentric world falls apart; at this
moment Davis suddenly recalls how this "verye white and freshe" kind of
ice is the same upon the "sea coastes of Desolation" (eastern Greenland)
that he has felt too well, and

> which I have seene incredible to bee reported, that upon the toppe of
> some of these ylls of yse, there have been stones of more then one hun-
> dredth tonnes wayght, which in his fall that snowe hath torne from the
> clyffs, and in falling maketh sich an horrible noyse as if there were one
> hundredth canons shot of at one instant. (217)

Davis knows this frightening sound of desolation in the never-silent space
of ice, a cold carillon of hard-soft sciences, like bone and flesh and sound
rattling in winter. "[A]ll the roaring which we heard . . . was caused onely

by the rouling of . . . yce together"—writes John Janes, a merchant aboard
Davis's ship, the *Sunshine*, and who authored the first voyage's account—
"making such yrksome noyse" (4). The nonhuman noise physically disturbs his subjective analysis. As mediary actants, the ice-torn boulders and
spinning pinball-bergs penetrate Davis's seemingly inviolable subject-
object border that his scientific know-how previously sustained. Glacial
activity takes place unobserved and in spite of him; the rocks move on
their own accord. Davis's ship and his "vessell" are made small within the
larger vessel of the cryosphere. Even if the creaturely icebergs flip outside his ship, even if the iceberg in his hand is grasped tightly, the noisy
ice breaks the easy distinctions between inside and outside, human and
nonhuman. To put it differently, the noise flips the one-way agency the
"vessell" is supposed to represent: the active experimenter and the lifeless experimented. Ice acts upon him. Davis is startled because he senses
that his scientific "passage[s]" are written by swerving with the ice rather
than against it. The glacial sounds glance ("glacer") off him, insert within
the human "vessell," collaborate in his laboratory, slip into the pages of his
hydrography by passing through his physical body and bloodwork. Davis,
in a phrase, *goes glacial* by listening to the sonorous cannon-shots of icespeak. If he had previously spoken of the contradiction between elements
(a kind of *versus*), he additionally summarizes conjunctions with living ice.
Thus the "passage[s]" have no conceivable end; they are "execut[ed]" in
perpetuity. Like Best's experience in the whirlpool, Davis feels the multisensory touch of the Northwest Passage via the noise of mingling sense-
bodies as they pass through the icescape. In the traverse book of the third
voyage he recalls seeing the "sea falling down into the gulfe with a mighty
overfal, and roring, and with divers circular motions like whirlepooles,
in such sort as forcible streames passe thorow the arches of bridges" (56).
The noise rattles him in a way that guides him to new prospects. The
touch of ice in his hand was not enough. It took more than a small "peece"
to move him, to send that chilling feeling that crawls up the spines of
both bodies and books.

Ice enters Davis by surprise, and a sensational new natural contract is
forged with cold contacts. He slowly begins to see ice differently than any
other early modern Arctic explorer before him (and few after). Whereas
his experiments had once proven his hypothesis of elemental opposition,

how he ends his observations-objections in the *Discription*, while lengthy, reads like a peace accord. Davis drafts an ecomaterial manifesto of our enmeshment with the physical world, one that I wish to quote in full for the magnificent *meta* turn that it stages, a new beginning of the beyond (the *hyper-*), of how to be desolate but never *solus*, "alone":

[I]n ordinary reason men should not suppose nature to bee monstrous, for if all such yse and snowe as congealeth and descendeth in the winter did not by natures benefit dissolve in the sommer, but that the cold were more actual then the heate, that difference of inequalitie bee it never so little would by time bread natures ouerthrowe, for if the one thousand parte of the yse which in winter is congealed, did the next summer remayne undissolved, that continual difference sithins the worldes creation would not onely have converted all those North Seas into yse, but would also by continuall accesse of snowe have extended himselfe above all the ayers regions, by which reason all such exalations as should be drawn from the earth and seas within the temperate zones and by windes driven into these stiffe regions, that moysture was no more to bee hoped for that by dissolution it should have any returne, so that by time the world should be left waterlesse. And therefore how ridiculous this imagination of the seas frysing is, I refer to the worlds generall opinion. (218)

Davis's Arctic dream imagines non/human lives in precarious imbalance. Nature and its icy agents could not possibly "bee monstrous," for without the natural cycle of freezing and dissolving the whole world would be rendered "waterlesse" after all its water froze. One might argue that Davis invokes the language of catastrophe here, but unlike modern visions of the Arctic ice, there is no predestined collapse unless something happens to prevent it. For Davis, the only danger is in meddling with a process outside of human knowledge and furthermore mistaking "natures benefit" as "monstrous." Ice is not a cause for trepidation; rather, Davis becomes an advocate for ice's flow. He illuminates for his readers the faraway dissolutions that they can never fully observe but must nevertheless appreciate. Let the earth breathe its hot vapors. In fact, Davis's rebuke is a proposal: a challenge to embrace the misconstrued monstrosity of nature and its elements and, in doing so, inhabit the world's flows. A planet bereft of water is a dry planet, indeed, but so is a planet bereft of ice. The most "ridiculous . . . imagination" here is not just the sea freezing, then, but freezing the icescape's living ice, to deny ice's ability to flip and sound, distill and congeal, mix and transport. Davis's attempts to analyze the ice of the Northwest Passage teach him about his desire for the icescape. He is in the grips of something even as he grips the ice world in his hand. Peering into the "vessell," Davis sees a reflection of his own cryocorporeality. He recognizes what he looks like through ice's eyes. Incredibly, the "turning" and resounding icescape instigates his own turning, his own transformation, a moment of cryophilia. Davis's experiment is really a thought experiment that beggars onto-epistemological proportions, collapses macro- and microcosmos, disrupts reliable scalar understandings of size and intimacy, inaugurates a desire for the "monstrous" at the northern end of the world. To make this announcement, Davis needs the ice to flip him. It is a likelihood not beyond our imaginations, either, or a dream beyond reality. (The harmony of perfect balance, sustainability, which specifies just the right amount of ice necessary to maintain sea levels exemplifies the opposite.) It is an "opinion," I hypothesize, that the current world could use when thinking about the unstable "slope" of climate change, when broking diplomacy instead of war, relations and negotiations instead of salvation or colonialization: a frigidity that strangely loosens rigidity, that catalyzes postsustainable times.

Facing Ice: Ellis

I have been arguing up to this point for revisiting early modern Arctic narratives in order to discover the delights and dangers of going glacial, and also to acknowledge the segregations imposed upon this process, whether between captain and kidnapped (Best), scientific subject and senseless object (Davis), silent and silenced (in general). These hydrographies, titled as such or not, oppose the idea of composition as exclusively human. I now want to build on the process of writing as a "common" task that can help construct a teeming non/human commons, how textuality itself—the touch of frost-nipped pages—may deliquesce even the most indurate non/human restrictions. I wish to take an ice-walk with Serres, for whom to visit is to compose. Composition, he claims, is not the patient observation of a visible landscape but a place of creativity; the page of the book is inextricable from the *pagi* of the land, as his own musing meandering meanderings prove: "Pages do not sleep in language, they draw their life from the *pagi*: from the countryside, the flesh and the world."[71] In their shared "life," pages, flesh, and landscape compose together in a writerly coexistence. Thus the geographer is one who both writes about the land-scape and is part of a "fleshy" conjunction with a sensual world. Allow me my own ramble, then, to consider the *pagos* (a Greek word meaning "ice") *as* page. The resounding ice in Davis's *Discription* is a significant example of how page and *pagos* enfold. The travel narratives of the North-west Passage are all pagographies, instantiations of glacial composition in as much as they illustrate examples of glaciality on their pages. Ice *-graphs* (or writes) just as it *-scapes* (or creates). With this scaping in mind, word-calving in mouth, I turn to my last primary passage, scrawled by chapped hands, that rethinks the nature of visiting and composing along these carved lines.

My example belongs to a minor figure in the history of Arctic explora-tion, Thomas Ellis, who was onboard Frobisher's flagship, the *Ayde*, during the third voyage of 1578 and wrote *A True Report* the same year. Though professing to be a "Sailer" in the preface, "more studied and vsed in my Charde and Compasse," any hydrographical skill Ellis possesses is under-cut by his flair for ostentatious poetry. "In praise of Maister Martine Frobisher," one out of several commendatory verses he includes as an epilogue—and that he penned himself—compares the captain to Jason:

> The glittering fleece that he doth bring,
> in value sure is more,
> Than Iasons was, or Alcides fruite,
> whereof was made suche store.[72]

As Ellis continues, Frobisher matches and then outshines the Grecian examples by bringing home the "glittering fleece" (the ersatz gold), tam-ing "cruell monsters" (the ice), and conquering "men of sauage kinde" in "countries straunge" (the Inuit). Following Best's example, Ellis fittingly lauds Frobisher, for Jason was supposedly the first to venture outside the ancient world. Despite the "glittering fleece" turning up as coarse cloth, or worthless rock, Frobisher at least had Jason's courage to his credit. Like other contemporary accounts of the third voyage, Ellis describes the monstrous icescape in terrifying detail to augment his captain's heroic feats. Passing Friseland, for instance, proves especially distressful: "There we might also perceive the great Isles of yce lying on the seas, like mountaines, some small, some bigge, of sundrie kindes shapes, and such a number of them, that we coulde not come neere the shoare for them."[73] Approaching the presumed "Streightes," Ellis feels straightjacketed: "the yce being round about us, and inclosing us, as it were within the pales of a Parke" (197). This fenced-in "Parke" is not a bucolic place. The company is enlimned, enclosed, and hopelessly claustrophobic: "Thus the yce coming on us so fast, we were in great danger, looking everie houre for death. And thus passed we on in that great danger, seeing both our selves, and the rest of our ships so troubled and tossed amongst the yce, that it woulde make the strongest heart to relent" (197). Ellis narrowly escapes the hoartempest on Bear Sound. Hopelessly "plunged in . . . perplexitie" of icy flux, he and his weary companions are forced to fend off the ice though the night: "the yce had so environed us, that we could see neither land, nor Sea, as farre as we could kenne" (197). Thus to read Ellis's narrative, nearly thirty pages in all, is to question the sincerity of his introductory praise: a trip to the far west for "Alcides fruite" does not yield its fabled golden apples; in this infertile Garden of the Hesperides, they only "tasted of" shipwreck, a cold "sauce," instead (197).

Eventually, the Bear Sound storm abates, and Ellis is left "praising God for our deliverance" (198). It is at his moment of salvation that the *Report* becomes exceptional. Contemporaries like Fenton, who was also on the same voyage as he, infrequently scribbled shorelines as seen from water level (as the log for the *Judith* attests). But Ellis, without precedent, pens several portraits of a tabular iceberg as seen from all sides, "[t]hese foure being but one Island of yce" (198). The storm literally delivers him to new ways of perceiving ice. As if strangely attracted to his vanquished enemy, he renders the iceberg for us in both word and picture:

> And as we thus lay off and on, we came by a marvellous huge mountaine of yce, which surpassed all the rest that ever we sawe: for we judged him to be neere a foure score fadams above water, and we thought him to be a ground for any thing that we could perceive, being there nine score

fadams deepe, and of compasse about halfe a mile, of which Island I have, as neere as I could, drawne and here set downe the true proportion, as he appeared in diverse shapes passing alongest by him. (198)

The attraction is a nervous one. Even as Ellis draws close, the ice remains harmful like a wounded beast. The caption to the first perspective calls it a "great and monstruous peece of yce." But as Ellis draws nearer to it, the ice loses its bite. His second, third, and fourth depictions involve careful attention to detail instead of quick judgment. As he nears the iceberg, he discovers a "hollow" cavity shown in sketch three: or, rather, an entryway. Neglecting its ice-mazes, however, Ellis moves on; and significantly, he is the only one moving, "passing alongest by him." He might have drawn the iceberg's negative space deliberately as a way to assert his own strength.

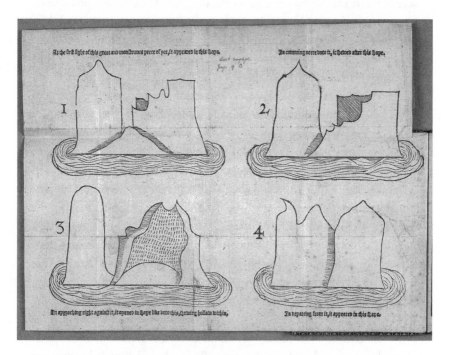

"A mounteine of yce appearing in sundrie figures," from Thomas Ellis, *A True Report*, RB 18070, The Huntington Library, San Marino, California. Captions read: "1. At the first sight of this great and monstruous peece of yce, it appeared in this waye. 2. In coming near unto it, it shewed after this shape. 3. I approaching right against it, it opened in shape like unto this, shewing hollow within. 4. In departing from it, it appeared in this shape."

Eviscerating the ice's body is a way to gauge and control the icescape by avoiding the complexities of the human–nonhuman relationship: only "it" melts, rendering each picture slightly different than the one before. Edges soften, sharpen; the "true proportion" Ellis outlines does just that: he undercuts the immensity of the iceberg by transferring it to a small page in a book he carries. He condenses ice's monstrous size into something manageable. The sketchbook becomes a method of escape. Ellis's act of composition, the drawing of ice on the page, is a means to compose his frightened senses in a harsh icescape. Moreover, his composition is avowedly human. He is writing about ice, not letting it glance, pass through, or slip "him," "him"-self, the human.

Ellis's prolonged dwelling on the "marvellous" aspect of the "huge mountaine of yce," however, betrays his report's brief desire for the icescape. There can be no "true proportion" of the iceberg, of course, since ice endlessly changes shapes. Ice itself is diversity in "diverse shapes." And the "marvellous" shapeshifting power of icebergs powerfully amazes the viewer as well. The mutability of the ice island is part of its splendor, and its mystery demands a type of love, a profoundly secular love for and with the physical world. Ellis's sketches are acts of shared life overtly denied. The stolid and monolithic form of the fourth sketch illustrates his apparent rejection. Yet he must go to the iceberg to know his opponent. Ellis performs an icy *ingesis*; his artistic interpretation of the iceberg leads him into, not out of, its cavernous domain. It is in the third sketch—when "approaching right against it"—that the iceberg opens to him. The caption describes a moment of proximity, perhaps even of touch: to feel right *against* something and not simply *against* it antagonistically. Crucially, Ellis "against" the iceberg narrates the physical mingling of human and nonhuman. Perhaps he felt something shockingly familiar when "against" the ice. Or maybe, like a passionate creature, the ice yearned for his embrace. Ellis anthropomorphizes the iceberg as if making its acquaintance: the ice is not always a creature, an "it," but is gendered as a male "him" as well. His encounter witnesses the moment where glaciality meets "faciality." Deleuze and Guattari interpret Perceval's red blood dripping on white snow—in Chrétien de Troyes's twelfth-century CE tale of the same name—as a razing of the "face-landscape," "facing" constituting an act of territorialization. The knight's numbing amnesia signals the effacement of subjectivity: "Find your black holes and white walls, know them, know your faces; it is the only way you will be able to dismantle them and draw your lines of flight."[74] The Arctic landscape affords Ellis just that opportunity as it did the wobbly Perceval: what the pago-logy of the page, the black ("hollow") holes of the illustration, does for us. What Ellis faces are mixtures: not mirrorlike reflections of himself in the ice-glass, but the shaky slide of deterritorialization, the unconscious incognita where the face of self e-scapes, where im/personal pronouns are lost in im/permafrost.[75] Yet by "passing alongest by him," Ellis passes on a chance to go fully glacial with the multifaceted iceberg, to realize the pleasurable potential of two beings in mixture rather than ontological players on polarized sides. The opportunity dissolves. The ice closes in the fourth sketch. His report is finished. Ellis leaves, "departing from it," forever.

We could take pause in this passage, listen to its ("his") glisten: returning to Ellis's opening poem, he surely doubted the "value" of the English enterprise at these unbelievably cold moments. But the crew's icy errancy holds much more "value" in "store" for us than we first imagined. If we revisit "Iasons" path, different "waye[s]" of non/human composition appear. Ellis takes the invitation to visit-compose into new territory. Although at times he desires distance from ice, both spatially and ontologically, his "marvellous" illustrations in fact illustrate the compositional abilities of living ice. The *Report* reports a true pagographical text. Ellis is not escaping ice through his art as much as he is *-scaped* by ice and, furthermore, pens with it, like an ice-etching that escapes the thaw and travels across time, off the "Charde." Ellis's multivalent "against" models the prepositions any writer may take with ecomaterial. There cannot be "true proportion," just endless perspectives, horizons, and positions, "sundrie figures" remaking "diverse shapes." Composition's greatest contribution is the promise of the *com-*: the ability to truly live with this life. Visiting ice islands—composing with them, through them—is the lesson lost on Ellis but not on us. We can revisit the desires in and of the icescape: pagophilia can be a peacemaker, an act of love, turning "passing alongest" into the passing through, the para- of "alongside" (of many sides); tracing how the ice world composes us; writing back; wondering how many other permutations and perspectives await, for us and for other shapes, for the love of ice.

The Ice Age Is Never Over

Ellis's island returns us to the meshwork of connections that icescapes are: shifting archipelagos of slips, flips, and slides into unknown mixtures, of going glacial. Once we understand ice as a lively composer, as I have argued, and not just some passive *pagi* waiting to be written about, the icescape cracks open, and more irenic ways of composure with and within a cold world emerge. In its very existence, Ellis's *Report*—all three narratives, and yes, even my own passages in which you find yourself this instant—demonstrate how ice de- and recomposes as it visits us and as we visit the icescape. In its plurality of Arctic actants, ice in the early modern English imagination "shew[s]" ecocompositionism at work; like this work that is its relations, its bodies are never at rest, never wholly finished. And somehow, though urgently, we need to remain composed in the face of this polar plentitude of prospects. Apocalyptic meltdowns and ice monsters are possible, but so is the potential for peaceful compromise. Similarly, abandoned mines, Inuit abduction, and territorializing Jasons are only several prospects within a multitude of trajectories; we can reconceive the icescape just like any other. At a time in which we are told that ice ages have been lost or have passed, the key is to keep moving, however slowly, *forward* while going back and forth in time. The past, never frozen in time, confronts us; let us face it because we must. The Ice Age is not over, and never can be, for it is a cacophonic calving of ice ages with which we interact. Even now, glaciologists question whether or not we have passed the end of the last Ice Age. The accepted view is that the most recent Ice Age, the Pleistocene Epoch, began 1–1.5 million years ago and ended 10–11 thousand years ago, giving way to the Holocene Epoch we live in today, this warm heaven some call the Anthropocene. Another opinion is that we may be in what is called an "interglacial interval" instead: the warmth between glacial phases. The *inter-* of the interglacial is significant; the ambiguity of our place in the linear chronology of glacial time is relative to being in the middle, or going glacial, with the flows and assemblages of the ecomaterial world: enter, "glacer." The interglacial is as much an untimely as a timely place to be in. Glaciers are natural storehouses of history; yet as time congeals into discrete chronological units, the ice stultifies. But the cores refuse by fusing multiple times; their "loss" not merely the loss of date but of legibility. Almost every Arctic explorer notes the bizarre elongation of day and night in the Arctic. Time moved, but just not in typical chronological progressions, offering midnight suns and day-long nights. Arctic temporalities bend normative lines of time; as Davis wrote, "their night is equall with twenty five weekes and three days such as we have, so that our whole yeere is with them but one night and one day, a wonderfull difference" (223). Being disoriented by time in the ice-scape reveals glacial layers of times as well as geographies. Arctic time queers that grand march of progress toward a pronounceable end via its endless days and nights. *Inter-* in time and space is the crispness of per-colation. Those sailors who were intimidated by the onslaught of icebergs around them inconceivably latched on to see where the ice would take them: forward, backward, sideways; they were polar time-travelers, and their ice ages are ours.

I propose in this co/l/da a shift from civilization's chronological march of *progress* to an interglacial *process* instead: a call to harness the temporal slipperiness of prospects (futures), if you will, as it arrives in a present that starts to melt as soon as it begins and in a place that is currently melt-ing; a move from Ice Age/s lost and found to the never-left. Sensing the world's living ice could not be timelier for us in a world in which glacial "retreat" has become a byword for disaster and drifting icebergs venture increasingly farther out to sea. The coldest war imaginable threatens to annihilate our warming world. Ice forces us to confront the "after" but also the "before" of this cataclysmic event. Without an organizing, holistic concept at the core—nature, culture, time, the human—one option is to recompose. To be with ice is to go glacial, go somewhere, visit elsewhere, but always compose together; it is a process that brings chilling catastro-phes alongside Arctic dreams. Nightmares will come: in Fenton's descrip-tion of a frigid English dreamscape, Captain Courtney dreams of his own drowning, "and so troubled therewith in his sleepe, that he cried with such lowdnes, Iesus have mercie upon me."[76] Similarly, Best narrates a vision that eerily transpires in waking. On the return journey of the sec-ond voyage, the boatswain and master of the *Gabriel* are swept overboard:

> Thys mayster . . . William Smyth . . . who beeing all the morning before exceeding pleasaunte, tolde hys captayne hee dreamed that he was cast overboorde, and that the boateson hadde hym by the hande, and could

not save hym, and so immediately uppon the ende of hys tale, hys dreame came right evelly to passe. (153–54)

Both of these dreams reinforce the dangers of the "eve[ll]" icescape. Ice penetrates the English mind in disastrous ways. Courtney fortunately survives; Smith's country of the mind in fact swallows him. The sinking feeling imagined here is not a desirable place of transformation, but a chilling ice tomb. While we cannot avoid the night terrors of Courtney and Smith, we cannot diminish Davis's world-change, or Ellis's labyrinth of feeling, either: the Arctic will always produce sensational dreams of creation in addition to destruction. The touch of cold life sponsors new ways of observing cryospheric connections between skin, heart, and mind; of composing, and living, well; of touching passages between C/c/reatures, like the one most associated with ice in the English imagination, a Romantic with touches of the early modern, Mary Shelley's "daemon": "And do you dream?" said he to Captain Walton before plunging into the Arctic night. We are told that "one vast hand was extended," certainly cold, moments before.[77]

Do we? Call me a dreamer, just keep dreaming; do not give up the search for passages, just *the* passage. Baffin's personal example (for whom the island was named) is instructive. In a letter to John Wolstenhome— one of the chief members of the Company of Merchants of London, Discoverers of the North-West Passage (formed 1612)—he announces that there is no passage north of Davis Strait: "Wherefore I cannot but much admire the worke of the Almightie, when I consider how vaine the best and chiefest hopes of men are in thinges vncertaine; and to speake of no other then the hopeful passage to the North-West."[78] Uncertainty may be humbling rather than defeating; it may rouse intimacy instead of jealousy. Henry Briggs (1561–1630), a lesser-known searcher, complained about maps' inaccuracies on account of these sailors' unfettered imaginations: "But how often are the usuall Charts reiected by experience in those Nauigations . . . recorded? Painters and Poets are not always the best Oracles."[79] I hope to have shown in this chapter that they are, for they point us to the tasks ahead: to find new labyrinths, to shiver with pleasure and pain, to embrace the cold even as things warm up (and they will). Foxe had likened authorship to working in a "Laborinth," his "pen and

selfe . . . growne weary";[80] let us remain, here, in the labyrinthine laboratory of collaboration. Since imagination tends to be the keyword that
links Arcticological studies, let us compose an imaginarium; let us reimagine ice as action with agency, with its own desires, even with dreams;
let us enter into new relationships with the cryosphere, face the multivalent "glace," extend hands of vastness. When we rethaw the ice and enter
the depths that we can only plumb but never fully understand, we might
predict what we will find, but we can find and face differently. When
we do not automatically curl up in the cold—when we feel our "withs,"
our coimplications with frosty stuff—the encounters at the northern end
of the world do not mark the end of *the* world but dream the end of *a*
world that is rife with ontological divides and epistemological hostilities.
"Dream" comes from the Old English word *drēam* ("joy, music"), and I
wonder what joys may ring. So here is my dream: not to live in a world
without ice, but one with it, one that tells the once and future stories
of Ice Ages, and that dreams on. Early modern travel writers prove that
both fears and joys may be found on the white horizon, that what was
supposedly the most inimical landscape can be the most enticing, that
their hyperbolic words bear the mark of the hyperboreal. We are, in the
end, right back in the vortical Arktikós with which I opened: the vibrant,
living world of the bear; Bear Sound's stormy sense-bodies enveloped in
sound; pellucid northwest passages. Ice says what we, as passengers, have
known all along but have recently forgotten. The Ice Age is never over:
glaciality is our reality, and one full of potential.

When that I was and a little tiny boy,
  With hey, ho, the wind and the rain,
A foolish thing was but a toy,
  For the rain it raineth every day.

But when I came to man's estate,
  With hey, ho, the wind and the rain,
'Gainst knaves and thieves men shut their gate,
  For the rain it raineth every day.

But when I came, alas, to wive,
  With hey, ho, the wind and the rain,
By swaggering could I never thrive,
  For the rain it raineth every day.

But when I came unto my beds,
  With hey, ho, the wind and the rain,
With tosspots still had drunken heads,
  For the rain it raineth every day.

A great while ago the world begun,
  With hey, ho, the wind and the rain,
But that's all one, our play is done,
  And we'll strive to please you every day.

—Twelfth Night, 5.1.376–95

CHAPTER 3

Making (It) Rain

Does life only make sense as one side of a life-matter binary, or is there such a thing as . . . a life of the it in "it rains"?

—Jane Bennett, *Vibrant Matter*

To *see* it rain is better then to be in it.

—John Ray, *A Collection of English Proverbs* (1678)

As I write this paragraph in early June 2015, a 113–16 degree Fahrenheit heat wave is dehydrating India. Nearly 2,500 people have died over the past two months, particularly in the southern states of Andhra Pradesh and Telangana. Many would wish to not only "*see* it" rain, but also to be "in it."[1] The annual southwest monsoon that supplies water for agriculture and relief from the heat is late this year: June 1 is the typical day when the rain makes landfall in the southeastern part of the subcontinent. But today, June 5, the monsoon finally reached Thiruvananthapuram, Kerala, and will begin to make its way northwest, reaching the capital of New Delhi later in the month. While this year is not too far behind schedule, hotter conditions driven by climate change and El Niño's interference with ocean currents—which brings less rain to Asian countries—have led many to worry that India's rains will be modest for a second year in a row, bringing drought once more and stymieing Prime Minister Narendra Modi's intended revitalization of national industry. Weak rains weaken the gross domestic product by decreasing demand for exports; at home, poor crop yields mean agricultural inflation, raising the cost of food for the citizens of one of the world's fastest growing economies.[2] The Indian Meteorological Department (IMD) predicts that this year's monsoon will shed less than 90 percent of the fifty-year period average, which is set close to 90 cm. Across the world in West Virginia, it is earlier in the day. My National

Weather Service forecast says that thunderstorms are likely tonight (60 percent or so). Outside my office window, I can see a dark cloud coming over the hill, as if rolling down into the Monongahela River. The air is still; it is not raining. Weather is sometimes about waiting, being in the pause before bearing witness to the flash of the flood; at other times, it is watching for rain that never comes, wishing *yes*, here: *no*, not there. It is rain that retains the *yet* of becoming-wet.

Rain Song

To find the wet entrance in William Shakespeare's play *Twelfth Night*, you must look elsewhere than the ocean's waves. For someone just shipwrecked off the coast of Illyria, the beachcomber Viola defies stage conventions and does not enter wet at her introduction in act 1, scene 2. Instead, the fool Feste's song, sung solo at play's end, provides, repeatedly, "the wind and the rain" (5.1.377) for which we have been waiting. In her famous essay on Shakespeare's "sense of an ending," Anne Barton states that "in the final act . . . a world of revelry, of comic festivity, fights a kind of desperate rearguard action against the cold light of day."[3] Her reading examines the forces of holiday and reality, fiction and fact, at odds in the play; these intransigent worlds, she believes, require the exclusion of certain characters, ill-willed Malvolio most notably, in order to maintain their contradistinction. Like the characters within the play, the audience members, too, must unavoidably leave the world of present mirth (the playhouse) in the past and return to the "normality" of their actual lives when it is over. The consequence of Barton's reading is to reinforce a "cold" sense of in- and exclusion and of semipermissible border crossings permitted, for a limited time only, between sides, despite Feste's energetic mediation between these supposedly opposed worlds. Barton is sympathetic; while the play reminds us that we have to go back to the "light" of reason, at least "the song [Feste sings] . . . is curiously consoling" and eases audiences into an acceptance that, in the "end," "the reality of wind rain wins out, the monotony of the everyday."[4] A sad song made even sadder: it is impossible not to feel depressed by its damp.

Reading the rain in this de/moralizing way, however, risks overlooking *Twelfth Night*'s ecological context, one that helps illustrate the collaboration between, not separation of, artistic and environmental skies. Audiences would have known the "cold light of day," indeed, not only due to the play's association with winter—Twelfth Night is January 6, the culminating night of Christmas revels, a wet day in the city still—but also because plays were performed, at least at the Globe, during the day in an intemperate climate like London's. According to the website of the rebuilt Globe, patrons are prohibited from unfolding their umbrellas during performances; the show will go on in sunshine, rain, or both at once: "Those standing in the yard are at the mercy of the elements."[5] The climate could be "cold" in another sense of being stiff, standoffishly "real"; recall John Stow's report that on Whitsunday 1599 (late spring), excessive rainfall produced a flood that surged toward the theater's construction site in Southwark; the building materials and the Lord Chamberlain's Men—the foundations of the great Globe itself—almost dissolved in the deluge. Feste's song must have certainly registered with Londoners who experienced periodic floods. Over the next thirty years, almost the entire lifespan of the Globe, dams and drainages along the Thames routinely failed. A sense of ending, then, might be one of resignation for those in- and outside the play facing harsh weather; and yet, the circumstances of 1599 suggest rain's potential to be both aesthetically pleasing and painfully sobering: the streets were made "more fresh and faire," the theater opened later that year, and the "extreame violence of this Tempest" Stow recorded is that same stuff that allowed a song of vicissitude—"With hey, ho, the wind and the rain" (5.1.377)—to be sung on an open-air site exposed to the elements' "mercy" two years, and four hundred years, later.[6] The song is "curiously consoling" not because it teaches us how to defer to the tediousness of the everyday—"All holidays come to an end; all revels wind down at last"[7]—but because it proves that the physical sensation of rain sponsors prolific festivity as well as catastrophic foreclosure: a temporary harmony of human and nonhuman joinings, not merely monotony; windings up as much as down; a sense of watery materiality that promotes openings in addition to "ends" each and every day. Feste's song reflects *Twelfth Night*'s environmental embeddedness, and in doing so, it invites us to see how rain allowed Shakespeare to explore the complex relationships between climate and culture, human and nonhuman, water and imagination.

What listeners typically perceive in the strains of Feste's melancholic song are the universal pangs of maturation, hearing a timeless tale of rain set against the lone and lonely human. Rain represents the inflexibilities of life and the inhospitalities of the world that push back. Wind and rain incessantly batter the "I" of "When that I was" (5.1.376), resulting in a strengthening of the I's protection rather than in a washing away of its autonomy, an encounter different from what we witnessed previously with the anonymous Thames watermen in 1641. It is fitting that rain is the most repetitive part of the song, then: "With hey, ho, the wind and the rain" appears four times in twenty short lines. To make this pitter-patter worse, Feste usually sings alone in performance. The rain falls only to promote the alienation he deplores. Its special ability to touch him only makes him feel isolated in its showers, like a soggy individual "I" singled out for assault. He must suffer the sleets of outrageous fortune. Thus rain supports Barton's summation of Feste as a simultaneous insider and outsider, a necessary carnivalesque energy who must, nevertheless, be "shut" from the "gate" and pushed to the margins (5.1.382). Shakespearean characters who stay in the rain are typically fools. The Fool in *King Lear* adapts Feste's speech, reiterating it to Lear who becomes a fool in a rainstorm:

> He that has and a little tiny wit—
> With hey, ho, the wind and the rain—
> Must make content with his fortunes fit,
> Though the rain it raineth every day. (3.2.72–75)

Just as his more tragic counterpart, however, Feste clarifies something that is often unrecognized, or rather, purposefully ignored. Rendering rain as the epitomic image of melancholy is an anthropocentric gesture, for it forces rain to convey exclusively human psychology and emotion; in Lear's case, especially so: as pathological madness, the famous "tempest in my mind" (3.4.13); the darker chance of being "minded like the weather" (3.1.2) by virtue of "[c]ontending with the fretful elements" (3.1.4); a battle against rain that "[i]nvades us to the skin" (3.4.8), whose outcome determines whether one keeps their wits dry or else suffers the dissolution of insanity; or, worse yet, a thought that rain might dig deeper, attacking the idea of humanness—with all the trappings of sovereignty—itself.

But confusion is what fools do best; they "mingle together": "Then shall the realm of Albion / Come to great confusion" (*King Lear*, 3.2.89–90). And so shall Illyria: from his earliest entrance, Feste proves to be an emphatic figure of elemental embodiment. His melancholy is important less for its psychoanalytic dimensions, actually, and more for the geohumoral insights into his song it provides. As a "melancholic," Feste would be literally de/pressed by barometric pressure, pushed down and closer to earth by the denser air, a body physiologically full of black bile and exhibiting cold and dry qualities. Yet we know his song is wetter than that; he correspondingly takes on a more phlegmatic attitude, a condition associated with the element of water and its qualities of cold and moist, the season of winter appropriate for early January, and the organ of the brain. Feste's first entrance, in fact, displays him readying his wet wit, the brain, for an attempt to prove his mistress Olivia a fool: "Wit, an't be thy will, put me into good fooling!" (*Twelfth Night*, 1.5.28). His intelligent wordplay is met with Olivia's curt enjoinder, "Go to, you're a dry fool" (1.5.35). Fools, it seems, should not be "dry" in her implied sense of "dull" and "thirsty." This predicament is easily solved: "give the dry fool drink, then is the fool not dry," he replies, "Anything / that's mended is but patched" (1.5.38, 40–41). Feste, with more water on the brain than Olivia will credit, chooses an appropriately slippery word; wet wits like him patently deal in "[m]isprision" in the highest degree" (1.5.48). "Mend" comes from the Latin *emendare* (*e-*, "out of" and *menda*, "a fault"). While the Illyrians amend in terms of correction, believing they may fix their faults, Feste mends altogether differently, through "drink." He confuses the dry (the language of stitching, the "patched") with the wet (language itself), weaving both into a moist mixture, a knotted network of the various, the particolored, an accretion that can only be described as the fool's motley: "I wear . . . motley in my brain" (1.5.49–50). Feste has us again, this time by the "mote": defining a tiny piece of something, "mote" derives from Dutch *mot* ("dust, sawdust"). In body, words, and now his costume, Feste teaches how water is the tie that loosens and binds. "Doth he not / mend?" asks Olivia (1.5.63–64) in exasperation. "Yes," answers Malvolio, who too will learn a lesson in being motley, "and shall do till the pangs of death shake him" (1.5.65).

For a play that invokes "element" often—five times, the most in Shakespeare's entire oeuvre—embodiment is properly construed as outright elemental: "Does not our life / consist of the four elements?" Sir Toby Belch, a windy figure, blurts (2.3.8–9). The word is used so often that Feste himself is able to jest with Viola: "Who you are and what you / would are out of my welkin—I might say 'element,' but the / word is over-worn" (3.1.50–52). Here "element" means moist air (Belch's exhalation) and the sky ("welkin"). But no one classical element can be separated from the others, of course, and Feste's eventual declaration that he is "for all waters" (4.2.56) only accentuates water's role in the play's "over-worn" elementalism. Feste's watery mediation extends to all other characters as well; their "lives" consist of water-bodies undergoing motley's multitude. In this sense, Olivia truly acts the fool for thinking that dry bodies exist; she herself has been watery, Valentine tells us, for quite some time, "water-[ing] once a day her chamber round / With eye-offending brine" (1.1.28– 29). Dry thoughts are not only routinely undermined but also exposed to laughter. When Malvolio chastises his aqueous oppressors Toby, Fabian, and Maria, believing his sobriety to be a mark of distinction from them— "You are . . . shallow things, / I am not of your element" (3.4.111–12)— he uses "element" as shorthand for "kind" but also for the element of water that constitutes their ale, that is their bodies, and that fuels their merry-making. Malvolio's parched piety is what leads him to "a dark room" where he is "bound" and tortured by protean shape-shifting (3.4.121). Feste disguises himself as Sir Topas, then transforms back into Feste: this is deep, not "shallow" subterfuge. Malvolio's treatment exposes how madness is defined in the play: not as the inability to tell trickery from truth, wet rhyme from dry reason, but as the refusal to recognize water's elemental powers of dissolution. Sebastian, from the sea, usefully puts this dilemma in watery terms: "Are all the people mad? . . . What relish is in this? How runs the stream? / Or I am mad, or else this is a dream" (4.1.24, 56–57). In short, trying to mend the bends of madefaction ("the action of making something wet or moist") is true madness. The jester ultimately gestures to running with the "stream" even though the destination is unknown; running against the current proves foolish, possibly damaging—in Malvolio's unfortunate case—even as the "for" of being elemental is uncertain.

With this elemental excursion in mind, I now wish to think about how rain is (on) the brain in Feste's saturated stanzas, the words driving like wet motes. His rain song is definitely in tune with the juxtaposition of romance and mortality in the play. This is the same fool, after all, who sings earlier, "Present mirth hath present laughter. / What's to come is still unsure. / In delay there lies no plenty" (2.3.46–48). In a play that leaves little we can be "sure" of at its end—Malvolio's vengeful vow, for one—Feste chooses the "plenty" of the present moment for us. But by his closing tune, "[w]hat's to come" is surely rain, and "plenty" of it. Rain keeps spilling over. And so does his body. Feste's "drunken hea[d]" in the fourth stanza describes him becoming liquid: in his drunkenness, he resembles a human "tosspo[t]" or brimming vessel (5.1.390). Like his song, Feste's body is attuned to the effects of rain: "I *am* for all waters." Some slight reordering lets slip the line's ontological profundity: I am waters. Feste's "laughter" is not so fleeting, not so dry; "[w]ith the hey and the ho" insinuates that things happen with weather, not despite or without it: this is weather really "with" you. Rebecca Totaro has tracked the "sublunary exhalations" in Shakespeare—treating emissions like sighs and curses as "the very meteors of the body"[8]—and it is worth noting that speaking onstage would create wet and moist air with every breath (not just belch) the actor takes. Phonetically, "h" is an aspirational consonant as well, meaning that words like "hey" and "ho" are pronounced with the exhalation of breath. (An appropriate classification, it seems, for a class-conscious play about social aspirations.) Pushing breath out literally speaks the body's weather. Similarly, Feste's "for" in the phrase "[f]or the rain it raineth" expresses both support and affect (5.1.379): things happen or they do not "for," or because, the rain rains. Rain allows him to "thrive" just as it thrives (5.1.386). The use of prepositions here is telling; rain is the ultimate catalyst, propelling Feste to endless prepositions and moments "when I came" (5.1.384). Although stymied in spots, he still comes and goes, again and again, through the world and with the rain.

The clearest example of thriving with the rain is the song itself, born from Feste's embodied experiences of being (in) it since he "was and a little tiny boy" (5.1.376). Just as rain drives him from station to station in life, the song moves from stage to stage, allowing audiences—who might be in the rain, depending on the theater—to contemplate how waters make "our play" (5.1.394), whether the wet Whitsunday of 1599 or the weather at the moment. As he enters and exits singing his rainy song, Feste makes connections between actor and audience that bring them into his rainy world. While there are no wet entrances written for characters in *Twelfth Night*, and no stage directions call for rain, there are explicitly rainy entrances in contemporary plays: "*It snowes, and raines, thunders*" in Thomas Drue's (ca. 1586–1627) *Duchess of Suffolk* (1631), and both Thomas Heywood's (ca. 1573–1641) *The Brazen Age* (1613) and Thomas Dekker's (ca. 1572–1632) *If This Be Not a Good Play, the Devil Is in It* (1611), staged at the Red Bull, call for rain.[9] The forlorn and future queen Elizabeth deictically describes her rainy imprisonment in Heywood's *If You Know Not Me You Know Nobody* (1604–5): "The piteous heauens weepe teares into my bosom / On this cold stone I sit, raine in my face."[10] Rain in your face: early modern in- and outdoor theatrical wetspaces rephrase Hamlet's request to "hear a play" (2.2.513) as hearing (in) the rain. Matter is not precipitated out of the dramatic medium but co-constitutes it. As Tim Ingold bemoans, "materiality is identified with everything that has . . . precipitated out from the medium, with the result that the medium itself is rendered immaterial."[11] Instead, he argues, rainwater evinces a "weather-world" that binds medium and substances, in which participation is a condition for perception and objects are abolished: "the weather is not so much an *object* of perception as what we perceive *in*, underwriting our very capacities to see, to hear and to touch."[12] The "wind and the rain" become underwriters, phenomenological participants that help sense the watery "I" in undulating interface. It is not far-fetched to imagine Feste singing *about* rain while *in* it as it falls *upon* a wet stage. Like John Heywood's (ca. 1497 – ca. 1580) *The Play of the Weather* (1533), written during a flood year, Shakespeare surely felt some of the prodigious rain of 1599 as he composed his play. The result is a lucrative actors' network that will be performed "every day" (5.1.379), a kind of positive feedback loop that builds profits exponentially as it falls upon the audience's ears "when" they come to the theater, making it rain—so the company hopes—liquid capital. Feste's song is economically motivated, but it is also, and perhaps more importantly, a rainy act of compositionism that reassembles the stage of culture and the matter of nature, revealing an ecopoetical relationship that resists pitting precipitable matter and media in isolation, or piling them into an undifferentiated "all one" (5.1.394).

For Feste, being caught in this "thriving" daily rain is a pleasurable thing; his "for" is an inclination toward rain that is not necessarily "for" financial gain. Interestingly, the word we most expect to rhyme with rain, "pain," is never mentioned. And although weather is notoriously un-predictable, rain is paradoxically the most stable part of the song. The second and fourth lines of each stanza repeat until the final stanza. Con-spicuously, "For the rain it raineth every day" (5.1.379)—probably the most melancholic line of the song—disappears in the last stanza when it is replaced by "And we'll strive to please you every day" (5.1.395). This surprising substitution of "rain" with "please" performs a metonymical exchange rather than a literal erasure. Feste suggests to the audience, and to us, that rain and pleasure are physically connected. His song truly is soaked in pleasure. The "thriv[ing]" of sexual pleasure he mentions in the third stanza resembles the procreative type of "thriving" sanctioned by matrimony. Too frivolous to "wive," and "bed[ding]" only when drunk, he does not bear children but performances of *Twelfth Night* instead (5.1.384, 388). The pleasure truly is in the performance; because "we'll strive to please," the players bring forth a play every day. Feste stays in his rainy role, birthing a play while simultaneously begetting future perfor-mances. "[B]eds" and the "world begun" (5.1.392) possibly allude to the classical analogy between rain and fertility, a metaphor that stretches as far back to the meeting of Heaven (male Uranus) and Earth (female Gaia) in Hesiod's ca. seventh-century BCE poem *Theogeny*. Despite this persis-tent, mythological, and hypermasculine equation of rain with insemina-tion, Feste's pleasure has a queerness to it that problematizes rain's inherent gendering and indelible mark of fertility. While the language of "done" (5.1.394) and finishing invokes sex, it need not be androcentric, espe-cially for a transvestite theater and in a cross-dressed play like this one that repeatedly challenges gendered essentialism (Viola-Cesario is a "poor monster," 2.2.32). Neither must the desire be heteronormative, divulging instead an in/organic coupling with a molecular compound like rain that moves from biological determination of sex to a determination simply to be with nonhuman *bios*. Feste's inability therefore to dry off is an im-portant point I think we miss; rain prevents him and the play from ever finishing since it prevents the consummation of his "thriv[ing]" (and just as crucially, he never achieves "wiv[ing]"). In other words, if rain keeps driving Feste onward and elsewhere, his song will never really be "done" even as he exits, wet; like his rainwater body that never finishes or reaches completion, a craving without surfeit and thus deliberately opposed to

Orsino's opening tune of the play and his pleas for an "excess of" music so that "[t]he appetite may sicken and so die" (1.1.2–3), Feste's open-ended number keeps the "thrive" alive. His strain "swagger[s]" on (5.1.386), the play continues to "thrive," and the pleasure behind one of the play's most famous lines is preserved: "For the rain it raineth every day."

The play's subtitle, *What You Will*, reflects the watery enjoyment that subtends it: "I shall have more of this happy wreck," Orsino gleefully vows (5.1.259). "What you will" is the pleasure you *will have* and that you *will* for yourself; in this light, the "you" of the song's last line ("please you") comes into contact with the "I" with which it begins. The song, as I have suggested, should not be read solely as an expression of the individual's separation from society, but at the same time, it certainly communicates the discomfort of those suffering from a sense of alienation, those unhappy "wrecks" whom Orsino overlooks. Rain could be associated with physical gold across the world (not just in the hands of the acting company's share-holders) and the enslavement necessary to retrieve it;[13] patriarchy's fear of a dangerous, because feminine, liquidity that threatens to dissolve the stolid male body;[14] and the risk of rape: Thomas Heywood's *The Golden Age* (1611) tells the story of Jupiter impregnating Danae as a golden shower. More specific to the song, being turned from "man's estate" and/ or tackling the complications that the "estate" of adulthood incurs are definite matters of concern. Feste gives voice to his era's preoccupation with increasing "vagrancy," what Patricia Fumerton calls "unsettled subjec-tivity":[15] the lot of many mobile, itinerant workers who were susceptible to placelessness and infrequently housed. To Fumerton's list of "unsettled" today we should add the world's rising number of environmental refugees, predicted to reach fifty million by 2020, many of them washed away by worsening storms or intentionally drowned (out) by corporate dams; we must raise questions of disability, those unable to move for reasons ranging from the socioeconomic to the toxicological; we are compelled to ask how and why human and nonhuman beings and their desires for dis/location are rendered im/mobile, forgotten, or expendable.[16] The "you" of the song in both second person singular and plural asks us to confront the stigmas that the early modern audience had (and we have) to notions of "vaga-bondage" in its strictest sense: those who "wander," those against whom morality is too easy to cite, as if John Taylor's (1621) "right . . . perpetuall motion" of the beggars' life becomes the fault of their own (unknown) perpetration.[17] This song, in sum, exposes the violence of rain in all of its vectors,[18] aligning the pour with the poor and interrogating any "all" in "all one" that would save *some* beings, for instance, from the territorializing "estate" of enclosure. But rather than settling or even diminishing these disputes, Feste strikingly points up our difficult world in ceaseless transition. His "anti-house behavior" of becoming with the rain helps challenge domestic fixity—the socially stratified household of labor— as well as the limits of the hierarchical household (*oikos*) dominated by an outmoded humanism that still sifts subjects from objects in the rain; he urges us to rethink and perhaps remake thriving spaces of community that account "for the rain" and "for" as many lives as possible.[19] The feelings of loss and nostalgia that permeate his song point to the problem of *not* being able to feel the rain, or anyone or anything, at all. Feste grieves the thought of the body cut off from the "heys" and "hos" of the rainy natural world, in perpetuity.

And thus the early modern "day" gets caught in "the whirligig of time[s]" (5.1.364) that swirls into our own "day." Their "day" is ours. Yet it is curious that despite water's refutation of temporal origins and singular causation, the play's first night has been fervently debated, fashioning *Twelfth Night* as a comedy about firsts. The first known staging was on February 2, 1602, because John Manningham, a law student at the Middle Temple—one of the Inns of Court, or law colleges, in London—wrote a pithy review of the play in his diary. To this rare example (for the time) of a recorded performance is added another origin story involving Don Virginio Orsini, Duke of Bracciano, who visited Queen Elizabeth's court on January 6, 1601, a coincidence that persuaded Leslie Hotson to spin a fabulous tale of the duke's mark upon the play, *The First Night of Twelfth Night* (1954). The search for firsts here betrays critics' desires for attributable sources and historical specificity. The song is surely invested in time; "[a] great while ago the world begun" (5.1.392) can be read linearly, especially as Feste progresses from station to station in life: a "boy," then part of "man's estate," and finally to "bed" (presumably, death). But the last stanza confuses temporalities: although the world "ago" (in the past) has led up to the play that is now done (the present), it will return to the stage as forthcoming performances (the future), thereby starting the cycle all over again. "Begun" and "done" look more like beginnings: each rendition of the "wind and the rain" guarantees repetition, but always as a version slightly different from the night before or after. Even the timeliness of the play's title is equivocal: it is specific only if read alongside the Christian liturgical calendar (twelve nights after Christmas), but if read more secularly, it suggests a performance twelve nights from an unspecified point of time. In other words, the rain comes another some/day, or *when* you *will* put on a play. Spurious connections like Orsini's visit are but nodes in the "whirligig" known as multitemporality, the eddy of rainy time, that unmoors calendric exactitude and promotes nonlinear loops of material exchange spearheaded by rain. It is not inconceivable to think of water that fell on Shakespeare's stage as still circulating today in unknown phase states. (Time scales for processes like evaporation and condensation vary widely from seconds to years.) Water "that's all one" slips through times, its untimelessness signaled by something as simple as a breath.[20] Just as the carnivalesque inverts social order, the time of the rains ushers in chronological misrule.

Rain might not fall all at once; on the subject of time, it imparts pauses and anticipation: a shivering sense of an approaching storm, the restless hours of not-quite rain when the world seems to prepare, and holds its shared breaths, for disasters that may or may not come "every day." I will conclude this section appropriately with the "for" of Feste's proclamation, for it wonders where and into what the "whirligig" world turns: indicating what we are getting wet "for" in terms of time and distance (measurable length) and in number of occurrences (succession), rains that barrage "for" multiple times without quieting. Rain has "swaggering" to it. England in the early seventeenth century was inundated by pamphlets detailing tempestuous events, a climatic predilection that would only grow throughout the century.[21] One report in particular is notable for its proximity to the time and season of the play: *The Wonders of This Windie Winter* from 1613.[22] The brief twenty pages relate what happens when the drama's "wind and the rain" take the dramatic turn of catastrophe (the denouement, "down turning," of Greek tragedy). The blasts for the past three months "every day and night affrighted us with fear," and the anonymous author enumerates a series of sorrowful relations and unfortunate events, some of them illustrated on the title page: dead bodies floating along the

The VVonders of this

windie winter.

*By terrible ftormes and tempefts, to the loffe of liues and goods of
many thoufands of men, women and children.*

The like by Sea and Land, hath not beene feene, nor heard of in
this age of the World.

LONDON.
Imprinted by *G. Eld*, for *John Wright*, and are to bee fold at his Shop neere
Chrift Church

The *Wonders of This Windie Winter* (London: G. Eld, 1613). Folger Shakespeare Library
Shelfmark STC 25949. Reprinted by permission of the Folger Shakespeare Library.

coast; "beasts" and human laborers blown out to sea, driven into fenny marshes, drowned under bridges, and crushed under toppling architecture. The picture raises without relief the underlying suspicion that "wel may we therfore (if we consider al these things arightly) call this the blacke fatall winter of mishaps." London is endangered yet again in 1613, just as it was in 1599 and will be forever after. The woodcut's "wonders" depict what might have been the play's "winter" and the playhouse's spring. Anthropomorphized wind and rain at opposing corners of the page, whose cheeky "surfeiting" faces and meteorological breaths belch water just as human bodies do, hang in comparison to the watery bodies drowned or sinking below. Yet this event at the same time exacerbates the Illyrians' and the company's discontent: the absence of onshore survivors insinuates that there is no becoming terrestrial or drying off; at first glance, the lack of devils (oftentimes present in other depictions) and religious signification prevents any attribution to demonic trickery or divine disorder. In fact, the destruction of a windmill (technology) and steeple (church) in the background empties the image of any security in either science or religion. Rain's slanted movement swerves buildings and the household—framed as an ecological focal point at center—demonstrating its forces of in- and declination, how its bends bend architectures. Naval debris and detached body parts of disproportionate size foreground how catastrophe and its expansive effects often appear out of scale, disorienting historically sanctioned ways of reading the skies. These pieces in general capture a word frequently used to describe rain, "unwholesome," usually meant to indicate its affiliation with disease (as we will see) but also, and more broadly, its refusal of wholes/wholeness, breaking and uprooting earth's fixity, shattering and sending out bodies at all angles. And by writing at the moment of inundation—at "this" time—the writer's eyewitnessing only adds to the windstorm's unprecedented reach: anyone out of the entire English population affected by it could give report, swelling the cries of those both within and without London. All together, the *Wonders* relates what it means to write with/in the submergence zone of rain: its whirling lines and thick ink betraying the gravity of dark, liquid times, "for" this winter and the next.

Further in the text, however, the pamphleteer resorts to religion to explain the cataclysm dealt upon sinning civic and rural English: in this case, the actual persona of Satan, a "most ugly shape," breaks into a church outside of Canterbury, "dasht the Ministers booke out of his hand," and causes the holy man's limb to break and blacken. Weather's terrors were frequently attributed to moral transgressions committed by those under heaven; Joshua Sylvester's (ca. 1563–1618) translation of Guillaume de Salluste Du Bartas's (1544–90) epic biblical poem starting from creation onward, *La Sepmaine* (1578) and *La Seconde Sepmaine* (1584–1603), published as the *Deuine Weekes* (1605), establishes a direct correlation between "blacke fatall . . . mishaps" of meteors and immorality: "When from the Clouds excessiue Water Spinnes, / Me thinks God weepes, for our vnwept-for sinnes."[23] Punishments "haue beene laied upon us for our sinnes," *Wonders*'s writer concludes, representing the "outward calamity to our inward griefes." Seeking reasons beyond divine causation or immaterial purpose proves to be morally charged as well, as when the writer condemns those who "accoun[t] [tempests] natural, common, and usuall, more like unto Atheists, then Christians, but, oh you temporizing naturallists except you repent, full vials of Gods wrath wil be powres downe upon your heads, and all your temporal purposes brought to nothing." To damn deliberation in this way is to commit double violence toward the rain and rainy day unbelievers. By not going over to the side of godly explanation, "temporizing" denotes delay but is also an attack against those who depart from teleo-theological lines to dwell on nonlinear temporalities, "the whirligig of time[s]" that make up the tempest of reality. Michel Serres notes how the French language, in its "wisdom," uses the same word for weather and time, *le temps*. Like time, "meteorological weather, predictable and unpredictable, will no doubt some day be explainable by complicated notions of fluctuations, strange attractors."[24] But inhabiting *le temps* does not mean that fears "for" what happens next suddenly disappear, or that pleasure in rainwater's spin is undetectable. Some came down to *Windie* Dover in 1613 to witness "strange battles, betwixt the wind and waters . . . waves like mountaines, danct in the skies, and the whole seas appeared like a fiery world." These few were attracted strangely to an elemental admixture where partners cannot be told apart, only shared, where drizzle dazzles. In this interstitial space known as the "wind and the rain" they might have thought intracatastrophically; embracing uncertainty, forecasting beyond the horizons of Christian argument; knowing that the "vials

of . . . wrath" were not the apocalyptic "nothing" the writer threatens, but
the material something—rain—of the cloudbursts in, around, and upon
them; imagining different stories than those a judgmental narrator would
place them in, alternate tales of what happens when it rains.

In Pluvia

If you have ever been "caught" in the rain, you, reader, have made such
an alliance. Or perhaps you gained a new position by running "out of"
it. Consider Jane Bennett's meditation on inorganic life: "Is there such
a thing as . . . a life of the it in 'it rains'?"[25] Here rain is not merely a
metaphor for life; it is lively, life defined in her own words as "a restless
activeness, a destructive-creative force-presence that does not coincide fully
with any specific body."[26] Rain materially represents "it": pure immanence, affect, a (liquid) life of things. Bennett's question identifies rain
as wet matter-movement that ceaselessly catalyzes new bodily forms. Rain
participates in her thought experiment, as it did in Shakespeare's. In a
single line—"for the rain it raineth"—Feste recognizes both the subject,
the "rain," and the impersonal affect, the "it." The impersonal is essential;
in her study of medieval rain and identity, Gillian Rudd personifies, that
is, anthropomorphizes, the rain by making it "personal": "we imbue rain
with something approaching intent while . . . denying it even the potential to be a self-realising system. . . . Rain, it emerges, is personal, it has
agency which may even suggest a personality, as it seems to delight in making us wet."[27] Rudd's insinuation that rain has "intent" and "delight[s]"
of its own leads to more speculative ways of thinking about rain as a
living element that is both impersonal and intimate at the same time.
Elsewhere in ecocriticism, however, the "it" is more problematic. According to Timothy Morton, the "it" or "there is" ironically upholds the
subject-object distance "it" supposedly collapses. The binary between in-
and outside remains.[28] This "outside" vibe is not the same impersonal
affect that Bennett discusses. The "intoxicating atmosphere of aura" is a
"vibe" that shakes the "I."[29] Writing about atmosphere still involves what
he calls a "re-mark": that which indicates mimesis and thus maintains the
inside-outside boundary. ("As I am writing this" and "it is raining," in
fact, are his examples.[30]) Each side of the binary is needed to define the
other. There is nothing we can do about it, and his point is precisely that
we should stay in the illusion of the in-between, something that "feels

like dualism," and love the thing as nonidentical to us.[31] The darkness of rain certainly supports his "melancholic ethics."[32] But to return to Bennett, the vibrating "I" is also a "vibrant" one that neither occludes its fragility nor marks its egocentricity. The "I" expresses its interdependence with in/organic stuff like atmospheric rain. Feste's "I" is shaken but nevertheless stirred into a vibrant climate-culture system. To have an agitated "I" is a form of humility that need not be reclaimed. It certainly appears that when *it* rains, it storms ecotheoretically; all this is to prove, I think, that the pluvial (from the Latin for "rain," *pluvia*) is good for ecological thought. Both critics have intimacy at stake and consider the force of the im/personal. The vital materialist track I take here configures coexistence with rain in relation, preferring a material monism in which rain is substantially shared instead of a dualistic approach that takes on the "darker" counterparts of irreducible difference to envision rain as essentially not-us.

If "it" feels like vulnerability, do not blame it: it should. Out of all the watery forms in this book, rain is arguably the most attentive to issues of exposure; rain captures and connects bodies at their most open and porous, and its piercing quality stresses the real violence of bodily penetrability. Rain's teardrop shape, bottom-heavy for bombardment, is capacious. (In actuality it looks more like a parachute.) While certainly melancholic, Feste's song is a meditation on how to "thrive" with the rain and what pleasures may come of it; likewise, the disastrous illustration of 1613 acknowledges the dangers of rainy weather while offering a glimpse beyond divinity and moral economy to one of spectatorship, even a desire to be drawn, not just drowned, in the glaze and blaze of rain. This chapter enters the "whirligig" of pluviality: as a literal "top," rain is far from being "[a] foolish thing was but a toy"; as a matter of fact, I argue, it would be foolish to discard it. It is our world, too, that spins like a top, although we are unable to forecast how much longer it will twirl and to where it will stray. In its Latinate form of *pluvia*, rain evinces the Lucretian dynamics of matter, void, and the *clinamen* (swerve) of crashing creation; admittedly, his first-century BCE poem *De Rerum Natura* bespeaks things' tendencies for inclination by negative example:

> Unless inclined to swerve, all things would fall
> Right through the deep abyss like drops of rain. There would be no

The manner of their sheltring themselvs from the Raine by the Tolipat leafe.

Robert Knox, *An Historical Relation of the Island Ceylon*, RB 139811, The Huntington Library, San Marino, California.

Collisions, and no atom would meet atom with a blow,
And Nature thus could not have fashioned anything, full stop.
 (2.220–23)[33]

But rain, like everything else, never falls straight down, and that is precisely the point of his analogy: rain realizes a universe in reinvention, for
the nature of matter is to be on the go—no stop—in spinning plurality.
    We should mind early modern weather exactly for this reason—we have
been told to come "in" when it rains[34]—for it signals that you are always
in a showering world of pluvial things that you cannot get "out of," and
yet one you can get many alliances "out of" still. As Cynthia Barnett
writes in her natural and cultural history of rain, "rain does not give up
its mysteries. . . . It is an opening to connect."[35] The question is what rain
does, and, just as importantly, how we react to and with what it brings
when "it raineth": whether to seek shelter from encounters—"by the Tolipat leaf" as Robert Knox (1641–1720) ingeniously displays in his 1681
description of Ceylon (Sri Lanka)[36]—or to trace its impacts; whether to
greet a "foolish thing['s]" material agency and (a) life, create a "thriv[ing]"
composition with rainy matter and the slipperiness of "when['s]" temporalities; whether to recognize within its onto-epistemological flux the
ethical, catastrophic, and gendered concerns all above-mentioned—the
"wreck" of floodwater, a "deliver[ance] to the world," like Viola's, "after
our ship did split" (*Twelfth Night*, 1.2.38, 8)—the juxtaposition of wet
births and deaths that is romance's hopeful hallmark. Through the writers
it touched and the texts it enabled, rain says that we are always-already
environmentally enmeshed—always in our element of water—and that
there is both distress and delight to be had with a showering world. Across
natural-cultural times and tales, rain, never still, relates this un/comfort-
able message clearly distilled: that exposure is our greatest risk and greatest potential at once. To listen to the rain is to hear the stories that rain
tells, literary "re-marks" that reflect the physical marks the rains made on
flesh and page, raindrops sprinkled on skin.
    My chapter has an inclination to it: to reconceive Stow's "fresh and
faire" 1599 rain as a wet thought experiment in the "extreame" for the
present day. I magnify early modern desires to be caught by the rain, that
tell what it feels like outside the emotional constraints of the pathetic

fallacy, and that forget the hydrological steps delineating rain's journey as recyclable stuff that "simply" floats through the atmosphere, percolates below ground, and "transpires" (evaporates) at sea.[37] By grasping rain's true transpiration, as a "happening," my wish is for the rains they witnessed to reconceive our own rainy relations in the present, helping us develop alternatives to technoscientific mastery—in longer irrigation canals, denser cloud seeding, or farther-reaching radar—and their promises for water-tight preparation from the next outburst or desiccation. When rain "brings in his revenges" (*Twelfth Night*, 5.1.364), it is typically situated around two sites: drought (too little) and flood (too much). The dilemma only worsens when a meteorological harmony between heaven and earth is assumed to have been lost: reservoirs are trusted to return balance in the former, storm barriers in the latter. But hard rains have fallen since the world "begun"; scientists affirm that four billion years ago rain finally fell during the Earth's Hadean Age, creating rivers, lakes, and oceans, hydrau-lically shaping the hot land.[38] The water world we live in today began with rain, and might end with it; forecasts will and do fail. By examining how rain washes away the nondivide between climate and culture in texts of the past, I believe we can develop an onto-ecological approach that builds on prevailing studies that track the conditions for how and why our knowledge of climate change is produced.[39] My hope is that "when" thinking about early modern rain, we imagine ecologies in which humans and nonhumans intersaturate, where the making of rain means a remaking of relations on Dover beaches. We are "for all waters" even if we do not know where we are going: true ombrophilia (Greek: "rain shower fond-ness") is learning how not to let go of a spinning world.

Whirl

Early modern weather writers are at an important junction historically to help redefine the hydrological cycle as a "whirligig" since the model was hotly debated at the time. Most natural philosophers, in their attempts to account for replenishing freshwater sources on land, alluded to the Aristotelian "alembic" idea that maintained that seawater rose up through the mountains to produce potable springs. In the mid-seventeenth century, poised between the mechanistic New Science and an Epicurean revival of vitalism, a desire emerged to deduce water's inner workings once and for all. As Yi-Fu Tuan's magisterial history of the water cycle shows, before the birth of the modern scientific discipline of hydrology, writers like John Ray (1627–1705)—who provides my epigraph above and whose *The Wisdom of God* (1691) supplies Tuan's title—commonly combined the two tracks of sacred and scientific in their pursuit of water's source. Ray's question concerning creation in *Wisdom* is instructive in this natural-theological way: "Where is the wisdom of the Creator in making so much useless sea, and so little dry land, which would have been far more beneficial and service-able to Mankind?"[40] Tuan's argument is that there was no sharp distinction between these two trains of thought; but the larger point worth noting here is that the water cycle is as much a God-given system as it is an invention wrought by the "ingenuity of the human mind," one, moreover, that is particularly prone to rendering the nonhuman environment into use-values, "service-able" or not.[41]

The variations of the cycle proposed by the era's argumentative protohydrologists are too numerous to list here, but it is correct to say that the publication of Pierre Perrault's *On the Origin of Springs* (1674)—in which he refuted the alembic theory after proving that rainwater was the cause of water's return to the ocean—brought about the so-called "death of water's social nature," as Jamie Linton laments: "Instead of allowing for the increasingly hybrid (socio-hydrological) nature of the circulation of water, the hydrologic cycle conditions an understanding that keeps water and people in separate, externally related spheres."[42] Caught up in these deliberations, early modern thinkers of rain could just as easily refuse to deploy the hydrological cycle with or without divine omnipotence, re-fashioning it as spiraling cycles of change rather than predictable (because set) circles of motion.[43] It is an important lesson to unlearn for us: doing so jettisons the circle's association with harmony, morality, and perfection. Circles still attest to our desires for sustainability and our beliefs in achievable, closed circuits. We have come to depend on rain, despite its surprises; we will need to know it as interdependability in future. The "whirl" of rain's "whirligig" comes from several Germanic languages: "turn around," "spindle," and "circle"; appropriately, "circle" (Old Norse *hvirfill*) shares the same base with "rotate." The water circle—the great spinning wheel of the sky—is more accurately an activity of undirected movement than a geometry of completion, loosening the homophonic but real reign of science over the rain. The material flow of rain is where the circumference of the circle meets the angle of the *clinamen*: "*turba* and *turbo*" as Serres sketches, "an incalculable population tossed by storms, by unrest, in vortical movement."[44] This is wisdom useful for us on the precipice of postsustainability, polychronically spur/t/r/ed on within early modern science's debate over the water cycle-circle. Here is precipitation that brings much-needed debate to scientific "discovery," liquefying its matters of fact, testing only the fallibility of tests, checking our own reasons to check rain gauges: true-blue hydro-theses.

If debating the cycle necessitates thinking postsustainably about the world's sloping—in- and declining—Feste's bodily weather, like Prospero's before him, seems made for our, and not just early moderns', concerns about strange weather, climate change, and living in the Anthropocene. Early modern dramatists and travel writers are participants within the non/human "socio-hydrological nature" of the rain cycle in this regard, less prescient of a hidden knowledge to be found later and more cognizant of its contingencies felt now, helping to destabilize the misleading search for "first" origins. Marjorie Hope Nicolson has traced late seventeenth-century poets' involvement in the "breaking of the circle"— the macro-, micro-, and geocosmic model of the body—around the same time that the cycle was rationally, and forcibly, separated into its natural (water) and cultural (people) components. But just as the embrace of the spiral need not be nostalgic, this unraveling of the "faithful" need not be sacred and should not be recuperated as such. What is collapsed is exactly the divine overlay; water's cycle and enfolding of the three -cosms promotes mystification, and unknowing, rather than mysticism.[45] Thus literature of and "for" a rainy day breaks not just a metaphysical circle but also *the* circle as concept altogether. Reading their works presents a unique situation, then; Shakespeare and the others introduced shortly are skeptical of any ordering of the rainy world and the resulting hierarchies. Rainy weather only unlocks the geographical unmooring inherent in the safety of "climate" as opposed to the mercuriality of "weather." (Shakespeare, recall, coined the word "climate" in another wintery context and tale.) "Climate" (from Greek *klima*) is a "slope, zone" on the map, but it is one that wavers; *klima* comes from *klinein* ("to slope"). As Steve Mentz points out in his postsustainable reading of *Lear*'s storm that "threatens 'to the skin,'" "neither receptive to nor reflective of human desires, this version of the elements re-draws the boundaries between self and world and puts the body-nature relationship in crisis."[46] Mentz importantly regards weather as one "agent" across a distributed "network," yet while the body is pervious, its permeability only goes so far: weather's violence may "restructure" the body–nature relationship, and it also redraws the body–nature boundary. Mentz's crisis announces a disequilibrium that checks our "hopes of sustainability or interdependence."[47] But I do not see the two as proximate as he; disregarding the former offers us an invitation to redefine the latter as intimacy, for ill—"declining," to be sure, also means "to perish"—and all else. *Twelfth Night* is utter unpredictability as well, a matter of what rain w/ills, but unlike the "hanged" fool of the high tragedy (5.3.304), its fool hung up in the rain presents a tragicomedy of unknown survival during strange weather and through cycles fast and slow.

It Raineth

Drama has accompanied us this far: I now pivot pluvially into this chapter's second half, turning to the stage's connections with global rains. Here we leave "the realm of Albion" but do not exit confusion: we enter performative wetspaces of unparalleled scope, the massive "whirligig[s]" of Indian monsoons. Drip for drip, the rest of this chapter falls thusly. (1) Early modern travel literature and its accompanying meteorological texts cohabit the "it" of living rain, exploring the strife and pleasures of absorptive interchange. (2) Rain "raineth" in that it precipitates nonhumans and humans out and through "gates" in the literal sense: it actively "throws" them "headlong" and "causes" events "to happen." Rainscapes are systems in cascade, and its interruptions are acts of creation; like their dramatic counterparts, whenever "it" rained, early modern author-travelers could theorize how ecologies are assembled: how things dis/charge to create random, wet affiliations that disrupt ontological binaries, disturb neat linearities of causation and chronology, and emphasize the aleatory nature of scientific methodology. (3) What makes these explorers exceptional, however, is their geographic location and the critical role it plays in the process: India's monsoons are prodigious events, the world's wettest phenomena, spectacular deluges considered both catastrophic and life giving. The state of Meghalaya is the rainiest place on earth. Hindi and Urdu in fact erase the "it" of English and French entirely. *Baarish hai* ("rain is") and *barsaat hai* ("monsoon is") signal (a) life of rain in their very syntax.[48] India is a contact zone on multiple levels—of East and West, human and nonhuman—and its monsoons challenged English visitors' ontological, epistemological, and temporal conventions, especially the "hydrological Orientalism" inherent in the northern temperate bias of the Western water cycle, driven as it is by a neo/colonial impulse to improve dry land.[49] The great rains continue to pose challenges to European and Indian alike (and more nations besides), applying pressure to how we know and interact with rainscapes that can no longer be considered localized experiences. Seventeenth-century passages to India—like Edward Terry's (1590–1660)—are superb stages on which to see "great confusion" play out, exposing and then battering Eurocentric biases toward India's unhealthy climate and parasitical rain. (4) In order to narrate physical experiences in the rain, members of the East India Company (EIC), established in 1600—one a chaplain, John Ovington (1653–1731), and the other a physician, John Fryer (ca. 1650–1733)—must coinvent with the sick/ening "seeds" rain represented: an etiology that is also strikingly eco-compositionist. While both narratives put Indian rain to the test, and both writers often retreat to the drier ground of reason and scientific calculation, their bodies are placed in direct contact with living rain, at times soaking them to points of pleasure as well as fear, even sponsoring visions of life within, not before or after, the deluge. Like them, we may reexamine our shared and soused materiality with rain: celebrating, not just complaining, when getting caught in and by *it*.[50]

Precipitation

It is difficult, even impossible, to think about rain without thinking about bodies with which it has mixed, from where it has ranged, and into what phases it has transformed across its transtemporal lifespan. The etymology of "precipitation" helps illustrate the life of rain in the early modern period. What we call "precipitation" today during our weather reports—"the condensation of moisture from water vapour and its fall or deposition as rain . . . an instance of this, a shower of rain"—was first set down during the days of the Royal Society in 1692.[51] Its meaning of "senses relating to descent" was first recorded in English in 1475: "The action or an act of casting down or falling from a height; the fact of being cast down; vertical fall or descent." The word "precipice," from classical Latin *praecipit-*, is related ("headlong, sheer"). Thus in its earliest meanings, "precipitation" merely *fell*; rain was a passive fluid that had been hurled from above. Precipitation is such because it *has been* precipitated. But "precipitation" comes from the Latin stem *praecipitāt-* ("to throw or cause to fall headlong, to ruin, destroy, to fall headlong, to suffer ruin, come to grief, to hasten, to rush"). Appropriately, a transitive verb form appeared in 1528: "To throw (a person) suddenly or violently *into* a particular state or condition, esp. an undesirable one." "To cast down . . . to throw over a precipice" followed shortly thereafter in 1541. By 1557, to "precipitate" could denote bringing about or hastening: "To cause (an event or series of events) to happen quickly, suddenly, or unexpectedly; to hasten the occurrence of . . . to bring about, cause to happen." To sum up, although the idea of "precipitation" as an atmospheric process that condensed water and precipitated it to the earth was not thought of until the end of the seventeenth century—and specifically as condensed, measurable water until the beginning of the nineteenth—early moderns could think of rain as an agentic precipitator that could (1) throw things "headlong" and (2) catalyze events and/or "hasten" preexisting ones. Aided by the Royal Society's definition, modern meteorology has come a long way from living rainfall. In contrast, early modern precipitation was felt in fell swoops. To qualify the OED's hasty conclusions, "precipitate" did not always involve "a person" in an "undesirable" situation. Early modern meteorologists theorized the thing-power of "precipitation" in one or both of these ways.

Raised Up

When William Averell (1556–1605) delivered "wonderfull and straunge newes"[52] out of Suffolk in February 1583—"it rayned Wheat"—he gave voice not only to his time's popular interest in reporting and receiving word of "straunge" meteorological events, but also to that timeless connection between life and rain, the essence of agricultural production, a metaphorical association made explicit when some folk "did bite and eate therof, whosoe affirme that it hath a more meatier inward substaunce then our Wheate hath." This is good rain, meaty *meteora*; in addition, as a self-titled student of divinity, Averell testifies to how these events were typically explained: "our God, who is Causa causarum." Despite his myopic take on manna-like meteors and satisfaction with divine causes—the rest reads as a theological exercise advocating faith in the skies—Averell could nonetheless admit that he could provide "[i]nnumerable examples, and most straunge wonders could I recite which haue happened in times past . . . which would . . . open too wide afeelde for me to wander in." It is his confession of a wider world of weird weather that opens up the rain and bespeaks its ability *not* to stop minds from wandering; it leaves the holes in knowledge unfixed. Indeed, as S. K. Heninger Jr.'s still-handy study shows, meteorology as a scientific pursuit was one in motion, slowly gaining momentum in sixteenth-century Elizabethan England and reaching its energetic apogee in the next century's source-quest for the hydrological cycle previously detailed.[53] Derived from the Greek meaning "something raised up," *meteors* included all atmospheric phenomena. Popular resources included the Bible, Seneca's *Quaestiones Naturales* (first century CE), and Bartholomaeus Anglicus's *De Proprietatibus Rerum* (thirteenth century CE). By 1625, many classical and medieval authorities had been translated into English. Most studies borrowed heavily from Aristotle's *Meteorologica* (fourth century BCE) that emphasized constant interactions between the four elements, their qualities (hot, cold, dry, and moist), and the two types of evaporations drawn up by the sun (exhalations and vapors). Writers often adapted and interpreted Aristotelian philosophy— supplementing it with the Roman encyclopedic tradition of Pliny's *Historia Naturalis* (first century CE), for example—rather than accepting or rejecting his views outright. English authors started to develop their own theories, and aided by the printing press that disseminated their ideas adopted from others, their opinions sold.[54] Envision the early modern meteorological book market as a commotion of buyers and sellers in conversation: here we find technical works like Thomas Hill's (ca. 1528 – ca. 1574) *A Contemplation of Mysteries* (1571); topical writings such as Arthur Golding's (ca. 1536–1606) *A Discourse upon the Earthquake* of April 6, 1580, and Abraham Fleming's (ca. 1552–1607) *A Treatise of Blazing Starres in Generall* of November 10, 1577; and wonder books like Stephen Batman's (ca. 1542–84) *The Doome Warning All Men to Judgemente* (1581). People might have wanted to be in the rain only proverbially or to sap the "straunge" from the sky, but they also wanted to make their acquaintance with its "[i]nnumerable examples," devouring the new and improved field's meaty substance.

Even as studies of its nature proliferated with no sign of abating, Renaissance rain was generally considered to be an atmospheric phenomenon of "vapor" with "cold" and "moist" attributes. It would take the seventeenth-century new scientists, many of them contestants in the hydrological debate, armed with inventions like the barometer (1643) and assured by advancements in thermometer mechanics, to believe that they had ultimately triumphed over the irrational discourses of astronomy, astrology, and sublunar influence. But it was a hard battle to objectify, to throw down, this meteor that had been previously raised up: the *Meteorologica* and so-called superstitious types of "forecasting" stayed current through the seventeenth century. William Fulke's (ca. 1537–89) *A Goodly Gallerye* (1563) is perhaps the most significant early modern English meteorological text, appearing in five editions and referenced for over a century. As the first to use the word "meteorology," he serves as a useful introduction to the intellectual climate at the time and its penchant for describing "straunge" precipitation in detail. Referencing Aristotle, Fulke divides meteors three ways: bodies "perfectly" and "imperfectly mixed"; "moist impressions and drie"; "fiery, aery, watery, and earthly."[55] Rain results from clouds thickened by cold, tempered by hot winds, and melted into drops:

> For after the matter of the cloud being drawen vp, and by cold made thick, (as is sayde before) heate followynge, which is moste commenlye of the Southerne wynde, or any other wynde of hotte temper, doth resolue it againe into water, so it falleth in droppes, to geue encrease of fruict to the earth, and moue men to geue thankes to God.[56]

Rain has a power in this process, a fructifying force that "doubtles . . . doth more encrease and cherishe thinges growyng on the earth, then any other water wher with they may be watered."[57] In this way, Fulke insinuates rain's paradox as matter that is life giving ("geue encrease") and yet not alive. The best fertilizer is not itself fertile, only a carrier of another's virtue, the sun's rays: rain "reteineth much of the sunnes heate" that then nurtures plants, and this unique blend of liquid sunshine also explains why rainwater "wyll sooner come to putrefaction, or stinking, then any other" when it mixes with earthy and "corruptible substaunces."[58] Fulke warms up to the idea of rain's life force only through insinuation—he must add organic "substaunces" to water—moving on to its "signes" (red skies in the morning, sweating stones, hungry birds) that ultimately, as he admits, "moue men" to praise a Christian, Protestant god of pluviality.

Besides a brief mention that rain "is sweet and not salt" even if it comes from the sea, Fulke's body is strangely absent from his observations.[59] Tellingly, in his section on "monstruous or prodigious rayne," he approaches rain power as a force for the "straunge": that is, not as an "external" thing, but as an impersonal affect. Addressing wondrous rainfalls such as milk, wool, and brick that the Averells of the world would appreciate, Fulke mentions how clouds creatively combine: they spawn fish near water, form flesh over bloody battlegrounds, and even forge iron by drawing into themselves quicksilver, brimstone, and "the special matter of mixtion."[60] But rain can also be a womb of more spontaneous generation, an exceptional "mixtion" that "it" names:

> Wormes and frogges may thus be generated, when fat Exhalations ar drawen vp into the ayre by a temperature of whott and moist, such vermyn may be generated in the ayr, as they are on earth, without copulation of male and female. Or els that with the Exhalations and vapors, their seede and egges are drawen vp, which being in the clouds brought to form, fal down among the rain.[61]

The "monstruous" rain of "vermyn" is an omen or warning of something to come: perhaps God's displeasure. As a Protestant clergyman, Fulke early on assigns all meteors and their anomalies to God's ordered plan, "first of the materiall cause" and "the vniuersall chiefe and last end of all thinges."[62] But there is hydrosocial hybridity at stake in this atmospheric and amphibious copulation. He seems unsure about the example into which he has wandered. Despite declaring meteors as "body compounde with out lyfe naturalle,"[63] Fulke's clouds suggest living precipitation indifferent to a divine plan or creator, and operating simultaneously within and without the bounds of heteronormativity, "without . . . male and female": conjoined seeds and eggs coexist alongside the asexualized, but no less generative, heated embrace between "fat Exhalations." Thinking of rain as swerving "seeds" of genesis without the restriction of gender approximates Jonathan Goldberg's reading of Lucretius's "seeds of things": "Ontological questions about the meaning of life cannot simply be glossed by means of heterosexual reproduction; it is, after all, only one means of reproducing human life, not the model for reproduction in general."[64] Rain's de/coupling collisions stress a form of reproduction in which the human is only one consort out of many; these seedy raindrops generate far afield and not into neat rows, failing to fall into Christian epistemology and a bio-teleological sense of germinal seed to germinating plant; rather, they conceive of constant, recrudescent births, rhizomatic creations. Fulke reveals an anxiety over this promiscuous companionship by relegating rain's "straunge," sometimes spontaneous, power as a creepy feeling—the verminous and venomous parasite, bad "seede[s]" and rotten "egges"—that will unfortunately prove endemic (as we will see) to future writing on the rain.

Emblem of Inconstancy

Through these unresolved openings in which breeding things get in—the wormholes and cracks in the foundation of Fulke's *Gallerye*—we can steal glimpses of climatic actor-networks that others were not so reluctant to follow; these are spaces English rain-men entered: monsoons, places of immense immersion and pouring power that exceeded the gentler European cycle they thought they knew, spinning its circle out of control, threatening to break its orbit. Readers of Averell or Fulke were enthralled by extraordinary climatic events, but it is safe to surmise that few had experienced the sheer size of the South Asian monsoons. Monsoons are seasonal prevailing winds that typically blow across the Indian subcontinent from the southwest during May to September and from the northeast during October to April. Known primarily for the heavy rains of summer, monsoons last long enough to constitute a season: the "rainy season" known as *barsaat* in Hindi and Urdu. For the first English merchant adventurers to India attempting to make a foothold in the spice trade—like Ralph Fitch (ca. 1550–1611), William Hawkins (b. ca. 1560), and William Finch (d. 1613)—the monsoons were often noted for their impediments to travel and competition (friendly and not) with the Dutch,

Spanish, and Portuguese.[65] Transportation to and from the major English factories and forts—at Surat, Madras (Chennai), and Bombay (Mumbai)—was extremely dangerous during these months. Peter Mundy (ca. 1596 – ca. 1667), who toured northwest India in 1622–23, wrote in "What a Monsoon Is" that during either wind "there is no putting to Sea . . . vessells beinge wither hailed [hauled] on Shoare or drawne up into secure places."[66] The English were forced to economically acclimatize; William Dampier (1651–1715), who sailed around the world in 1679–91, could argue in a lengthy passage that "most of the Navigation in *India* depends on the *Monsoons*."[67] Traveling (or not) by monsoons' rhythms created climate-culture hybrids, or what Robert Markley calls "monsoon-cultures" in their wake.[68] Such collectives promote a deeper understanding of rain's role within political ecologies and other material networks, an "eco-cultural materialism" of Latourian scope, "heterarchical networks of mutually constitutive identities and relations."[69] Even the monsoon's etymology bespeaks a swirling nature; usually attributed to the Arabic *mawsim* ("season," from *wasama*, "to mark, brand"), the word is a composite of merchant-travelers' tongues: taking on the Portuguese *monção* and Dutch *monson* as well.[70]

The climate–culture interchange of monsoons (and rainscapes in general) means that there is no overriding idea of a "familiar" Eurocentric nature, culture, or temporal mode to serve as a "secure plac[e]," a dry dock from which to keep nature and culture separated and times straight. To the four classical seasons (winter, spring, summer, and fall) monsoons presented a problem, and the year could be variously split into three seasons—"*The Rains. The Cold Season. The Heats*"[71]—as Fryer would have them, or a biannual wet and dry season, a summer and a winter monsoon. And any "season" of the monsoon (from the Latin *serere* "to sow") could not only commence in different regions but also arrive late or early, challenging time's chronicity in its dilatoriness and rapidity. Notoriously un/predictable, what could be certain was an epistemological crisis, a time storm whose "seeds" defied Europeans' chronological definitions and distinctions. Dampier mentions that "monsoon" can signal a storm (as "Violent, Terrible") as well as a trade wind ("East or West") and that, despite their regularity, can go out of season: "by the Account I have lately had from Fort St. George [in Madras], they have suffered very much by one of the April Monsoons (if it may be so called) for it came before its usual time, even before it could be expected."[72] In short, monsoons are turbulent networks of wind, rain, traveler, and times; they are time's "meteorological weather" reports: times (as seasons) that put time out of season; the time of the monsoon is a monsoon of times, punctual only in the point they make about unknowing "usual time" and time as usual. Time itself is upset. The question of determinacy in fact depends upon monsoonal turbulence: deviation is their sole certainty. Dampier and many others discovered the combined flux of weather and time by being "brand"-ed by monsoons. Seasons in Europe certainly fluctuated in time and experienced drastic changes, yet the idea of a (literally) moveable season that encroaches on temporal borders is uniquely complex. Monsoons are periods of un/expected rain that reveal time's messiness. The truth of rain's progress always arrives soon, never in the now: sometime indefinitely in the future, someday later.

Or to put this percolating process of *le temps* another way: as one passenger to India, Thomas Herbert (1606–82), said about the "anniversary wind" that blows one way half the year and in the other half the opposite direction: "doubtlesse it is the Emblem of inconstancy, experience taught it us; so long time proving our Antagonist."[73] Whether configured as economic interdependence or not, encounters with monsoons could easily be pitched as wars against an indefatigable enemy. Cognizant of its nonhuman anima, the particularly violent storm that announced the arrival and departure of the monsoons was called the "Oliphant," from the Portuguese *elephante*, a translation of Hindi *hathiya*, an asterism known as the sign of the elephant.[74] This bestial rain gives a global analogy to Fulke's worst nightmares about virulent "seede and egges" that ran rampant in English imaginations (and Europe at large) and that served to bolster prejudices against India's sickly airs. Edward Terry was chaplain to the ambassador Sir Thomas Roe (ca. 1581–1664) at the Mughal emperor Jahangir's court from 1616 to 1619. His *Voyage to East-India* (1655) starts with water tornadoes off the coast of Africa, a fate most journeying to India from Europe would face. Winds blow from all points of the compass at once— thirty-two, by his count—scattering the seeds of rainy procreation:

These strange Gusts were accompanied with much Thunder and Lightning and with extreme rain, so noysome, that it made their cloths who stir'd much in it presently to stink upon their backs; the water likewise of those slimy, unwholsome, hot, and unsavorie showres, wheresoever it stood, would presently bring forth many little offensive Creatures.[75]

It is incredible to think that the compiler of English travel voyages, Samuel Purchas (ca. 1577–1626), called Terry's tempestuous travelogue "a good fare-well draught of English-Indian liquor."[76] The omen in this "monstruous" rainwater is the prophecy of death by water, *aqua mortis*. Although stuck together, the two sides of human and culture—with all their gusty creatures—are opposed. Terry employs a word we have seen before to describe water: "noysome," related to "annoy," which only exacerbates the infectious and parasitic tone of the passage. The physical passage to India involves unwanted things passing through the body: rain both engenders pests and is a pest, doubly dangerous in this regard; the factor to blame for its perniciousness and the birth of these "Creatures"—whether still water ("stood"), rainwater ("showres"), temperature ("hot"), or a combination of all three—was disputed and varied.[77] Whether the designation of "Creature" stands for a prescient view of microbiology or a basic synonym for disease is peripheral. Avoidance of this "unsavorie" and "unwholsome" substance of rainwater—words the contemporary *Wonders* repeats—was paramount. "[S]limy" stuff of generation that "stink[s]" and that sticks to the human the harder it tries to escape: this is the more sensual meaning of "noisome," matter we could call monsoonal "ooze."

Terry's terror at how rain creaturely works—passing across bodies and space—seems incongruous with his admission elsewhere of "those fat enriching showers" reviving "as it were by a new Resurrection"[78] the parched Indian landscape that inconceivably endures drought for nine months. But soil is one material substrate and the English body another; contrasting a human's nine-month gestational period with the "fat" fertility of the monsoonal rains puts the embryos at odds. The full-grown English, Terry complains, "stew in their own moisture" every day before the monsoon arrives,[79] and yet, as he has already mentioned, their bodies wither in the rain once wet. There appears to be no relief for the English in India: whether in the wet or dry season, torrid is all. Terry's *Voyage* proves that it is hard to *be*, not just publish, "English-Indian liquor." His estimation of climatic embodiment is pithily provided long before reaching India: "[T]hus together / enraged gusts oppose each other."[80] Although he is discussing those "self-opposing blasts,"[81] the African tornados, at an early point in the narrative, Terry might as well be addressing the "strange Gusts" of monsoons, a similar eddy of countering water-air currents. ("Tornado" comes from Spanish *tornar*, "to turn.") His choice of sentiment, from the fifth-century BCE Greek tragedian Aeschylus, is telling: to split the human from the weather is tragic; it pits the "self" as its own enemy, "opposing" the ontological two-as-one by staging a one-on-one match, a battle of breaths, in which rain's "Resurrection" is presented as a zombie-like onslaught of un/dead pestilence that keeps falling, somehow, and from someplace unknown. Writing against the wind and the things it carries, Terry is unable to conceive of "self-opposing blasts" as meteorological forces that lose and loosen the autonomous self, blasting bodies off-compass and off-kilter, away from and into composite conceptions, a strange "stew" that *opposes* the very split between human subjects and nonhuman "showres."

It is time to shift from such widespread and pejorative perceptions of precipitation: importantly, the insufferable un/predictability of monsoons is also a corporeal experience. Much of Madras's rain comes from the late summer northeast monsoon. The inhabitants of Fort St. George, Dampier explains, waiting for the winds to change at the "usual times"—September and April, known as the "turning months"—try to block the "hot Blooms" that blow from June to August: "They . . . shut up their Windows and Doors to keep them out; and I have heard Gentlemen that lived there say, that . . . they have been sensible when the Wind shifted by the Change they have felt in their Bodies."[82] A "felt" monsoon motivates either defensive or offensive actions; "[b]odies," in short, always take sides. But in addition to the politico-cultural language of "economy" (meaning "household management") and acculturation that are prevalent in studies of English encounters with Indian monsoons in the seventeenth and "long" eighteenth centuries should come a closer engagement with rain's penchant for "anti-house" dis/rule; similarly, critical treatments of sickness—a topic tracked extensively, and underpinned by interests in (failed) techno-scientific imperialism, etiological methods of othering, and the corresponding genealogies of knowledge that support such practices[83]—would only be enhanced, I think, by relinquishing the human and its hold, no matter how fatuous, on the weather, stressing permeation, bodily becomings, and the monsoonal materialism of more-than-human embodiment. Here is where I depart: to reference other sites of climate–culture interchange and interanimation, including desire, when bodies trade fluids and the fragile vulnerability of the human body's constitution gives way to an ever-shifting assemblage of co-constitutiveness with rainy things. The monsoonal narratives that follow, while examples of "sick ethnography," point up the "ambivalent pleasure" that Jonathan Gil Harris has identified as one potential outcome of "becoming-Indian."[84] I build on the role ecology plays in the writing of "India" and the "Indian"— what he terms "Indography"—by identifying water's part in hybridization ("becoming-Indian" rain) as well as by suggesting its capacity to write (the -graphy of "Indography"), all in an attempt to amplify the pleasures of porosity: the sematic equation of "thirst" with "desire," rain's ability to truly slake ("relax") bodies as much as put them at dis-ease. There are those who did not catch rain in order to explain it, but who described its strange effects and nonlinear processes feelingly, who redefined capture as a kind of intimacy, who wanted to be caught by the "strange attractor" of rain and would not wish to wait another day for it. Imagining an Indo-hydrography committed to alternative, pleasurable possibilities besides the pernicious parasite and antagonistic blast required rethinking "economy" altogether, what it meant (and still means) to be "alongside," *para-*, to be bodily English-Indian liquor caught in monsoonal middles.

Cascade

It will take a brief detour: down the hall from Fulke's *Goodly Gallerye* are damper corridors. In *The Parasite*, Serres expresses that "parasite" signifies three things at once in French: a biological eater, a human (social) parasite, and noise (static). What the parasite communicates, in short, is relationality in action. The parasite is absolutely relational, *para-*, next-to, "[having] a relation only with the relation itself."[85] Each parasite tries to outdo its predecessor, spurred into parasitism by the sudden eruption of a third, noise: "A parasite, physical, acoustic, informational, belonging to order and disorder, a new voice, an important one, in the contrapuntal matrix."[86] The system "is parasitic in a cascade,"[87] and to inhabit this cascade is to enter collectives. Subjects and objects persistently switch positions, scrambling the ontological chain of command between host and interrupter. The system incorporates rather than paints over the "chance, risk, anxiety, and even disorder" that constitute it.[88] Fluctuation therefore is no longer an affront to the house of reason: it is the actual foundation upon which reason is built. There can be no system without parasites. Far from a closed system, the cascade invents new systems precisely because of its dis/equilibrium. Refuse to "restore" harmony to ecosystems; we are better off allowing for disputability, error, and disruptions: "One must write . . . of the interceptions of the accidents in the flow along the way between stations—of changes and metamorphoses."[89] The exact form of the noisy flow, the crossing of cascading things, is left to the listener to ponder in this parasitical model.

It is back at the house: observe hungry occupants chasing each other down the hallway. A fable by the French poet Jean de La Fontaine (1621–95) serves as Serres's prime scene of parasitism. A country rat is sent into the house by a noise outside; this rat joins a city rat on a Persian rug where they feast on a tax farmer's scraps; the farmer chases the rats from under the table; and the chain goes on. Beating on the house, however, has been the rain, the noise in the first position that provides a sense of in- and exclusion for these creatures, even as its acknowledgment seems delayed:

> But the excluded one, just a while ago, was making his way through the countryside; the passer-by goes out again in the rain that, as far as we know, never stops, beating incessantly on the roof of the host and guest. That noise too interrupted a process: a trip. And from this noise comes the story. Hosts and parasites are always in the process of passing by, being sent away, touring around, walking alone. They exchange places in a space soon to be defined.[90]

Just as rain falls in a cascading form, rain's noise crucially reveals how the cascade works: it brings collectives into dis/order. The noise of the Serresian cascade is the same as the noise of rain as it cascades upon our bodies, our architecture, our constructed houses of life and knowledge; it is what generates "the story" like La Fontaine's, Serres's, and mine, right now: my fingers' "physical, acoustic" taps upon the keyboard resounding like rain on roof. Consider that the Latin root of rain, *imber-* ("shower of rain") comes from *imbrex* ("roof tile"). In this passage, the literal meeting of material rain and the medium of tile creates a literary type of rainy ecopoesis. Wet writer and world overlap; in a word, they *imbricate*. Rain materializes aloud a system in cascade, non/human characters at a run across haphazardous lines of poetic invention. Although he is addressing the house of scientific reason in particular, we can extend his argument further; these ramblings and errors are fundamental to ecology's foundation: "Mistakes, wavy lines, confusion, obscurity, are part of knowledge; noise is part of communication, part of the house."[91] Yet we must not mistake Serres's concern for the moldy house as an act of redemption. Unlike Fulke, he is showing us ecological openings on purpose, preferring to enlarge (not fix) them in order to let the rain get, and set, in. In this dank house buffeted by the rain, we hear alternate voices: be it rain, farmer, rat, or "unsavorie showres." The parasite offers an erring and errant kind of ecocriticism that denounces the human's position as prime parasite.[92] Rain reminds us that there are only things in relations and as relations, beings in cascade with everywhere to fall: "The thing is nothing else but a center of relations, crossroads or passages."[93] We leave one house only to find new relations in an/other. We are drawn in and out by the noise of rain as it swerves us in a cascade that "as far as we know, never stops." Read in this way, Terry's "noysome" rain of annoyance illustrates the noisiness of transmissions that create chains of relations. Early modern passages to India exhibit bodies being parasitically passed through and, as a result of this transfer, composing textual passages that exemplify rain's salutary as well as sickening effects: bodies and texts both are "spaces soon to be defined" that never quite reach resolution. Rain's "it" was their "trip," and it is ours still. With this more commodious definition of parasitical profligacy in mind, I turn to two English authors most associated with monsoonal sickness in India, intensifying rather than curing them of their cascading interruptions in an effort to follow rainfall's plenteous impress.

Refreshment

John Ovington, EIC chaplain and author of *A Voyage to Suratt in the Year 1689* (1696), is perhaps best known for his deplorable summation of health conditions at the English factory in Bombay: "*Two Mussouns*," he pronounces, "*are the Age of a Man*."[94] While Ovington does not attribute the region's devastating sicknesses and exponentially increasing fatality rate specifically to rain—the monsoons are known to bring relief from "tedious Pestilence," actually, by cooling the air—they nurture diseases nevertheless: "For the excess of earthy Vapours after the Rains ferment the Air, and raise therein such a sultry Heat, that scarce any is able to withstand that Feverish Effect it has upon their Spirits, nor recover themselves from those Fevers and Fluxes into which it casts them."[95] The two months after the monsoon leaves Bombay, around September–October, are the worst: these misty exhalations precipitate a water cycle of death by physically "cast[ing] them" into physiological sickness. Vermin find a way to swell during the monsoons as well: "The prodigious growth of Vermin, and of Venomous Creatures, at the time of the *Mussouns* . . . demonstrate the malignant Corruption of the Air."[96] The rain breeds spiders as big as thumbs and toads as large as ducks; frogs drop from buildings above; wounds refuse to heal. The English body is ever-open and overexposed. Swarms of locusts buzz Ovington's ship while approaching the port of Bombay, and nests of water snakes trailing the ship mean land is close because serpents always flee "the violence of the Rains in the times of the *Mussouns*."[97] The water-airborne parasites are ominous indicators of how rain will treat the arriving English—ex-habitants soon to be—and the inevitable violation of bodily borders that await them there. This awareness of an oncoming violence that the English cannot flee but only face explains why Ovington promises, while still onboard and barely into his description of "The Island of Bombay," that he "shall . . . describe" these virulent weather systems for his readers. Here he is able to report the approximate time of the monsoons' onset on the west and east coasts, but also, and less predictably, his amazement that the monsoons can bring unprecedented changes in climate across short distances: "Travellers, who are unacquainted with it, are at a stand to find two different Seasons of Winter and Summer in 20 [70 miles] or 30 [100 miles] Leagues distance."[98] Space (geography) and time (season) are supposed to designate a semistable climate (region) and what one is to expect from its slope. Ovington's awe is informative, for it instructs how meteorological acquaintances are made and understood, and just as importantly, it shows how easily these informational signals can be confused. The eventful "*Ele-phant*," for example, has intention: the monsoons "resolv[e] to try their utmost effort, sooner than tamely resign their Empire."[99] The admission of imperial empyrean forces says much about Ovington's own territorial-ized rubric for writing the weather—the monsoons frequently slide into medicinal breakdowns and colonial anxieties concerning the botched Mughal War from 1689–90—and his steadfast interest in better fortifi-cations for both body and mind. But the parasitical breaches and their "utmost effort[s]" he admits, however, demonstrate the contingency of demarcation. That is, if "Nature must needs be under great Conflicts and disorder, by such a suddain Change from an uninterrupted Sun-shine to such constant Rains,"[100] he begs the question of how one can make long-lasting, even nonviolent, acquaintances with rainy and raining "Creatures."

For even within this Indian oven, Ovington finds pleasure in the atmo-sphere; in fact, it is the monsoons' seasonal variation and difference from familiar water cycles that he welcomes. Contrary to European classifi-cations, when the sun comes closest to earth at midyear, it initiates the "fowlest" (stormiest) weather in India—instead of the "fairest Weather" the "Natives of Europe" would expect—due to its "Vertical Exaltation, which with great violence Exhales the Vapours of the Earth, and returns them as plentifully again."[101] Foul is fair, and fair is foul: "And that abun-dant moisture which is always powerfully drawn up, near the *Æquator*, from which the sun is never very far distant, abates that scorching Heat of his Influence, which otherwise would be scarce tolerable to either Ani-mal or Plant."[102] Or an animal such as himself: like Dampier, Ovington assuredly felt his body temperature "shift" when the winds finally came. Indeed, there are several moments in the *Voyage* in which he "plentifully" enjoys rainwater. He and his shipmates dry up long before reaching India. Off the African coast, near the mouth of the Congo, they reduce water rations to a quart a day, plugging their noses to put the "unsavoury and corrupt" drafts down. As the crew fears the worst, the sky miraculously opens: "But that Misfortune was drown'd by the Pleasure we receiv'd in the refreshment of abundance of Rain which fell that Night, a Drop of which we had not seen for at least two Months before. The richest Wine could not please our Palates with half that Delight, as this Blessing which descended from Heaven in Showers upon us."[103] Where once rainy vapors dangerously "ferment[ed] the Air" in Bombay, here the process of fermentation sends them a delicious vintage: "this fresh Liquor drink . . . cheer'd our Hearts, as if they had been refresh'd with the noblest Wine."[104] Ovington is outright intoxicated by rain, pleasurably corrupted, cheerfully infected; ingesting rainwater deliquesces any previous distinctions between animal, plant, and human. The ethnographic tone of the narrative slips here as well, since the "Bannian," what he calls the male trading-class Indians of Surat, commonly drinks rainwater, "which he esteems a more pure and Ethereal Liquor for descending from above."[105] Rain's "Blessing" is twice blessed by soaking "Misfortune" and "Palates," a watery exaltation that need not go vertical into ontological hierarchies or higher up (still) into divination, but horizontally into distribution and dissemination that is precipitation, drowning everything in a freshwater sea of joys. A thirst for rain is a desire that unites all beings—"greedy Soil"[106] is one hungry host out of many—endowing even the thirsty rain with its own longing for quaffable connectivity.

Ovington details what it is like to be literally refreshed ("back fresh," from Old English *fersc*, "fit for drinking") just as he recognizes how, "refresh'd by Nature's Seminal Juice," the "Vegetable Race below . . . grace[s] the World with infinite variety of delightful Forms, and pleasant Colours."[107] The sight and smell of rain is an aesthetic that still appeals: today, perfumes claim to bottle the nose (we might say) of rain-wine. Overall, Ovington's organic and "infinite variety" relates the endless possibilities of "Forms" and "Colours" that the nosy, noisy, and noisome rain produces: a veritable and verdant rainscape of desire. This refreshingly arousing "attractor" continually brings beings "back" for more. On deck in Africa the rain becomes the swirl at the center of attention: "For impatient of letting it fall into the Tubs, which were placed upon the Decks on purpose to receive the falling Water, no Wine was more greedily catcht at by the Vulgar out of publick Conduits on a solemn Day, that the Rain was by the Sailers in their Bowls and Hats."[108] Terry's ecclesiastical clothes, unlike Ovington's, could not tolerate the wet; here, the sailors are far less solemn and more than willing to sacrifice their clothing for a chance to catch and be "catcht" by the rain. Like the conduits of London, the ship's ingenious water-capture mechanism is a civic ecosystem in miniature, congregating watery human and nonhuman citizens, and momentarily dissolving "Vulgar" class- and species-based contours by making rain public. This catching feeling and propulsion for assembling with others extends, extraordinarily, to Ovington's own writing. Surat's air is so hot before the rains come that it "licks up the Moisture in the Pen, before we are able to write it out."[109] He needs the ink of rain, and it is this confession that spells out a monsoonal hydrography: in these dehydrated moments when even thoughts could dry up, he sprinkles water on his chamber floors for the practical reason of cooling, but also, he notes, "to create a kind of *Fresco* in them."[110] "Fresco," a watercolor painting on wet plaster, is from the Italian for "cool, fresh." Art, Ovington avows, is the ultimate refreshment, the outcome of a "fresh" rain that solicits (potable) draft after (penned) draft. To paraphrase Purchas's encomium, this composition—the *Voyage*, an English-Indian liquid body and narrative done al fresco in the Indian-African rainscape—is a good drink.

But despite Ovington's idyllic passages and sporadic horizontal relations sponsored by rain on the tongue and the pen, the "Vulgar" and the "Bannian" harden into derisive designations. His evergreen rainscape reaches too far above, out of the real world and into the immaterial realm of protection, perfection, and immutability: that which "gives *India* the lovely Aspect of those Blessed Seats," he concludes, are "sweetly described by the Poet," Lucretius, as fit only for the gods: "And where they dwell, wind never lashes them, cloud never rains."[111] Suddenly there can be no chance for peace in the rain, even within the fluctuations he helps us to recognize; that beautiful "Aspect" that runs with refreshing "Seminal Juice" belongs above the weather, up where ordinary humans and nonhumans do not belong. It seems only appropriate, then, that he turns his attention at this moment to Bombay's unhealthful months and the proverbial proclamation about monsoonal ages for which he has become famous. He grows judgmental, unfortunately, swerving away from the thirsting and thirsty connections he had found and felt elsewhere: outlining, for instance, his fears of miscegenation and imperfect mixture that undergird his approval of the company's plan to send marriageable English women to the fort. How quickly the seeds of things supply a sermon on human sin, transforming its blessings into a curse: the "Seeds of . . . a thousand . . . black Infernal Vices"[112] not only exacerbate the consistently contagious condition of the Indian air, but now present immorality as a new kind of climate change. If wickedness does not cease on the island, delugic "Divine Justice" will be forced to intervene. Do not be surprised, he preaches, "if the pure Luminaries of Heaven should set themselves against their Impieties, and dart their mortal Poysons on the Earth; of the Planets should wisely shed their venomous Aspects upon profligate Men, and thereby in Vengeance produce the mortal Fruits of Death."[113] All races—"Vegetable" and what else—will drown in this hydro-humoral hell. Ovington portrays the monsoons as a watery apocalypse in another oft-quoted passage of his: "The whole Hemisphere then is most sullenly Dark, and the Sky overcast with the thickest weighty Clouds, so that the Earth seems rather inclosed within a huge Ocean of Water . . . that it gives the fairest representation imaginable of the terrours of a second universal Deluge."[114] As if retracting his earlier thoughts on rain, the liquor here misfortunately drowns "Pleasure" and the lives, certainly, of the unfortunates he has hurriedly condemned. Ovington will be a survivor when that time comes, at least he hopes, transported to unreal "Blessed Seats" unbelievably preserved in an evergreen state where the rains cannot touch him but that have been touched, strangely, by rain already. In the end, his prayer is not for others: it is one, instead, that attempts to leave behind the material world with its "refresh'd" and diseased bodies undergoing unpredictable cycles wrought by rain; it is one that, in trying to stop this full-flooded potential of monsoons, proves ignorance to be an injustice.

Predicament

Several of the physician John Fryer's eight years in the east (1673–81) were spent in India. Cambridge-educated, he conveys in his *New Account of East-India and Persia, in Eight Letters* (1698) a more cerebral air than Ovington when it comes to analyzing the correlation between climate and health. In general, and somewhat predictably by now, rain temporarily cools but eventually kills; as Fryer sails to India, "the Rains . . . became intemperate; not but that they mitigated the Heat *in actu*, tho as to its effects, it proved more virulent, impregnating the Air with a diseased Constitution, whereupon we had many hung down their Heads."[115] On this twelve months' voyage through "Divers Climates," as he calls it, the passage proves insufferable, rain once more assaulting the pregnable English body with its pregnant poisons. Surprising for the sailors but

perhaps not for his readers accustomed to the "violence of the Rains" and
its multiple forms of infliction, "virulent" vermin run amok amidships:
"the kindest and the softest downfal on [their] Bodies is productive" if
drenched clothes are not changed immediately.[116] Once he lands at Eng-
lish-occupied Mechlapatan (Machilipatnam) in the southeastern part of
the subcontinent, the heat is on: the monsoon fosters the perfect conditions for a pernicious storm—temperature, insects, and disease—ingre-
dients that "breed and infest them" with pimples, rash, and worse.[117] In
Surat, Fryer pronounces, "Diseases reign according to the Seasons";[118]
although rain cleanses the "Filth" from the city streets, it also, like the
precipitative version of the *pharmakon*, sows the seeds of "Fluxes, Apo-
plexies, and all Distempers of the Brain, as well as Stomach" in its victims.[119] All of these dire diagnoses of incontinence—including the aptly
named aquatic "Fluxes"—may be summed up in the doctor's quotable
conclusion that the company members in Bombay "walk but in Charnel-
houses, the Climate being extremely Unhealthy."[120] Once set up in India,
the English "Constitution" and its constituent body parts are knocked
right down by the rain.

At this point I do not wish to pursue Fryer's "bioregional" consid-
eration of disease any further, but instead move to his unconventional
interests in making the monsoon's acquaintance that sets him apart from
some of his more incurious contemporaries. On the surface, his description of the monsoons' lifespan is hardly unique; his notes on when which
wind arrives on what coast are accurate. What is remarkable, however, is
his explanation of the word "monsoon": "being the Name imposed by the
first Observers, *i.e. Motiones*."[121] Technically, Fryer is incorrect (see above),
and yet his error of w/etymology importantly grasps the singular quality of the monsoonal eddy. Herbert, gazing upon waterspouts, observed
"Cataracts in their violent and precipitious fluxes";[122] Terry, peering into
the same phenomena, witnessed "precipitant Motion."[123] Both were hesitant, as we know, to go through these meteorological motions. Fryer's
mistake, then, is actually his accidental recognition of the monsoons' endlessly "precipitant Motion" he is made aware of by passing through the
cataract ("down rush") of water. His derivation of "monsoon" arrives from
climatic deviation, *le temps*, as he ultimately decides to name "*Monsoons*"
as "Tempestuous Seasons" in his glossary. Incredibly, for one trained in

medicine's cause-and-effect logic, Fryer is uninterested in prescribing the operations of monsoons; as he sails on his way to Bombay, his mind "deviate[s]" from lists of forts and factories and threats to the company: "Concerning the Regularities of these Winds," he muses, "perhaps some others may give patter Guesses than my self, who am not conceited enough to dogmatize."[124] This deference does not mean that he is indifferent to the patter of rain, however: as if the allure of the monsoon pulls him in, he conducts a little trial; the sun, he conjectures, is the reason why the winds annually blow, according to the circumrotation of the earth, just as the moon impresses upon the air and makes the tides adhere to monthly revolutions. But any type of Copernican Revolution that would posit stability in human-engineered scientific fact falls apart. Fryer's conceit purports to know only the instability of reason. Using René Descartes's (1596–1650) theories on magnetism and the lodestone in the *Principia* (1644) as an example, he claims that the French philosopher "acquiesces only in modest Hypotheticks, not any ways informing the Understanding to a clear Apprehension; but after he has brought it through the Maze of Probabilities, he parts with it at the same Predicament it entred."[125] While the "Maze" for Descartes is "Metaphysical Notions,"[126] for Fryer it is the physical space of the cascade. Scientific inquiry for him—entering, wet epistemologically—is not a quest for attainable truth or a guarantee of any such thing, but just another bend in the labyrinth of "Probabilities" that sets other inquiries into motion, an aleatory realm without a center in which the re-searcher wanders through the randomness of rain and its inconstant subject-object positions. Fryer's miniature essay is a true attempt to think with the rain: a veritable experiment in errancy, about "Guesses," on the true rain/cloud of unknowing. Monsoons are spaces soon to be defined, then later to be, but always deferred to be. Fryer understands weather's whirl, writing in word-wind. His quick "conceit" is worth lingering over since it avoids simple Cartesian motion-mechanics, and, even more importantly, it challenges those (like Ovington) who "dogmatize" the workings of the world by attributing a religious core to its "Maze" of difficulties: it is an interruption, if only for a moment, that suggests maybe God and the gods do not know the nature of rain, after all.

The same monsoons that propel Fryer's epistemological deviation also veer his body-environment split off track, redirecting rain's intractable predisposition for violence into more amiable modes. Returning to his *Account*, as if his mind blew away with the monsoon, Fryer bizarrely narrates "we are now winding about the *South-West* part of *Ceilon*; where we have the *Tail of the Elephant* full in our mouths."[127] Presumably, he means that he has been drinking rainwater during the stormier "*Tail*"/end of the monsoon. Carnivorous and yet refreshingly ambiguous, this unusual passage puts zoomorphic, inhuman weather into the human body, demonstrating a connection that has always been there: Fryer is where mind, body, and "*Elephant*" meet. The *Account*, too: this "full" line intimates what a monsoon feels like in the mouth—of taste (drinking), and also speaking (narrating)—collapsing the compositional aspects of body and writing that is his hydrography, to stomach the rain and be "full" to the skin. Rain in the mouth puts the non/human water-body into motion; sends watery skins into orbit around rainy constellations; speeds, slows, and swerves their trajectories. Heavy rainfall during the monsoon season often meant that travel decreased considerably (or stopped altogether) until the rains ceased; yet even in these pauses, the seeds of things retain their speed. It is rain's pronounced quality of ac- and deceleration—the halting for and in the rain, the hiccups of stop and go—that allows seemingly immobile things to be organized into energetic groupings. Fryer notes a particularly pregnant pause in Bacein outside Bombay: "And now the Rains are set in, all Hostilities and Commerce cease, and every one provides for this time . . . here being no stirring out to Sea, or travelling in the Country; the best Pastime now being good Fellowship."[128] The "Hostilities and Commerce" refer to the Dutch, Spanish, and Portuguese trade rivals in the area, but also to the cessation of the Mughal emperor Aurungzeb's war efforts, who, "by reason of these interruptions [the tops of trees are underwater] cannot go on to overcome the *Pagans*."[129] The monsoon becomes a time of gathering together, just like on Ovington's ship, a season of "Fellowship" in which nonhuman and human things partner up, parasitically poised on the precipice of war and peace. The ceasefire cannot last forever; Fryer's Christian religiosity and derision for nonbelievers throughout the *Account* is undeniable: the Bombay "*Banyans*, assisted by their *Brachmins*" who march to the sea at the end of the rainy season and make offerings to the water to bring about "*Mare Pacificum*" and reopen trade are clearly superstitious.[130] Even if occurring as a flash on the page, peace does happen in Bacein nonetheless—the "Probabilities" had arrived in the same way—encouraging a sense of "stirring" stillness. Rain means war—a chance of violence in "full"—and yet Fryer's "Pastime" also predicts a chance of peace.

For peace to stand a chance in an area and era of chanciness, the cascade must paradoxically keep its "*Motiones*" in "precipitant Motion" because of, and not despite, the risks involved. While he is in fluid "Fellowship" in "Bombaim and the parts adjacent," Fryer takes note that "[t]hus lies this place afloat, and the Rains and Thunder are violent enough to convince the incredulous of a possibility of a General Deluge."[131] The possibility of "Deluge" is one that all pluvial places must face, and the "Predicament" of floods constitutes a definite matter of concern. Fryer elsewhere dwells not just on "place[s] afloat" but those that have been submerged, its citizens sunk. At the end of his sixth letter dated December 31, 1679, he describes "Two Portentous Calamaties, the one Inland, a Shower of Blood for Twelve Hours; the other on the Sea-Coast, *Mechlapatan* being overturned by an Inundation, wherein Sixteen thousand Souls perished."[132] Incarnadine rain is the ultimate message of murder, a bloody accident without cause that turns the terrestrial into the tidal by inverting the sea and sky, making the green-blue one red. At the end of 1679 he appropriately turns to end times, rain apparently "the sum of this Anniversary."[133] The "Pastime" of becoming the rain must necessarily include past times of "Calamaties" and an acknowledgement of those "Sixteen thousand Souls" who have passed on. The sum of the anniversary winds known as monsoons include both disaster and desire running on both a variable seasonal basis and a fixed yearly time scale without the manipulation of a godly hand. It was an uncomfortable position to be in, as it is for us today, coming at this "farther discovery of India" late in the *Account*, impossible to forecast what will be unveiled by going farther into India's liquid labyrinths, by staying in the "Predicament" predicated by downpours, where scientific discovery only uncovers more doubt, where "Apprehension" ("lay hold of") does not clearly lead to answers but to the "Understanding" of literal seizure by the rain. Rain is a puddling puzzle that requires reacquaintance with the "Pastime" that is writing: Fryer's actual letters posted from drowned lands. He adds a postscript at the end of his fifth letter: "Sending you with this the General

Account of *Persia*, which I had time to write during almost Forty Days
floating upon these Waters; which had like to prove as fatal to Us, as the
great Deluge did once to the Old World in that space of time."[134] By
invoking Noah's "Forty Days," Fryer's ark appears supersessionary, the
"Us" floating onward into a Christian future, its pilot secure in the faith
(like Terry) that he will survive the "General Deluge" of monsoons this
year and the next. But "this" is writing with the monsoon's tail trailing in
his mouth. To write on water, in other words, is to wonder about living
intracatastrophically in zones that have been—and will be—devastated
by portents to some extent legible: climates of no rain and of plenty. A
monsoon is a capacious "space of time," Fryer relays to his original patron
from the noisy ark of transmission, tasting rain, floating for now. Yet his
letters are epistolary time capsules that come addressed to us as well, that
read we have never been postdiluvial: that we have always been here before,
all in this "space," at the precarious scene of water writing.

Come (Again) Another Day

Dampier once had an inspired daydream. Imagine in your mind what he
saw in his: a chart of monsoonal weather patterns, split into quadrants,
and centered on the Tropic of Cancer. In April, "whereas the West *Monsoon* is accompanied with Tornadoes and Rain in North Lat. the S.S.W.
Monsoon, which blows at the same time in South Lat. is accompanied
with fair Weather."[135] The sections swap in September: above the line,
the east monsoon brings fair weather while the winds blowing N.N.E
south of the line usher in the fouler weather of the N.N.E. monsoon. The
"turning months" of September and April are especially bad as the two
latitudes "participate of both sorts of Winds. For these *Monsoons* do as
constantly shift by turns, as the Year comes about."[136] Dampier's chart
is not just another puffed up attempt at catching winds' shifting epistemology; instead, it is a thought experiment about inventive turbulence: because his entire aerial cartography depends on one quadrant in
flux, Dampier anticipates what physicists now call the "hairy ball theo-
rem" that states that a sphere, including the earth, must have at least one
vortex spinning on its surface at all times; in other words, the planet's
vectors, its winds, are necessary fields of dis/equilibrium that hold the
whole world together. But with this knowledge of constant inconstancy

comes nightmares: Dampier was tormented by the winds. He notes the commonplace practice of sleeping on deck in torrid climes at sea:

> I have many times spread my Lodging, when the Evening has promised well, yet have been forced to withdraw before Day; and yet it was not a little Rain that would afright me then; neither at its first coming could I have thought that such a small Cloud could afford so much Rain: And oftentimes both my self and others have been so deceived by the appearance of so small a Cloud, that thinking the Rain would soon be over, we have lain till we were dropping wet, and then have been forced to move at last.[137]

Always unpredictable—no matter how many "coming[s]" and goings he has felt in his body—the volume of even the smallest cloud "deceive[s]" them. (Trinculo, at least, could rely only on the "same black cloud" [*The Tempest*, 2.2.20] striking twice.) Dampier's entry begs the question of how long these watermen, reluctant at first to find shelter, lying until "dropping wet," were asleep before they were "forced to move," or if they moved at all. He, not "we," seems haunted hereafter, a tempest of mind-body who paranoically watches the skies for the slightest chance of rain: "'tis impossible for me to forget how oft I have been disturbed by such small Clouds that appeared in the Night."[138] Nowhere on the globe— from the East to West Indies, North to South Seas—did the "afright[ed]" circumnavigator find shelter from these clouds he believed were following him.

Nor could he: Dampier's day and night dreams underscore the unrelenting question of what to do when the rain clouds roll in, when the hairy "whirligig" hails us. The authors present here who attempt to straighten out these climatic irregularities betray a larger dilemma of doubt, as Vladimir Janković argues, that ran from early modernity to the Enlightenment: "The history of meteorology may . . . be conceived as an effort to resolve . . . uncertainty, or, better yet, as a series of recurring failures to do so."[139] Many of them configure rain as beginnings (seeds), ends (floods), and sickening in-betweens (disease) across phases from drought to deluge. We have inherited their "effort[s]." If we are to be "for all waters," then, it is with waters that will repeatedly rise and fall. Responding to

Britain's record rainfall in the first years of the twenty-first century, Brian Cathcart's *Rain* seems to bring more of it: "It is only when things go wrong that our dim consciousness of scientific meteorology rises to the surface."[140] For Cathcart, scientific analysis provides a false sense of security. We are to make a "managed retreat from the assumptions that science has the answers, that even if the price is high we can always buy protection, that we can cope with downpours and their consequences."[141] Two-thirds of the world's population currently lives under the influence of southeast Asian monsoons, weather patterns whose internal clocks are rapidly shifting due to climate change. Even as twenty-first-century technology has improved upon Dampier's understandings, they have also pointed to more "uncertainty" and "recurring failures" ahead, airy apparitions all day and night. Rain's un/predictability and variable effects are still frustrating—one ecosystem's flood may very well be another's source of life—and a little more decipherability would certainly be desired in order to stop environmental degradations like acid rain, stymie the global stream of ecological refugees, and initiate early (and earlier) warning systems to better predict the clouds' "first coming." Climate change deniers could just as easily point to these early inundated English narratives to claim that death by rain's abundance or its dearth cannot be attributed to expanding industrialization post-Enlightenment, even if these pronouncements obviously extend Ovington's damnation to those communities literally damned and drowned out—surrounding India's Sardar Sarovar Dam, for example—exchanging Christian eschatology for neoliberal capitalism.

Some humility of rain-fed humidity is timely, I think, and the early modern writers of monsoonal storms I have tracked in this chapter supply the perfect refresher. Arguing against inevitable catastrophe, Cathcart believes that only a "new humility" can shake our egocentric delusions of domination: simply put, "there is no such thing as getting above the rain."[142] These authors rephrase his warning against climate control to ponder what would happen if we stayed *in* the rain rather than held our egos and our knowledge systems *below* it. (The preposition, as always, is crucial.) Inadvertently or not, they challenged and then broke the water cycle built by scientific-theological wisdom by revealing how the nimbus and the nebulous routinely mist-ify knowledge. Whenever it rained, these authors reacted widely: falling back on theological explanation

(Fulke, Terry); composing a noisy contract (Ovington's frescos, Fryer's letters); dreaming turbulent contact zones (Dampier); drinking their fill of desirous, intersaturated becomings; and embracing, momentarily, the momentous pauses in the rain blame-game to reinterpret nonhuman and human parasites as cascading fellowships that may weather predicaments. Whether or not it is welcome, whether drizzly or diluvial, living rain resists any solid position; drip after drip, is a trip to both pleasure and catastrophe. Julian Yates has described Serres's parasite ingeniously as "agentic drift": "a way of representing agency as a dispersed or distributed process in which we participate rather than as a property which we are said to own."[143] Agentive drift epitomizes the distributed agency of rainscapes. Rain is "ecological" drift that we catch and are caught in. It asks what and who is floating underneath and above and through us in the drift, "Creatures" known and unknown, Caliban-ic, who cry out for rain or for the rain to stop:

> in dreaming
> The clouds methought would open and show riches
> Ready to drop upon me, that when I waked
> I cried to dream again. (*The Tempest*, 3.2.135–38)

It means to sail the ark not of apocalypse but of shared futurity, to redefine the ship of salvation for one as a story of survival for many;[144] to reconsider architecture not as a (leafy) shield but as just another layer of skin that is, like everything, susceptible to permeation; to find in the arc of a rainbow a covenant written in water of non/human convening, a bond of relationality as opposed to servitude or determination. Our precipitation-participation begins by hearing the rain on our rooftops, taking umbrage at umbrellas, feeling it on our bodies, and listening to the stories it tells. At the same time, it means reexamining the kinds of stories we are told and the types of embodied experience we narrate. It does not take an avowedly postcolonial ecocritical reading to connect EIC narratives to the eventual colonization of India and the harmful extraction of its resources. Theorists of living rain show us to be always-already with/in rainy weather. Once we realize that a house (*oikos*) "out of" the rain is illusory, once we stop tiling our houses of reason in vain efforts to protect them, we begin to build new houses altogether—together—to really let *it* rain.

To get to the end we must go full circle: always repeating, of course, with a difference. "He does smile his face into more lines than is in the new map with the augmentation of the Indies" (*Twelfth Night*, 3.2.66–68), says Maria about the gulled Malvolio, making reference to Edward Wright's nautical world map, the *Hydrographiae Descriptio* (1599), that we know John Davis helped scribe. An incomplete map replete with lines that lead into uncharted Indian territory and make up the human: here, finally, is Shakespeare's hydrographic being.[145] Feste touched by a living rain "every day," and maybe even Shakespeare by an English-Indian liquor that circled his world, should not sound so foolish by now. The trick is on us. From Feste's first days, he realizes that rain does not stop at the skin, does not halt at the supposed limits of the human. His mantra of moisture—a processional chant that processes the rain, that celebrates and demonstrates the individual indivisible from the physical environment—emphasizes the mandatory "cares" we must have in a diluvial world; it recognizes rain's real violence against those who are forced out of their own "gates," out of homes, and barred from others'. But it also highlights the pleasures, the festiveness, of an eco-ontological approach over the tired, and damaging, duality of climate and culture. The "estates" of nature and culture were not, and have never been, severed ever since "the world begun." Shakespeare came to this realization on a rainy day in 1599. The "great rain" did dissolve the Globe: at least the idea of a globe made out of discrete human and nonhuman parts. When *it* rained, it ushered in a new world, the play of *Twelfth Night*, which sings our interdependence with things and the promises of newer worlds once willed, to be "for" *it* when *it* comes (again) another day (and *it* will), to write and ride out stormier times, to form contingencies through contingency, assemblages via the aleatory, and, above all, to love the whirl that is your world.

CHAPTER 4

Mucking Up

To love a swamp . . . is to love what is muted and marginal, what exists
in the shadows, what shoulders its way out of mud and scurries along
the damp edges of what is most commonly praised. . . . A swamp is a
poor place to go for a steady reflection.

—Barbara Hurd, *Stirring the Mud*

Come Brethren of the water, and let us all assemble,
To treat upon this matter, which makes us quake and tremble;
For we shall rue it if't be true that Fenns be undertaken,
And where we feed in Fen and Reed thei'le feed both Beef and Bacon.

—William Dugdale, *The History of Imbanking and Drayning* (1662)

Swamps are *great*—"big" in size, from Old English *grēat*—and *gross* in
affect. Two of the most famous swamps in the United States sprawl across
its eastern seaboard: the Great Swamp (Morris County, New Jersey) and
the Great Dismal Swamp (southeastern Virginia and northeastern North
Carolina). The former's nearly eight thousand acres became the first wilderness area within the Department of the Interior after Congress passed
the Great Swamp Wilderness Act of 1968.[1] The latter's over 112,000 acres
were also protected as a refuge under the Dismal Swamp Act of 1974. A
swamp's greatness, however, does not necessarily lead to its aesthetic appreciation; monetarily, perhaps, it does: facing land scarcity and poor soil in
the developing east coast, the Dismal Swamp Company was founded in
1763 to cultivate what the surveyor William Byrd II in 1728 had called
"a miserable Morass, where nothing can inhabit."[2] Among the wealthy
Virginian shareholders charged with "draining Improving and Saving the
Land"[3] was George Washington. He and his workforce (including sixty
slaves) could not turn a profit over the next decade, and the plans for

draining the swamp were eventually abandoned in the late 1790s. In the nineteenth century, the Great Dismal Swamp sheltered maroon communities of runaway slaves who rode the Underground Railroad's slough. A swamp, then, designates greatness at the same time that it questions the capacity for "refuge": of whom and by whom, humans and nonhumans. As the aforementioned acts detail, draining the "dismal" at one point reversed to conserving it.[4] Thus if "refuges" are so named due to an "exceptional example of the natural history of the United States," as the country's Fish and Wildlife Service declares, this "natural" narrative is troubling. Thinking through a swamp's troubled history is a draining proposition that saps strength, leading and leaving one down in the dumps.

Drain You

England now rues the day its people ransacked the wetlands, having established the Great Fen Project to save what once was sermonized as unseemly and in need of correction.[5] Centuries earlier, they trembled during debates about how to "treat upon" the country's wet matter that thwarted their intents for population expansion, experiencing a series of protests over the draining of its fens in the eastern part of the country like Lincolnshire, attempts that ultimately gave way to the conversion of wetland into arable ("Beef and Bacon") land and the displacement of the poorer, "Reed"-feeding, rural peoples.[6] It was a wet earth policy sponsored by leaflets like A Discourse Concerning the Drayning of the Fennes (1629), later reprinted as The Drayner Confirmed (1647).[7] Thus if early modern citizens learned the difficulties that all swamps harbored, they were also told how to improve them in manual form, how to eat a more civilized diet. This scientifically engineered practice of water domination was tied to the colonial ambitions in the British archipelago to squash rebellion, the "flying enemie" of the lurking Irishman, who, according to Edmund Spenser's A View of the State of Ireland (1596), "hi[d] himselfe in woodes and bogges" and pestered English planters and soldiers.[8] Further out, those "Fen"-skulkers in the New World only exacerbated hostility at home by extending it geographically abroad; some of the first landscapes sighted in North America were swampscapes. When the Spanish conquistador Hernando de Soto landed in Florida in 1539, he was plagued by the gelatinous Everglades, a "countrie . . . cumbersome with woods and bogs, where the horses stacke fast."⁹ The New World was really a new swamp world. Solid-seekers found only aqua firma in which to plant; facing unruly assemblies eager to stir things up and down, the projectors of marshland reclamation sought to stomp out those human and nonhuman inhabitants near and far who could foil their plans (temporarily and long-term), dis/assembling at will in the quaking zone of wet/land politics, subverting through submergence. There were ample reasons, in short, to fear the swamp in the sixteenth and seventeenth centuries.

The early modern English imagination struggled with framing the "matter" of mud; traveling within, without, or stuck with swampy stuff was a prevalent predicament in popular culture. Caliban's "unwholesome fen" in *The Tempest* (1.2.325), previously discussed, conveniently gums the three aspects of thinking in and with the swamps: colonization and conversion (Prospero's "dry convulsions" [4.1.255]); indigenous resistance at local and global level (Caliban's "wicked" castigations [1.2.324]); and the physical and not just ideological matter of marshland (the island's "dew" [1.2.324]). Authors like William Shakespeare could theorize how moisture infiltrates the human body because travelers had trudged through the massively mossy sites of the continent and then penned accounts of their travails, conflating the globe's two hemispheres of "new" and "old." Todd Andrew Borlik has reevaluated the critical proclivity to see the play as essentially mid-Atlantic, Caribbean, or both: "the chimera known as Caliban is in part inspired by legends of Lincolnshire fen spirits, and . . . his plight comments on the displacement of local cottages by land reclamation projects."¹⁰ The geographical swampscapes explorers entered enfolded into the playwright's (and others') art, thereby generating newer, and even more pernicious, images of toxic muck. Caliban curses from the early modern stage, the east English fen, and the Floridian swamps. When Othello thinks on the green-eyed monster of jealousy, for instance, he thinks on a "toad" and "vapour" of a green-brown "dungeon": the swamp (3.3.275–76). As *Othello* suggests, swamps represented inner fears as well as harbored external creatures. The swamp personifies the sick mind of jealousy, a psychoanalytical dumping ground for repressed desires and the muddy Freudian id. Mind and body collapse into each other; just as the inner thoughts of the mind were to be cleansed from exterior pollutants, the swamps outside the European body required control and, ultimately, purification. The swampscape was not an easy site to pay a visit: calling for a lamp to illuminate—or purge—his slimy dungeon, Othello quickly "put[s] out the light" (5.2.7), horrified by what he sees within himself, tragically bent upon smothering still.

The beating goes on, unfortunately: early modern forays into the fens tell us about humanity's ongoing fight against the quagmire, a transhistorical assault that can never seem to reach a ceasefire. Slung critically at foes, scrubbed obsessively off skin, the soft and squishy stuff too easily turns hard.[11] Michel Serres's *The Natural Contract* opens under the banner of "War, Peace," accompanied by Francisco Goya's painting of two men, knee-dip in sludge, dueling to the death, *The Fight with Cudgels* (ca. 1820–23):

> Who will die? we ask. Who will win? they are wondering—and that's the usual question. Let's make a wager. You put your stakes on the right; we've bet on the left. The fight's outcome is in doubt simply because there are two combatants, and once one of them wins there will be no more uncertainty. But we can identify a third position, outside their squabble: the marsh into which the struggle is sinking.[12]

As Serres points out, swamps typically serve as battlegrounds for human struggles, where armed belligerents exchange diatribes just as Prospero and Caliban before. In fact, humans are still fighting *the* swamp. "Fen" is one of the oldest words in the English language (from the Old English *fen*).[13] While shipwrecks are some of world literature's earliest subjects, swamps have been around since stories were first recorded in English: Grendel and his mother, dwellers on the "mere bottom," are Caliban's kin in *Beowulf* (ca. 700–1000 CE).[14] To love the sticking stir, like Barbara Hurd does, is aberrant; most humans do not like to be "swamped," "mired," or "bogged."[15] Black water conjures up the usual stereotypes— darkness, disease, disorientation, death—according to what Susan Signe Morrison calls the "waste-ern literary canon in the waste-ern tradition."[16] In African American histories of runaway slaves, swamps promote "eco-melancholia."[17] As spaces in which fear is easily met with force, they epitomize "ecophobia."[18] Sticks in the mud are better left alone, we are told. Neither beautiful nor useful, and mysteriously withdrawing into the dark, swamps mark the danger zone, areas of interstitial terror, the spatial borders of civilized development that somehow fan out and hem in at the same time. Aldo Leopold, the famous founder of the "land ethic," rhetorically asked in a "Marshland Elegy," "What good is an undrained marsh anyhow?"[19] Although he was being sarcastic—at least I assume he was—his question remains a good one to ask about the purposes of ecological valuation: how "worth" turns too readily into a fighting word. First comes war, then comes peace: or is it first war, then war? Enter at your own risk. "Every third thought" (5.1.314) of Prospero's pertains to his "grave" in Milan, but the "thought" contains the "third" (space) of the swamp that he cannot completely banish from his mind. In sum, if a contract is only made "good" through contact, the tactility of swamp things perennially retains the bad touch: bodies tagged, cudgeled, dead in the mud.

It is not all death from below in bogland, fortunately: Laura A. Ogden's notion of "swamplife" helps imagine a more perspicacious, materially networked framework for thinking through swampy assemblages, including their dislodgment. Her "landscape ethnography" strategizes "a practice of reintroducing and reinscribing the human back into the multispecies collective while at the same time being attuned to the politics of asymmetrical relations."[20] The "reintroduction" is not anthropocentric, however, but a way to understand "how what it means to be 'human' is constituted through changing relations with other animals, plants, material objects, and the like."[21] Thus if we are to ask how we are geographically losing wetland in the present—to industry, to private ownership—we must additionally inquire into how we have historically rendered swamps and their inhabitants mute, dead, and deadly through longer traditions of violence. Interrogating the fraught question of agency entails seeing the swamp for its suction ontology: an inherent flatness of being (nature–culture symmetry) *given* varying depths and hierarchical determinations (hence Ogden's "asymmetrical" worry) by various social factors. If the danger is now what humans do to swamps, it is harder for swamps to answer back. The two efforts at reviving the role of swamps in the modern environmental imagination with which I opened—preservation and sanctification— are helpful to a certain extent. Yet their underlying idea of rescue effectively robs the swamps of their sphagnous agency and thus jeopardizes any attempt at a politics of nature. By reclaiming the swamp as a meditative site, spiritualized forms of nature writing risk silencing human and nonhuman voices by occluding acts of environmental destruction. If we think that all we have to lose is a measurable area on a map, we delude ourselves. Nature writing on land-water—John Muir's recognition of "disputed empire" and Henry David Thoreau's dictum "[n]ature abhors a straight line"—are promising avenues that postcolonialist critics have importantly advanced, impugning acts of linearity and ethnographic purity.[22] Indeed, the swamp tales below tell of the interstitial parahuman that Monique Allewaert has identified in the early modern Caribbean, a "creolized ontology" of ecological personhood that contests colonialist ideas of the bounded body and that "offers grounds for an ethics of relationality . . . an engagement in which a body is recognized as a medium that extends into (and is extended into by) media that are proximate to it, and sometimes even into media that are not proximate to it."[23] The mixed medium of in/organic mud reaches white and other races, incorporates terror and desire, encompasses humid subtropical (Virginia) and continental (New England) climates, and smears temporal distinctions: time periods peel back like sloppy sediments, revealing their shared material sympathies undermuck.

Swampspeak

I will make a wager: staying in and exploring the mud, specifically the early modern mud of thick possibility, can help promote livable lives for both human and nonhuman things in the swamp while allowing them to voice their past and present grievances. Even if we recognize the "third position" underfoot and over which the squabble slimes, we still risk going to war whenever we grant priority to *either* human or nonhuman interests (between Goya's belligerents or the background), combat the associated logic of cultivation-civilization or let unadulterated wilderness run amok (bifurcating nature and culture), or embrace one affect of uncertain intimacy at the expense of the other (by hate or love). It is easy to pick opposing sides. Stuck in this ethical quagmire, the more we struggle with one side of the question, the more we exhaust ourselves. But the fight in the swamp might abate when fighting *the* swamp stops, when unpacking its contents is an effort to pack in, to "assemble" into assemblages. At the bottom of the mud is only more mud; by concluding that there is no way out of the morass—that we are always-already enmarshed—we gain a critical point of entry. The sphagnous sucks away stability, empties the illusion of solid ground, darkens the elusive transparent. Opaque and exudative, the swamp is an unsteady place to go "for a steady reflection," and that is precisely *why* we should go.[24] Rather than simply recuperate swamps from early modern environmental imaginations, I reach deeper into them, staying in the sink. Early modern swampscapes show us what is at stake when the human attempts to sever itself from the environment. Andrew Pickering persuasively argues that humans are constantly in medias res, "in the thick of things."[25] And so does Shakespeare: we are "dancing up to th' chins" (*The Tempest*, 4.1.183), we are chin-deep (and deeper) in sites of potential, rewriting a swamp epic of isolation and connectivity, of mud baths that please as well as poison. As Caliban's separated form of stymie, "sty me," suggests, it is clear that swamp becomes a "sty"—an inflamed swelling of the eyelid, pigsties in miniature—whenever it and its multiple meanings and possibilities are penned up into stale descriptions. If we hope to challenge the unstoppable momentum of the bellicose, painted with its clubs raised in midstrike, we must cohabit the fluidity of the supposedly stagnant swampscape; dwell with the ooze; proliferate new meanings rather than stick to the old, mired stereotypes; get and go down with the thickness.

I stake that early modern conversations with the swamp, including its curses, help enlarge the lopsided (one-sided) lexicon in use today. Postmodern wetlander Rodney Giblett defines "swampspeak" as the language we use to speak about swamps, calling for a "counter-tradition" to oppose the more derogatory terms like "dismal" we have inherited.[26] I wish to rephrase his "swampspeak" by proposing a posthumanist wet/land ethic that refuses to put its wetness outside of our interpretations and our bodies. To a degree, popular culture trains us to speak a certain dialect of swampspeak: be it the exaggerated masculinity of the television show *Swamp Loggers* (2009–12), the classism of another, *Swamp People* (2010–), or the comic book character and chemically created monstrosity known as Swamp Thing (1971). These examples prove that we need to focus on what kind of "swampspeak" is spoken at any historical moment as well as who is, and who is not, allowed to speak it. Caliban vents his autobiographical tale to Prospero and members of the audience. The native tribes of seventeenth-century New England, as we will see, were less proclamatory although no less audible. The swamp, perhaps out of all my watery shapes herein, best controverts the degradative logic of cultivation and convertibility; if a swamp is on its way *to* something else, this transition, like any sort of forced exodus, is fraught. Their sites are often theaters of violence, and yet, as witnessed with the violent matter of penetrative rain in the previous chapter, they are always more. As spongy collaborations of things tightly packed together, and places full of creatures that have a hold, swamps are ideal sites for exploring our material enmeshment. When things stick together they may desire extraction; they may also wish for grosser connection and intimacy, their "darkness" a token of proximity, of a black "wilderness ontology" that does not escape the stigmas of race and class but confronts them.[27] As some of the planet's most diversified and nutrient-rich ecosystems acting as natural filtration systems, swamps intimate fragility in full;[28] percolating precarious relations, their thickness not so much provides a barrier or shield but pronounces a population of talking things at risk. It is precisely for the trenchant terminology (pure or impure) and cultural valuations (bad or good) used to demarcate them that swamps emphatically recall the stakes humans have in the world of things today. Early modern speaking swamps and writers who spoke of them stymie the dead-"straight line" of empire and the fantasies of the hermetically sealed human in addition to delimiting messy, seemingly impossible desires. They encourage us not to "sty" ourselves on drier land until the swamps—and their stories, layered in biblio-stratifications— are truly irretrievable. To speak up, for, and with the swamp is a means of getting closer and reimmersing ourselves in the language of swamp-composition, of forming allies in outcry against the concrete.

Mucking Up

This chapter inspects the life of "swamplife" in an unlikely way: by entering one of the most violent, and deadliest, conflicts in North American history, King Philip's War (1675–76), that pitted the United Colonies of New England—Connecticut, Massachusetts, Plymouth, and New Haven along with their Mohegan and Pequot allies—against Metacom (Philip) of the Wampanoags in league with the Narragansett, Nashaway, Nipmuck, and Podunk peoples. I argue that swamps muddy the social-political divide between English and native and, more importantly, the greater ontological divide between human and nonhuman. Beleaguered by dark bodies that surface from and withdraw into the swamp, English authors conflated the baleful environment that surrounded them with the threatening native who was born from a merger with its scum. But contrary to Puritan attempts, there is no escape from the entangling swampscape and the things it harbors. Swamps are non/human networks of intergenerational strife that constructively interrogate harmful ideologies, like the racist beliefs, for example, that equated the odious and invasive blackness of the terrain with the pervasive nuisance of the natives. Early modern New England swamp skirmishes—culminating, tragically, in the Great Swamp Fight of December 1675—offer a compelling stage for inquiring about how environmental and human rights are inextricably conjoined. With this point, I confess, I feel *stuck*: detailing, exclusively, the horrible injustices of conflict not only seems at odds with this study's interest in re- and configurations of fleshy desire, but also threatens to neglect smart critical work that has scrutinized hybridized and highly mediated moments of interchange. The mixed media of ecological mixture I detail—that is, ecomaterialist and ecocompositionist bodies in proximity—approximates Matt Cohen's work on the "networked wilderness" that defined the "communication encounters" of early New England, for instance.[29] In other words, by focusing on conflict I might be replicating the exact dichotomization I am attacking. Reading through these primary sources, however, I am astonished at the extent of their stigmatization; and, to be totally honest, I am haunted by their ontological strategy of genocide, the "darker side of the Renaissance['s]" con- and inscriptive techniques.[30] I feel urged to ask how and why such acts of interspecies commingling were suppressed, justifiably (if inexplicably) pressed down into the dark not just of relations but of marginalization and attempted, even accomplished, extirpation. This is my argumentative tactic—my own *great* fight, if you will—to develop a different agenda, a more generous policy of political inclusion that takes the non/human phrase "Brethren of water" seriously to heart. If distracting, I trust the reader to forgive my own feelings laid bare, seeing this final chapter as my own experiment in sensitization rather than a lapse of scholarly diligence on my part.

I outline three slurpy footprints for us to follow. (1) Seventeenth-century narrators of the English-native strife of New England thought of swamps as living things, full of creepy poisons and lacking creeping pleasures, noxious networks of nonhuman and human actants engaged in spontaneous generation. The etymology of "swamp" itself (as rhizomatic "mushroom") illustrates this liveliness, as does their obsession with swamp things that could enmesh the human body. Narrators try in vain to stick to their binary terms: the Puritan is clean, enclosed, and firm, while the Indian is dirty, permeable, and fluid. (2) These narratives of conflict show the violent consequences of a Puritan belief system, guided by religious rhetoric, that insisted upon pure nonhuman and human divisibility. William Hubbard's *A Narrative of the Troubles with the Indians in New-England* (1677)—written out of fear, malice, and obedience to the will of God—will be my main focus for both points, a lengthy account of the Puritans' struggle with the excremental indigene whose body was typecast as a darkly present (even when invisible) danger. To be clear: reading the swamp as a defenseless victim would only make its inhabitants stagnate. The question I pose is not how to "save" the wetlands of the past: hence, in a salvific gesture, repeat the colonial move of making wetlands livable or knowable. This solution entails a similar form of cultivation that reinforces human superiority and perpetuates violence. Neither do I convert swamps into objects worthy of critical attention: this only repeats the Puritan policy of purification I refuse. Early modern swamps instead show us how some actors distribute and/or manipulate agency to the detriment of others. (3) By apprehending these (unheard) voices and (unmarked) bodies hidden in the mud, we envision new ways to address the plight and flight of both nonhumans and humans alike, feeling spaces where emergence and emergency impinge, in which the gobs of conglomeration do away with ontological divides but never with material repercussions and concomitant accountability. The world is a vast swamp of connections—some dangerous, some supposed to be— and better understanding mud's unpredictable slings of mis/fortune, their effects upon bodies, and our participation with them is our task ahead. Going into the darkness of this dark ecological matter can also be a de- and recompositional effort with decay. With a little reflection, steady or not, we learn that a descent into the mud affords us a chance to recompose our shared and sphagnous, more-than-human selves. Swamps quake in anticipation; they are the zones of the virtual, the murky and messy examples of how to make a more-than-human, how to generate a new kind of posthuman ethics in a quaking society: a veritable Slough of Respond. But in order to become better attuned to this vociferous place of violence as well as love with/in the shadows, we have to keep mucking up.

Lifequake

One of the most common misconceptions about swamps is that they are standing bodies of water. But the brackish water does roll: they are "living black waters" with flow.[31] Even if stuck with and to its things, we are never immobile. What is supposedly the most stagnant matter turns out to be the most vibrant and vibrational. Indeed, the word "quagmire" comes from the "quaking zones" we call swamps.[32] We are all shook up: going with the flux of swamp things unsettles claims of human mastery, shakes up traditional knowledge practices and modes of understanding. Giblett's historical study of "postmodern wetlands" is useful to envision nature and culture in a newer temporal paradigm. Still, the nominal "postmodern" might be too tied to the language of the "modern constitution" Bruno Latour critiques, as if we have moved past or *post-* the modernists' epochal divide between nature and culture.[33] The swamps of "early modernity"—by now, a term I use only for convention's sake and for its suggestion of chronological inexactitude—do not just predate the modernist split, they have always been amodern places whose quivering and quaking quasi-objects early modern mudrakers knew well. Writers interested in living swamps could refer to the theory of spontaneous generation located in Aristotle's *History of Animals* (fourth century BCE). Edward J. Geisweidt's reading of "excremental life" in Shakespeare's *Antony and Cleopatra* "questions humans' ability to rise out of the dung heap and attain a nobleness of life that sets them above the animals."[34] Citing Arthur Golding's and Raphael Holinshed's (ca. 1525 – ca. 1580) experiments with hair as well as with English and Egyptian soil, Antony's attestation of the "nobleness of life" (1.1.35–39) in the play "demands a broader understanding of life, that is, as a phenomenon that animates various forms of being."[35] The Nile is crucial in his estimation; as a muddy place of generation as well as putrefaction, a "repository[y] of the planet's own excreted waste," it epitomizes the wider earth's "excremental topography" that "usually feature[d] moist, fenny land, or pools of stagnant water."[36] Geisweidt's ultimate gift is an ethically imperative alternative to the Great Chain of Being: "for although 'forms of life' can be said to substantiate the categories of Being on the Chain, life for the early modern English also involved a shared experience of the world, a mode of relations between humans and other species that did not prioritize one over the other."[37] Dung, or excrement in general, is the great leveler. Significantly, composition and decomposition creatively coexist; "being in excrement" is "stinking evidence of life and death dancing."[38] Spontaneous generation is a rotten dance in which all beings in and of ordure are invited: no questions asked at the door, all partners on the same floor, mangling in the ontogenetic manure.

Geisweidt's excremental emphasis is useful for recognizing another example of early modern "excremental topography": swamps. North American mud could generate lifeforms to boot—perhaps not the beetles, crocodiles, and toads of Cleopatra's Egypt, but its own creatures—in its "repositories," and even, according to the Puritan imagination, human-like shapes. Benjamin Tompson's prefatory encomium to Hubbard's "impartial *Pen*" praised the historian for his high-handed treatment of the region's blurry rebels: "Former Adventures did at best beguile / About these *Natives Rise* (obscure as *Nile*)." But if spontaneously generating excrement is the great leveler, not everything is always on the same level. Focusing on level "nobleness" would mean that even the slots between nonanimal forms are bridged as well: this is not always the case in Geisweidt's view that tends to privilege relations between humans and animals. I find it useful to disgorge the definition of "life" beyond vitalist (animist) terms to a more vital materialist philosophy. Swamp matter itself is lively, not simply dead sphagnum infused with an animating force. Geisweidt's restriction of "life" to the animal kingdom retroactively pushes us to reconsider what forms are allowed to bridge the gaps, both in early modern literature and material ecocriticism at large. We need to expand the terms of swamp *life* and living in order to firmly grasp, in his remarkable phrase, a "shared experience of the world."[39] It requires a return to vocabulary, actually, for early modern swampspeakers wrestled with the sticky predicaments in which they found themselves every time they used language to describe the situation: each time the problematic "swamp" was uttered, black water rolled off their tongues.

Mushroom

Early modern wet writers articulated ideas of generative mud and water-land life whenever they deemed something a "swamp." The most common meaning of the noun "swamp"—"a tract of low-lying ground in which water collects; a piece of wet spongy ground; a marsh or bog"— is of dubious origin.[40] "Swamp" was possibly taken from Low German— where *swampen* denoted quaking or boggy land—and is related to multiple Germanic prefixes with the shared meaning of "sponge" or "fungus": *swamp-, swamb-,* and *swamm-*. These root words are more fungal than arboreal, comprising a network of Germanic languages including Low and Middle High German, Old Norse, Middle Swedish and Swedish, Danish, and early modern Dutch. "Swamp," in a word, is a fascinating specimen of linguistic spongiform. More importantly, "swamp" owes its etymological inception to the North American landscape. Although it had probably been used in local speech around England for some time, the first recorded use of the word "swamp" as a noun applied, unsurprisingly, to the fledgling colony of Jamestown founded in 1607: England's first "permanent" colony that was, in reality, on shaky and impermanent ground. John Smith's (1580–1631) *The Generall Historie of Virginia, New-England, and the Summer Isles* (1624) imprints the swamp for the first time: "In this tract of *Iames* Towne Riuer I know very few; some small Marshes and Swamps there are, but more profitable then hurtfull."[41] In its earliest recorded uses, "swamp" pertained only in the North American colonies, where it denoted a tract of soil with trees and other vegetation too moist for cultivation. As Smith's citation points out, the word from its bemired beginnings is already divisive even if it is etymologically dubious: a negative fecundity set against the positive plenty of agrarian aspirations. Polarized by and to the letter, a "swamp" is "profitable"-to-be once drained and sown. If not met with this steady hand of plantation-making, it remains "hurtfull."

The second sense of "swamp" in English, "mushroom," comes from the Old English *swamm*, most likely as a borrowing from a foreign source.[42] This rarely observed meaning, now obsolete, is supremely significant for my purposes here, for it showcases the mushrooming qualities of muck. "Swamp" meaning "mushroom" appears in a 1621 English translation of Wilhelm Adolf Scribonius's (fl. 1576–83) *Naturall Philosophy*: "In the bodie of the [larch] tree groweth Fungus Agaricus, a swamp or mush-rome. The best is white, thin, full of pores, light, and easie to breake: it purgeth fleame."[43] Scribonius renders the swamp not just as an organic and vegetal place, but as a fungal organism. (Modern science classifies fungi separately from animals, vegetables, and bacteria.) Swamp-as-mushroom by definition emphasizes the swamp's rhizomatic characteristics, a network of sporal actants that sporadically "groweth" and "purgeth" and more. Incidentally, the verb form of "swamp" with which we are most familiar—"to plunge or sink as if in a swamp or in water; to overwhelm with difficulties, or esp. by superior numbers, so as to render inefficient"—first appeared in 1818.[44] Yet the swamp's transitive powers were observed centuries sooner. Medieval authors (ca. 1480) gestured to its embodied effects, establishing parallels between a *swank* ("depression in the ground, deep hollow, bog") and being *swank* ("thin in the belly").[45] "Swank" referred to "a body that may be or is normally distended: that has sunk and become flat; thin from emptiness, as the breasts, the belly, etc." This *swank*-y conjunction perhaps explains the long-standing association of swamps with depression: they literally "depress" bodies by "pressing down," making them feel mentally and emotionally swamped because of physiologically mushrooming connections. Historically, "swamp" became a process and gained its "mushroom effect" (I call it) once it materially interacted with the geographic swamps of North America. Overall, in both senses of the word, "swamp" grew out of marshy ground, generated new language—its own "swamp-speak"—in dialogue with fungal others. Thus the very word "swamp" describes what a swamp *is* and what a swamp *does*; in short, a swamp is an assemblage of mud-packed things that shakes things up, creates, connects, and mushrooms.

The linguistic mobility of "swamp" was pronounced enough, in fact, that when the theologian and founder of Providence Plantation, Roger Williams (ca. 1606–83), put swamps in *A Key into the Language of America* (1643) he listed them in his eleventh chapter titled "Of *Travell*." Algonquian "Cuppi-machàug" translates into "*Thick wood: a Swamp*."[46] He provides an annotation for this "*Obs.*" word: "These thick Woods and

Swamps (like the Boggs to the *Irish*) are the Refuges for Women and children in Warre, whil'st the men fight."[47] As a simultaneous pushing away (into obsolescence) and bringing closer (into censure of the Irish), the swamp's persistent links to gendered violence demonstrate that a vocabulary of the "swamp" was not so obsolete, after all, but could be used for discriminating ends, even as its incessant travel was disapproved or its multiple roots immobilized. In the same way that Williams handled words like "Cuppi-machàug" in his dictionary—translating them not for the benefit of acculturation but to mark them as defunct—writers widely repudiated the rhizomatically inflected "swamp" and the teeming "nobleness of life" for which it stood. These actual, never "*Obs.*," lives sought "Refug[e]" from a puritanical disdain that defined swamp things as unspeaking as well as unspeakably abhorrent.

Black Turf

From the first seeds sown in the new northeastern lands of "Virginia" and "New-England," the English plantation agenda resembled that of a dutiful gardener's: emplacing themselves by re- and displacing the human and nonhuman inhabitants who preceded them. (It is an analogy apparent enough, I think, that I will avoid overstating it here.)[48] What was there previously—and unable to be commodified—could easily become expendable to the colonial project, and the nearly ubiquitous early modern aversion to swamps fit neatly into this mold. The swamp's conflation with miasma and sickness is the clearest indictor of its denigration. When George Gardyner (ca. 1610 – ca. 1677) compares the weather in the "*America* Islands and *Continent*" to that of England in 1651, he describes the source of the region's rampant summer heat: warm exhalations from "wood swamps, and such moist crudities, as are not in Europe."[49] And while he attributes the planters' recurrent sicknesses to the fickleness of the weather, the "unwholsome" air bred by the "standing-waters" of swamps is especially pernicious.[50] But the moistness of such "crudities" could be vaporized properly through hard work, a directive that was commonly disseminated; texts like William Wood's (fl. 1629–35) *New Englands Prospect* (1634), for example—and there are many others[51]—extolled the prospective richness of marshy soil for agriculture and were, in essence, manuals for labor. Wood's motto for home improvement caught on: "[A]ll

new *England* must be workers in some kinde."[52] Smith himself had advertised the region as richly rewarding, claiming that "Nature in few places
affoords any so conuenient [for building], for salt Marshes or Quag-
mires."[53] Yet these early to midcentury advocates were only preludes to
the straight lines of territorialization set down by Ferdinando Gorges
(1568–1647), whose *America Painted to the Life* (1658) draws pictures
in words of towns like Ipswich literally sprung up from the muck, making clear that even a "most hideous swamp of large extent, even for many
Miles" can be civilized.[54] Gorges founded Maine but never travelled to
the continent himself; still, the picture of typical life that he paints for
his readers, such as this one of Roxbury ca. 1631, indicates a prolific pattern in publications at this time that portrayed the English as industrious
gardeners,

> a very laborious people, whose labours the Lord hath so blest, that in the
> roome of dismall Swampes and tearing Bushes, they have very goodly
> Fruit-trees, fruitfull Fields and Gardens, their Heard of Cowes, Oxen and
> other young Cattell of that kind about 350. and dwelling-houses neere
> upon 120.[55]

In Gorges's *America* the conversion of swampland by New England residents meets the greater Puritan work ethic: the "prospect" (as picture) of
agricultural imperialism and a newer England to which Wood prospec-
tively looked forward.[56] As the English numbers mushroom at a "blest"
and accelerated rate, they are configured as stocky planters in a confined
"roome," trees with roots that avoid the language of assemblage. There is
little "roome" for "dismall Swampes" at first. "Fruit-trees" and "dwelling-
houses" alike must be planted. And both require the "tearing" of "Bushes,"
a rending wetland ethic of conquest that dominates dismalness, its tearing a manifestation of their intended separation from sick and unwanted
marshland, a puritanical protocol that will eventually leave these exact
same garden states like Ipswich, Roxbury, and their roomy environs war-
torn. The prospect laid out in these moist manifestos—although they
would never be identified as such—establishes the lines of normality and
expectations for others' trajectories to follow: do not be "crud[e]" in your
new home.

It is with Samuel Hartlib's (d. 1662) *Legacy of Husbandry* (1655) that the seeds of systemic stigmatization bear fruit, describing swamp bodies discarded from the northeastern prospect. His "legacy" is a form of socio-economic fungal generation that disparages certain social groups by associating them with the engrossing and outspreading ooze. Explaining the types of wood that "do grow wonderfully thick" in the region's swamps, he conflates the swamps with the poor, rendering both human and non-human harmful to society: "I suppose these *Moors* are *Commons*, to the which the poor have used to resort for siring, and how soon great woods will be consumed by them, every one making what havock he pleaseth, all men know."[57] The "them" is the outlandish poor; Hartlib's concern is not only that humans will chop down the woods, but also that the forests will be "consumed" by the poor, those who can make as much "havock" as they want and thereby mangle the proper agricultural model just delineated. It is clear that he is not simply arguing for (what we would now call) better conservation practices but for firmer social divisions. Less sympathetic and more sententious, the ecological "*Commons*" he allocates is discriminatory, segregational. Swamp-bodies are the least desirable in society, the worst-off, the consumers who cannot afford to live anywhere else and continue to infect the land. (Notably, other forms of consumption, like his own, escape these condemnations.) These "poor" bodies consume, but they also generate, amass, and mushroom, becoming the swamps they flee into. In the same passage, Hartlib publicizes the swamp's "vegetative" powers:

As concerning their being so deep in the ground, and their blackness; I suppose that when wood was abundant in those places, every one did cut what they pleased, and left what was not for their turns, which being in moist places, was soon glutted with moisture, and made ponderous; by which means it soon buried it self, as Ships do, on Quicksand, or perhaps the *Turf* (which hath a peculiar faculty vegetative, for where it is exhausted, it soon groweth again) in time hath grown over them.[58]

The swampy "*Turf*" houses vegetation like trees and productively vegetates as well, possessing the inexhaustible "peculiar[ity]" to bring forth ("groweth") things. In Hartlib's mind, this positive fecundity or "faculty" is detrimental, negative; his social anxiety, then, relays an even greater panic about being "made ponderous" by the swamp, "glutted" (from Latin *gluttire*, "to swallow") by the crudities of moisture, depressingly *swank*ed socially, psychologically, and physically.[59] "[I]n time," the vegetal landscape will overcome class aspirations, body, and mind. Like wet wood permissible only when it is useful, not by its own existence, those "being[s] so deep" down the ranks of social stratification—stumps and the poverty-stricken—are better left to fend for themselves in the fens: "because that wood, once *sobbed* in wet, is of little use, as we see by *Piles* on the *Marshes*-side, scarce any man vouchsafing to carry them home."[60] Recognizing his own corporeal risk of contamination, Hartlib states that swamps belong to the poor because their bodies alone share affinities with it: they are the "ponderous" not deserving of pity; a contagion of impecuniousness to be avoided; piles of poverty wrecked in shallow ponds "as Ships do," sobbing their brackish tears, sinking in the quick-"*Turf*" outside the prospects that will not envision them. Yet one foot is always in the frame: to see "a citty upon a hill" is to look up, after all, never down at the dirt striding the water table.[61]

As his attention not just to the depth but to the color of the swamp makes unpleasantly apparent, Hartlib uses swamp's "blackness" to code any intolerable thing of darkness that he does not want to husband. In doing so, he prefigures a materially based form of racism that would be levelled against dark bodies and that fueled English fights in and against the swamps. To Hartlib's dismay, inhabiting the black-brown hues of onto-logical inseparability—the horizontal plane of "ponderous" interactions—is a creeping sensation; no matter how harangued, the blackness of "*Turf*" is not just penetrative of certain bodies, the poor, but is a precondition for life and lives in the quaking zones. Granted its own desires, the glut-tonous swamp would attempt to gorge on everything within its sprawl-ing maw:

> The blackness of this wood proceedeth, as I suppose, from the sooty fume, or *evaporation* of the black *turf,* (which endeavoreth, as all earths do) to reduce all things into its own nature; which though it be not able fully to accomplish; yet it introduceth divers dispositions, and qualities, as blackness in the Wood. Some suppose, that these *Moor-logs* have lain

there ever since the *flood*, with whom I will not contend; seeing that any wood, if it be kept from the Aire continually moist or dry, will endure even thousands of years without putrefaction.[62]

Here Hartlib conceives of swamp-life in his theory of the earth's "*evaporation*," just as he did in its vegetative powers; again, this life is rendered dangerous by its ability "to reduce all things into its own nature," even if "not able fully to accomplish" it. The earth imparts "qualities" like "blackness" into the bodies with which it comes into contact. (Contemporary anxieties over the vapors emitted by another local item, tobacco, are similar.)[63] The swamp "endeavoreth," and it always gets in, "as all earths do." In thinking about the source of wetland's "sooty fume," Hartlib introduces a problematic materiality of race—the uneasy juxtaposition between "*Moor-logs*" and Moors, perhaps—and, more urgently, the absent-presence of New England natives from his analysis. All bodies can become black, but some are significantly blacker than others. Hartlib is on the verge of a swampy ecomaterialism that accounts for difference without granting certain swamp things (the human, whiteness) automatic superiority, a deduction, if made, that would openly evince the irreducibility of relations. The "black *turf*" has its own desires, he "suppose[s]"; it wishes to draw things, and transform things, "into" it. Regardless of its ability to assemble "divers dispositions" across all non/human bodies, blackness is firmly associated with the world's dark undesirables. Hartlib tries to hide the fact that blackness can slip in at any time, including the present. He betrays himself in his temporal comment; these black logs are not from a bygone antediluvian age he "contend[s]," but from multiple times, washed up in the era of endless swamps surrounding them: the land of "the *flood*," the poisonous now. Brought closer and not blown completely off the margins, the gaseous potential of the swamp's "black *turf*" is ushered in— and inhaled—only to exhibit the dangers of relation. No body is safe at any moment of time; the "fume" must be fought if the English were to "endure even thousands of years" in a purer air rather than the paradoxically preservative space of the swamp: as we will see, it was a mission that disastrously linked trenchant racism with entrenched environmental degradation, a lamentable legacy that proved predictable to foresee and hard to forestall.

One illusory hope of safeguarding the bounded body from "blackness" was the conversion of the fumy unfamiliar into familiar substance. The commodification of materials applied to the salvation of souls. Place-based melees with mephitic *"Moor-logs,"* combated by heavy-handed gardening, and endorsed by early English writers, stretched to their ideological limits once combined with Puritan religious ideology, which involved, in the most general terms, an injunction to improve a fallen nature. The Puritans' work ethic was not just tilling fields but doing God's work on earth. Conversion of land dovetailed (not so) neatly with conversion of persons. Thomas Hooker (ca. 1586–1647) claimed in *The Application of Redemption* (1656) that purifying the "dunghil heart, a soul like a dirty swamp," takes labor, just like turning a putrefying piece of ground into arable land does.[64] In his printed series of arguments and counterarguments with Roger Williams, *A New-England-Fire-Brand* (1678), George Fox (1624–91) wrote of swamps as surmountable impediments to Christian self-fashioning: "So we are not in a *Bog* and *Swamp* . . . *between Christ* within and *Christ* without; our Understanding is clear, it's his own State."[65] The swamp supplies Fox's metaphor for a theological hard place stuck between inner and outer Christ. Typically representing the negative aspects of religious doubt and uncertainty allegorically, the real and ubiquitous wetlands of New England fed the populace's fervent religiosity. Even if they wished to denigrate the *"Bog* and *Swamp"* as sites of extreme sloth or moral lassitude, the swampscape was an essential player in the articulation of Puritan philippic. Reading these religious texts ecopoetically proves that the Puritans could not deny the swamps' stentorian voice: in fact, their language only amplified it. Utilizing, not purging, the metonymic ties between wetland and language, however, swamps were the depths of darkness, a veritable hell-on and down-to earth where native tribes lived, resisting the seeds of Christianity by worshipping Satan who ferried tempted believers into the black. Richard Gilpin's (1625–1700) *Demonologia Sacra* (1677) cites native service to the damp devil, while William Gurnall's (1616–79) *The Christian in Compleat Armour* (1655) compares the devil's strategy of concealment to a body lurking in a swamp.[66] The puritanical Christian-warrior therefore did double duty: cleaning up the slough meant that one could baptize its black waters with fire while simultaneously proselytizing (or anesthetizing) the heathen hordes they anathematized.

Religious rhetoric of darkness faithfully served the dual purposes of racial differentiation and ecological mastery, plating soldiers who believed in the rustproof logic of bodily impermeability as they marched onward into darkness and toward the darker-skinned minions who served, as a contemporary poet of Puritanism put it, the "Prince of Darkness."[67] Hubbard, for example, glories in taking prisoners, meaning King Philip's "black Regiment of *Wempanoags*," out of "those habitations of darkness."[68] Tones of skin, place, and religion are uneasily enfolded in this one convenient phrase, strung together in a nasty sermonic syllogism.

The conflation, not just the letter, kills. Although not exonerated for the incendiary illustrations they painted and helped disseminate in perpetuity, Hartlib and the rest of his anhydrous congregation had historical reason to view swampscapes and their black things as inimical: the Pequot War (1634–38) that resulted in the enslavement and near elimination of the Pequot tribe in present-day Connecticut. But this was just a spar compared to King Philip's War forty years later, a conflict that shook the quaking zone to unspeakable depths, where the association of "black *turf*" with foreign others, bolstered by Puritan bombast, became a propagandistic

Walter Blith (fl. 1649), *The English Improuer Improued* (London, 1652). Detail from page 31. Folger Shakespeare Library Shelfmark B3195 Copy 1. Reprinted by permission of the Folger Shakespeare Library.

call to cudgels. Walter Blith's (1605–54) advice in 1652 for making marshland's wayward "water work most gallantly" was to fashion a homemade
leveler. "[B]eat over all thy Land. . . . You cannot possibly beleeve how
fast worke will goe forward."[69] This tamping tool of England's "improue-
ment" was but one sort of ontological weapon used—ironically in this
instance—*against* the horizontal leveling of relations. My brief survey of
swamps within the discourses of colonial planting and religious conversion is intended to prepare us for what happens when religious doctrines
of sin and death intersect with physiological discourses of malodorous
dark matter; as a result, the native human and nonhuman populations
often exclusively felt the repercussive weight. If being in the swamp is
evidence of "life and death dancing," Puritan responses to the opaque
bodies of New England are unequivocal examples of how the dance can
be deadly in the main. In 1689, but a decade after the war, the most
polemical Puritan ideologue, Cotton Mather (1663–1728), could write
about the altered landscape: "there are scarce any of them [the Narra-
gansett] that we know of, to be now seen upon the face of the Earth."[70]
Conversion entails the extermination of the earth's "face" and its faces, of
wetlands and wet people, those "tawny Infidels" Mather rebukes.[71] Mus-
keg meets musket, the modernist work of purification, the bloody point
where subjects sever from objects, literally purged by firebrands wield-
ing fire: a *dismal* protocol to prevent further putrefaction, by all means.[72]
Because I assume the conflict is lesser known, allow me to briefly sketch
its key events before delving, in medias res, into Hubbard's retelling, at
which time I will ponder, myself, whether swamp things from the past can
tell us anything about how to change prescribed futures.

(Wet) War, Peace

Put your stakes. The four bellicose English colonies who fought in King
Philip's War—Massachusetts, Plymouth, Connecticut, and New Haven—
were a barely united band of disparate Puritan sects that had been stitched
together as the New England Confederation in 1643. The earliest colonists "were convinced that they had a mission, a divinely appointed 'Errand
into the Wilderness,'" note historians Richard Slotkin and James K. Folsom, "and that in going to the New World they were fulfilling an evident
purpose of God."[73] But this mission could be interpreted secularly to

divisive effect. Living in a fertile land, desires for economic independence jarred with the communitarian principles of the congregation-colony. When borderers pursued the fruits of the wilderness, their nonreligious spirit left a class struggle pertaining to church membership and ministerial authority for future generations to inherit. Because of strains like these, the relative prosperity they had achieved after decades (1620–40) of initial hardship with little outside support—tribal land treaties, peace with the Dutch and French, and victory over the Pequot—was imperiled. Writers viewed the past as a kind of golden age, attributing to it an Exodus-like tenor of puritanical heroism. What is more, the restoration of the Stuart monarchy in 1660 and its efforts to reassert the primacy of royal government in the colonies added stress. The settlements had prospered during the Interregnum; Charles II, however, tried to revoke the charters that had previously allowed them virtual self-governance for nearly forty years. As a result of these numerous pressures, King Philip's War literally "exploded in a society that was already riven by an internal crisis: at war with itself over Indian policy and over economic, social, political, and religious issues, and divided along lines of class, race, interest, and generation."[74] It is crucial to understand the New England colonies not as a molar unit bound by common faith, enjoying the relative ease of security and religious identity, and succumbing to an invasive force (whether Carolingian or aboriginal). Instead, the war highlighted and exacerbated the internal crisis that had already begun: "The Indian war precipitated conflicts inherent in the structure of colonial society and offered the model of a conflict of races as an analogy for the internal and external conflicts of that society."[75] Puritan writers forecast an unraveling unity, able to anticipate the end of one conflict only to visualize new ones ahead, both within themselves and with their neighbors across humid horizons.

Who will win? The tension plaguing Puritan–"Indian" relationships was characterized chiefly as "clientage politics": disputes respecting landownership and other inheritable entitlements with vast economic importance. The English proved to be coercive and exploitative in their dealings, "unscrupulous in their pursuit of *realpolitik*."[76] Metacom (Philip), chief of the Wampanoags, inhabited the islands of Narragansett Bay and the Mount Hope Peninsula. The Wampanoags had a long history of friendship with the English: Metacom's father, Massasoit, dealt with the Pilgrims. Along with his brother Wamsutta (Alexander), they remained "free sachems" who swore obedience to the king rather than colonial jurisdiction.[77] Their principal dealings were with the Plymouth and Rhode Island colonies, two settlements with questionable charters that needed to possess primitive land tenure in order to validate their claims: Plymouth had settled in the wrong location granted to them, and Rhode Island had controversially split from Massachusetts. Arguably, the war started when business-as-usual "clientage" politics went wrong: John Winslow seized Wamsutta in 1644 and forced him to sell land to Plymouth (his home colony) rather than Rhode Island. His captive, however, grew ill and died; when Metacom succeeded him, he was accused of conspiring to raise a rebellion in retaliation for his brother's death, whereupon he swore his innocence and promised not to broker land without Plymouth's blessing. Plymothians used this agreement to expand their territories from 1665 to 1671. When the natives began menacing settlers in objection to the increasing number of English incursions, Metacom was brought to trial at Taunton, fined, and compelled to swear his allegiance again (this time to Charles II as well). When he appealed to Massachusetts for help—hoping to flame intercolonial rivalry—the colony surprisingly supported its neighbor, coercing Metacom into signing a revised version of the Taunton agreement, after which he began to foment discontent amongst outlying tribal bands while diplomatically placating the English. Thus the exploitative dealings with native "clientage" help explain the large numbers Metacom was able to amass so quickly, "testimony more to the ubiquitous effects of English encroachment," it must be said, "than to the power of Philip as a conspirator."[78]

Who will die? Metacom's first attack was on Swansea, Massachusetts, in June 1675. By August the offensive moved north, where the English were routinely beaten due to their inept organization and general ignorance of indigenous tactics. In the middle of the month the most exposed parts of Massachusetts were descended upon, and the English confederation officially declared war on September 9. The fighting spread north and east over the next two months, during which time the English endured ambushes in devastating repetition, abandoned multiple towns, and felt constrained enough to break a consequential peace treaty with the Narragansetts. In November, the colonial commissioners sent a force of one thousand soldiers under the command of Winslow to destroy the Narragansetts in their winter stronghold. The English marched into the chilled swamps of Rhode Island on December 18 and attacked the next day; the Great Swamp Fight left approximately seventy English and three hundred natives dead and marked the turning point in the war. But 1676 began with a massive onslaught led by Metacom, who stormed the Massachusetts border and penetrated deep into Plymouth territory. He and his allies pushed to within just ten miles of Boston, attacked the capital Plymouth Town, and invaded Connecticut. Surviving a major epidemic in the spring, the natives prepared for the biggest assault yet; in April they were repelled at Sudbury, and while both sides suffered major losses in the combat, the native forces could not fight a long war of attrition like their enemies. They suffered a similar defeat at the Falls of the Connecticut in May, allowing the English to effectively sweep through Narragansett country in June and July. The loss of leading chiefs and the defection of tribes depleted an already-weakened native morale. His friends surrendering, Metacom retreated to his swamp home at Mount Hope Neck where he was betrayed, murdered in August 1676 by one of his own men while walking in the woods. His widow and young son were sent to slavery in the West Indies. By late August the last war band had surrendered, signifying the end of native resistance in southern New England. Many faced the same fate as Metacom's family: either shipped off to plantations or withheld as a domestic source of labor. Peace at last. If there were, according to Mather, "scarce any of them" left shortly after the war, by 1830—when the U.S. Congress passed the Indian Removal Act—disease and cultural dissolution had made "them" even scarcer.

Frustrated Ends

In a word, Hubbard's account of the troubles that I have chronologically traced is "troubled" as much as it is troubling.[79] Little is known of the Reverend William Hubbard (ca. 1622–1704). Born in Essex, he arrived in New England in 1635, graduated from Harvard in 1642, and entered the ministry at Ipswich, Massachusetts, where he distinguished himself through sermons and histories, including his embattled archive to which I now turn, the *Narrative*. Hubbard's prefatory material proves that he did not sit easy on his laudations as the great Puritan chronicler. The war with all its muckiness—"*the Late Troubles in the Two Last Years, 1675 and 1676*," as his full title discloses—was still too close to home in 1677. He seems vexed by the very reason that he has to write a narrative in order to set the record straight: he says as much in his "Advertisement" about the "matters of fact" that his profession obliges him to "make good." Even so, he cannot avoid the "barbarous inhumane outrages" that come at him from the past, and, moreover, he must reluctantly return to the inhospitable places in which the events occurred, "which no Geographers hand ever measured, scarce any vultures eye had ever seen." Hubbard's solution is to start making lines, reverentially translating the events of the previous years into safer metaphors by assigning them places in ordered providence. His epistolary dedication opens the narrative organically, configuring the New England colonies as an ecosystem under duress—"*from the First Planting Thereof in the Year 1607*"—and one that necessarily must be so: "It is with young Colonies, as it is with trees newly planted, which those winds, as one saith, that are not so boisterous as to blow down, doe so far advantage as to shake them to a greater fastness at the root." Tribulations, simply put, strengthen roots. The arboreal metaphor is telling for its linearity, progressing the Puritans to their present moment ordained in divine time. Likewise, the narrative is a thing newly planted, a sprouting seed that will grow to help those in the future, a promise of continuance that is dependent upon his bookish brethren to nurture it:

> [I]t might have remained in the place where it was first conceived & formed, or been smoothered as an imperfect Embrio, not worthy to see the light, if some such as your selves had not both quickned the being, and hastned the birth thereof. Something of this nature may be of use to post[e]rity.

Hubbard writes a living history that is shared with specific "selves": those saved spiritually and carnally who are able to recall their collective woe. Drawn into the swampy unknown that cannot be accurately mapped by himself alone, he must refer to the reports of the "Actors, or Spectators" who were there. His narrative is a beacon of hope for making the unknowable knowable through colonial encounter, bringing "it" to "light" in both historical and theological terms, so that "post[e]rity, as well as to those of the present Generation" can remember the "special preservations granted by divine favour to the people here." The arboreal method he "conceive[s]" spruces up the murky and too-recent past in an attempt to make a troubled history untroubled in its facticity, pruning the messy offshoots of multitemporality when necessary. As past troubles are straightened out in sequential order, and finally superseded on a fixed timeline of history, they become irretrievably "former"—so he thinks—and fall into the past.

Smooth time depends upon "smoother[ing]" the swamp, of course, the stuff his seedy history is watered by and militates against. As if anticipating this contradiction, Hubbard enters right into the heart of the "quickned" matter: the war's first raid on quag, is, in fact, the story's opening skirmish, and therefore offers an overarching way to understand Hubbard's annoyance with the swampscape. The war begins, in the historian's estimation, with the death of translator John Sausaman, Metacom's close associate and a Christianized native who divulges his warlord's malicious intentions to the English and is subsequently murdered for his betrayal. The English, denouncing the crime as one of religious intolerance, mistakenly believe that war will be avoided if they do not arraign Metacom. He has gathered too much force, however, and native families flock to the nearby Narragansetts for security. And so, Hubbard decrees in a grave tone, it was in "*Swanzy . . .* on the 24*th.* of *June* 1675. [that] the Alarm of War first sounded in *Plimouth Colony*" (16). The English quickly discover that this war will be fought differently. Thomas Savage, in charge of the Massachusetts company, forces his savage foes off of Mount Hope and into the swamps but must delay further advance due to foul weather. The next day at noon they come upon a sad scene: houses "newly burned," Bibles "newly torn," and, down the highway, "some Heads, Scalps, and Hands cut off from the bodys of some of the English, and stuck upon Poles . . . in that barbarous and inhuman manner bidding us Defyance" (19). Hubbard frequently paints pictures of fragmentation such as this for his readers, situating "Defyance" beside the shores of swamps for added shock value and vilification. He continues to a point: the English "espyed a company of Indians burning an house; but could not pursue them by reason of several Fences, that they could not goe over till the Indians had escaped into a Swampe" (20). The English are always one step behind the retreating natives who unfairly use the swamp for fighting—"by skulking behind Trees" (38)—for refuge, and for flight.[80] Soldiers only enter the swamps upon orders, not by their own volition, as Savage hits on: "it was resolved that a more narrow search should be made after them, both upon *Mount-Hope*, and upon the ground between *Swanzy* and *Rehoboth* to scoure the Swamps, and assault them if they could find where they were entrenched" (20). Swamps terrify the English; they prefer to bide their time on the fences they had once constructed to keep the swale beyond the pale. Hubbard's battle hymn against "them," the swamp-"Indians," will incorporate several key components in its refrain: the simultaneously "entrenched" and fleeing native unable to be found; the English follow-ing their disappearing tracks, predictably halted by anything unincorpo-rated or transmutational, such as "bodys" in pieces, apostasy, *the* swamp on/as a whole. Although they will eventually make peace treaties with certain native groups and fight alongside them, these agreements will always be done with a "Sword in their hands" (20–21). The idea of trans-cultural and transcorporeal exchange is a nervous one by default, and swamps are the material representatives for nerve-wracking ecological mix-ture in essence.

Swamps are consistent sites of ontological scrambling between human, animal, and vegetable: places, to Hubbard's horror, "in a continual motion" (86). King Philip's War is named for its rebellious protagonist, but it is really a war against the swamps that harbor him and where he hides "like a wild Boar kept at a Bay" (25). The native body, not the English one, is that which runs the constant risk of undertaking taboo metamorphosis; bestial imagery is often employed to describe their adversaries: they are boars, "*Serpents*" (94), "Monsters" (41–42), "Wolves" (33), and flushed-out "Fox[es]" (101) seemingly at random. How this zo/ontological polic-ing holds up in the confusion of battle is less clear, yet the English soon discovered that a "Sword" or musket in hand could be useful to conquer their onto-epistemological fears of the bush. After the first swamp fray the English retreat, reluctant to "figh[t] with a wilde Beast in his own den" (27). But Benjamin Church rallies the troops, pressing Metacom further into the swamp around Pocasset. Here the English learn how to "scoure the Swamps"—that is, "clean away" (from Latin *excurare*)—and the first large-scale swamp fight begins:

Af[t]er the first shot, the Enemy presently retired deeper into the Swamp, deserting their Wagwams (about an hundred in all) newly made of green Barks, so as they would not burn. . . . The Commander in chief, (night drawing on apace) not thinking it safe to tarry longer in so dangerous a place, where every one was in as much danger of his fellows as of his foes, being ready to fire upon every Bush they see move (supposing *Indians* were there) ordered a Retreat to be sounded. (26)

The swamp is the ultimate arena of disorientation on multiple levels. In terms of space, bodies have nowhere and everywhere to retreat at once: one can always tread "deeper." Socially, distinctions between "*Indians*" and English muddle: allegiances dissolve as comrades incorrectly meddle with their "fellows" in their frightened desperation. Ontologically, boundaries between human and nonhuman break down: natives attack by becoming verdant middles, taking "advantage of the thick under-wood" (26) and living in "green Barks" like a virulent species of tree, who can grow right around the English—as the swamp does—everywhere and anywhere at once. While the English characterize their opponents as deserters, they themselves are actually the most mired. Swamps are places of immobility for the English, but for the natives they are places of mobility: newness "newly made" of the holm with which to blend their bodies and build their homes. Becoming moving "Bush" is supposedly a trait belonging solely to "the Enemy," yet it proves an unreliable marker as friends as well as "foes"—as humans—turn unidentifiable in the fading light. Fire's illumination will not avail them here, either, refusing to enlighten their nonsensical classifications upon closer inspection; their misleading senses seem to feed rather than dispel their parahuman paranoia.[81] When the English try to sieve the swamp into principal parts they deceive themselves; with their weary attempts to "scoure" dirty entities into pristine lines and bodies, they might as well sound a retreat, for the fantasy of making a clean break with their surroundings is just that: a fatiguing and fatuous wish for impossible inextricability.

Hubbard's unburnable "Bush" is his signal for the swamp as a live and unruly creature. But the chronic English response to this greatly discombobulating bog is inflammatory force, tireless bushwhacking that decisively debases beings within it. When the sword fails to cleave cleanly or dominate discernibly, as "Commander" Church realized, their automatic reaction is to seek solid ground; not exactly able to drain adversarial fens through impromptu feats of engineering, they mud-brick up temporary houses for themselves in vain, stiff efforts to deter not just their vegetative enemies but dissolution entirely. Told that Philip is lodged in the same swamp, and remembering Church's persecution, Daniel Henchman and his men decide to starve out the opposite side, and "[t]o that end they began to build a Fort, as it were to beleaguer the enemy, and prevent his escape out of the place, where they thought they had him fast enough" (27). There is no thought of going in and staying there, simply one of commandeering "the place": an entrance into the swamp is a roundtrip ticket for the English. The necessary return means that they can muck up only so far. The English refuse to get dirty, at least willingly, and this betrays their un/flagging attempts, again, to strain the swampscape into discrete things: "swamp," "English," and "Indian." What is easy to miss, however, is why Henchman's crew initially choose "to build a Fort"; debating their next course of action, "their eyes were muffled with the leaves, and their heads pinnioned with the thick boughs of the trees, as their feet were continually shackled with the roots spreading every way in those boggy Woods" (27). The English begrudgingly grasp swamps' surprise of action at this instant: manacled by moss, "muffled," and "pinnioned," they are insufferably "shackled" by "those boggy Woods." The "thick boughs" of the Englishman-tree illustrates the body's wretched (to Hubbard) interconnectedness with the swampscape, just as the "green" natives had done before.[82] What infuriates them repeatedly is just how this leafy open-ended state could translate into speed for the enemy's war machine that, like them, faced the same smooth—albeit tangled and tentacular—swampscape. Metacom makes off from this sticky situation, one out of many frustrating times to come, his getaways reinforcing the English standpoint that wetlands defy capture as well as empire. (Not all were so lucky in avoiding the Christian-State apparatus, however: women and children were regularly left behind as prisoners.)[83] The Puritans' saving grace from the advancing-retreating wilderness was to cite or return to God's will. Hubbard supplies a quick sermon for the ultimately unfortified soldiers: "the most likely meanes are often frustrated of their desired end" (28). The message to push on, to convert the hybrid swamp into an organized system of straight lines and immaculate edges—to erect shining forts in "the networked wilderness"—was a matter of faith, of believing that all trajectories teleologically point to God above, not the muck below. Praying for divine intervention to disavow the swamps' materiality that preyed upon them, their words "muffled" and their thoughts frustrated about the lack of "ends"—both embodied and heuristic—the English, for now, are not merely ambushed: they *are* the dreaded "Bush."

Fair Fight

Keeping dissoluble and disaggregated "bodys" in the swamp compact is an endless war the English can never win, serving up a series of Pyrrhic puritanical victories that inflict each entity involved. One captain, Samuel Mosely, pursued the enemy so "through and through," we are told, that he "took a little breath [and] was almost melted with labouring, commanding, and leading his men through the midest of the enemy" (40). Significantly, Mosely *almost* melts. But the swamp, as I have been insisting, smears all. Hubbard's holistic fantasy would take a miracle to happen: or a massacre. As the natives' association with animal and vegetal forms hardens over time, the narrative's notoriously ethical impasse, the Great Swamp Fight, approaches. Their courage emboldened after success at Hatfield, and with winter coming, the English sense an opportunity to drive the natives, God-willing, into the afterlife, the swamp-pit of hell. Hubbard's delight in recollecting their counteroffensive is alarming by being almost gleeful in its anticipation: "the greatest number of them to be sure were found in the winter at the *Narrhaganset Fort,* where we shall leave them for the present till the Forces of the United Colonies shall fire them out of their nests" (47). This "nes[t]"—like a troublesome insect's—will be burned. By attacking the hive, Hubbard explains, every single pest can be exterminated at once to prevent any pesky reprisal: "there were before this time so many hundreds gathered together into one Body, and that there was great reason to fear, if they were let alone till the next spring they might all rise together as one man round about us" (47). Hubbard lets slip another, far more injurious reason for their elimination besides militaristic opportunity (harmful in itself): the ideological fear of "Indian" infestation. In the spring, the consolidated and cocooned "Body" will hatch "hundreds" and "could on a sudden on any occasion

spread themselves like grashoppers all over the Country" (47). When
Hubbard compares the English to insects—bees, for example—it is to
applaud their industry: a "little Regimental Army, as busie as Bees in a
Hive" (53). The entomological likenesses denigrate the natives as pests,
contrasting the regimented apiary order of the English to the reckless
migratory marauding of their rivals, couching fears of their multiple
and multiplying competition in biblical typology: buzzing bodies misbe-
have like the Egyptian plague of locusts detailed in the book of Exodus.
("Mosely," as leader of a company in the Massachusetts regiment, looks
conspicuously like "Moses.")[84] These insectile remarks harken to the language used against their larger opponent, the swarming swamp. Insecti-
cide and genocide combine in attempted topophobic murder, divulging
Hubbard's undying efforts to exterminate entirely the material *non*distinction shared by bespattered beings; those earlier "roots spreading every way"
undulate in a rhizomatic spread, "melt[ing]" the swamp lives present, halting only when these soiled selves are dead.

On December 19, 1675, the English march through the snow until
they reach the swamp in which their guide-hostage said they would find
"Indians enough" (51). Arriving undetected around one o'clock in the
afternoon, they are so surprised by their good fortune that they prema-
turely open fire, exchanging shots with the sentinels at the fort. "[R]aised
upon a kind of Island of five or six acres of rising land in the midst of
a Swamp" with impenetrable "palizadoes," the fort resists English entry
until God, "who as he led Israel . . . through the Wilderness" reveals a
small entrance upon the side of the fort that only one man can enter at
a time (51–52). Once inside the "nes[t]," "the English seeing their advantage, began to fire the Wigwams, where was supposed to be many of the
Enemies Women and Children destroyed, by the firing of at least five or
six hundred of those smoaky Cells" (53). "Indians enough" either burn
alive or are smoked out of their insectarium; those who survive appropriately reabsorb into the bushy backdrop, "forced to hide themselves in
a Cedar Swamp, not far off, where they had nothing to defend them from
the cold but Boughs of Spruce and Pine Trees" (53). Polder smolders.
The Great Swamp Fight is over. The native bodies are left to fester in the
sphagnous substance from which they sprung. Though the English lose

soldiers during and after the assault (to the snow), the natives' loss of crops and habitation spelled "the occasion of their total ruine" henceforth (54). Hubbard cannot tally the native dead: "the number of old men, women and children, that perished either by fire, or that were starved with hunger and cold, none of them could tell" (54). (Later he coolly calculates between three and seven hundred.) His matter-of-fact narration is sinister; after commending the valor of the men and "the goodness of Almighty God" (55), he confesses that the war cannot end so long as swamp-bodies are on the loose, and they always are. Swamp fights will come and go, but the English are not to blame:

> [A]s was said of old, *God hardned their hearts to their own ruine and destruction afterwards.* For as soon as our Souldiers were able to March, finding that all the Enemies overtures of peace, and prolonging of treaties, was only to gain time that they might get away into the Woods. They pursued after them, and sometimes came upon their Rear, but then they would immediately fly an hundred wayes at once into Swamps, so as our men could not follow them. (55)

The Great Swamp Fight is nothing entirely new in its violence, just *great* in the extent of its viciousness and in its numbers. It is the culmination of the grand Puritan environmental ethic still at large, epitomizing the epic battle against heterogeneity that demands an act of "*destruction*" to turn the inseverable non/human into non|human oppositional sects— the vertical bar [|] indicative of the cut—a mission supposedly meant to resist the possibilities of proliferation even as it strangely, perhaps sadistically, unleashes actors for more purifying "*ruine*." How pharaonic: swamp things are allowed to be brought up in order to put down a theological point; they are object lessons discarded when done, buried back in the mudpack when their human teachers, or historians, see fit.

As Hubbard himself admits, however, the flying swamp into which insectan things "fly" houses the irreducible, indestructible, and indissectible parahuman that recedes "into Swamps" yet is constantly nearby; it is still possible, therefore, that not all things take the purgative path purposely given to them by their Puritan masters, but instead deterritorialize it, taking route-y (not rooty) trajectories of "an hundred ways." In this flight against fight, the victory belongs to that which veers. Any narrative of troubles cannot be over with Hubbard at the helm: they pile up. Going and going, he does not want to "follow them"—the unanswerable unknowns—but he does anyway, believing that he can finally convert the frustrating open-ends of bodies and of storylines into hardier Christian roots. But by entering moist, as he must, he and his project crudely fail. The fights in the narrative symbolize Hubbard's own fight against the narrative's erraticisms. In short, the amount of energy it takes for him to settle the ontological and not just cultural disorder within belies his promise of orderliness without. Despite Hubbard's attempts to hold things firmly, the pro- and antagonists start to "get away" from him. His repeated attempts at literary unification reflect the compulsive English anxiety about keeping the body together. The dilemma has an authorial dimension: "But to return," as if he has forgotten (Prospero-like), "and pursue the Rebelious Indians, and keep pace with them in our History, though our Forces as yet could never overtake them in the Woods" (31). Hubbard pursues diversions and asides, chases biographies and anecdotes pertinent to the lives of numerous characters; while this stream of mis/remembrance tends to reach its destination—mainly, the treacheries enacted upon the English by specific tribes—it does not always "keep pace." The Great Swamp Fight should be the fight that ends all fights, a justification commonly applied to the atrocities of war today. His tone at these moments is remorseful, his inability to "overtake" elusive ends—of the war, of the native—and not have to take up their return, an embarrassment.[85] This eagerness for translating intransigent hybrids into stalwart subjects and objects that will no longer exhaust their ontological attention spans is strikingly conveyed in a terse account of the Great Swamp Fight published just months after the actual event. The anonymous author revels in the jubilation felt by the English after they hurt the enemy, at last, in their own homes: "It did greatly rejoice our Men to see their Enemies, who had formerly sculked behind Shrubs and Trees, now to be engaged in a fair Field."[86] Such rejoicing exposes the deep-rooted English desire to drain the swamp and deracinate its things we have already witnessed. The unruly and endlessly generating native body can actually be uprooted, slashed, burned, and proven, to "our chiefest Joy . . . mortal."[87] Once completed, that storied seed of "an imperfect Embrio" is planted in the hole left behind, but its tale—we know differently now— is contingent, "imperfect" by its narratological nature, shameful in its supercessionary aspirations, and vulnerable to change.

In fact the "fair Field" is a fine way, once we appropriate it, to counterbalance and counteract the English tactics of silencing; I have faith that the errant voices and errors that check the effectiveness of Hubbard's project, in making their escape, may allow us to enter alternative modes of environmental justice as well as being: "[we] never could come to charge them," he complains, "for they would presently betake themselves into Swamps, and not two of them run together, so as they saw it was an endless work to proceed further in the chase of such an enemy" (60). A "fair Field" is a prospect lacking in tousled tangles and woody knots, one free from assemblages' complexities and ethical implications: a New England Puritan's wet dream. Yet fighting fairly is not exactly a fair fight if the beings on the field begin on unequal ontological standing; indeed, while the widespread issue of discrimination is briefly mentioned in the anonymous report—"It hath been the great care of our Council to distinguish between Friends and Enemies"[88]—Hubbard's "endless work," ironically, has been better discernment *in order to* discriminate more effectively. As a question left inconclusive but still hammered out in his swampy workshop, he has taken "great care" to separate English from "*Indians*," human body from nonhuman swampscape. But like a blacksmith afraid of the dark materials at his disposal, and frustrated by his "endless work" on ends, he turns to another, final end in conclusion, the divine fire of eschatology: "God grant that by the *Fire* of all these Judgments, we may be purged from our Dross, and become a more refined people, as Vessels fitted for our Masters use" (115). Hubbard closes with more purgation and purification, leaving us with his own vision of bodies washed clean of the mud. But it is too late; he has already "quickned the being" of swamp-being and, by giving times the "chase," revealed its intrinsic interminability. Transcorporeal mixtures cannot be separated by even the greatest fight, but the blows can still be gauged, nevertheless, and they still register over time. This transtemporal responsibility to take "great care"—to painstakingly ask what is "fair," for whom, and what counts as such—sponsors different visions than Hubbard's, however, because it imagines how to bring about "fair" play on any given "Field" by bringing up the muck.

The Slough of Respond

I have a confession to make: my conclusion is actually a wish that something of this investigation "may be of use to post[e]rity," sparking endeavors for care and not for the scour/ge, an unequivocal quickening of prosperity posthaste. I have argued thus far that the Puritans' attempts to exonerate themselves from King Philip's War, done in the name of divine justice, are in tandem with their extreme exertions to separate themselves from the New England swamps. All swamp things suffer terribly, and unequally, within their aggressively overarching discourse of purification. I have also argued that the swamp is a transcorporeal space that refuses straight lines, pure forms, and binary logics. While all waterscapes harbor these faculties, to be sure, few can be portrayed as forcefully—and as drastically—as the early modern swampscape. The swamp's materiality is always more than an anxiety over exogenous miasma or a secret desire for what one overtly repudiates. One possible reaction to this enmeshment, the Great Swamp Fight, is undoubtedly malign. But the fight is neither singular nor does it end, here, in Hubbard's "*Fire*" of revelation and Hartlib's "black[ened] *turf*." Although marketed as history and husbandry, respectively, these writers reverberate relationships with the swamp that their readers *wanted* at present and in future, demonstrating the un/easy repetition of violence that looks to previous events for justification as well as inspiration: from the Parliament-backed General Draining Act of 1600, to the congressionally mandated reclamation of forested swamps in the United States mid-twentieth century. In both their predictability and impulsiveness, these historical continuations require regarding swamps as ethical spaces where all actions have material effects. The swampscape's thick and bottomless embeddedness refuses any attempt at self-distance; just as the English struggled in the bogs of connections, so, too, are we in the mushrooming mire of ecomateriality. One step to achieving a ponderous politics of nature—in the sense of "weight," the Latin *pondus*—is a reconsideration of swamp stories and their things that stick to us up and down the years. If it seems like these swamp accents of and with which I speak can be "delivered," only and duly, "under the similitude of a dream,"[89] then I will slide into one of the stickiest places in art—dreamed up by a Puritan preacher, no less— to help us think through the gravity of composition, what does and does not endure (and why), and whether the pond/erous can still be a portal to new worlds.

John Bunyan (1628–88) published his long religious allegory *The Pilgrim's Progress* (1678/84) only a year after Hubbard's history, yet his "Slough of Dispond" has pervaded English literature and popular culture much more thoroughly than Hubbard's swamps, becoming a catchphrase for depression, low spirits, and a general lack of confidence. "As [he walks] through the wilderness of this world," Bunyan falls asleep in a "Denn."[90] In his dream he sees a man, Christian, who is seeking the path away from death's condemnation but "could not tell which way to go."[91] Evangelist, a conveniently named character, instructs Christian to venture beyond the fence that marks the border of his home. As Christian runs out onto what appears to be firm ground, another person, Pliable, joins him on his journey; almost as soon as he gains his new companion, however, Christian loses him in one of the story's most famous places:

> Now I saw in my Dream, that just as they had ended this talk, they drew near to a very *Miry Slough*, that was in the midst of the Plain, and they being heedless, did both fall suddenly into the bogg. The name of the Slow was *Dispond*. Here therefore they wallowed for a time, being grieviously bedaubed with the dirt; And *Christian*, because of the burden that was on his back, began to sink in the Mire.[92]

Pliable chastises Christian for leading him into this mess and, with a great heaving, lifts himself out of the swamp near his own house, leaving Christian to "tumble in the Slough of *Dispondency* alone."[93] It takes the hand of Help to pull him out, who then proceeds to tell Christian why the way is miry: "It is the descent whither the scum and filth that attends conviction for sin, continually run, and therefore it is called the Slough of Dispond."[94] Here the soul's fears, doubts, and apprehensions come "grieviously" together in confluence, explaining why the matter of being "bedaubed" is so burdensome.

Bunyan's allegorical swamp encroaches upon Hubbard's historicized version: the "badness" of swampy ground must be rendered good.[95] The solution, Help says, one that parallels his peers' efforts on the continent, is cultivation. The king's "Labourers . . . have by the direction of His Majesties Surveyors, been for above the sixteen hundred years, imploy'd about this patch of ground, if perhaps it might have been mended."[96] They labor in vain; the slough has "swallowed up . . . Twenty thousand Cart Loads; Yea Millions of wholsom Instructions, that have at all seasons been brought from all places of the Kings Dominions."[97] This "king" is the pinnacle of ecoimperialism, proclaiming that the right amount of surveying and draining will successfully "men[d]" the land. It is wishful anthropocentric thinking, of course: just as the first visitors to New England discovered, swamps are sucking sites that defy human control; mud keeps guzzling the best-laid plans. "[I]t is the *Slough of Dispond* still; and so will be; when they have done what they can."[98] Help helps Christian discover the futility of human industry amidst the intractable marsh: it is here to stay whether he likes it or not. But to decenter the human superficially is not necessarily to redefine it carefully, for as much as Bunyan's slough reasserts its powers—ceaselessly, even if "Slow"-ly—over civilization, this only seems to bolster an antagonistic, rather than co-constitutive, view of the swampy environment. Like Prospero's cell, the swamp is at Christian's and the Christians' door, and yet, somehow, fens are fenced out, permanently cordoned off. The two houses of nature and culture remain separated like "*Wicket-gate*[d]" communities.[99] Although humanity's sins replenish the filth, saturating the ground to maintain its unhealthy levels, this influx bespeaks spiritual rather than material commingling. If Christian cannot be wholly cleansed of his embeddedness, he can at least be shown the way out. Help lends another hand:

True, there are by the direction of the Law-giver, certain good and substantiall Steps, placed even through the very midst of this *Slough*; but at such time as this place doth much spue out its filth, as it doth against charge of weather, these steps are hardly seen; or if they be, Men through the dizziness of their heads, step besides; and then they are bemired to purpose, notwithstanding the steps be there; but the ground is good when they are once got in at the Gate.[100]

Because there are laws within this system—faith in Christ, according to Bunyan—it is the errant who "bemire[s]" him- or herself by straying from the "good" path. The progress of the *Progress* is a linear one, a one-way trajectory that opposes "substantiall" deviations with swamps' substance. Despondence is merely a stop to spiritual transcendence. Let the swamp swallow what it will, let it "spue out its filth," the steps will always "be there." The path of righteousness will wash Christian/s clean. There is method in this Puritanical mire, and these laws are without disputability. Bunyan seems to anticipate the modernist view of science that fallaciously separates matters of belief from matters of fact.[101] Theo-, teleo-, and hydrological laws like his interpret swamps as manageable, "purpose[ful]" places, distancing the observant subject from the observed object: this is how "facts" are tendered, and once converted into gospel truth, how they resist critique.

Here is the true good news, however: we need not be *stuck* with the "*Miry Slough*" of puritanical forebears. Try as he may to circumvent "this *Slough*," Christian has to be "bemired" in order to reach what he believes to be his final destination nonetheless. Bunyan's and his confederates' texts found herein are all borne out of "dirt[y]" material interactions with the agential swampscape; and yet, writers could still argue that coextensiveness with "filth" is something to avoid even as they "wallowed" through this fallen, but no less real world to develop their ecospiritual jargon. (Perhaps after a "fall suddenly into [a] bogg.") Because evangelicalism breaks the human free from the "Denn" (prison) that swamps represent, Bunyan's slough is intended to be read metaphorically rather than as an accurate geographical description; in comparison, Hubbard stages a material as well as metaphorical "descent" in which his in/firm Christian soldiers curb the metaphysical threats of sin, death, and imprisonment that linger in the quite physical mud. Hubbard's war on the matter-phor—which I have presented and wholeheartedly protest—hubristically backfires, concurrently enchaining both humans and nonhumans. Yet it must be said at this point in my own narrative that attachment does not automatically guarantee the "dizziness" of freedom; there were, and are, beings "pinnioned" and "shackled" in the packed bonds of slavery. Some swamp things really are *stuck*, that is, forcefully set in place by another. Bunyan's title page looks forward to another world—"from this world, to that which is to come"—his pilgrimage clearly intended to "progress" from one point to the other. But the world "to come" need not be a transcendent one, but instead be recognized as the imminent realm of immanence at our thresholds right now, not above (super-) or below (sub-) the natural or the human on a God-given hierarchical scale, but beside, and next to (para-), even if spatially down below. It need not designate a destination, either, but create "pilgrim[s]" who herald the wandering of the word (from Latin *peregrinus*, "foreign," from *peregre* "abroad"), traveling the swamp world with its unsteady streams of strangers. By confronting the chains of human and nonhuman bondage and reconverting the language in which they are written and employed, we may learn new lessons from histories like Hubbard's about how to temper a swampscape's (or any -scape's) chains of injustice into long mycological chains of transformations, into endless sequences of sphagnum that resist embryonic causality in favor of the "every [which] way," seeking a turbulent "charge of weather," processing quivering dreams unlike any that have come before.

I still feel *stuck*, but that is precisely where I want to be, exactly where I think we should be, stuck together with this present-day world.[102] Early modern swampscapes reveal how we are "up to th' chins" in things, always-already enmeshed with the world despite the clean narratives of the Hubbards and Bunyans among us. The question I have routinely poised is not how to free things but how to better appreciate the coimplication of human and nonhuman, to dwell deeper in our sticky attachments, to enhance the "nobleness of life" for all swamp things, even if it entails putting their "burden[s] . . . on [our] back" at times. Reemphasizing the swamp's shaky agency can shake loose detrimental ways of thinking that sever the human from the environment. Early modern swamps are therefore of real Help: they help us become more responsible by being more responsive to the calls of things, better attuned to "other speaking" (the literal meaning of "allegory"). Because I am closing with Bunyan's concretized vocabulary of swampspeak, this ethical as well as spatial place I imagine can only be called the Slough of Respond. Tracking voices and bodies buried in the mud—beings who were and are without helping hands—allows us to mourn for lost lives but also hatches plots to improve nonhuman and human lives together, together. Unfortunately, the slough-ciology for which I advocate will not spontaneously generate. We must pay attention to the human and nonhuman bodies divided by purifying lines of territorialization, hold those dead-"straight line[s]" of divisions and their implementers accountable, and try to remedy their wrongs. In 1776, almost one hundred years after King Philip's War, the American War of Independence delivered New England and its swamps to fire yet again. So "[c]ome Brethren of the water": let us ask what we are fighting *for*—be it interdependence—and not just against; let us have garrulous conversations in swampspeak and see the world in slough motion; let us quake in the Slough of Respond and plan campaigns of great care. We have to keep mucking up in these ways if we hope to prevent future swamp fights, both great and small, in the world "which is to come," if we ever want war to give way to peace, and for "overtures of peace, and prolonging of treaties," finally, to *stick*.

Exit, Wet

[Sebastian:] I am standing water.

—William Shakespeare, *The Tempest* (1611)

Here we stand, down in the slough: I admit that the swampy slowness of the sociological response might not seem to be the best place to end a book. But we never exit wetness, as I have been arguing in these pages, only exit one assemblage and enter another. In a similar way, our hopes might not always be high; they may start (and stay) low. This outro is meant to echo Eileen A. Joy's brave "attempt . . . to think about depression as a shared creative endeavor, as a transcorporeal blue (and blues) ecology." My own "attempt" is a refrain in phases, an "endeavor" that engages hope as a methodology, that risks reopening the hydropolitical and storied spaces that are water and that are us.[1]

Elk

On January 9, 2014, in Charleston, West Virginia, a neglected tank owned by Freedom Industries leaked seven thousand gallons of 4-methylcyclohex-anemethanol (MCHM), a toxic chemical used to clean coal, into the Elk River, one-and-a-half miles upstream from the region's water treatment facility. Nearly three hundred thousand residents in the state's "Chemical Valley" went without water. The first ban was lifted on January 13; a few days later, the Centers for Disease Control cautioned pregnant women against drinking what had just been declared "potable." Governor Earl Ray Tomblin told residents that "it's your decision" to use the water or not, unable (or unwilling) to promise that one could enter wet safely; the day after his press conference, however, it was reported that another substance, polyglycol ethers (PPH), had also leaked. Ninety percent of citizens polled that summer remained distrustful of the water management system, even after a series of indictments and Freedom's bankruptcy. They had, and still have, good reasons: not only did a slew of different coal-related spills occur in the region in the weeks following the initial incident, but one of those contaminations occurred on the exact same site on June 12. Since at least one of the (known) effects of MCHM is "reproductive toxic discharge" in women and men, and "developmental toxicity" in children, many of the damages are yet to be told. WV FREE, a women's reproductive health, rights, and justice organization launched a "Change the Current" campaign before the midterm elections in the fall of 2014 to pressure government officials into improving the state's substandard water, distributing photos of a young girl innocently chewing her wet hair with the slogan "We are bodies of water" displayed menacingly across her eyes.[2] The connection between speaking and silencing—muffled mouths and the eventual sickness that invades them—the return of aqua- and geohumoral concepts, and the performativity of drinking (or not drinking) on a public stage parallel the water politics, for example, of events like London's 1641 double tide. Puritans and Catholics in England's capital, just as Democrats and Republicans in West Virginia's, interpreted the event as an instance of civil war: martial in the case of the first, ontological in the case of the second. Even with evidence of the nonseparation between humans and waterscape, the chemically trespassed body remains divided like congressional (or parliamentary) houses, sick instantiations are attributed to a lapse of bureaucracy and lax industrial oversight, backward stereotypes of the region repeat, classism is evoked like the dry-clothed aristocracy of *The Tempest*. "Materializing ignorance," as Nancy Tuana states.[3] Cleanups leave slow and fast violence unresolved: an oil tanker derailed and exploded in Fayette County in February 2015, releasing its cargo into the Kanawha River, another drinking supply. Despite the dreams of water-men and water-women, *the fantasy of dryness dies hard.*

Library

On the Snæfellsnes Peninsula in western Iceland is a town called Stykkishólmur, famous for its Library of Water, the permanent home of Roni Horn's *Water, Selected.* Within each of the twenty-four plastic tubes that reach from floor to ceiling is water from a different glacier in Iceland.

Roni Horn, *Water, Selected*, 2003/2007. Twenty-four glass columns filled with water from glacial sources, each column diameter 12 inches (30.5 cm), column height 110 inches (279.4 cm), approximately 1,500 square feet (457 square meters) overall. Permanent installation at VATNASAFN/Library of Water, Stykkishólmur, Iceland. Courtesy of the artist and Hauser & Wirth.

Along their rubber bases run Icelandic and English words, all difficult to translate, but every syllable speaking the interpermeability of weather and personality: from *blautt* ("wet") to *hráslagalegt* ("rough, cold, and wet"), *rakt* ("moist, soaked, wet") to *vott* ("damp, wet"). The cylinders, one might say, ominously resemble a prison's bars. My own impression, I will admit, was of loneliness—pensive *kyrrt* ("calm")—mainly due to the library's diffracted sunlight and hushed tones, perched as it is on a hill with a panoramic view of Breiðafjörður Bay. For a country that holds the largest glacier in Europe, Vatnajökull, and that depends on glacial activity for much of its everyday functions, Iceland's once-ice water certainly deserves a library. The clarity is a reminder that ice is retreating, not advancing; it seemed particularly withdrawn the day I was there in the summer of 2014. The light at the base of one of the tubes had burned out, and although the bulb had been recently replaced, it simply refused to cooperate. The curator told me it was a mystery; when I asked to what glacier the water had

originally belonged, she informed me that this glacier was the only one
in the room that no longer existed. I shivered; I felt as if I was witnessing
environmental catastrophe that was both past and yet to come twenty-
three more times. World-melts in recess: this was the unbearable truth
of these tubular ice cores, time capsules who relayed to me chronology's
scientifically verified progress and the globe's unstoppable warming. I
stayed for almost the entire afternoon, but not in an effort to decipher a
code. I recognized in these words embossed on the floor—just as I had
done in the wet textual passages of early modern drama and travel literature—a kind of cryo- and hydrosemiotics at work, a realization that as
we talk in the language of uncertainty (that *is* the water-world's weather),
and walk on the thin ice of possibilities (that *are* relations), it is through
these stories of both delight and destruction that resilience is best taught.
A library of water houses the potential for de- and recomposition with
wet things, a disorienting labyrinth of hydrological haunts and -graphical
entrances, a desire to dwell and a discovery of dwelling as a desire. It is
what the previous writers of waterscapes felt and found: the potential for
glettið ("frisky, playful") action in the *glórulaust* ("clueless, blind, out of
control") of assembly.

Solution

"Be part of the solution," one motto of environmentalism goes. A literary
labyrinth of storied matter tests this phrase's limits: the liquid rods resemble the test tubes of water sampling on the polluted banks of the Elk, the
chance of being one (out of a million or more) parts toxic "solution." The
clear bars reveal our imprisonment in an onto-epistemological maze of
material attachments we cannot escape, the inability to "solve" questions
of environmental health and justice in order to prevent future tests and
their dim results. If there was a word missing from the floor of this library,
then, it is *draumur* (Icelandic for "dream"). But this is not the point with
and at which the book exits; since many (if not all) of its chapters have
related a dream, it is now time for me to take a turn. It is a misprision,
in fact, to think of these prisms of water as prison bars; instead, I have
argued that water-bonds are actually forces of liberation, and that to be
truly industrious with freedoms means sinking deeper into complicated
and coimplicated relations instead of dissolving them. To put it another

way: if materially we are solution, and if environmental justice necessitates the solution of problems, negotiating their terms might not mean to automatically "solve"—in the sense of "find an answer to"—but to further plumb our incomplete, interminable, and loosened liquidity (*solvere*). It would mean to rethink the prison of unpredictability (reality) as prisms of attachment *from which selected things are barred*; but like every overflowing "*Chart*" or illustration each chapter of mine contains, it redesigns containment as a magnification of ever-present uncharted powers, waters' expressive possibilities in shudder. With four different forms of water that emphasize, and exert, four different types of action—river (flow), glacier (assemblage), rain (permeability), and swamp (enmeshment)—I submit to you my own wish to swell in the potential of watery things: (1) to translate how water-bodies "testify" ills into the legal testimonies of indictment, to reimagine how power relations are witnessed in the hope that such harmful currents may be better fought against; (2) to perceive how stories written with water contain, explain, and promote the promise of multiple hues of blue, how compositions and the libraries that house them are held in a delicate hydrographical solution of questions without answers.

One last voyage: "Yet sure me thinkes the water should be free / For passage, for all men [*sic*] of each degree."[4] I have more hopes for hope; there is much work to be done by water poets and politicians alike: the liquefaction of sovereignty, a refreshing reminder that to abjure mastery is not the same as abstaining from it. The final aim of this book is to make an entrance into wet "reactivism," by which I mean any sociopolitical movement that reacts to present injustices by reactivating the water-works of the past and, in doing so, inspires alternate modes of activism in future. Just as "be part of the solution" became a catchphrase for environmentalist problem-solving, so, too, might a reinvented ecomaterialist motto like "we are bodies of water" advocate different histories and champion more-than-human forms of just, ecological futures. The "we," the water of "we" that runs through these lines, cannot protest too much. We need these diffusive (not divisive) stories that spread across genres, temporalities, theories, and pedagogies. We will always have more to gain than to lose by avoiding stopgaps in periodization, discipline, field, and subspecialty, by refusing to claim, for instance, that pre- and early modern forms of art like John Taylor's 1641 search for the aqueous commons—

"water . . . free . . . [f]or passage"—while imperfect, do not "evince any-thing like a modern ecological sensibility."[5] Each of my chapter titles, like my w/etymologies of language, has tried to grasp this "doing" of w/ethics, the "gerunds" (from Latin *gerere* "do") as manifestations of prepositional movement: becoming, going, making, mucking, *entering*. So, in this exit *in-*, not "out": let us look forward to futures; turn "I am standing water" from the stance of neutrality to standing and speaking up, "for" and with, "all waters" in protest. Let us sing in chorus, like Gower of *Pericles*, "a song that old was sung" (1.1). To make new songs of our selves aquatic: those that testify to life, and to love.

Acknowledgments

Come, oh my friends, on a clear morning to sing the stream's vowels!
—Gaston Bachelard, *Water and Dreams*

Friends, this is the part of the book where I can be at my most effusive, where I can thank you for helping me realize my dream of writing a book (my first) about a substance I love. Know that you are within these pages—and (oh) forgive me if I have not mentioned you by name—for you have always been collaborating with me, teaching me how to sing.

This desiring-project began as a dissertation at the George Washington University, where I had the most desirable committee ever assembled: my director, Jonathan Gil Harris, who introduced me to Wa/l/ter Ralegh in my first graduate seminar, who helped me find my element, and who never failed to give brilliant feedback even while he weathered the monsoons of India: *adbhut shukriya ada karta hoon*; Jeffrey Jerome Cohen, whose generosity of heart and mind kept both me and my work flowing, and who believed in me during the most turgid times; Holly Dugan, who asked the tough questions I was afraid to answer, who opened up new routes for me to travel. My internal examiner, Jonathan Hsy, contributed more than a designated reader should; I thank him for reminding me how fluid language really is, that translation should never be taken for granted. I must also thank Steve Mentz, my outside examiner, true-blue scholar, and sometimes swimming partner, for making waves for me to follow. Countless influential voices swirl outside this committee. Ayanna Thompson started my love affair with *Pericles* as my MA director

249

at Arizona State University; I would not be "singing to an ocean" if she had not made up my mind for me at a critical point of my graduate career. There are many others whose work has significantly shaped my own; to name a few: Stacy Alaimo, Serenella Iovino, Serpil Oppermann, Alfred K. Siewers, and Julian Yates. I was fortunate enough to meet thinkers like these through the Medieval and Early Modern Studies Institute (MEMSI) at GWU, a center whose mission should be an inspiration to all disciplines. Special thanks to the BABEL Working Group, my wet lab of academic experimentation, for its intoxicating intellectualism: Eileen A. Joy and Myra Seaman, I will buy you both a drink.

Two internal grants from West Virginia University financed this book, for which I am grateful: a Riggle Fellowship in the Humanities and a Summer Senate Grant for Research and Scholarship. I thank my past and present colleagues in the English department for their encouragement, especially those in attendance at the Faculty Research Colloquium at which I presented the overarching frame for this book: you reimagined it (on a clear afternoon) in a way that I could not, and its final form I owe to you. Audiences of pieces presented at BABEL, the Modern Language Association, the International Congress on Medieval Studies, the Shakespeare Association of America, and the Association for the Study of Literature and the Environment (including UK-I) similarly contributed to the book's development. My graduate and undergraduate students thought *with* water with me, helping to hone almost everything here. I particularly thank Jordan Lovejoy and Andrew Munn, two outstanding Appalachian voices from whom we will certainly hear more, for pushing me to think early modern waters through environmental justice and health at home. Elise Keaton from Keeper of the Mountains (an anti–mountaintop removal organization), Catherine Venable Moore, and the Friends of Decker's Creek took my classes to sites where we could witness environmental degradation firsthand. I applaud the work they are doing to improve the wetness of non/humans; my exit could not have been written without them, for the better water worlds they believe in and intend to bring about.

Richard Morrison originally solicited this project for the University of Minnesota Press. Doug Armato's editorial hand (true Help) narrowed its overflowing ambitions without staunching its energy. I cannot think of a better place to publish than under his guidance at the University of Minnesota Press. Erin Warholm-Wohlenhaus answered any questions I had, no matter how incidental. Rachel Moeller and Deborah A. Ooster-house skillfully set wet words to page. The anonymous readers (I wish you are reading this) proved to be the perfect interlocutors. I thank the following presses for granting me permission to republish material in this book (by chapter): Manchester University Press, Palgrave Macmillan, Indiana University Press, and punctum books. The digital imaging teams at the British Library, Folger Shakespeare Library, and Huntington Library made rights acquisition prompt and painless. Andre Ermolaev, Roni Horn, and Colleen Ludwig graciously allowed me to reproduce their art, and I am honored by their kindness as much as I am motivated by their art.

Growing up in the wetscapes of the Pacific Northwest sent me on searches for saturated others. No ecocritical project would be complete without acknowledging the wet places that made my writing possible: Assateague Island National Seashore, the Potomac River and Rock Creek Park, Iceland's glaciers, Ebey's Landing, India's Himalayan foothills, Michigan's Upper Peninsula, the falls of Niagara and Snoqualmie, the coasts of Oregon and Maine, Santa Barbara, Dolly Sods, Crater Lake, Jenny Lake, Chuckanut, Kalaloch, Liberty Bay, Cyprus. These (streams) and more have impressed my work in ways I am not quite certain, yet I know their touch is in my writing. Waterscapes (vowels) run through every word.

So here we come, finally. I thank my family and friends who accompanied me on this long liquid journey, who stayed with me through its ridged ups and downs, who never failed to give me a spurt when I needed it, apothecaries all: Rick and Dee Feutz; Daniel Remein's "w[h]atery" ornament; the humans and nonhumans of the Hagen Avenue household; Brady and Marilena who tutored me in *endaxi*. Jeffrey Jerome Cohen and his family were (and are) a source of strength for me; even as Jeffrey and I enter our third collaboration together, his friendship continues to astonish. (I gush at the thought.) To my mother: you centered me in Seattleite art. To Elisabeth, Christina, Collette, Jude, and Loralei: you might say that I take *you* places, but the feeling is mutual; you have given me the hope for the futures I imagine herein. Thank you, Jessica, Ken, and the entire "C7" ranch for proving to me that recreation can re-create and, most important, that creation truly is an act of love. Singing of which, all my dreams constantly and clearly return to one person who is eager to get her feet wet, who likes walks on the beach, and who continues to keep me on course: Erin, you have my deepest water love.

Notes

Preface

1. All technical details and quotations are from the artist's website: http://www.colleenludwig.com/SHIVERpages/Research.html.

2. Vitruvius, *Ten Books of Architecture*, ed. Ingrid D. Rowland and Thomas Noble Howe (Cambridge: Cambridge University Press, 1999), 96.

3. See Lisa Robertson's *Occasional Work and Seven Walks from the Office for Soft Architecture* (Toronto: Coach House Books, 2011). "What if there is no 'space,' only a permanent, slow-motion mystic takeover, an implausibly careening awning? Nothing is utopian. Everything wants to be. Soft Architects face the reaching middle" (21).

4. Michel Serres, *The Five Senses*, trans. Margaret Sankey and Peter Cowley (London: Continuum, 2008), 52.

5. Richard Doyle, *Wetwares: Experiments in Postvital Living* (Minneapolis: University of Minnesota Press, 2003).

6. See Ian Bogost, *Alien Phenomenology, or What It's Like to Be a Thing* (Minneapolis: University of Minnesota Press, 2012), chap. 4, "Carpentry."

7. For more on the "onto-story," see Jane Bennett, *Vibrant Matter: A Political Ecology of Things* (Durham, NC: Duke University Press, 2010). "The story will highlight the extent to which human being and thinghood overlap, the extent to which the us and the it slip-slide into each other" (4).

8. The "noisy" conversations I communicate derive from Michel Serres's *The Parasite*, trans. Lawrence R. Schehr (Minneapolis: University of Minnesota Press, 2007).

9. Jamie Linton, *What Is Water? The History of a Modern Abstraction* (Vancouver: University of British Columbia Press, 2010), 3.

10. Bruno Latour, *Politics of Nature: How to Bring the Sciences into Democracy*, trans. Catherine Porter (Cambridge, MA: Harvard University Press, 2004), 21.

11. Mick Smith, *Against Ecological Sovereignty: Ethics, Biopolitics, and Saving the Natural World* (Minneapolis: University of Minnesota Press, 2011), 63.

12. One prominent example is Vandana Shiva, *Water Wars: Privatization, Pollution, and Profit* (Cambridge, MA: South End Press, 2002).

13. See Rob Nixon, *Slow Violence and the Environmentalism of the Poor* (Cambridge, MA: Harvard University Press, 2011).

14. Nancy Tuana, "Viscous Porosity: Witnessing Katrina," in *Material Feminisms*, ed. Stacy Alaimo and Susan Hekman (Bloomington: Indiana University Press, 2008), 188–213.

15. Stacy Alaimo, *Bodily Natures: Science, Environment, and the Material Self* (Bloomington: Indiana University Press, 2010), 2, 48.

16. Karen Barad's tripartite probe in *Meeting the Universe Halfway: Quantum Physics and the Entanglement of Matter and Meaning* (Durham, NC: Duke University Press, 2007), 3.

17. See s.v. "water" (n.) in the *Oxford English Dictionary*: "Popular language recognizes kinds of 'water' that have not all these negative properties; but (even apart from any scientific knowledge) it has usually been more or less clearly understood that these are really mixtures of water with other substances."

18. Herman Melville, *Moby-Dick* (New York: Penguin Books, 2003), 4.

19. Cecilia Chen, Janine MacLeod, and Astrida Neimanis, eds., *Thinking with Water* (Montreal: McGill-Queen's University Press, 2013), 9–10. The introduction, "Toward a Hydrological Turn?," is refreshing.

20. Philip Ball, *Life's Matrix: A Biography of Water* (Berkeley: University of California Press, 2001), 182.

21. See "Eleven Principles of the Elements," the introduction to *Elemental Ecocriticism: Thinking with Earth, Air, Water, and Fire*, ed. Jeffrey Jerome Cohen and Lowell Duckert (Minneapolis: University of Minnesota Press, 2015).

22. "Always look for the molecular, or even submolecular, particle with which we are allied. . . . Write, form a rhizome, increase your territory by deterritorialization, extend the line of flight to the point where it becomes an abstract machine covering the entire plane of consistency." Gilles Deleuze and Félix Guattari, *A Thousand Plateaus: Capitalism and Schizophrenia*, trans. Brian Massumi (Minneapolis: University of Minnesota Press, 1987), 11.

23. Recent studies of water's role in the building of "civilized" communities tend to configure water as a tool for human history and progress. See Brian Fagan, *Elixir: A History of Water and Humankind* (New York: Bloomsbury Press, 2011).

24. Michel Serres with Bruno Latour, *Conversations on Science, Culture, and Time*, trans. Roxanne Lapidus (Ann Arbor: University of Michigan Press, 1995), 108. For more on the counterrevolution, see Bruno Latour, *We Have Never Been*

Modern, trans. Catherine Porter (Cambridge, MA: Harvard University Press, 1993), 82.

25. Bennett, *Vibrant Matter*, 2. Her first chapter on "The Force of Things," containing the mantra that "matter itself is lively" (13), propels this book.

26. See Viktor Schauberger's (1885–1958) work on water's natural energy that he attributed to its "double-helical motion—a spiral within a spiral." He believed that "more energy is encapsulated in every drop of good spring water than an average-sized power station is presently able to produce" (1 cm^3 = 25 million kilowatt hours). *The Water Wizard: The Extraordinary Power of Natural Water*, trans. and ed. Callum Coats (Dublin: Gill & Macmillan, 1999), 61.

27. The phrase is, of course, Zygmunt Bauman's. See *Liquid Modernity* (Malden: Polity Press, 2000).

28. Serres with Latour, *Conversations*, 58–60. His handkerchief is famous for espousing a crumpled view of time; here I invoke his fondness for the filter (the origin of the French verb *couler*, "to flow"). The writers herein will promote theirs: "The traveller . . . percolates like time. . . . He proceeds horizontally. The time of this great work, both unexpected and expected, percolates along the whole length of the navigation route or ramble, as it could be called, up and down, adventurous, but a knot in the volume of space, with repetitions, rediscoveries, novelties, and sudden grandiose visions" (Serres, *Five Senses*, 238).

29. Manuel De Landa, *A Thousand Years of Nonlinear History* (New York: Zone Books, 1997), 21. His work is potentializing in its scope: "The call for a more experimental attitude toward reality and for an increased awareness of the potential for self-organization inherent in even the humblest forms of matter-energy" (273).

30. Linton, *What Is Water?*, 23.

31. Jeffrey Jerome Cohen has rightfully critiqued the calcification of periodization in "In the Middle of the Early Modern," *Journal for Early Modern Cultural Studies* 13, no. 3 (2013): 128–32.

32. "Actant is a term from semiotics covering both humans and nonhumans; an actor is any entity that modifies another entity in a trial" (Latour, *Politics*, 237).

33. Serenella Iovino and Serpil Oppermann, "Theorizing Material Ecocicism: A Diptych," *Interdisciplinary Studies in Literature and Environme* no. 3 (2012): 450.

34. All quotations from Shakespeare refer to the *The Norton S* 2nd ed., ed. Stephen Greenblatt, Walter Cohen, Jean E. Howard, ar Eisaman Maus (New York: W. W. Norton, 2008).

35. Gail Kern Paster discusses "the hydraulic modeling that links organs and psychological functions" in *Humoring the Body: Emotions and the Shakespearean Stage* (Chicago: University of Chicago Press, 2004), 65; see also 72–74.

36. John Stow, *The Abridgement of the English Chronicle* (London, 1618), 415.

37. Ibid.

38. James Shirley, *The Lady of Pleasure* (London: Thomas Cotes, 1637).

39. Thomas Nabbes, *Totenham Court* (London: Richard Owen, 1638). "Mischiefe on you sir," she complains, "you have spoild mee a paile of conduit water cost mee many a weary step the fetching" (36).

40. Richard Brome, *The Court Begger* (London, 1653). For more on Taylor, see Simon Schama, *Landscape and Memory* (New York: Vintage Books, 1995), 320–32.

41. David Macauley, *Elemental Philosophy: Earth, Air, Fire, and Water as Environmental Ideas* (Albany: State University of New York Press, 2010), 5.

42. Michel Serres's final line in *The Birth of Physics* (Manchester: Clinamen Press, 2000), 191, and one that I continue: "Invent liquid history and the ages of water."

43. For more on mapping fluidity, see Serres with Latour, *Conversations*, 105–7.

44. See Annette Kolodny, *The Lay of the Land: Metaphor as Experience and History in American Life and Letters* (Chapel Hill: University of North Carolina Press, 1975) for an in-depth study of the "land-as-woman" motif. The seminal texts about pre/colonial treatments of nature are Alfred W. Crosby, *Ecological Imperialism: The Biological Expansion of Europe, 900–1900* (Cambridge: Cambridge University Press, 1986) and Richard H. Grove, *Green Imperialism: Colonial Expansion, Tropical Island Edens and the Origins of Environmentalism, 1600–1860* (Cambridge: Cambridge University Press, 1995).

45. An accessible overview is Brian Fagan, *The Little Ice Age: How Climate Made History, 1300–1850* (New York: Basic Books, 2000). For the early modern period, see Robert Markley, "Summer's Lease: Shakespeare in the Little Ice Age," in *Early Modern Ecostudies: From the Florentine Codex to Shakespeare*, ed. Ivo Kamps, Karen L. Raber, and Thomas Hallock (New York: Palgrave Macmillan, 2008), 131–42.

46. Keith Thomas's *Man and the Natural World: Changing Attitudes in England, 1500–1800* (Oxford: Oxford University Press, 1983) remains the foundational study. John F. Richards's *The Unending Frontier: An Environmental History of the Early Modern World* (Berkeley: University of California Press, 2003)

47. Some of my greatest influences are in wet medieval studies: Alfred K. Siewers, *Strange Beauty: Ecocritical Approaches to Early Medieval Landscape* (New York: Palgrave Macmillan, 2009); Sebastian I. Sobecki, *The Sea and Medieval English Literature* (Cambridge: D. S. Brewer, 2008); and James L. Smith, who formerly blogged at http://fluidimaginings.wordpress.com, and whose monograph, *Fluid Models of Thought in Twelfth-Century Western Monasticism: Water as Medieval Intellectual Entity*, is forthcoming from Brepols.

48. The last decade has witnessed a notable upsurge in early modern ecocriticism, one that seems settled on several key terms: the pastoral genre, such as Ken Hiltner, *What Else Is Pastoral? Renaissance Literature and the Environment* (Ithaca: Cornell University Press, 2011) and Todd Borlik, *Ecocriticism and Early Modern English Literature: Green Pastures* (New York: Routledge, 2010); the color green, such as Leah Knight, *Reading Green in Early Modern England* (Farnham: Ashgate, 2014), Bruce R. Smith, *The Key of Green: Passion and Perception in Renaissance Culture* (Chicago: University of Chicago Press, 2009), Robert N. Watson, *Back to Nature: The Green and the Real in the Late Renaissance* (Philadelphia: University of Pennsylvania Press, 2006), and Rebecca Bushnell, *Green Desire: Imagining Early Modern English Gardens* (Ithaca: Cornell University Press, 2003); the animal, such as Karen Raber, *Animal Bodies, Renaissance Culture* (Philadelphia: University of Pennsylvania Press, 2013), Laurie Shannon, *The Accommodated Animal: Cosmopolity in Shakespearean Locales* (Chicago: University of Chicago Press, 2013), and Bruce Thomas Boehrer, *Animal Characters: Nonhuman Beings in Early Modern Literature* (Philadelphia: University of Pennsylvania Press, 2010); feminism, Jennifer Munroe and Rebecca Laroche, eds., *Ecofeminist Approaches to Early Modernity* (New York: Palgrave Macmillan, 2011); and pedagogy, Jennifer Munroe, Edward J. Geisweidt, and Lynne Bruckner, eds., *Ecological Approaches to Early Modern English Texts: A Field Guide to Reading and Teaching* (Farnham: Ashgate, 2015). This list is meant to be suggestive, not comprehensive. All in all, if the field of early modern ecostudies is growing, it is an expansion I only hope to accelerate through the genre of travel literature, different shades of blue, and (a) life of the inorganic.

49. Dan Brayton's *Shakespeare's Ocean: An Ecocritical Exploration* (Charlottesville: University of Virginia Press, 2012) and Steve Mentz's *At the Bottom of Shakespeare's Ocean* (New York: Continuum, 2009) are indispensable. Also see the "Oceanic Studies" cluster in *PMLA* 125, no. 3 (2010) and Elizabeth Jane Bellamy's *Dire Straits: The Perils of Writing the Early Modern English Coastline from Leland to Milton* (Toronto: University of Toronto Press, 2013).

50. See the "Ecomaterialism" issue of *postmedieval* 4, no. 1 (2013), ed. Jeffrey Jerome Cohen and Lowell Duckert. Also vital are Jeffrey Jerome Cohen,

ed., *Prismatic Ecology: Ecotheory beyond Green* (Minneapolis: University of Minnesota Press, 2013), Jean E. Feerick and Vin Nardizzi, eds., *The Indistinct Human in Renaissance Literature* (New York: Palgrave Macmillan, 2012), and Axel Goodbody and Kate Rigby, eds., *Ecocritical Theory: New European Approaches* (Charlottesville: University of Virginia Press, 2011).

51. We could benefit from unmooring the Bard's celebrity a bit, even though many titles on this list are superb: Randall Martin, *Shakespeare and Ecology* (Oxford: Oxford University Press, 2015); Gabriel Egan, *Shakespeare and Ecocritical Theory* (London: Bloomsbury, 2015); Gwilym Jones, *Shakespeare's Storms* (Manchester: Manchester University Press, 2015); Cary DiPietro and Hugh Grady, eds., *Shakespeare and the Urgency of Now: Criticism and Theory in the 21st Century* (New York: Palgrave Macmillan, 2013); Lynne Bruckner and Dan Brayton, eds., *Ecocritical Shakespeare* (Farnham: Ashgate, 2011); Simon C. Estok, *Ecocriticism and Shakespeare: Reading Ecophobia* (New York: Palgrave Macmillan, 2011); Gabriel Egan, *Green Shakespeare: From Ecopolitics to Ecocriticism* (New York: Routledge, 2006); and Jeanne Addison Roberts, *The Shakespearean Wild: Geography, Genus, and Gender* (Lincoln: University of Nebraska Press, 1991). Greg Garrard has gone so far as to announce in his foreword to *Ecocritical Shakespeare*: "Enter Shakespearean ecocriticism. By that I do not mean only the application of pre-existing ecocritical approaches to Shakespearean texts, but rather the possibility . . . that ecocriticism itself might *be Shakespearean*" (xxiv). Such a "natural" conflation of Shakespeare and ecocriticism is worth investigating. We should ask not just *how* Shakespeare is ecocritical, but *why* he—and primarily he—leads the field. Some of the abovementioned authors are more inquisitive than others; indeed, Julian Yates and Garrett Sullivan query the conjunction "and" in the introduction to their forum on "Shakespeare and Ecology," *Shakespeare Studies* 39 (2011): 25–26. Also see Tiffany Jo Werth, ed., "Shakespeare and the Human," a special section of *The Shakespearean International Yearbook* (Farnham: Ashgate, 2015).

52. Graham Huggan and Helen Tiffin, *Postcolonial Ecocriticism: Literature, Animals, Environment*, 2nd ed. (New York: Routledge, 2015), 12. Also significant is Upamanyu Pablo Mukherjee's chapter on "Towards Eco-Materialism," in *Postcolonial Environments: Nature, Culture and the Contemporary Indian Novel in English* (New York: Palgrave Macmillan, 2010), 59–81. Noteworthy early modern examples are the "Nature and Empire" section of Kamps, Raber, and Hallock, *Early Modern Ecostudies*; Jonathan Gil Harris, "Sick Ethnography: Recording the Indian Body and the Ill English Body," in *Indography: Writing the "Indian" in Early Modern England*, ed. Jonathan Gil Harris (New York: Palgrave Macmillan, 2012), 133–47; and Markley, "Summer's Lease" (see chapter 3).

53. William Shakespeare, *The Comedy of Errors* (1592–93), 1.2.35–36.

54. Patricia Yaeger, "Sea Trash, Dark Pools, and the Tragedy of the Commons," *PMLA* 125, no. 3 (2010): 523–45.

55. Bruno Latour, "An Attempt at a 'Compositionist Manifesto,'" *New Literary History* 41 (2010): 487.

56. Watson, *Back to Nature*, 7.

57. For a smart reading of early modern wooden media, see Vin Nardizzi, *Wooden Os: Shakespeare's Theatres and England's Trees* (Toronto: University of Toronto Press, 2013).

58. John Stow, *The Survey of London* (London, 1633), 25.

59. Borlik, *Ecocriticism and Early Modern English Literature*, 140, 206, 208.

60. Ibid., 209.

61. Bruno Latour, *Pandora's Hope: Essays on the Reality of Science Studies* (Cambridge, MA: Harvard University Press, 1999), 200.

62. See Sharon O'Dair, "Is It Shakespearean Ecocriticism if It Isn't Presentist?" in Bruckner and Brayton, *Ecocritical Shakespeare*, 71–85. Also of note is the "strategic presentism" Brayton outlines in *Shakespeare's Ocean* (5–6), while Craig Dionne's *Posthuman Lear: Reading Shakespeare in the Anthropocene* (New York: punctum books, 2016) announces outright: "I think it is worth taking the risk of sounding incoherent or boorish in the face of ecological catastrophe. It is not risking all that much when considering the stakes" (16).

63. "Rose Theatre Looks Up from Watery Grave," *BBC News*, April 13, 1999: http://news.bbc.co.uk/2/hi/entertainment/315419.stm. The theater's website provides pictures and more information about the "Rose Revealed Project": http://www.rosetheatre.org.uk/.

64. Ivan Illich, *H₂O and the Waters of Forgetfulness: Reflections on the Historicity of "Stuff"* (London: Marion Boyers, 1986), 25, 36.

65. See the "Theories and Methodologies" cluster of *PMLA* 127, no. 3 (2012).

66. From the King James version (1611): "And the earth was without form, and void; and darkness was upon the face of the deep. And the Spirit of God moved upon the face of the waters" (Genesis 1:2).

67. Ulrich Beck's indelible phrase from *Risk Society: Towards a New Modernity*, trans. Mark Ritter (London: Sage Publications, 1992).

68. Macauley, *Elemental Philosophy*, 89–90.

Introduction

1. Roni Horn, *Another Water (The River Thames, for Example)* (Göttingen: Steidl, 2000), n. 410.

2. Ibid., n. 226.

3. Mentz, *At the Bottom of Shakespeare's Ocean*, 1.

4. Brayton, *Shakespeare's Ocean*, 18.

5. Ibid., 7.

6. Ibid., 200, 164.

7. See Mark McMenamin and Dianna McMenamin, *Hypersea: Life on Land* (New York: Columbia University Press, 1996).

8. The classic study is E. M. W. Tillyard, *The Elizabethan World Picture* (New York: Vintage, 1959). While some early modern ecocritics consider re-appropriating the chain, I argue throughout that these vertical links, no matter which way they are arranged, may actually thwart a true ecology of freedom. See Gabriel Egan, "Gaia and the Great Chain of Being," in Bruckner and Brayton, *Ecocritical Shakespeare*, 57–69. In her introduction to "Shakespeare and the Human," Tiffany Jo Werth justifiably "proposes that we shift metaphors from a 'chain of being' in favor of a 'scale of creatures'" (4).

9. Andrew Gurr, *The Shakespearean Stage: 1574–1642*, 2nd ed. (Cambridge: Cambridge University Press, 1980), 170.

10. Shakespeare's predilection for water was rivaled only by Thomas Heywood's. With the help of Alan C. Dessen and Leslie Thomson's *A Dictionary of Stage Directions in English Drama, 1580–1642* (Cambridge: Cambridge University Press, 1999), I have amassed the following list (and counting) of titles with stage directions that mention water, in chronological order: Thomas Lodge and Robert Greene, *A Looking Glass for London and England* (1588); Christopher Marlowe, *Doctor Faustus* (1592); Thomas Heywood, *The Four Prentices of London* (1594); William Shakespeare (muddily), *The Merry Wives of Windsor* (1597); anonymous, *The Merry Devil of Edmonton* (1602); George Chapman, Ben Jonson, and John Marston, *Eastward Ho!* (1605); Thomas Heywood, *The Silver Age* (1611); William Rowley and Thomas Heywood, *The Thracian Wonder* (1611–12); anonymous, *Two Noble Ladies* (1619–23); Thomas Dekker, John Ford, and William Rowley, *The Witch of Edmonton* (1621); Thomas Heywood, *The Captives* (1624); anonymous, *Loves Changelinges Change* (1630); Thomas Nabbes, *Totenham Court* (1633); and James Shirley, *The Lady of Pleasure* (1637).

11. George Chapman, Ben Jonson, and John Marston, *Eastward Ho!* (Manchester: Manchester University Press, 2006), 149.

12. Andrew Gurr, "*The Tempest*'s Tempest at Blackfriars," *Shakespeare Survey* 41 (1989): 101.

13. Ibid., 99.

14. The "tug-of-war between storm noise and the spoken words" can be negotiated by actors who successfully "rely solely upon their voices and bodies rather than upon special effects involving lightning, sound, and water." Alan C.

Dessen, *Recovering Shakespeare's Theatrical Vocabulary* (Cambridge: Cambridge University Press, 1995), 268. Gwilym Jones briefly touches on the stormy stage directions as part of his larger argument about separation and spectatorship—"When an actor delivers lines that prompt the audience to imagine the elements of the play-world, an automatic ironic relationship with the elements of the real world is established" (*Shakespeare's Storms*, 2–9)—a gap which maintains, I worry, the ontological divides dramatic wetness disavows.

15. See Anne Barton, "'Enter Mariners, Wet': Realism in Shakespeare's Last Plays," in *Realism in European Literature*, ed. Nicholas Boyle and Martin Swales (Cambridge: Cambridge University Press, 1986). "The theatre audience, already disoriented by Shakespeare's cunningly inconsistent use of the dramatic code of 'playing wet,' could not have been quite sure what it was meant to believe" (46).

16. Trevor R. Griffiths, *The Tempest* (New York: Palgrave Macmillan, 2007), 4.

17. Stow, *Survey*, 24.

18. Ibid., 688.

19. Ben Jonson, "On the Famous Voyage," in *Ben Jonson: The Complete Poems*, ed. George Parfitt (London: Penguin, 1975), 88.

20. Nedra Reynolds, *Geographies of Writing: Inhabiting Spaces and Encountering Difference* (Carbondale: Southern Illinois University Press, 2004), 16. See especially chap. 1, "Between Metaphor and Materiality": "We should . . . be asking how metaphors result from, rather than simply shape, our experience in the material world" (46).

21. Ibid.

22. Latour, *Pandora's Hope*, 24–79.

23. Griffiths, *The Tempest*, 17.

24. Philip Sidney, *The Countess of Pembroke's Arcadia*, ed. Maurice Evans (London: Penguin, 1977), 64.

25. Julian Yates, *Error, Misuse, Failure: Object Lessons from the English Renaissance* (Minneapolis: University of Minnesota Press, 2003), 22.

26. *Loves Changelinges Change*, ed. John P. Cutts (Fennimore: John Westburg and Associates, 1974), 2.

27. Todd Andrew Borlik has smartly corrected this; see "Caliban and the Fen Demons of Lincolnshire: The Englishness of Shakespeare's *Tempest*," *Shakespeare* 9, no. 1 (2013): 21–51. I return to the swamps and Borlik's dirty work in chapter 4.

28. See Julia Reinhard Lupton, "Creature Caliban," *Shakespeare Quarterly* 51, no. 1 (2000): 1–23.

29. Deleuze and Guattari, *A Thousand Plateaus*, 3.

30. I have Michel Serres's *The Natural Contract*, trans. Elizabeth MacArthur and William Paulson (Ann Arbor: University of Michigan Press, 1995) in mind, but also see Latour's explanation of attachment within the actor-network: "It was impossible before to connect an actor to what made it act, without being accused of 'dominating,' 'limiting,' or 'enslaving' it. This is no longer the case. The more *attachments* it has, the more it exists. And the more mediators there are the better." *Reassembling the Social: An Introduction to Actor-Network Theory* (Oxford: Oxford University Press, 2005), 217. "Nonhumans are born free, and everywhere they are in chains. . . . As to emancipation, it does not mean 'freed from bonds' but *well*-attached" (*Pandora's Hope*, 172, 218).

31. Stow, *Survey*, 698.

32. One of the oldest stories is war-torn: the flogging of the Hellespont by Xerxes. See Herodotus, *The Histories*, trans. Aubrey de Sélincourt (London: Penguin, 1954).

33. Steve Mentz, "After Sustainability," *PMLA* 127, no. 3 (2012): 589. Such "shipwreck hermeneutics" are further developed in Mentz's *Shipwreck Modernity: Ecologies of Globalization, 1550–1719* (Minneapolis: University of Minnesota Press, 2015).

34. Mentz, *At the Bottom of Shakespeare's Ocean*, 68.

35. Andrew McRae, "Fluvial Nation: Rivers, Mobility, and Poetry in Early Modern England," *English Literary Renaissance* 38, no. 3 (2008): 534.

36. Ibid., 506.

37. Ursula K. Heise, *Sense of Place and Sense of Planet: The Environmental Imagination of the Global* (Oxford: Oxford University Press, 2008), 10.

38. Mark S. R. Jenner, "From Conduit Community to Commercial Network? Water in London, 1500–1725," in *Londonopolis: Essays in the Cultural and Social History of Early Modern London*, ed. Paul Griffiths (Manchester: Manchester University Press, 2000), 265.

39. William Blake, "Auguries of Innocence," in *The Complete Poetry & Prose of William Blake* (New York: Anchor Books, 1988), 490; Latour, *Politics of Nature*, 40. According to science writer David Blatner, the number of stars in the universe is equal to the number of water molecules in ten drops of water; see *Spectrums: Our Mind-Boggling Universe from Infinitesimal to Infinity* (New York: Bloomsbury, 2012).

40. Mentz, *At the Bottom of Shakespeare's Ocean*, 80, 69.

41. Ibid., xiii, xii, 18.

42. All quotations sieved from the company's website: http://www.synetic theater.org/event_pages/the-tempest/.

43. Consider Serres's confession to Latour: "What I seek to compose, to promote—I can't quite find the right word—is a *syrrhèse*, a confluence not a

system, a mobile confluence of fluxes" (Serres with Latour, *Conversations*, 122). My wish here is to compose with wet matter.

44. Iovino and Oppermann, "Theorizing Material Ecocriticism," 451; and Serenella Iovino and Serpil Oppermann, "Introduction: Stories Come to Matter," *Material Ecocriticism* (Bloomington: Indiana University Press, 2014), 1.

45. Iovino and Oppermann, "Introduction," 8.

46. The "articulation" I detail follows Latour's definition of a distributed agency that need not be verbal or linguistic: "Propositions do not have the fixed boundaries of objects. They are surprising events in the histories or other entities. The more articulation there is, the better. . . . *We are allowed to speak interestingly by what we allow to speak interestingly*" (*Pandora's Hope*, 143–44).

47. Latour, *Reassembling the Social*, 244.

48. See Steve Mentz, *Romance for Sale in Early Modern England: The Rise of Prose Fiction* (Burlington: Ashgate, 2006).

49. Joan Pong Linton, *The Romance of the New World: Gender and the Literary Formations of English Colonialism* (Cambridge: Cambridge University Press, 1998), 1. Also note Mary C. Fuller, *Voyages in Print: English Narratives of Travel to America, 1576–1624* (Cambridge: Cambridge University Press, 1995).

50. Serpil Oppermann, "From Ecological Postmodernism to Material Ecocriticism: Creative Materiality and Narrative Agency," in Iovino and Oppermann, *Material Ecocriticism*, 34.

51. My use of ecotone builds on Mary Louise Pratt's influential "contact zone." See *Imperial Eyes: Travel Writing and Transculturation*, 2nd ed. (New York: Routledge, 2008).

52. Monique Allewaert, *Ariel's Ecology: Plantations, Personhood, and Colonialism in the American Tropics* (Minneapolis: University of Minnesota Press, 2013), 2, 25. See "Ecomaterialism" especially, 17–20.

53. *The Court and Times of Charles the First* (London: Henry Colburn, 1848), 1:113.

54. Michel Serres, *Biogea*, trans. Randolph Burks (Minneapolis: Univocal, 2012), 175. "Every existence thus shows something stable in divergence from stability" (178).

55. *A Strange Wonder, or, The Cities Amazement* (London, 1641), unpaginated.

56. Gaston Bachelard, *Water and Dreams: An Essay on the Imagination of Matter*, trans. Edith R. Farrell (Dallas: Dallas Institute of Humanities and Culture, 1983), 5, 15. "By grouping images and dissolving substances, water helps the imagination in its task of de-objectifying and assimilating. It also contributes a type of syntax, a continual lining up and gentle movement of images that frees a reverie bound to objects" (12).

57. Ibid., 134.

58. Stow, *Survey*, 20.

59. Ibid.

60. "*The more nonhumans share existence with humans, the more humane* a collective is" (Latour, *Pandora's Hope*, 18).

61. See Alaimo and Hekman, *Material Feminisms*. My use of "testify" and "attest" (both derive from the physiological "testicle"), for example, is meant to point out the gendered bias of social activism that ecofeminism targets.

62. See Munroe and Laroche, *Ecofeminist Approaches to Early Modernity;* Sylvia Bowerbank, *Speaking for Nature: Women and Ecologies in Early Modern England* (Baltimore: Johns Hopkins University Press, 2004); and Carolyn Merchant, *The Death of Nature: Women, Ecology, and the Scientific Revolution* (New York: Harper & Row, 1980). An example of said "persistence" is Bachelard's masculine, exclusionary encouragement: "A man [*sic*] should be defined by the sum of those tendencies which impel him to surpass the *human condition*" (*Water and Dreams*, 16).

63. See s.v. "landscape" (n.) in the *Oxford English Dictionary*.

64. Bennett, *Vibrant Matter*, viii.

65. Ibid.

66. Eduardo Kohn removes water's voice while granting it to stone in *How Forests Think: Toward an Anthropology beyond the Human* (Berkeley: University of California Press, 2013). "*Tsupu* . . . refers to an entity as it makes contact with and then penetrates a body of water; think of a big stone heaved into a pond" (27). And yet later he admits that "life thinks; stones don't" (100). For a convincing argument against this point, see Jeffrey Jerome Cohen's *Stone: An Ecology of the Inhuman* (Minneapolis: University of Minnesota Press, 2015).

67. Latour, "Attempt at a 'Compositionist Manifesto,'" 487.

68. Ibid., 484. A "thirst for mixed connections" is where I want you to be, and it is, coincidentally, how Latour likens our current situation to the Renaissance (481).

69. Janine MacLeod, "Water and the Material Imagination: Reading the Sea of Memory against the Flows of Capital," in Chen, MacLeod, and Neimanis, *Thinking with Water*, 49. By contrast, Maggie Kilgour, "Writing on Water," *English Literary Renaissance* 29, no. 3 (1999), reads water as a nationalistic trope in the late sixteenth and early seventeenth centuries: "If Britain gained a sense of itself as a nation through its control of the waters that surrounded it, it also created a new image for itself based on the internal relation between its waters" (284). Likewise, David J. Baker relegates the fluidity of Coryate's body to the analogical in "'My Liquid Journey': The Frontispiece of *Coryat's Crudities*," in *Environment and Embodiment in Early Modern England*, ed. Mary

Floyd-Wilson and Garrett A. Sullivan Jr. (New York: Palgrave Macmillan, 2007), 118–36. I do not mean to disparage these (and other) contributions, of course, only to enlarge their scope.

70. Julie Sanders, *The Cultural Geography of Early Modern Drama, 1620–1650* (Cambridge: Cambridge University Press, 2011), 9–10. "Liquid Landscapes" is the title of her first chapter, interested in "the complex relationship between the literary understandings of watery environments and the everyday practice and representation of the same" (52).

71. Ibid., 177, 100.

72. Ibid., 10.

73. Ibid., 64, 42–43.

74. Ibid., 21.

75. Ibid.

76. Ken Hiltner makes a similar claim regarding pastoral poetry, arguing that pastoral writers chose *not* to represent nature, "choosing instead to gesture to what lies outside of the work" (*What Else Is Pastoral?*, 3).

77. Sanders, *Cultural Geography of Early Modern Drama*, 64, 12.

78. Sidney I. Dobrin and Christian R. Weisser, *Natural Discourse: Toward Ecocomposition* (Albany: State University of New York Press, 2002), 176.

79. Ibid., 177.

80. Laura Gries, "Agential Matters: Tumbleweed, Women-Pens, Citizens-Hope, and Rhetorical Agency," in *Ecology, Writing Theory, and New Media: Writing Ecology*, ed. Sidney I. Dobrin (New York: Routledge, 2012), 70.

81. Jack Selzer and Sharon Crowley, eds., *Rhetorical Bodies* (Madison: University of Wisconsin Press, 1999).

82. Raúl Sánchez, "In Terms of Writing as Such," in Dobrin, *Ecology, Writing Theory, and New Media*, 25.

83. Serres, *Biogea*, 24.

84. For starters, see Catriona Mortimer-Sandilands and Bruce Erickson, eds., *Queer Ecologies: Sex, Nature, Politics, Desire* (Bloomington: Indiana University Press, 2010).

85. See Beth Stephens and Annie Sprinkle, dirs., *Goodbye Gauley Mountain: An Ecosexual Love Story* (2013).

86. By "ecophobia," he means humanity's "irrational and groundless fear or hatred of the natural world" fed by our anxieties over control and unpredictability (Estok, *Ecocriticism and Shakespeare*, 4).

87. Deleuze and Guattari, *A Thousand Plateaus*, 76.

88. Sharon O'Dair, "Water Love," *postmedieval* 4, no. 1 (2013): 55–67.

89. Tim Ingold, *Being Alive: Essays on Movement, Knowledge, and Description* (New York: Routledge, 2011), 131, 126.

90. Charles S. Brown and Ted Toadvine, eds., *Eco-Phenomenology: Back to the Earth Itself* (Albany: State University of New York Press, 2003), xi.

91. Serres, *Five Senses*, 81.

92. Alphonso Lingis's fourth chapter in *The Community of Those Who Have Nothing in Common* (Bloomington: Indiana University Press, 1994), 69–106. "To live is to echo the vibrancy of things. To be, for material things, is to resonate" (96).

93. Gail Kern Paster, "Becoming the Landscape: The Ecology of the Passions in the Legend of Temperance," in Floyd-Wilson and Sullivan, *Environment and Embodiment in Early Modern England*, 139, 140.

94. Ibid., 139.

95. Ibid.

96. Ibid., 137.

97. Mary Floyd-Wilson and Garrett A. Sullivan Jr., "Introduction: Inhabiting the Body, Inhabiting the World," in Floyd-Wilson and Sullivan, *Environment and Embodiment in Early Modern England*, 3.

98. Ellen Mackay, "Water, Absorption, Uncontainment, and Cleopatra's Barge," in Werth, "Shakespeare and the Human," 147–66, concentrates on how water expands the play's emotional range—"Given the evanescence of the performance world of early modern England, it is easy to underestimate the extent to which absorbing theatricality took place within an aquatic register" (150)—a thorough soaking I detail throughout.

99. William Caxton, *Caxton's Mirrour of the World* (New York: C. Scribner, 1913), 109. Other examples are George Sandys's (1578–1644) *A Relation of a Journey Begun in A.D. 1610* (London: Thomas Cotes, 1637): "the waters thereof [the Nile] there is none more sweet being not unpleasantly cold and of all others offers the most wholesome [draught]. So much it nourisheth, that the inhabitants think that it forthwith converteth into blood retaining that property ever since thereunto metamorphosed by Moses" (99); and Phineas Fletcher's (1582–1650) *The Purple Island* (Cambridge: Thomas Buck and Roger Daniel, 1633): "The first [vein] in single chanels skie-like blue, / With luke-warm waters di'd in porphyr hue, / Sprinkle this crimson Isle with purple-colour'd dew" (2.10).

100. See Barad, chap. 2, "Diffractions: Differences, Contingencies, and Entanglements that Matter," in *Meeting the Universe Halfway*.

101. Mary Floyd-Wilson, *English Ethnicity and Race in Early Modern Drama* (Cambridge: Cambridge University Press, 2003).

102. John Donne, "Holy Sonnet 15," in *John Donne: The Major Works*, ed. John Carey (Oxford: Oxford University Press, 1990), 179; Max Haiven, "The Dammed of the Earth: Reading the Mega-Dam for the Political Unconscious

of Globalization," in Chen, MacLeod, and Neimanis, *Thinking with Water*, 219.

103. "The material imagination dramatizes the world in its depths" (Bachelard, *Water and Dreams*, 148).

104. Timothy Morton, *Ecology without Nature: Rethinking Environmental Aesthetics* (Cambridge, MA: Harvard University Press, 2007), 205. According to him, "There is *not even nothing* beyond inside and outside" (78).

105. Timothy Morton, *The Ecological Thought* (Cambridge, MA: Harvard University Press, 2010), 50. I agree that thinking the ecological thought is about "considering others, in their interests, in how we should act toward them, and in their very being" (123).

106. Ibid., 50.

107. Ibid., 33.

108. Alaimo, *Bodily Natures*, 2.

109. For more on these terms, see Deleuze and Guattari, *A Thousand Plateaus*, chap. 14, "1440: The Smooth and the Striated."

110. Serres with Latour, *Conversations*, 105.

111. Bennett, *Vibrant Matter*, 12.

112. The year of my writing, 2015, is the final year of the UN's "Water for Life Decade": http://www.un.org/waterforlifedecade/human_right_to_water .shtml; and Kate Shuttleworth, "Agreement Entitles Whanganui River to Legal Identity," *New Zealand Herald*, August 30, 2012, http://www.nzherald.co.nz/ nz/news/article.cfm?c_id=1&objectid=10830586.

113. In fact I am a cosigner of one, the Friends of Decker's Creek Watershed Bill of Rights, part of the community organization's ongoing Citizen Scientist program: http://deckerscreek.org.

114. Yates and Sullivan, "Shakespeare and Ecology," 25.

115. Latour, *Pandora's Hope*, 61.

116. Vicki Kirby's point precisely in *Quantum Anthropologies: Life at Large* (Durham, NC: Duke University Press, 2011). "What happens if Nature is neither lacking nor primordial, but rather, a plenitude of possibilities, a cacophony of convers(at)ion?" (88).

117. Émilie Hache and Bruno Latour, "Morality or Moralism? An Exercise in Sensitization," trans. Patrick Camiller, *Common Knowledge* 16, no. 2 (2010): 312.

118. Ibid.

1. Becoming Wa/l/ter

1. I gathered the following information from Floodlist: http://floodlist .com/.

2. Walter Ralegh, *The Discovery of the Large, Rich, and Beautiful Empire of Guiana*, ed. Robert H. Schomburgk (London: Hakluyt Society, 1848), 41. All quotations from Ralegh's *Discoverie* refer to this edition and are hereafter cited in the text.

3. Thomas Fuller, *The History of the Worthies of England* (London: J.G.W.L. and W.G., 1662), 262.

4. Walter Ralegh, *The Discovery of Guiana: With Related Documents*, ed. Benjamin Schmidt (Boston: Bedford/St. Martin's, 2008), 25.

5. Ibid., 31. For more on the *Discoverie*'s afterlives, see Benjamin Schmidt, "Reading Ralegh's America: Texts, Books, and Readers in the Early Modern Atlantic World," in *The Atlantic World and Virginia, 1550–1624*, ed. P. C. Mancall (Chapel Hill: University of North Carolina Press, 2007), 454–88.

6. C. A. Patrides, ed., *The History of the World* (Philadelphia: Temple University Press, 1971), 1.

7. Charles Nicholl, *The Creature in the Map: A Journey to El Dorado* (New York: William Morrow, 1995), 15.

8. See D. B. Quinn, *Raleigh and the British Empire* (New York: Macmillan, 1949).

9. David Hume, *The History of England from the Invasion of Julius Caesar to the Revolution in 1688* (Indianapolis: Liberty Fund, 1983), 4:296.

10. See, respectively, Stephen Greenblatt, *Sir Walter Ralegh: The Renaissance Man and His Roles* (New Haven: Yale University Press, 1973); Mary B. Campbell, *The Witness and the Other World: Exotic European Travel Writing, 400–1600* (Ithaca: Cornell University Press, 1988); and William N. West, "Gold on Credit: Martin Frobisher's and Walter Ralegh's Economies of Evidence," *Criticism* 39 (1997): 315–36.

11. Latour, *Pandora's Hope*, 304.

12. Andrew Pickering, "New Ontologies," in *The Mangle in Practice: Science, Society, and Becoming*, ed. Andrew Pickering and Keith Guzik (Durham, NC: Duke University Press, 2008), 7.

13. Ibid., 8.

14. Ibid., 10.

15. Schama, *Landscape and Memory*, 312.

16. See Joyce Youings, *Ralegh's Country: The South West of England in the Reign of Queen Elizabeth I* (Raleigh: North Carolina Department of Cultural Resources, 1986).

17. Walter Ralegh, "The 11th: And Last Booke of the Ocean to Scinthia," in *The Poems of Sir Walter Ralegh*, ed. Agnes M. C. Latham (Cambridge, MA: Harvard University Press, 1951), 42.

18. Quoted in Nicholl, *The Creature in the Map*, 46.

19. In a letter written from Thomas Naunton, secretary of state, to Thomas Wilson is an "inventory of such things as were found on the body of Sir Walter Rawleigh, Knight, the 15th day of August, 1618." The inventory was compiled shortly after Ralegh's failed escape attempt from the Tower. See Ralegh, *The Discovery*, ed. Schomburgk, 228.

20. Greenblatt, *Sir Walter Ralegh*, 99.

21. Schama, *Landscape and Memory*, 307.

22. Walter Ralegh, *The History of the World* (London: William Stansby, 1614), 30.

23. Walter Ralegh, *The Discoverie of the Large, Rich and Bewtiful Empyre of Guiana*, ed. Neil L. Whitehead (Norman: University of Oklahoma Press, 1997), 100.

24. Nicholl, *The Creature in the Map*, 15.

25. Linton discusses Ralegh in *Romance of the New World*, chap. 2, "Sea-Knights and Royal Virgins," 39–61.

26. Walter Oakeshott has catalogued his impressive collection in "Sir Walter Ralegh's Library," *Library* 23 (1968): 285–327.

27. Ralegh, *Poems*, ed. Latham, 17–18.

28. Deleuze and Guattari, *A Thousand Plateaus*, 156.

29. Ibid. Hugh Raffle's "account of rivers, trade, and the grounded prosaics of everyday political economy" in Amazonia—while advancing the poetical phrase "fluvial intimacies"—differs from my approach in its strict attention to "the production of difference and power": "Fluvial Intimacies," in *Waterscapes: The Cultural Politics of a Natural Resource*, ed. Amita Baviskar (Ranikhet: Permanent Black, 2007), 315, 317; it approximates my method, however, in that it "offers a way into thinking about how people . . . live with their rivers, and how rivers inhabit both places and people" (ibid., 317).

30. Schama, *Landscape and Memory*, 312.

31. Elsewhere in the narrative Ralegh considers the ingestive agency of things. Armadillo "horne" possesses medicinal powers (74). Although the Amazons exchange plates of gold for spleen stones, Ralegh does not automatically condemn them as fetishistic. "[F]or a kinde of greene stones, which the Spaniards call *Piedras Hijadas* . . . we vse for spleene stones, and for the disease of the stone we also esteeme them" (28–29). Jane Bennett argues that eating demonstrates "the formation of an assemblage of human and nonhuman elements, all of which bear some agentic capacity" (*Vibrant Matter*, 49).

32. Eating is an aesthetic experience, though solid food does not seem to move him as much as imbibing the liquid landscape does: "On the banks of these riuers were diuers sorts of fruits good to eate, flowers and trees of that varietie as were sufficient to make ten volumes of herbals, we releeued our selues

manie times with the fruits of the countrey, and sometimes with foule and fish: we sawe birds of all colours, some carnation, some crimson, orenge tawny, purple, greene, watched, and of all other sorts both simple and mixt, as it was vnto vs a great good passing of the time to beholde them" (40).

33. The other unknown presence in the landscape—the "keepers call"—could come from "a shamanic keeper or 'master-of-animals'" (Ralegh, *Discoverie*, ed. Whitehead, 163n70).

34. Deleuze and Guattari, *A Thousand Plateaus*, 381.

35. Ibid.

36. See entries s.v. "prospect" (n.) and s.v. "prospect" (v.[1]) in the *Oxford English Dictionary*.

37. Schama, *Landscape and Memory*, 15.

38. Stephen Greenblatt, *Marvelous Possessions: The Wonder of the New World* (Chicago: Chicago University Press, 1991), 20.

39. Ibid., 24.

40. Serres, *Parasite*, 38.

41. Wyman H. Herendeen, *From Landscape to Literature: The River and the Myth of Geography* (Pittsburgh: Duquesne University Press, 1986), 7, 3.

42. John Taylor, *Drinke and Welcome* (London: Anne Griffin, 1637).

43. "Hope, suspense, and uncertainty are what sustain colonial narratives; they fill the gaps between expectations and results, and so allow the narrator to continue to work on his tale, to buy on margin, and to defer the final reckoning of loss and gain." West, "Gold on Credit," 318.

44. Mary C. Fuller, "Ralegh's Fugitive Gold: Reference and Deferral in *The Discovery of Guiana*," in *New World Encounters*, ed. Stephen Greenblatt (Berkeley: University of California Press, 1993), 223.

45. Fuller, *Voyages in Print*, 66.

46. Quoted in Nicholl, *The Creature in the Map*, 278.

47. See Katherine Eggert for a notable introduction to alchemy in the period, "*The Alchemist* and Science," in *Early Modern English Drama: A Critical Companion*, ed. G. A. Sullivan Jr., P. Cheney, and A. Hadfield (Oxford: Oxford University Press, 2006), 200–212. Ralegh built his own chemical still and left behind a collection of chemical and medical recipes. Nicholl's chapter on the balsam provides a quick overview, *The Creature in the Map*, 278–87. Also see Oakeshott, "Sir Walter Ralegh's Library," 288. Deborah Harkness's work on "Big Science" in Elizabethan England, *The Jewel House: Elizabethan London and the Scientific Revolution* (New Haven: Yale University Press, 2007), traces the connections between mining, alchemy, and royal patronage, implicating the emergent adventures to the New World and those close to Ralegh: Robert Dudley, Humphrey Gilbert, and William Cecil.

48. Lee Patterson, "Perpetual Motion: Alchemy and the Technology of the Self," *Studies in the Age of Chaucer* 15 (1993): 35.

49. Ibid.

50. Ibid., 39.

51. Ralegh, *Discovery*, ed. Schmidt, 472, 473.

52. Shannon Miller, *Invested with Meaning: The Raleigh Circle in the New World* (Philadelphia: University of Pennsylvania Press, 1998), 2. Joyce Lorimer's edition, *Sir Walter Ralegh's "Discoverie of Guiana"* (London: Hakluyt Society, 2006), allows readers to compare a discovered manuscript edition to the printed version of 1596. Her conclusion likewise distributes authorial agency: "The [1596] version . . . was not an unmediated account of his experiences in Guiana but rather a carefully edited version of them. The comparison . . . demonstrates that the final product was not what Ralegh had wanted, but rather what already engaged investors . . . felt it was advisable to publish" (xcv). I would consider Ralegh's questionable collaboration another instance of his narrative's liquidity.

53. George Chapman, "De Guiana, Carmen Epicum," in *The Poems of George Chapman*, ed. Phyllis Brooks Bartlett (New York: Russell & Russell, 1941), 353–57. Chapman's commendatory poem compares Ralegh to Jason. The "*Argolian* Fleet" should be sent forth by Elizabeth upon the "*Guianian Orenoque*": "Then most admired Soueraigne, let your breath / Goe forth vpon the waters, and create / A golden worlde in this our yron age" (159, 161, 30–32). Also see book IV, canto xi of Edmund Spenser's *The Faerie Queene*, ed. Thomas P. Roche Jr. (London: Penguin, 1978), in which the noble *Thame* and his train surpass the rivers of the world. The Amazon River is fit for taking: "And shame on you, ô men, which boast your strong / And valiant hearts, in thoughts lesse hard and bold, / Yet quaile in conquest of that land of gold" (22.3–5).

54. Ovid, *Ovid's Metamorphoses*, trans. Arthur Golding (Baltimore: Johns Hopkins University Press, 2001), 1.115–16.

55. Linton, *Romance of the New World*, 1.

56. Ralegh, *Discoverie*, ed. Whitehead, 30.

57. Ibid., 92–93.

58. Ibid., 163n71.

59. Henry David Thoreau, "Sir Walter Raleigh," in *Collected Essays and Poems* (New York: Literary Classics of the United States, 2001), 57.

60. Ibid.

61. Ralegh, *The Discovery*, ed. Schomburgk, vii.

62. Quoted in Raleigh Trevelyan, *Sir Walter Raleigh* (London: Allen Lane, 2002), 552. For the persistence of his "martyr" persona, see Mark Nicholls and

Penry Williams, *Sir Walter Raleigh in Life and Legend* (New York: Continuum, 2011), "The 'Martyr,'" 299–324.

63. Schama, *Landscape and Memory*, 320.

64. Paster, "Becoming the Landscape," 142.

65. Alden T. Vaughan describes Hariot's and Ralegh's successful attempts in language education, both in England and in the "language lab" of the New World, in "Sir Walter Ralegh's Indian Interpreters, 1584–1618," *William and Mary Quarterly* 59, no. 2 (2002): 341–76. Vaughan considers Ralegh a figure of transculturation, "the principal link . . . between native interpreters and English overseas ventures" (375). Intriguingly, several natives stayed with Ralegh in his Thames-side mansion. This domestic ecology is but one example of the fluvial "conference" I have in mind.

66. Schama, *Landscape and Memory*, 307.

2. Going Glacial

1. Laurence C. Smith and Scott R. Stephenson, "New Trans-Arctic Shipping Routes Navigable by Midcentury," *PNAS* 110, no. 13 (2013): E1191–E1195.

2. Bill McKibben, *Eaarth: Making a Life on a Tough New Planet* (New York: Times Books, 2010), 3.

3. Ibid., xiv.

4. See Kirsten A. Seaver, *The Frozen Echo: Greenland and the Exploration of North America, ca. A.D. 1000–1500* (Stanford: Stanford University Press, 1996).

5. For examples, see Robert McGhee, *The Last Imaginary Place: A Human History of the Arctic World* (Oxford: Oxford University Press, 2005) and Gwen Schultz, *Ice Age Lost* (Garden City: Anchor Press, 1974). Both are engaging studies of the Arctic and the imagination but, as McGhee's title suggests, tend to privilege the human as the end point of becomings. Schultz, for instance, argues for a "friendly Ice Age" since "the human race thrived and progressed in spite of [it]. Or did it do so *because* of it?" (303). Even while working together as friends, I fear, the human dominates the conversation.

6. Latour, *We Have Never Been Modern*, 1–3.

7. Consider Hampton Sides's recent work of nonfiction, *In the Kingdom of Ice: The Grand and Terrible Polar Voyage of the USS "Jeannette"* (New York: Doubleday, 2014).

8. Bernd Herzogenrath, "White," in Cohen, *Prismatic Ecology*, 1–21, critiques white ("Western Christian") ecology as "the default mode of ecology," offering plurality in its place: "a white ecology might provide a context in which different eco*logics* (different ecological fields, such as human, viral, chemical, etc., that all follow their own logic and trajectories) resonate with each other"

(1). His emphasis on "sonorous materiality" and "sonic materiality" impress this chapter.

9. Robert Frost, "Fire and Ice," in *Robert Frost: Collected Poems, Prose, and Plays* (New York: Literary Classics of America, 1995), 204.

10. Paul Arthur Berkman, "Preventing an Arctic Cold War," *New York Times*, March 12, 2013.

11. Mamillius here; Leontes, later: "The blessed gods / Purge all infection from our air whilst you / Do climate here!" (5.1.167–69). I argue for the play's cocreative relation with coldness in "Exit, Pursued by a Polar Bear (More to Follow)," *Upstart: A Journal of English Renaissance Studies* (2013), https://up start.sites.clemson.edu/ Essays/exit-pursued-by-a-polar-bear/exit-pursued-by-a -polar-bear.xhtml.

12. Jean-Christophe Valtat, *Aurorarama* (New York: Melville House, 2010), 25, 328.

13. See Mick Smith, "Apologue," in *Against Ecological Sovereignty*, 219–23.

14. I am reminded of another passage forged six years before the *Camilla*'s voyage, Latour's argument in *War of the Worlds: What about Peace?* (Chicago: Prickly Paradigm Press, 2002): "What is needed is a new recognition of the old wars we have been fighting all along—in order to bring about new kinds of negotiation, and a new kind of peace" (4). For Latour, it is better to be at war and to think about diplomacy than to imagine that there is no war at all and to hold fast to modernity's progress. The member states of the Arctic Council are Canada, the Kingdom of Denmark, Finland, Iceland, Norway, the Russian Federation, Sweden, and the United States of America. Indigenous organizations with permanent participant status are Aleut International Association, Arctic Athabaskan Council, Gwich'in Council International, Inuit Circumpolar Council, Russian Association of Indigenous Peoples of the North, and the Saami Council.

15. See Mark Carey, "The History of Ice: How Glaciers Became an Endangered Species," *Environmental History* 12, no. 3 (2007): 497–527. "Critiquing the endangered glacier narrative . . . does not propose to ignore or disregard global warming. To the contrary, it ultimately strives to refine and redirect climate change responses to make them more effective and just" (501).

16. "Ice is only another form of terrestrial love." W. F. Badè, *The Life and Letters of John Muir* (Boston: Houghton Mifflin, 1924), 9:266. Muir's *Travels in Alaska* (New York: Modern Library, 2002), while not cited here, motivates this chapter.

17. Timothy Morton, *Hyperobjects: Philosophy and Ecology after the End of the World* (Minneapolis: University of Minnesota Press, 2013), 1, 94–95.

18. Ibid., 100.

19. "The Titanic of modernity hits the iceberg of hyperobjects" (ibid., 19).

20. When John Playse recounted Henry Hudson's first voyage of 1607 in search of the Northeast Passage, he included the captain's own notes. On the evening of July 11, Hudson complains, "we had the company of our troublesome neighbours, ice with fogge." Quoted in *Henry Hudson the Navigator*, ed. G. M. Asher (London: Hakluyt Society, 1860), 12. While noting such dangers is commonplace for travel writers of the north, calling ice a "neighbor" is not. "Neighbor" is a composite word from the Old English *nēahgebūr*, from *nēah* ("nigh, near") and *gebūr* ("inhabitant, peasant, farmer"). See my "Arctic-Oceanic New York," in *Oceanic New York*, ed. Steve Mentz (New York: punctum books, 2015).

21. Henry David Thoreau, *Walden*, in *The Portable Thoreau*, ed. Carl Bode (New York: Penguin, 1947), 538.

22. Carey, "History of Ice," 518.

23. See also chap. 3 in Deleuze and Guattari, *A Thousand Plateaus*, "10,000 B.C.: The Geology of Morals (Who Does the Earth Think It Is?)."

24. François Rabelais, *The Histories of Gargantua and Pantagruel*, trans. J. M. Cohen (London: Penguin, 1955), 569.

25. Gretel Ehrlich, *The Future of Ice: A Journey into Cold* (New York: Vintage, 2004), 54.

26. George Weymouth, *Narratives of Voyages towards the North-West, in Search of a Passage to Cathay and India, 1496 to 1631*, ed. Thomas Rundall (London: Hakluyt Society, 1849), 65, 68.

27. Barry Lopez, *Arctic Dreams: Imagination and Desire in a Northern Landscape* (New York: Vintage Books, 1986), 279.

28. Ibid., 252.

29. Robert Boyle, *New Experiments and Observations Touching Cold* (London, 1665), 575.

30. Her case study is the international park system within the St. Elias mountain range that borders Alaska, British Columbia, and the Yukon Territory, designated a UNESCO World Heritage Site in 1979; protecting these parks threatens the livelihood of indigenous peoples like the Tlingit and Athapaskan. Julie Cruikshank, *Do Glaciers Listen? Local Knowledge, Colonial Encounters, & Social Imagination* (Vancouver: University of British Columbia Press, 2005), 17 (and introduction), 258–59.

31. Ibid., 243, 8.

32. John Taylor, *The Colde Tearme, or, The Frozen Age, or, The Metamorphosis of the Riuer of Thames* (London, 1621).

33. Alvin Snider, "Hard Frost, 1684," *Journal for Early Modern Cultural Studies* 8, no. 2 (2008): 27.

34. Mary C. Fuller, *Remembering the Early Modern Voyage: English Narratives in the Age of European Expansion* (New York: Palgrave Macmillan, 2008); "Where Was Iceland in 1600?" in *A Companion to the Global Renaissance: English Literature and Culture in the Era of Expansion*, ed. Jyotsna Singh (Chichester: Wiley-Blackwell, 2009), 149–62; "Arctics of Empire: The North in *Principal Navigations* (1598–1600)," in *The Quest for the Northwest Passage: Knowledge, Nation and Empire, 1576–1806*, ed. Frédéric Regard (London: Pickering and Chatto, 2013), 15–29.

35. For instance, see Gerald MacLean, "East by North-East: The English among the Russians, 1553–1603," in Singh, *A Companion to the Global Renaissance*, 163–77.

36. Francis Spufford, *I May Be Some Time: Ice in the English Imagination* (New York: Picador, 1997), traverses only the tip of the iceberg: the nineteenth and twentieth centuries. For the Romantic phenomenon, see Eric G. Wilson, *The Spiritual History of Ice: Romanticism, Science, and the Imagination* (New York: Palgrave Macmillan, 2003). For the Victorian period, see Jen Hill, *White Horizon: The Arctic in the Nineteenth-Century British Imagination* (Albany: State University of New York Press, 2008). A general overview is Peter Davidson, *The Idea of North* (London: Reaktion Books, 2005). A notable medieval example is Gillian R. Overing and Marijane Osborn, *Landscape of Desire: Partial Stories of the Medieval Scandinavian World* (Minneapolis: University of Minnesota Press, 1994). Geographer John Wylie's Antarctic approach closely parallels mine: he pays attention to "the manner in which material, corporeal practices produce contexts which persist without solidifying, contexts which produce an ingoing *resonance* of bodies, visions, landscapes." See "Becoming-Icy: Scott and Amundsen's South Polar Voyages, 1910–13," *cultural geographies* 9 (2002): 263.

37. Joseph P. Ward, "The Taming of the Thames: Reading the River in the Seventeenth Century," *Huntington Library Quarterly* 71, no. 1 (2008): 57.

38. Virginia Woolf, *Orlando: A Biography* (New York: Harcourt, 1928), 35–36.

39. Ibid., 36.

40. Lopez, *Arctic Dreams*, 16.

41. My terse scientific notes come from Robert P. Sharp's accessible volume, *Living Ice: Understanding Glaciers and Glaciation* (Cambridge: Cambridge University Press, 1988), 2.

42. All etymological references are from the *Oxford English Dictionary*; see entries s.v. "glacier" (n.); s.v. "glace" (n.¹); s.v. "glace" (n.²); and s.v. "glace" (v.) especially.

43. George Best, *The Three Voyages of Martin Frobisher*, ed. Richard Collinson (London: Hakluyt Society, 1867), 127; see also 126 and 234. All quotations from Best's *Discourse* refer to this edition and are hereafter cited in the text.

44. For more than the cursory historical sketch I provide here, see Helen Wallis, "England's Search for the Northern Passages in the Sixteenth and Early Seventeenth Centuries," *Arctic* 37, no. 4 (1984): 453–72.

45. See E. G. R. Taylor, "A Letter Dated 1577 from Mercator to John Dee," *Imago Mundi* 13 (1956): 56–68.

46. Snider, "Hard Frost," 24. "Bitterly cold winters provided experiential evidence that Britain should perhaps count itself among the frigid places on Earth, that her claim to a privileged position in the temperate zone and among civilized nations required iteration and even defense" (24–25). Also see Floyd-Wilson, *English Ethnicity and Race*, chap. 1, "The Ghost of Hippocrates: Geo-humoral History in the West," 23–47.

47. Quoted in Ward, "Taming of the Thames," 59.

48. William Bourne, *A Regiment for the Sea Conteining Very Necessary Matters* (London: T. East, 1580), 77.

49. In full: "the BwO is that glacial reality where the alluvions, sedimentations, coagulations, foldings, and recoilings that compose an organism—and also a signification and a subject—occur" (Deleuze and Guattari, *A Thousand Plateaus*, 159). Cf. Michel Serres's icy image of reality: "a sort of fluctuating picture of relations and rapports—like the percolating basin of a glacial river" (*Natural Contract*, 105).

50. Mariana Gosnell's amazing book, *Ice: The Nature, the History, and the Uses of an Astonishing Substance* (Chicago: University of Chicago Press, 2005), 27, details these queer properties of ice (in the sense of material deviancy) I include throughout. Uncovering more strangeness is an "exercise that will continue" (412) and to which I wish to contribute.

51. See Deleuze and Guattari, *A Thousand Plateaus*, chap. 10, "1730: Becoming-Intense, Becoming-Animal, Becoming-Imperceptible . . . ," especially 266.

52. Lloyd E. Berry and Robert O. Crummey, eds., *Rude and Barbarous Kingdom: Russia in the Accounts of Sixteenth-Century English Voyagers* (Madison: University of Wisconsin Press, 1968), 16.

53. Quoted in Robert McGhee, *The Arctic Voyages of Martin Frobisher: An Elizabethan Adventure* (Seattle: University of Washington Press, 2001), 32, the text that supplies my historical information.

54. Thomas Churchyard, *A Prayse, and Reporte of Maister Martyne Forboishers Voyage to Meta Incognita* (London, 1578), unpaginated.

55. Luke Foxe, *The Voyages of Captain Luke Foxe of Hull, and Captain Thomas James of Bristol, in Search of a North-West Passage, in 1631–32*, ed. Miller Christy, 2 vols. (London: Hakluyt Society, 1894), 1:7.

56. See, respectively, West, "Gold on Credit," and D. D. Hogarth, P. W. Boreham, and J. G. Mitchell, *Martin Frobisher's Northwest Venture, 1576–1581: Mines, Minerals & Metallurgy* (Hull: Canadian Museum of Civilization, 1994).

57. Lopez, *Arctic Dreams*, 279.

58. Quoted in Ward, "Taming of the Thames," 66.

59. Serres, *Five Senses*, 60.

60. See Fridtjof Nansen, *In Northern Mists: Arctic Exploration in Early Times*, trans. Arthur G. Chater, vol. 1 (London: Ballantyne Press, 1911), chap. 2, "Pytheas of Massalia: The Voyage to Thule," 66.

61. Serres, *Five Senses*, 274. "This new map of knowledge reproduces the old world map, or a present-day view of the North-West passage: great oceans invaginated into seas, then straits and gulfs or bays, scattered archipelagos and islands redrawing immensity on a small scale; ice flows, variable through freezing and melting, projecting into time the complexities of space, overlaps and dead-ends, reliable passages and obstacles, a mixed landscape in a fluctuating state, an intermediate and complex state between two plains of water on which constant, methodical routes are ensured" (ibid.).

62. "Fog betrays, completely fills the environment with potential things . . . mist disturbs ontology" (ibid., 70).

63. "[S]he not acquainted with such kinde of surgerie, plucked those salves away, and, by continuall licking with hir own tongue, not much unlike our dogges, healed uppe the child's arme" (143).

64. When Charles Francis Hall visited the bay in the 1860s, he heard a story about Eloudjuarng, an Inuit leader who had protected several *quadlunaat* (a local term applied to Norsemen) after they had been left behind. The following spring the men set off in their makeshift boat, never to be heard from again. The five men might have quickly perished; nevertheless, it is tempting to think that these *quadlunaat* were Frobisher's men and, furthermore, that they were attracted to an Inuit lifestyle in their captain's forbidden icescape (McGhee, *Arctic Voyages of Martin Frobisher*, 56).

65. Serres, *Biogea*, 175.

66. Lopez, *Arctic Dreams*, 405–6.

67. Woolf, *Orlando*, 36.

68. John Davis, *The Voyages and Works of John Davis the Navigator*, ed. Albert Hastings Markham (London: Hakluyt Society, 1880), 223. All quotations from Davis's *Discription* refer to this edition and are hereafter cited in the text.

69. Quoted in Gosnell, *Ice*, 5.

70. Sophie Lemercier-Goddard, "George Best's Arctic Mirrors: *A True Discourse of the Late Voyages of Discoverie . . . of Martin Frobisher* (1578)," in Regard, *The Quest for the Northwest Passage*, 56, 63.

71. Serres, *Five Senses*, 238.

72. Thomas Ellis, *A True Report of the Third and Last Voyage into Meta Incognita* (London: Thomas Dawson, 1578), A3, C.

73. Thomas Ellis, *The Third Voyage of Martin Frobisher to Baffin Island 1578*, ed. James McDermott (London: Hakluyt Society, 2001), 195. All quotations from Ellis's *Report* hereafter refer to this edition and are cited in the text.

74. Deleuze and Guattari, *A Thousand Plateaus*, 188. See chap. 7, "Year Zero: Faciality." In making this connection, I mean to expand the "face-to-face" of Emmanuel Lévinas, whose ethical imperative is too dependent, in my view, on the physiological, mammalian face for the "Other."

75. "You don't so much have a face as slide into one" (ibid., 177).

76. Quoted in Ellis, *Third Voyage*, ed. McDermott, 158.

77. Mary Shelley, *Frankenstein* (London: Penguin, 1992), 222, 221.

78. Quoted in Weymouth, *Narratives of Voyages*, ed. Rundall, 145.

79. Foxe, *Voyages*, 242.

80. Ibid., 423, 442.

3. Making (It) Rain

1. John Ray, *A Collection of English Proverbs* (Cambridge: John Hayes, 1678), 200.

2. See articles from the *Times of India*, June 3, 2015: http://timesofindia .indiatimes.com/business; I watched the monsoon's progress on the IMD website: http://www.imd.gov.in/pages/monsoon_main.php.

3. Anne Barton, "Shakespeare's Sense of an Ending in *Twelfth Night*," in *Twelfth Night: Critical Essays*, ed. Stanley Wells (New York: Garland, 1986), 308.

4. Ibid., 309, 310.

5. One of the most frequently asked questions: "What happens when it rains?" http://www.shakespearesglobe.com/your-visit/frequently-asked-questions/first-time-visitors.

6. Stow, *Abridgement of the English Chronicle*, 415.

7. Barton, "Shakespeare's Sense of an Ending," 310.

8. Rebecca Totaro, "'Revolving This Will Teach Thee How to Curse': A Lesson in Sublunary Exhalation," in *Literary and Scientific Cultures of Early Modernity: Rhetoric of Bodily Disease and Health in Medieval and Early Modern England*, ed. Jennifer C. Vaught (Farnham: Ashgate, 2010), 135–51.

9. Gurr, *Shakespearean Stage*, 170. Heywood's stage direction reads "Hercules . . . *kils* Busyris *and sacrificeth him upon the Altar, at which there fals a shower of raine*," in *The Dramatic Works of Thomas Heywood* (London: John Pearson, 1874), 3:183. Dekker's is "*Rayne, Thunder and Lightning*," in *The Dramatic Works of Thomas Dekker*, ed. Fredson Bowers, vol. 3 (Cambridge: Cambridge University Press, 1958), 4.2.33.

10. Heywood, *Dramatic Works*, 1:213.

11. Ingold, *Being Alive*, 130. See chaps. 9 and 10 especially: "we do not hear rain, but hear in it" (138).

12. Ibid., 130.

13. The English circumnavigator William Dampier, *A New Voyage Round the World* (London, 1697), had this to say about the Spanish mines near Panama: "Yet the Mines are so nigh the mountains, that as the Rivers soon rise, so they are soon down again; and presently after the rain is the best searching for Gold in the Sands: for the violent rains do wash down the Gold into the Rivers, where much of it settles to the bottom and remains" (195).

14. See Russell West-Pavlov, chap. 5, "The Aporias of Masculinity: Systemic Interpenetration and Systemic Instability," in *Bodies and Their Spaces: System, Crisis and Transformation in Early Modern Theatre* (Amsterdam: Rodopi, 2006). Feste's "fugitive plentitude of masculinity is once again deferred, reduced to derivative 'posturing' by a corrosive liquaeous other" (117–18).

15. Patricia Fumerton, *Unsettled: The Culture of Mobility and the Working Poor in Early Modern England* (Chicago: University of Chicago Press, 2006), xviii. See also Sanders, "Wandering and Making Progress on the Road," in *Cultural Geography of Early Modern Drama*, 135–47.

16. In his chapter on megadams, for example, Rob Nixon compares the plight of "oustees" and "unimagined communities" rendered disposable by economic development in submergence zones. Apprehending this slow violence, making it visible, is one way to counteract it. While the economic stakes are different, the similarities are enough, I believe, to see the fate of enclosure and flood victims as Feste's and Poor Tom's. See chap. 5, "Unimagined Communities: Megadams, Monumental Modernity, and Developmental Refugees," in *Slow Violence*.

17. John Taylor, *The Praise, Antiquity, and Commodity, of Beggery, Beggers, and Begging* (London: E.A., 1621), unpaginated.

18. Shakespeare elsewhere makes this connection: rain congregates witches, stabs skin, and anticipates the thrust of daggers in *Macbeth* (1606); "It will be rain tonight," Banquo states before he is murdered: "Let it come down" (3.3.16).

19. Catherine Richardson, *Domestic Life and Domestic Tragedy in Early Modern England: The Material Life of the Household* (Manchester: Manchester

University Press, 2006), describes "anti-house" behavior as that which is opposed to typical domestic productivity, such as sexual dalliance in hedgerows off-road, and invisible: "Intimate actions necessarily, inevitably, create a kind of domesticity, but it is one which is relocated outside, under the hedge or in the ditch, in between legitimate areas of jurisdiction, needing to be unmade at every liaison" (37).

20. The matter of rain breaks the levees of periodization: see Jonathan Gil Harris, *Untimely Matter in the Time of Shakespeare* (Philadelphia: University of Pennsylvania Press, 2009).

21. To name a few: *The Last Terrible Tempestious Windes and Weather* (London: Joseph Hunt, 1613); *A Wonderful Cry from the Country; or, The Wonder of Wonders* (London, 1674); *Sad News from the Countrey; or, A True and Full Relation of the Late Wonderful Floods in Divers Parts of England* (London, 1674); and *England's Most Dreadful Calamity by the Late Floods* (London: P. Brooksby, 1682).

22. *The Wonders of This Windie Winter* (London: G. Eld, 1613), unpaginated.

23. *Bartas: His Deuine Weekes and Workes*, trans. Joshua Sylvester (London: Humfrey Lownes, 1605), 58.

24. Serres with Latour, *Conversations*, 58.

25. Bennett, *Vibrant Matter*, 53.

26. Ibid., 54.

27. Gillian Rudd, "'Why Does It Always Rain on Me?': Rain and Self-Centredness and Medieval Poetry," *Green Letters: Studies in Ecocriticism* 11 (2009): 71.

28. Morton, *Ecology without Nature*, 77.

29. Ibid., 166–69.

30. Ibid., 47, 60.

31. Ibid., 205.

32. Ibid., 186.

33. Lucretius, *The Nature of Things*, trans. A. E. Stallings (London: Penguin, 2007). Rain's relation to permeation is not lost upon Lucretius: "The steady drip of water causes stone to hollow and yield" (1.312); but more uncomfortably unless taken out of context since he is describing how to win love from a woman: "For anything that's hammered by a blow, day after day, / However softly struck, at length is conquered and gives way. / Haven't you seen how drops of water falling, on their own / Have the power, over time, to wear their way through stone?" (4.1284–87).

34. We have been called foolish for doing so; for the proverbial connection between fools and rain, see Richard Levin, "Proverbial Fools in the Rain in *Twelfth Night* and *King Lear*," *Shakespeare Newsletter* 49, no. 2 (1999): 31–32.

35. Cynthia Barnett, *Rain: A Natural and Cultural History* (New York: Crown Publishers, 2015), 11, 12.

36. Robert Knox, *An Historical Relation of the Island Ceylon* (London: Richard Chiswell, 1681), 14.

37. In the simplest terms possible, the sun evaporates seawater to make vapor; vapor rises and condenses into clouds; water falls upon mountains as rain; and rain makes rivers that flow back to the sea. See the National Oceanic and Atmospheric Administration: http://www.srh.noaa.gov/mrx/hydro/hyd _cyc.php.

38. Earliest fossil records of rain are 2.7 billion years old; see "Origins," Barnett's prologue to *Rain*.

39. See W. E. Knowles Middleton, *A History of the Theories of Rain and Other Forms of Precipitation* (London: Oldbourne, 1965).

40. Quoted in Yi-Fu Tuan, *The Hydrologic Cycle and the Wisdom of God: A Theme in Geoteleology* (Toronto: University of Toronto Press, 1968), 9–10.

41. Ibid., 6. The 1613 pamphlet, for instance, translates disaster into economic loss: "The very Riuer of Thames, is also a . . . hereof, where by the rigorous strength of the windes the water (with the tyde flowing ouer-fiercely) made a most dangerous breach ouer the banks into the Medowes & Marshes by Stratfrod le . . ., & Dam, where many thousand akers of faire grounds are quite over-flowne and drowned, to the great hurt and hindrance of many the Inhabitants of London, as those Townes thereabouts, the recovery wherof, by men of such understanding, wil cost much time, with inualuable sums of money, to the great greife and care of many hundreds."

42. Linton, *What Is Water?*, 104, 106. I am purposefully brief here; for much more on the subject, see Linton's chap. 5, "The Hydrologic Cycle(s): Scientific and Sacred," and Tuan, *The Hydrologic Cycle and the Wisdom of God*, chap. 2, "Trails and Intimations."

43. I specifically have in mind Tuan's assuring (it seems) point that "mutability orderly enacted within a cyclic frame could be interpreted as a pattern of the good. In the sublunary sphere perfection may find its image in the cycles of change rather than in the circles of motion. . . . It was possible to expound the cyclic transmutation of elements together with the cyclic changes in the state of water" (*The Hydrologic Cycle and the Wisdom of God*, 37). While optimistic and engaged in cyclical change, I worry over the moral valence ("the good"); instead, the model of change is the eddy of change susceptible to more change, akin to Serres's "confluence of fluxes" (*Conversations*, 122).

44. Serres, *Birth of Physics*, 28. "Neither circle nor line, everything is stable and unstable at the same time" (58).

45. For instance, see Paracelsus: "It contains in its body all the minerals of the world. . . . There is a vast variety of things contained in the body of the Microcosm which elude the observation of the senses, though God, the Creator, has willed them to exist in that structure." Quoted in Marjorie Hope Nicolson, *The Breaking of the Circle* (New York: Columbia University Press, 1960), 23. "Correspondence between macrocosm, geocosm, and microcosm, long accepted as basic to faith, was no longer valid in a new mechanical world and mechanical universe, nor is it valid in the modern world" (7).

46. Steve Mentz, "Strange Weather in *King Lear*," *Shakespeare* 6, no. 2 (2010): 140.

47. Ibid., 147.

48. *Shukriya* to Jonathan Gil Harris for bringing this to my attention.

49. Linton, *What Is Water?*, 123.

50. For a different rainy route taken—François Bernier's mid-seventeenth-century journey through the Mughal Empire—see my essay "When It Rains," in Iovino and Oppermann, *Material Ecocriticism*, 114–29.

51. See s.v. "precipitation" (n.) and "precipitate" (v.) in the *Oxford English Dictionary*.

52. William Averell, *A Wonderfull and Straunge newes* (London: Edwarde White, 1583), unpaginated.

53. I must give only a cursory view here on the history of early modern meteorology: see S. K. Heninger Jr., *A Handbook of Renaissance Meteorology* (New York: Greenwood Press, 1968); Vladimir Janković, *Reading the Skies: A Cultural History of English Weather, 1650–1820* (Chicago: University of Chicago Press, 2000); and Craig Martin, *Renaissance Meteorology: Pomponazzi to Descartes* (Baltimore: Johns Hopkins University Press, 2011).

54. "The press provided texts to suit all intellectual needs and tastes, and thereby assured the greatest diffusion of recognized theories. Meteorological notions of all sorts, regardless of their wide variety, were easily accessible to everyone; and even those conceived in scientific spirit had readily passed into the commonplace of everyday life" (Heninger, *Handbook of Renaissance Meteorology*, 33).

55. *A Goodly Gallerye: William Fulke's Book of Meteors (1563)*, ed. Theodore Hornberger (Philadelphia: American Philosophical Society, 1979), 26.

56. Ibid., 90.

57. Ibid.

58. Ibid., 90–91.

59. Ibid., 90.

60. Ibid., 95.

61. Ibid., 93.

62. Ibid., 27, 30.

63. Ibid., 25.

64. Jonathan Goldberg, *The Seeds of Things: Theorizing Sexuality and Materiality in Renaissance Representations* (New York: Fordham University Press, 2009), 4, 45.

65. For more historical context than I provide, see William Foster, ed., *Early Travels in India, 1583–1619* (Delhi: S. Chand, 1968).

66. Peter Mundy, *The Travels of Peter Mundy, in Europe and Asia, 1608–1667*, ed. Sir Richard Carnac Temple (London: Hakluyt Society, 1914), 2:31.

67. Dampier, *New Voyage*, 22. See "Of the Coasting Trade-Winds That Shift" (ibid., 17).

68. Robert Markley, "Monsoon Cultures: Climate and Acculturation in Alexander Hamilton's *A New Account of the East Indies*," *New Literary History* 38 (2007): 527.

69. Ibid., 530.

70. See s.v. "monsoon" (n.) in the *Oxford English Dictionary*.

71. John Fryer, *A New Account of East India and Persia. Being Nine Years' Travels, 1672–1681*, ed. William Crooke (London: Hakluyt Society, 1909–15), 2:93.

72. Dampier, *New Voyage*, 72–73.

73. Thomas Herbert, *Some Yeares Travels into Divers Parts of Asia and Afrique* (London: R. Br., 1638), 9.

74. See Sir Thomas Roe's account in *The Embassy of Sir Thomas Roe to India, 1615–19*, ed. William Foster (London: Humphrey Milford, 1926), 217.

75. Edward Terry, *A Voyage to East-India* (London: T.W., 1655), 6–7. Herbert, passing through the same area, has almost the exact same thing to say. However, unlike Terry, he uses the language of infection and disease that renders the rain a little less strange, its "Creatures" more defined: "The infectious raines most damnifying the poore saylers, who must be upon the decks to hand in their sailes, abiding the brunt, and (which is worse) commonly get forthwith into their beds (or hamackoes) resting their tyred bodies in wet nasty clothes, thereby breeding many furious and mortall diseases, as burning Feavers, Calentures, Fluxes, Aches, Scurvy, and the like; which doubtlesse, did they moderate their bibbing strong waters, and shift their filthy apparell, might be prevented" (*Some Yeares Travels*, 7).

76. Quoted in Foster, *Early Travels in India*, 288.

77. John Ovington, *A Voyage to Surat*, ed. H. G. Rawlinson (London: Oxford University Press, 1929), 36; Fryer, *New Account of East India and Persia*, 1:46 and 1:99.

78. Terry, *Voyage to East-India*, 100.

79. Ibid., 125.

80. Ibid., 5.

81. Ibid., 6.

82. Dampier, *New Voyage*, 47.

83. Robert Markley has written about this elsewhere: "'A Putridness in the Air': Monsoons and Mortality in Seventeenth-Century Bombay," *Journal for Early Modern Cultural Studies* 10, no. 2 (2010), 105–25. See also "Early Encounters, c. 1600–1750," in Mark Harrison's *Climates and Constitutions: Health, Race, Environment and British Imperialism in India, 1600–1850* (Oxford: Oxford University Press, 1999).

84. "The process of becoming-Indian, despite not congealing into a solid identity—indeed, even because it refuses identity altogether—can also provoke an ambivalent pleasure": Harris, "Sick Ethnography," 134–35. For the various "Forms of Indography," see the introduction to *Indography*: "Indography is as much a writing (and displacement) of the European self . . . as of the Indian" (3).

85. Serres, *Parasite*, 39.

86. Ibid., 6.

87. Ibid., 5.

88. Ibid., 14.

89. Ibid., 11.

90. Ibid., 16.

91. Ibid., 12.

92. He does not put it mildly: "History hides the fact that man is the universal parasite, that everything and everyone around him is a hospitable space. Plants and animals are always his hosts; man is always necessarily their guest. Always taking, never giving" (ibid., 24).

93. Ibid., 39.

94. Ovington, *Voyage to Surat*, 87.

95. Ibid., 203, 85.

96. Ibid., 88.

97. Ibid., 79.

98. Ibid., 83.

99. Ibid., 84.

100. Ibid.

101. Ibid., 82.

102. Ibid.

103. Ibid., 40.

104. Ibid.

105. Ibid., 183.

on material culture, respectively, *Learning to Curse: Essays in Early Modern Culture* (Routledge: New York, 1990) and *Things of Darkness: Economies of Race and Gender in Early Modern England* (Ithaca: Cornell University Press, 1995).

11. For more on mud's elemental role in literary criticism—as a "*normative* tactic in the diffusion of ideas and the building of careers: through the application of mud, one builds turf" (141)—see Sharon O'Dair, "Muddy Thinking," in Cohen and Duckert, *Elemental Ecocriticism*. Steve Mentz addresses mud's material basis for repulsion in "Brown," in Cohen, *Prismatic Ecology*: "To be ecological is to be brown, disturbingly" (193).

12. Serres, *Natural Contract*, 1.

13. *Oxford English Dictionary*, s.v. "fen" (n.¹). The word first appears ca. 888 CE.

14. *Beowulf: A New Verse Translation*, trans. Seamus Heaney (New York: W. W. Norton, 2000), line 1366.

15. Barbara Hurd, *Stirring the Mud: On Swamps, Bogs, and Human Imagination* (Boston: Beacon Press, 2001), 8.

16. Susan Signe Morrison, *The Literature of Waste: Material Ecopoetics and Ethical Matter* (New York: Palgrave Macmillan, 2015), "Introduction," 1–14.

17. See Jennifer C. James, "Ecomelancholia: Slavery, War, and Black Ecological Imaginings," in *Environmental Criticism for the Twenty-First Century*, ed. Stephanie LeMenager, Teresa Shewry, and Ken Hiltner (New York: Routledge, 2011), 163–78.

18. Estok, *Ecocriticism and Shakespeare*, 4.

19. Aldo Leopold, *A Sand County Almanac* (Oxford: Oxford University Press, 1949), 107.

20. Laura A. Ogden, *Swamplife: People, Gators, and Mangroves Entangled in the Everglades* (Minneapolis: University of Minnesota Press, 2011), 29.

21. Ibid., 2.

22. Badè, *Life and Letters of John Muir*, 1:118; Henry David Thoreau, *Journal*, ed. B. Torrey and F. H. Allen (New York: Dover, 1962), 9:281.

23. Allewaert, *Ariel's Ecology*, 6, 19.

24. Hurd, *Stirring the Mud*, 39.

25. Pickering, "New Ontologies," vii.

26. Rodney Giblett, *Postmodern Wetlands: Culture, History, Ecology* (Edinburgh: Edinburgh University Press, 1996), 228–29.

27. Levi R. Bryant, "Black," in Cohen, *Prismatic Ecology*, 298–302.

28. See the United States Environmental Protection Agency's information on swamps: https://www.epa.gov/wetlands/wetlands-classification-and-types# swamps.

29. "An ongoing exchange of anxieties, imaginations, resources, and performances. . . . The communication encounters of the early settlement era offer
a provocative evidentiary challenge for rethinking theories about the relationships among representation, media, and the social order." Matt Cohen, *The
Networked Wilderness: Communicating in Early New England* (Minneapolis: University of Minnesota Press, 2010), 4–5. The material forces of swamp-
space are certainly part of this effusive "rethinking" (22). In the same way, only
through medicine, Kelly Wisecup, *Medical Encounters: Knowledge and Identity in Early American Literatures* (Amherst: University of Massachusetts Press,
2013), has shown that "early American medical writing—the textual manifestation of the medical knowledge communicated in cross-cultural encounters—
was shaped by Native, African, and colonial responses to medicines and diseases in the New World" (4). Intermingling examples are frequent, even if they
are few in my analysis; consider this account of alder by John Josselyn, *An
Account of Two Voyages to New-England* (London, 1674): "of which wood there
is abundance in the wet swamps: the bark thereof with the yolke of an Egg is
good for a strain; an Indian bruising of his knee, chew'd the bark of Alder fast-
ing and laid it to, which quickly helped him. The wives of our West-Countrey
English make a drink with the seeds of Alder, giving it to their Children troubled with the Alloes" (70).

30. Walter D. Mignolo, *The Darker Side of the Renaissance: Literacy, Terri-
toriality, and Colonization*, 2nd ed. (Ann Arbor: University of Michigan Press,
2003).

31. Giblett, *Postmodern Wetlands*, xii.

32. See s.v. "quagmire" (n.) in the *Oxford English Dictionary*.

33. Latour, *We Have Never Been Modern*, 13–15.

34. Edward J. Geisweidt, "'The Nobleness of Life': Spontaneous Generation and Excremental Life in *Antony and Cleopatra*," in Bruckner and Brayton,
Ecocritical Shakespeare, 90.

35. Ibid., 89.

36. Ibid., 92.

37. Ibid., 102.

38. Ibid., 103.

39. Ibid., 102.

40. See s.v. "swamp" (n.) in the *Oxford English Dictionary*.

41. John Smith, *The Generall Historie of Virginia, New-England, and the
Summer Isles* (London: I.D. and I.H., 1624), 162–63.

42. See s.v. "swamp" (n.²) in the *Oxford English Dictionary*.

43. Wilhelm Adolf Scribonius, *Naturall Philosophy* (London: I.D., 1621),
38.

44. See s.v. "swamp" (v.⁴) in the *Oxford English Dictionary*.

45. See s.v. "swamp" (adj.) in the *Oxford English Dictionary*.

46. Roger Williams, *A Key into the Language of America* (London: Gregory Dexter, 1643), 68, 72.

47. Ibid., 72–73.

48. Begin with William Cronon, *Changes in the Land: Indians, Colonists, and the Ecology of New England* (New York: Hill and Wang, 1983).

49. George Gardyner, *A Description of the New World* (London, 1651), 89.

50. Ibid., 99–100.

51. To name just a few: Francis Higginson, *New-Englands Plantation* (London: T. & R. Cotes, 1630); Edward Johnson, *A History of New-England* (London, 1653); and Edward Winslow, *Good News from New-England* (London: I.D., 1624).

52. William Wood, *New Englands Prospect* (London: Tho. Cotes, 1634), 48.

53. Smith, *Generall Historie*, 162.

54. Ferdinando Gorges, *America Painted to the Life* (London: E. Brudenell, 1658), 66.

55. Ibid., 44.

56. Native American cultures, of course, were just as adept at transforming the land; Shepard Krech III debunks the trope of indigenous harmony prior to European contact in *The Ecological Indian: Myth and History* (New York: W. W. Norton, 1999).

57. Samuel Hartlib, *Legacy of Husbandry* (London: J.M., 1655), 19.

58. Ibid.

59. For more on the region's "concatenation of corporeal encounters" at this time, see the excellent collection of essays Janet Moore Lindman and Michele Lise Tarter, eds., *A Centre of Wonders: The Body in Early America* (Ithaca: Cornell University Press, 2001), 8. Of particular note is Martha L. Finch, "'Civilized' Bodies and the 'Savage' Environment of Early New Plymouth," 43–59. Also of interest is Karen Ordahl Kupperman, "Fear of Hot Climates in the Anglo-American Colonial Experience," *William and Mary Quarterly* 41, no. 2 (1984): 213–40.

60. Hartlib, *Legacy of Husbandry*, 19.

61. The enduring (1630) phrase of the governor of the Massachusetts Bay Colony, John Winthrop, from *A Modell of Christian Charity* (Boston: Collections of the Massachusetts Historical Society, 1838): "For wee must consider that wee shall be as a citty upon a hill. The eies of all people are upon us" (7:47).

62. Hartlib, *Legacy of Husbandry*, 19.

63. Joyce E. Chaplin unpacks the racial tensions underlying the area's natural philosophy in "Natural Philosophy and an Early Racial Idiom in North

America: Comparing English and Indian Bodies," *William and Mary Quarterly* 54, no. 1 (1997): 229–52. For tobacco specifically, see Kristen G. Brookes, "Inhaling the Alien: Race and Tobacco in Early Modern England," in *Global Traffic: Discourses and Practices of Trade in English Literature and Culture from 1550 to 1700*, ed. Barbara Sebek and Stephen Deng (New York: Palgrave Macmillan, 2008), 157–78.

64. "Look now into thy condition with this resemblance, and be thine own Judg; thou hast a dunghil heart, a soul like a dirty swamp, those hellish abominations which have taken up thy mind, and will, and affections, in which thou hast continued, and unto which thou hast been accustomed, so that thy heart is like a standing puddle of prophaneness, which have weakened and wasted the very faculties of thy soul." Thomas Hooker, *The Application of Redemption* (London: Peter Cole, 1656), 345.

65. George Fox, *A New-England-Fire-Brand* (London, 1678), 45.

66. "Our Countrymen have noted of the Natives of New-England, that the Devil appeared to them in ugly Shapes, and in hideous Places, a[nd] in Swamps and Woods." Richard Gilpin, *Demonologia Sacra* (London: J.D., 1677), 52; William Gurnall, *The Christian in Compleat Armour* (London: Edmund Calamy, 1655), 100–101.

67. John Milton, *Paradise Lost* (London: S. Simmons, 1674), 10.383.

68. William Hubbard, *A Narrative of the Troubles with the Indians in New-England, from the First Planting Thereof in the Year 1607, to This Present Year 1677, but Chiefly of the Late Troubles in the Two Last Years, 1675 and 1676* (Boston: John Foster, 1677), 97. All quotations from Hubbard's *Narrative* refer to this edition and are hereafter cited in the text. (Benjamin Tompson's prefatory encomium, cited above, as well as Hubbard's prefatory material and dedicatory epistle are unpaginated.)

69. Walter Blith, *The English Improuer Improued* (London, 1652), 30–31.

70. Cotton Mather, *The Way to Prosperity* (Boston: Richard Pierce, 1690), 4.

71. Ibid., 3.

72. Latour, *We Have Never Been Modern*, 10–12.

73. Richard Slotkin and James K. Folsom, eds., *So Dreadfull a Judgment: Puritan Responses to King Philip's War, 1676–1677* (Hanover: Wesleyan University Press, 1978), 11.

74. Ibid., 8.

75. Ibid., 18.

76. Ibid., 29.

77. Ibid., 30.

78. Ibid., 31.

79. An extensive and yet accessible study is Jill Lepore, *The Name of War: King Philip's War and the Origins of American Identity* (New York: Alfred A. Knopf, 1998). Kathleen J. Bragdon, *Native People of Southern New England, 1650–1775* (Norman: University of Oklahoma Press, 2009) is also useful.

80. "For the Indians, notwithstanding their sublety and cruelty, durst [not] look on Englishmen [in t]he face, in the open field, nor ever yet were known to kill any m[a]n with their Guns, unless when they couldly in wai[ting] for him in an ambush or behind some shelter, taking him undiscovered" (39).

81. A sense of panic that was endemic to everyday life and not just to times of war, as two notable works in sensory studies point out: Peter Charles Hoffer, *Sensory Worlds in Early America* (Baltimore: Johns Hopkins University Press, 2003); Richard Cullen Rath, *How Early America Sounded* (Ithaca: Cornell University Press, 2003), especially chap. 1, "'Those Thunders, Those Roarings': The Natural Soundscape."

82. In an anonymous account of the conflict, *A Farther Brief and True Narration of the Late Wars Risen in New-England* (London: J.D., 1676), the colonial agenda is inverted along vegetal lines. The natives ironically "plant" the English, mocking their religion and taunting them: "[S]ome they took alive and sat them upright in the Ground, using this *Sarchasm; You English since you came into this Countrey have grown exceedingly above Ground, let us now see how you will grow when Planted into the Ground*" (4).

83. "About an hundred or more of the women and Children, which were like to be rather burdensome then serviceable were left behind," Hubbard states, "who soon after resigned up themselves to the mercy of the English" (27). I borrow the terms "war machine" and "State apparatus" from Deleuze and Guattari, *A Thousand Plateaus*, chap. 12, "1227: Treatise on Nomadology—The War Machine."

84. "And the locust went up over all the land of Egypt, and rested in all the coasts of Egypt: very grievous were they; before them there were no such locusts as they, neither after them shall be such" (Exodus 10:4).

85. See Lepore, *Name of War*, 14–18, for "The Circle" of writers aiming to explain the war.

86. *A Farther Brief*, 10.

87. Ibid.

88. Ibid., 4.

89. John Bunyan, *The Pilgrim's Progress*, ed. Cynthia Wall (New York: W. W. Norton, 2008), 3.

90. Ibid., 11.

91. Ibid., 12.

92. Ibid., 15.

93. Ibid., 16.

94. Ibid.

95. Ibid.

96. Ibid.

97. Ibid.

98. Ibid.

99. Ibid., 12.

100. Ibid., 17.

101. See Bruno Latour, *On the Modern Cult of the Factish Gods*, trans. Catherine Porter and Heather MacLean (Durham, NC: Duke University Press, 2010).

102. "Let's find out if we can forge new pleasures by feeling ourselves stuck," implores Lara Farina in "Sticking Together," in *Burn after Reading*, vol. 1: *Miniature Manifestos for a Post/medieval Studies*, ed. Eileen A. Joy and Myra Seaman (New York: punctum books, 2014), 36.

Conclusion

1. Eileen A. Joy, "Blue," in Cohen, *Prismatic Ecology*, 213. For a breathtaking example of hope as a critical methodology, see Teresa Shewry, *Hope at Sea: Possible Ecologies in Oceanic Literature* (Minneapolis: University of Minnesota Press, 2015).

2. For more information about the valley's chemical spills and ongoing environmental health campaigns, see http://www.wvfree.org/water/ and http://www.wvfree.org/research/women-water/.

3. Tuana, "Viscous Porosity," 207.

4. John Taylor, *Iohn Taylors Last Voyage* (London: F.L., 1641).

5. Bruce Boehrer, *Environmental Degradation in Jacobean Drama* (Cambridge: Cambridge University Press, 2013), 166. "Ecology itself only emerges as a recognizable discipline some three centuries after the reign of King James I, and in King James's own day neither ecology nor science in its broadest sense is yet capable of providing a cohesive intellectual framework for understanding and responding to environmental change."

Index

LOWELL DUCKERT is assistant professor of English at West Virginia University, specializing in early modern literature, ecotheory, and environmental criticism. With Jeffrey Jerome Cohen, he is editor of *Elemental Ecocriticism: Thinking with Earth, Air, Water, and Fire* (Minnesota, 2015) and *Veer Ecology: A Companion for Environmental Thinking* (Minnesota, 2017).